THE NEW WORLD NEGRO

SELECTED PAPERS IN AFROAMERICAN STUDIES

THE
NEW WORLD
NEGRO

MELVILLE J. HERSKOVITS

EDITED BY

FRANCES S. HERSKOVITS

Indiana University Press

BLOOMINGTON   *1966*   LONDON

To the
Community of Scholars
in the
Afroamerican Field

CONTENTS

VI: *Cult Life in Brazil*

VII: *The World View of an Urban Community*
PARAMARIBO, DUTCH GUIANA (1936)

VIII: *Reinterpretations*

Introduction

In a preface written a month before his death, Melville Herskovits summarized his commitment to interdisciplinary approaches to the basic problems that concern students of man in this way:

"It has been said that the research value of an area lies in the fact that it affords a *locus* for the study of problems. In somewhat different terms, it is to be thought of as a place which provides those in the behavioral and historical sciences with a laboratory in which they can test their hypotheses. But more than this, it encourages focus on a problem, and there is no problem in the context of area studies that does not impel the student to stray outside the bounds of his discipline."

As early as 1930 my husband saw the field of the Negro in the New World as such a laboratory. "We realize the importance of knowing the extent to which cultural phenomena, like physical form, are tenacious. We know, in a very rough sort of way, that a simple material culture will give way before a more efficient one much more quickly than one type of social organization will be given up for another. But when an aboriginal culture is vigorously suppressed will anything remain?"

His field experience in Suriname in 1928 and 1929 had a profound influence on his thinking, and though he was scarcely conscious of this at the time, the findings in both the Bush and the city of Paramaribo began shaping his concepts on acculturation. In the Guiana Bush, among the Saramacca peoples, he saw, as he often told his students, nearly all of western sub-Saharan Africa represented, from what is now Mali to Loango and into the Congo—and the Loango chief who came to our base camp invoked both the Great God of the Akan of the Gold Coast, *Nyankompon,* and the Bantu *Zambi.*

In the coastal capital of Paramaribo, where we were assured, because of generations of schooling and Christian teaching and worship, nothing more than some African-derived *Anansi* stories would be found, our first session with a literate young woman who came to teach us *taki-taki* (the Negro-English spoken on the coast in Suriname) brought us a full description of a prolonged illness caused, she explained, by her offended soul. She used the Twi word *akra* for soul. Her mother, when moving from Albina to Paramaribo, had forgotten to perform the ritual of asking her soul to accompany them to their new home, and she, being a child then, was especially vulnerable. She added that there was sickness for which doctors had cures, and sickness which came from spirits and for which someone knowledgeable in things African had remedies.

My husband began outlining the opening paper of this volume on board a cargo boat that was taking us from Trinidad to the United States in the late summer of 1929, after our second field trip to Suriname. It was a leisurely voyage, and he welcomed the opportunity to visit several islands in the Caribbean where the Dutch freighter that had taken us down to Paramaribo did not stop. Here in Barbados, Antigua, St. Lucia, St. Kitts, and Dominica, he played the African game *wari* (which he had learned in Suriname) with the men on the docks, and talked to them about his stay among the Bush Negroes and his enjoyment of the drumming at the *winti* dances in the city of Paramaribo. He was already well on his way into his ethnohistorical researches.

This was still the period in his research when the emphasis was on African carry-overs—"pure" Africanisms—for he was seeking firm leads that would point to regional and tribal origins of the African-derived populations of the New World.

Field work in western Nigeria (and Kano), in Dahomey, and among the Ashanti, followed by research in Haiti, opened up broader horizons, with new hypotheses to be tested in the laboratory of Afroamerican cultures.

His first research orientation had sent him to the early accounts of explorers, slave traders, missionaries, historians, and to existing ethnographic materials. This research experience he put to good use not only in establishing the provenience of the dominant African groups represented in the New World, but also in structuring a baseline for the analysis of what happened to the cultures in contact.

"It came to be recognized that the problem was vastly more complex than a statement merely drawn in terms of the presence or absence of Africanisms in the New World." The problem, which is at the heart of acculturation theory, was rather how the cultural elements of Europeans, Africans, and American Indians interacted with one another, each as recipient and donor in the cultural interchanges. Many years later, in other historical and cultural contexts, he was concerned with the same problems in Africa.

To the concept of *cultural tenacity*, phrased by him at a time when influential anthropologists were urging massive research into the far corners of the earth to "rescue" materials still available from "vanishing primitive" societies, he added the concepts of *retention* and *reinterpretation*. These he felt confident would raise research effort "from the elementary level of description and comparison to that of the analysis of process."

Finally, with the inclusion of the concept of *cultural focus*, which the study of the belief systems of Africans and their descendants in the New World brought into such sharp relief, he came more and more to shape his theoretical framework in terms of the importance of *values*. And this brought him to the moot philosophical problem of *cultural relativism*.

When he became director of the Program of African Studies, in 1948, his Afroamerican research was necessarily interrupted, but his commitment to the field never was allowed to recede into the background. In the same year he published *The Contribution of Afroamerican Studies to Africanist Research*, which is included in this volume. During my husband's travels in Africa, he took every opportunity to talk with villagers in the former areas of intensive slaving about their kinsmen in the New World, and he learned from them their attitudes toward their earlier traditions. In the western Congo (and the Kasai), and in Angola, he would tell the Africans he visited about the *nkisi* worshipped in Brazil and he, where conditions permitted, played some of the cult songs of the Congo-Angola rites which we had recorded in Bahia.

With the Yoruba graduate students, he reviewed the versions of the *orisha* myths as told in Brazil, and how they differed from those which continue to be given in the literature on Yoruba religion. He used the technique of the *hypothetical situation*, described in this volume, to compare the structure of family worship of the *orisha* among the Oyo both with the family *vodun* "service," which is detailed in *Life in a Haitian Valley*, and with the worship of the *Santos* in Bahia. This information reinforced his thinking about the need to broaden the perspective on the kind of syncretisms and reinterpretations that are found in Afroamerican cultures. He was able to incorporate this important conclusion, though only in a passing comment, in his *Social Organization of the Candomble,* included in this book.

He wrote: "There is reason indeed to question on both ethnographical and historical grounds the typicality of the candomble which, in its various forms has served in Afrobrazilian research as the model of African carry-overs. The only systematic investigation of the phenomenon in a rural area, made by Eduardo in Maranhão, showed no comparable organization. . . . This makes the historical question a fair one: Do the candombles, that have been assumed to be the only valid expression of African religious retentions in Brazil, rather represent special and restricted forms of organization found in the urban centres of western Nigeria and Dahomey, transplanted to the urban centres of Brazil?"

We might well add to this the parallel situations in the larger cities in Cuba and Haiti, and Port-of-Spain in Trinidad, among others.

He continues: "This, of course, leaves unanswered the further question of whether intensive study of Afrobrazilian religion in the rural areas may not reveal retentions of more widely spread African patterns organized in terms of family and lineage worship of the deities reinterpreted as saints, or under African designations as well, with specialists called in to perform more complex and extensive rituals when these must be given."

For this last observation he had the supporting comment of cult-heads in Porto Alegre, as will be seen in the article entitled "The Southernmost Outposts of New World Africanisms," published in 1943, and reprinted in this volume.

My husband's colleagues in the Afroamerican field also saw to it that his interest in their common field did not flag. Many of the papers he published after the early 1940's were done at their invitation—some were written in honor of colleagues, some for special issues, and others were addresses he was called upon to make.

He had looked forward to his retirement, when he could return to uninterrupted research and bring together his more than forty years' experience in studying a single area—Africa and Afroamerica—in terms, as he put it, not only of the "What?" and "Where," in the study of man, but also the "How," and the "Why?"

This volume includes only those contributions predating the publication of *The Myth of the Negro Past* (1941), which (1) there were either given only passing reference or were treated in summary form, and (2) others which appeared in generally inaccessible journals. The abridged discussion of the religious beliefs of the Paramaribo Negroes is included at the instance of a number of my husband's African and Africanist colleagues who feel that it documents the unities in underlying belief of much of sub-Saharan Africa. The essay on "Some Modes of Ethnographic Comparison" is also abridged.

Each discussion is headed by a quotation from the body of the text; in one instance only, in the section on Paramaribo beliefs, is a heading derived from another publication.

Considerations of space make it impossible to bring together the full evidence supporting the fact that African value systems enter into the forms of mating which in the New World can be designated as common-law marriage. A close reading of the papers where offerings to the ancestors are mentioned will demonstrate that the family dead do not disapprove of these arrangements. This can be contrasted with Christian belief, and the condemnation of all but the syncretized churches, such as the Shouters (Spiritual Baptists) of Trinidad.

I am much indebted to Alan Merriam of Indiana University and to Fred and Dorothy Eggan of the University of Chicago for urging me to undertake the selection of papers which constitute this volume, and to Peter Hammond of Indiana University for valuable suggestions about the contributions he wished to see included. Igor Kopytoff of the University of Pennsylvania helped measurably with the structuring of the book, and was unsparing in his readiness to solve technical problems.

I am also deeply grateful to Donald and Lola Campbell of Northwestern University for reading the Introduction and giving me their comments, and to the anthropologist and publisher, Robert Plant Armstrong, also of Northwestern University, who has given unstinted advice and help.

I am grateful to the following for permission to reprint the materials in this book: Alfred A. Knopf, Inc., *American Anthropologist, The American Scholar*, Association for the Study of Negro Life and History, Inc., *Bijdragen tot de taal-, land- en Volkenkunde*, Columbia University Press, *Institut Français d'Afrique Noire, Journal of American Folklore, The Musical Quarterly, The New Republic*, Routledge & Kegan Paul Ltd., *Southwestern Journal of Anthropology, Tomorrow*, and the University of Chicago Press.

FRANCES S. HERSKOVITS

Evanston, October 5, 1965

THE NEW WORLD NEGRO

: I :

THE AFROAMERICAN FIELD

A LABORATORY FOR THE STUDY OF MAN

The Negro in the New World

THE STATEMENT OF A PROBLEM

What is innate and what cultural? Investigation into the manner in which the Negro has accommodated himself to all the different cultural backgrounds into which he was brought as a slave should constitute a significant step toward an understanding of the interrelation of the processes of culture and physical form.

❉   ❉   ❉

The Negro in the New World has given rise to a situation which is of the utmost scientific importance, and which, in the final analysis, may have far-reaching practical significance. In affording an opportunity for study of a problem which is not only of itself worthy of consideration but which may also contribute impressively toward the understanding of some of the basic questions which confront the study of man, it deserves far greater attention than it has received, if advantage is to be taken of the peculiarly fortunate alignment of data which only await gathering to be utilized.

I

Let us restate some of the fundamental problems with which we are confronted in the study of mankind. We may group them under two principal headings,—those which arise from the consideration of Man's physical form, and those which present themselves in the study of his languages and cultures. To what extent, the physical anthropologist

American Anthropologist, XXXII, no. 1 (1930), 145–55.

asks, may it be said that a given physical type holds its aboriginal form through the vicissitudes of its historical experiences? What is the effect of environment on human types? Does Man retain his different racial characteristics no matter where he may be transported? Thus, it is said that American environment is making the hair-form of Caucasians straight like that of the aboriginal Indian. Or, again, one hears that the development of pigmentation in a race is the function of the amount and intensity of sunlight to which it is exposed, and the Caucasoid Hindu is pointed to as affirming this position. Again, there are the whole group of problems which center about the question of the physical results of racial crossing. Is there a decrease of fertility with race-mixture? What is the effect on the behavior of the crossed individuals when compared with pure breeds? To what extent are the processes of Mendelian heredity that the biologist has observed in non-mammalian forms operative in Man? All of these troublesome questions await data, and data of a nature not too easily obtained. Man is a slow-breeding animal, and the life of the student appears almost hopelessly short in view of the length of time necessary to bring about the conditions to be observed.

The same is true of our linguistic and cultural problems. The student of language and of culture is himself conditioned by his own culture, and this makes it difficult for him to obtain adequate and satisfactory data bearing on them or sometimes even to see clearly the problems he attacks. Thus, we realize the importance of knowing the extent to which cultural phenomena, like physical forms, are tenacious. We know, in a very rough sort of way, that a simple material culture will give way before a more efficient one much more quickly than one type of social organization will be given up for another. But when an aboriginal culture is vigorously suppressed, will anything remain in spite of everything? Will there be any residuum so subtle that only painstaking research will bring it to light? Again, we see that the problems of the manner in which cultures intermingle is of the utmost importance to our understanding of cultures as a whole. Yet we ask almost in vain the extent to which the differential rate of acceptability of new cultural traits makes for the harmonious combination of elements which are quite diverse in historical reality. This may perhaps be observed most satisfactorily in linguistic forms, yet on the problem as a whole we are almost completely at a loss.

More difficult than all are the problems which arise from our attempt to study the interaction between the biological form of man and his cultural behavior. As we survey a people, we are at once arrested by the questions: What of their culture is racially conditioned and what culturally? Why does the white child, when presented with a picture-puzzle, tend to put it together more quickly than the Indian but with more mistakes? Is this the result of the different cultural patterns of the social groups in which the children have been brought up, or is it caused by something inborn which will manifest itself in all aspects of their cultural behavior as they mature? We find an amazing variety of types of cultural behavior in the world, yet, if these are sketched in large enough perspective, they will seem curiously alike. Whether we observe similarities or differences, in physical form or cultural behavior, depends, in the final analysis, on the type of problem to be solved. But we all realize that differences both in race and civilization are to be found, and that if we can establish any correlation between the two, there will at least be the possibility of investigating more clearly any possible causal relationship which may exist.

II

Perhaps the fundamental difficulty in our study of these problems is the absence of control conditions. The biologist, working with the short-lived lower forms of life, can breed them in great numbers and through many generations, and thus observe the processes of heredity. He can cross various types at will, and in numbers permitting statistical analysis of his results. Not so the student of human biology. His laboratory is the world over, and he can only at best approximate laboratory conditions. The problem is even more perplexing when we approach the study of cultural or linguistic data. At least, in the study of physical anthropology, we may take reasonably exact measurements by means of which, through statistical manipulation, we may approximate results coming from controlled laboratory experiments. At least, for the physical anthropologist, the length of the head is something directly comparable on all human beings, no matter what the racial type or the cultural background. But when we attempt to compare cultural data we come at once into difficulties arising from definition. Is a paddle in one culture really the same as that in another? Is totemism one thing, or many? In order to answer even such fundamental questions, we must know the setting of the phenomenon we are studying in the cultures of which it forms a part. And it is on the rock of disregard of the cultural associations which adhere to a given trait in different cultures that the extreme diffusionists may well come to wreck.

We must agree, then, that the only way in which problems of this sort are ever to be answered is through searching out situations in which we find the necessary controls presented to us, and studying these. Thus, in the consideration of the processes of cultural change, if we find a people of a known cultural background, who have been presented with known cultural alternatives and have accepted some and rejected others, we may obtain light on the implications of their action by studying what they have done. If, further, we find that people with the same general cultural background have been presented with different cultural opportunities, then by analyzing what they have refused and retained in each case we may make our conclusions clearer and more acceptable. The same holds true for the consideration of problems involving change in physical form. And it is because the Negro offers almost the most accessible and most easily verifiable conditions of this sort, that we may regard him as offering one of the most promising possibilities for investigation.

III

What, then, is the nature of the data obtainable from the Negro in the New World and in Africa, which will contribute to the understanding of some of our fundamental problems? Let us first consider the aspects of the situation which bear on the problems of man's physical form and the processes of racial amalgamation and change. To begin with, the unmixed Negro is found in numerous environments. In West Africa, in South America, in the West Indies, and in the United States, there are hundreds of thousands of persons of unmixed Negro blood. The tropical West-African provenience of the New World Negro is not climatically different from many localities where he is found in the western hemisphere. Are any differences manifest between unmixed Negroes in the two regions? Has the pure Negro in tropical America and tropical Africa the same physical form and physiological processes? Furthermore, the Negro is not only found in the tropics, but also in the sub-tropical Bahamas and the southern United States, and in the temperate zone both in the United States and Brazil. Can it be said that he clings to his essential racial characteristics? Or has the descendant of the West African made fundamental physical adaptations to the colder climates to which he has been exposed? We cannot for a moment minimize the difficulties which lie in the path of the student who attacks these problems; the difficulty of gathering his data, and the greater difficulty of evaluating them. But they are there, both in Africa and the Americas, and need only the patience, the time, and the workers to collect and analyze them.

Ever since the seventeenth century, the Negroes in all this region have lived in contact with whites, with extensive mixture between the races resulting, while, although to a far lesser degree, there has been contact with American Indians as well. The availability of the data for studies of race-crossing and its results is obvious. And the material is present in such quantity that the difficulty which Fischer found in his study of the Bastards of South Africa, that of small numbers available, need not be feared. The problem becomes the more enticing when we realize, also, that there are not only large differences between these races but within them as well. Africans from all portions of the West Coast and the Congo are represented in the New World, while in the United States, Brazil, and the islands and littoral of the Caribbean sea they have crossed with English, Spanish, Dutch, French, Danish, and other European types. In a word, we find all degrees of mixture between numerous types both of whites and Africans present in the region.

When we turn to the field of cultural investigation, however, we become even more impressed at the amount and kind of data the Negro offers. To begin with, the problem which is the bane of most ethnological research is not present; for as far as the Negro is concerned, we know, within reasonably precise limits that are capable of more precise definition where the New World Negroes came from. The cultural background of Africa is better understood than the physical form of the African, to our resulting advantage in this aspect of the study. On the other hand, much is known, and it should not be difficult to gather more and more cultural information concerning the Negro on this side of the Atlantic. The folklore collections are impressive in their extent, linguistic studies and those of Negro dialects are beginning to be given the attention they deserve, while religious and ceremonial practices have for many years fascinated students in various portions of the Americas. With better knowledge of the African cultures we shall have an adequate basis to investigate the affiliation of those cultural traits the American Negro has retained in his contact with white and Indian civilizations. On the other hand, further investigation on this side of the Atlantic must result in more data from which to draw conclusions as to the nature of the African cultural survivals which are manifest in the behavior of the Negro in the Caribbean, the United States, and in South America.

It is quite possible on the basis of our present knowledge to make a kind of chart indicating the extent to which the descendants of Africans brought to the New World have retained Africanisms in their cultural behavior. If we consider the intensity of African cultural elements in the various regions north of Brazil (which I do not include because there are so few data on which to base judgment), we may say that after Africa itself it is the Bush Negroes of Suriname who exhibit a civilization which is the most African. As a matter of fact, unless the observer omitted to take their language into consideration, and unless he were familiar with small elements obtained from the whites with whom these people were in contact while they were in slavery and the Indians whom they drove out of the Guiana bush, he would assume, at first glance, that their culture was wholly African. Next to them, on our scale, would be placed their Negro neighbors on the coastal plains of the Guianas, who, in spite of centuries of close association with the whites, have retained an amazing amount of their aboriginal African traditions, many of which are combined in curious fashion with the traditions of the dominant group. Next on our scale we should undoubtedly place the peasants of Haiti, especially their religious life and their folklore, as they present numerous aspects which would at once be familiar to the Africanist. And associated with them, although in a lesser degree, would come the inhabitants of neighboring Santo Domingo. From this point, when we come to the islands of the British, Dutch, and (sometime) Danish West Indies, the proportion of African cultural elements drops perceptibly, but in their folklore, in such matters as the combination of aboriginal African with their Christian religious practices, and in the curious turns of phrase to be noted in their tales, we realize that all of African culture has not by any means been lost to them. Next on our table we should place such isolated groups living in the United States as the Negroes of the Savannahs of southern Georgia, or those of the Gullah islands off the Carolina coast, where African elements of culture are still more tenuous, and then the vast mass of Negroes of all degrees of racial mixture living in the South of the United States. Finally, we should come to a group where, to all intents and purposes, there is nothing of the African tradition left, and which consists of people of varying degrees of Negroid physical type, who only differ from their white neighbors in the fact that they have more pigmentation in their skins.

The importance of the mere fact that there is a racial type for which such a list can be made is enormous. To what extent are cultural elements which are constant in all this varied list to be discerned? What do the Africans do that the inhabitants of the Negro quarter of New York City also do? May we find perhaps, on close examination that there are some subtle elements left of what was ancestrally possessed? May not the remnant, if present, consist of some slight intonation, some quirk of pronunciation, some temperamental predisposition? And if we do find these, may we ascertain the extent to which they are increasingly present as we find Negroes removed from white influence? That such factors are to be discovered is quite possible, and this fact is something to be reckoned with in all studies of the Negro.

And the important part of the matter is that the discovery of any constants will throw as much light on the behavior of the African as it will on that of the New World Negro. For in the final analysis, and in the nature of the case, the most illuminating method of studying the presence of cultures is by considering conditions in which culture has maintained itself under stress and strain. What is retained and what discarded will point our way to understanding what is found in Africa, as it may well make for a greater understanding of the processes of culture as a whole. Certainly if we find that whatever has been retained by the Negroes in all these varying cultural adventures is constant throughout all the groups, we shall at least have a lead as to what to look for when we attempt to unravel situations arising out of an unknown historical past. And this is the sort of problem that presents itself to the anthropologist as the rule and not as the exception.

Data of this kind should also point toward an understanding of the nature of the interrelation of physical form and culture, as merely a cursory consideration of the Negro in his cultural wanderings is conducive to thought on the matter. That the problem is a very practical one is patent to one reading the literature of the Negro in the United States. Almost everything that he does has been attributed to innate qualities. Yet if in our survey of all these cultures we find some elements always the same, while others vary with differences in historical background and cultural contacts, the problem will be restricted by that much, and we can then go on from that point in our attempt to determine whether these results have been determined biologically or culturally. Has the Negro, for example, a definite temperament? Is he always happy? What is it that makes him like to sing and to dance? Is he, by and large, to be regarded as extraverted wherever found? A Negro economist who is making a study of Negro business activities in the United States finds himself puzzled by just this sort of problem. "Why is it," he asked me, "that Negroes living in a civilization essentially pecuniary turn to poetry, music, and painting rather than to business as soon as they have acquired a social surplus?" And that this question is not an idle one is apparent to those who are conversant with the development of the so-called "New Negro" movement in the United States, which has attracted so many of the younger Negroes.

There is the matter of folklore. How stable is the folklore of the Negro? We know that Negro tales are affected by the cultural contacts of their tellers; that the Dutch Negroes have Dutch elements in their stories, the French ones French elements. But aside from this, what common elements, African and not European, are to be discerned in all of them? Are the "voodoo" of the southern United States, the dances of Haiti, the winti of Dutch Guiana all manifestations of the biological make-up of the Negro which is to be seen in the pure form in the dances and other religious rites of the Africans and in attenuated form in the hysteria shown in the "revivals" of the Christian Negro churches from time to time in the United States? Or are these latter cultural carry-overs? Why does the Negro in Dutch Guiana use "tjari ko" [carry come] for the expression "to bring," and why do we find exactly the same expression in the folktales of the comparatively Europeanized Negroes of Jamaica? Why has the Twi day-name Kofi (Cuffee) persisted in the United States in spite of the rigorous manner in which the African elements of culture have been weeded out?

What of Negro music? It has been claimed by Professor von Hornbostel that the spirituals of the United States are essentially European folksongs created by the innate musical genius of the African, and that only the motor behavior which biologically determines the manner in which they are sung is African. But would this type of motor behavior persist in crossing? For the appearance of the mixed Negroes and the pure ones when singing these songs is quite the same. Or shall we find that there are gradations of intensity of African stylization in the music of these peoples to correspond with the degree of intensity of African elements in the general culture? In all these problems, the question comes up: What is innate and what cultural? Investigation into the manner in which the Negro has accommodated himself to all the different cultural backgrounds into which he was brought as a slave should constitute a significant step toward an understanding of the interrelation of the processes of culture and physical form.

So much for the problem and opportunities for gathering data contributing to its solution. That the Negro in the New World offers a wide and profitable field for study, which should result in findings of the utmost importance for Africanists, Americanists, and those who are interested in the larger aspects of human existence, should be apparent. We must consider the kind of information needed for an understanding and solution of the problem presented by the Negro.

IV

In the consideration of physical form, the problem must be first attacked in Africa itself. Until we know more of the essential nature of the people and cultures of the region from which the New World Negro was brought, studies made on this side of the Atlantic can have little general significance. What distinct tribal differences are found in West Africa and the Congo? What is the variation of pigmentation in the native African? What is the range of nostril width? Of lip thickness? What are the differences to be found in facial form, in bodily proportions, in functional processes? The measurements of families, especially adults of both sexes and of children of both sexes and all ages, are badly needed. How does the African child grow? In what manner are African physical characteristics inherited? All of these points need elucidation, for we have had too much measuring of cephalic index on a miscellaneous group of Africans, and not enough systematic study of other traits in related descent lines. In the case of the American Negro, having the necessary comparative data, we may do two things. In the first place, we may point with greater certainty to the African provenience of certain isolated New World groups. And for studies of racial crossing and its effects, we can have the greater certainty as to the nature of the basic stocks from which this African portion of the ancestry of the mixed American Negroes came, which we have for the other, the European portion.

Another aspect of the attack on the problem is the cultural one. Any serious contribution to this phase must also be based on far greater knowledge of African cultural processes than we possess at present. This is especially true of linguistic material. Thus, we know almost nothing about the significance of tone in the vast majority of West African and Congo languages. We know almost as little about their basic phonetic elements, thus it is here that we may find the most subtle survivals. Both in Haiti and in Suriname we find that the double closure (gb) is employed in certain terms, while it is reasonable to suppose, on the basis of present knowledge, that the tendency toward tonal inflection which characterizes many languages of West Africa is one of the most tenacious elements in the New World Negro's culture. That there is tone, no longer significant but none the less present, few who have heard the American Negro talk under stress can doubt. Much more definite information as to its rôle both in Africa and here is essential before we can draw conclusions of any validity. Furthermore, such a matter as the use of the falsetto to express surprise, so characteristic of the Negroes of the New World wherever they are found, is one concerning which no Africanist has enlightened us; perhaps because it has not been realized that it was a point of importance. But if we can establish such unconscious behavior patterns as present among Negroes wherever they may be found, will it not be of significance when fitted in with other data?

Religion, folklore, social organization will all repay the most careful study. And not only the reports of these cultural manifestations themselves, but the consideration of the attitudes of the people are needed. Why did the Negro acquiesce in slavery itself as complacently as he seems to have done? Was it something essential in his make-up, or was it because the only cultural fact that was familiar to him in the civilization of the Americas was that of slavery? What is the significance of the great family solidarity of the Negroes, something noted by all who have had contact with them? It is not strange that we find a form of social organization in Suriname, that is almost typical of West Africa, but why in the United States is there such great objection among Negroes to allow their children to be cared for in institutions? Why is it that families, themselves almost on the poverty line, will take under their wing a homeless child rather than give him to strangers? What is the relation of the phenomena of religious hysteria so familiar to students of the Negro in the United States, Haiti, the Guianas and the West Indies to similar African phenomena? And to what extent is the folklore of the Negroes western today, to what extent has it been deflected by the culture of the whites? Until we know more of African folk-material we cannot adequately answer these questions.

On the other hand, this is not to say that were African physical types and cultures much better known than they are, sufficient information would be available regarding the Negroes of this side of the Atlantic to make important progress with the problem. The first line of attack is one essentially historical, and a matter for the trained archivist. Where did the slaves brought to the New World come from? It is not enough to know that they represent tribes from Sierra Leone to Saõ Paulo Loando. It would be strange were no tribal names found tucked away in the records of the slavers; if a careful investigation into the problem of the places where shipment was made from Africa did not at least reveal the towns on which slave caravans converged from the interior. In the records of the ports of the southern United States and the West Indies, of Suriname and Brazil; in the archives of Lisbon and Rotterdam and Gothenburg and Gloucester and Liverpool and other shipping centers of the 17th and 18th centuries, it is fairly certain that careful search will reward us with a flood of light as to the exact provenience of the Negroes. We know that "Coromantynes" were brought to the New World, but who were these people? Ashanti, perhaps, but we cannot be sure. And although the names of some tribes are known to us, this, again, is not enough, and even the scattered references to these have not been collected and made available to us.

Data on the physical anthropology of the Negroes of the western hemisphere is also sadly lacking. Up to five years ago, nothing had been done to study the Negroes of the United States, and today relatively little is known of their physical form. Of the West Indians we know less, while of the Negroes of central America and northern South America we know practically nothing. And the culture and physical form of Brazilian Negroes are *terra incognita*. Studies of pure-blood and mixed Negroes in all these regions are badly wanted, and, although progress has been made in the United States, almost all the questions which were posed for the Africanist working in physical anthropology might also be posed for the student of the Negro in the New World. Work in this hemisphere takes on added importance, since measurements on some of the islands of the West Indies, and in Brazil, where there has not been the insistence on the color-line which has characterized other islands and the United States, should reveal the influence which prejudice, a cultural fact, has had in forming the physical types to be found.

In the realm of culture, only in folklore has work been carried on to an extent to be of use to us, and even here there are far more data to be collected. What of the lore of the Negroes in the Spanish-speaking countries of Central America? We know nothing of it, and practically the same is to be said of Brazil and many of the West Indian islands. In linguistics, studies of variations of dialect in the European languages spoken by the New World Negroes are practically non-existent, nor has any notice been taken of the manner in which the tonal survival to be noticed is employed. Yet the scientific importance of such studies, especially if carried on by one familiar with African linguistics, should be of the first order. No systematic study of the religious practices of the Negroes of the United States from the point of view of the ethnologist has been carried on to my knowledge. Yet survivals of African religious practices offer a fertile field for study. We have many collections of Negro spirituals, but the extent to which they are similar or different from the songs of the Africans and the West Indians and South American Negroes is unknown. Indeed, the point becomes striking when it is realized that a book review by Professor von Hornbostel, perhaps the only man conversant both with African music and the spirituals, threw more light on the problem of the rise of American Negro music and on the cultural processes involved, than any of the lengthier works dealing with the music of the Negroes where his comparative knowledge was lacking. Certainly it is in folklore, religion, and music that much of the attack must be centered. For it is principally here, certainly as far as the Negroes of the United States and most of the West Indies are concerned, that possible African cultural survivals are to be salvaged.

The problem is not a small one. But that it is of great significance for the study of man's physical form and culture, and particularly for an understanding of the Negro both in Africa and America, cannot be doubted. And if we realize that it deserves far more attention than it has received, and that it must be perceived and approached by many workers on a vast scale, we shall have made the first step toward its solution.

The Contribution of Afroamerican Studies to Africanist Research

Studies of culture contact in Africa have tended to stress that native cultures are giving way before . . . European ways of life. New World Negro studies, however, give pause to such assumptions. . . . If New World Negroes have met the impact of European culture without complete loss of ancestral tradition and behavior . . . there is little reason to anticipate that Africans in Africa will not meet the far less massive attack on their ways of life. . . . Applying the results of Afroamericanist research to Africanist studies . . . unfolds structural unities in African culture that touch not only tribal groups, or contiguous geographical . . . regions, but that . . . extends this horizon significantly to afford an over-all view of West African and Congo cultures in general.

*   *   *

The contribution that the study of New World Negro cultures can make to Africanist research has become apparent only recently, as the data on Afroamerican societies have come to be more adequate, and the concepts and techniques used in studying them have been sharpened. The control of materials from the areas of Africa from which New World Negroes were derived has, however, from the first been a basic methodological postulate of anthropologists who have worked in the Afroamerican field. It is the thesis of this paper that an understanding of New World Negro cultures will reciprocally deepen our comprehension of the relevant African cultures themselves, give unity to a broader field of research, and open the door for an interchange that cannot but be fruitful for Africanists and Afroamericanists alike.

A paper delivered as part of a Symposium on Africa, sponsored by the Committee on African Anthropology, National Research Council, and held at the annual meetings of the American Anthropological Association, Chicago, 1946. *American Anthropologist*, I (L), no. 1, pt. 1 (1948), 1–10.

I

Certain theoretical formulations that have crystallized from the study of Afroamerican cultures may first of all be indicated to provide a conceptual framework for the ensuing discussion. These are as follows:

1. The hypothesis of *cultural tenacity*, achieved through the psychosocial mechanism of *enculturation;*

2. The hypothesis of *cultural focus*, which points the way toward a comprehension of the primary concerns of a people, and, in contact situations, illustrates the carry-over of aboriginal modes of custom in unequal degree as the different aspects of culture lie within this focal area or outside it.

3. The hypothesis of *retention*, under borrowing, of aboriginal meanings of such conventions as are carried over into the new setting, and the corollary that retentions may manifest themselves in new forms by means of the mechanism of *reinterpretation.*

Let us now examine briefly the usefulness of these hypotheses in analyzing New World Negro cultures, and their application to furthering our knowledge of significant aspects of the cultures of Africa from which they have been derived.

1. Studies of culture-contact in Africa have tended to stress that native cultures are giving way before the impact of European ways of life. New World Negro studies, however, give pause to such assumptions. For, though in Africa Africans are experiencing a condition of accelerated—and at times of enforced—cultural change, any pressures against their indigenous cultures that may confront Africans in most of Africa are as nothing compared to those which the enslaved Africans faced in the Americas. In most of Africa, tribal groups retain their identity, the subsistence base of their cultures has not been too seriously dislodged, native languages persist, kinship structures function, the core of ancestral sanctions and values is there to guide the life of the people, religious expression and music and art in the accepted tradition can go on.

In the New World, on the other hand, the functioning bases of aboriginal African culture were removed. Economic institutions and political structures were, in the nature of the case, impossible to continue. African kinship groupings—at least in the sib–extended family–polygynous immediate family equation—were similarly suppressed. Persons of varied linguistic habits were thrown together, so that only with the aid of a kind of *lingua franca* could they communicate. Yet the fact remains that the present-day New World descendants of

Africans have everywhere retained Africanisms, even though the degree of purity of these Africanisms varies widely with locality, socioeconomic class, and religious affiliation.

If we have recourse to the hypothesis of the tenacity of culture as a result of early enculturation, this is not difficult to understand. The conditioning force of culture, as felt in the earliest experiences of the human organism—that phase of the entire enculturative process whereby an individual is adapted to the ways of his group—here operated to give continuity to tradition by passing on as learned behavior the motor habits and skills, the linguistic modes, the food patterns, the attitudes and goals and anxieties of the older generation. This process of cultural conditioning is carried on in the household and transmits to the child what the members of the household have learned in *their* earliest years, as modified by *their* later enculturative experience. Here, then, we recognize not alone the mechanism that makes for continuity in culture, but for change within a matrix of traditional shaping.

The relevance of this for the study of African cultures is patent. If New World Negroes have met the impact of European culture without complete loss of ancestral tradition and behavior, but rather have achieved an integration of both within the larger framework of Euroamerican norms, there is little reason to anticipate that Africans in Africa will not meet the far less massive attack on their ways of life that is for them comprehended in their contact with European culture. Here we are not dealing with questions of policy toward native peoples, or procedures, but with the fact of scientific perspective. Afroamerican studies, then, offer to students of African cultures a documentation of the tenaciousness of African ways of life under contact, and point out the socio-cultural processes by means of which this tenacity was achieved in the New World—processes that are operative in Africa as well.

2. The hypothesis of *cultural focus*, applied to the study of New World Negro cultures, brings into relief the values which different aspects of culture hold for Africans themselves. As students of custom, we know that every people is concerned more with certain phases of its activities than with others. In some groups, concentration on economic and technological pursuits overshadows other aspects of life; elsewhere religion, or social organization, or art, or prestige phenomena will play that role. Because the focal unit of any culture is the one that commands greatest interest, it comes to hold a dynamic significance. That is, in a fairly stable situation, the focal aspect is the one most dwelt upon, with the result that here multiple possibilities and elaborations are envisaged, and change becomes most acceptable.

As a consequence, the focal aspects of stable cultures manifest more complexities and greater variation than do those less stable. Where a culture is under pressure from another way of life, however, ranks are closed and the sanctions and institutions of the focal aspect come to take on great—one might almost say obsessive—importance. In such a situation, the focal aspect thus becomes that part of the culture where we find the greatest resistance to change.

In the New World, it is in that general field of culture we may denominate as supernatural sanctions that peoples of African descent manifest the widest range of Africanisms, and the purest. The many recorded instances indicative of this phenomenon document the determination of the enslaved Africans to rescue from the debacle of slavery as much as possible of their aboriginal beliefs. Where Catholicism was the religion of the masters, the problem of retention of African religious practices was simpler than in Protestant countries. For example, in countries like Brazil, Cuba, and Haiti, West African and Congo cults flourish in such purity that, as we shall presently see, they lay bare significant facets of African religion that have heretofore been shown most difficult, if not impossible of study in Africa itself. The analysis of the Shouters sect in Trinidad documents the manner in which the aboriginal patterns were transmuted into Protestantism.

The materials everywhere underscore the fact that religion gives color and coherence to these cultures of Africa, a fact that had much impressed earlier students, but has tended to be overlooked by later emphasis on social, economic and political structures. Yet every student who has worked in those regions of the continent from which the New World Negroes were predominantly derived—even where he was limited by his problem to giving religion only cursory study—has testified to the basic role that religion plays in these cultures. To study agriculture without taking into account its supernatural sanctions as these bear on beliefs concerning ancestors and gods, or to investigate African social organization, or property rights, without probing the role of the ancestral cult is to obtain and present a truncated version of the phenomena being studied, and fail to grasp that core of cultural reality in terms of the integrative norms which inhere in these practices, however vulnerable they may appear from the point of view of economic expediency. The reaction of informants documents this, for it is actually difficult to hold an informant to a discussion, let us say, of kinship terminology, or land tenure, and not have him move at once to a consideration of the role played by the family dead.

3. As Africa comes into closer contact with Europe, and the acculturative situation comes to demand more of the ethnographer's attention, there is need of a full grasp of how the retention of older

ways may take on devious reinterpretations. How significant this process may be, and in what different outer forms the inner belief-systems and values sanctioned by African conventions may appear, can be perceived both conceptually and graphically from the New World experience of the Negroes.

Let us consider, as an example, an element of West African and Congo family structure that tends to go unrecognized, not only because of its humble place in the life of the peoples of these areas, but also because of the difficulties of studying it in Africa itself. Under slavery in the Americas, one institution, the nucleus of African kinship structures, came to dominate the social organization of New World Negro groups. We have reference to the individual woman's hut in the West African compound, where she and her children live, and which she leaves periodically to go, in her turn, to the hut of the man she shares with her co-wives, for her allotted time with him.

In the New World, the reinterpretation of this element in African social life was far-reaching indeed. The family unit came to be dominated by the mother or grandmother, and included her children and the man with whom, at a given period of time, she was living. The effect of this reinterpretation in family structure on the respective roles of men and women calls for a re-examination of African social structure. We need to understand better the several nuclear units within each compound, how they function individually, and in relation to each other, and to the male-dominated aspects of their lives. For the New World materials make clear that the women have traditional modes in hand to take over in the interest of cultural stability, even against great odds. By the same token, the study of New World Negro cultures suggests that the place of women in other aspects of African life, especially in its religious and economic phases, should be the subject of intensive research.

II

In addition to the leads for Africanist research offered by the analysis of New World Negro cultures in terms of the theoretical postulates just mentioned, there are certain methodological considerations that aid the student who comes to the African data with Afroamerican materials in hand. These are to be subsumed under two headings:

1. Where New World Negroes have retained Africanisms in relatively pure form, these are found to be less complex than their African counterparts. This means that institutions that, in West Africa and the Congo, present the student with such an overlay of elaboration as to obscure the foundation of belief or the rite that validates belief,

appear in the New World cleanly outlined. As a result, the Africanist comes to these more complex aboriginal parallels with a grasp of their essentials. His problem can in consequence be phrased in terms of a recognition of basic unities over a given area, and a perspective toward variants that can counteract descriptions of seemingly fragmented belief, or of amorphous practices, autonomous and unrelated to any common world view.

But the factor of seeing a specific problem in small compass is but one advantage. The New World data permit also a greater refinement in attack in terms of the particular, the detailed aspects of belief. In many West African cultures, the forms of worship have been institutionalized under a priestly hierarchy. Under the direction of specialists, cult-initiates, as surrogates for their families, perform the complex rituals whereby the gods are served. But to serve the gods requires knowledge that can only come with training—with schooling, that is, in the strictest sense. The training of novitiates is carried on in the seclusion of the priest's compound, or in the courts of the temples where the gods are worshiped.

As far as is known, not only have the details of this process of initiation not been recorded, but, in addition, the details of the cycles of ceremonies known to exist have defied attempts to set them down in systematic form. The rites of public worship in West Africa are so long, involve so many persons, and take on such varied forms that, even granted a willingness to reveal them to outsiders, and to discuss their meaning for the people who participate in them, they would be beyond the scope of anything less than a corps of observers to describe with any degree of adequacy. Moreover, informants who control the theological doctrines underlying these rites are to be found among the priesthood. But priests in West Africa are typically the least willing to give away their professional secrets, and become evasive and preoccupied once the probing goes deep.

Now it must be said for the priestly hierarchy that such reaction to probing is not motivated by economic self-interest alone. Such information is not to be had at a price. The nature of the methodological problem facing the ethnographer is rather one of traditional sanction, the factor of secrecy that throughout much of African life is a recurrent motif—secrecy of soul-name, of the nature of the founding phenomenon of the kinship group, of cult rites, of tabus that individualize charms, of initiatory practices, of remedies. Folklore richly illustrates this theme, and the spiritual and even legal penalties for violations.

We may say, then, that to clarify much of the present picture of a multiplicity of deities and rites, differing in concept as well as in name from group to group, the ethnographer must overcome both the factor of high specialization, and traditional emphasis on the mystic role of secrecy.

It follows, therefore, that insofar as high specialization is recognized to be a concomitant of population mass, where numbers are smaller, specialization is not so marked. As for the mystic value assigned to secrecy, even though present in the New World, it gives way to a desire, where this can be done with confidence, to demonstrate a fulness of esoteric knowledge. With definite leads at our command, therefore, or better still an outline of rites and their meanings, more than half the problem is met. Discussion becomes a matter between specialist and specialist, and no longer either a breach of professional safeguards or of spiritual jeopardy. The rest is in the hands of the ethnographer—and chance.

How is this demonstrated in New World Negro societies? In many Haitian peasant communities, or in the Shango cults that cluster about the city of Port-of-Spain, Trinidad, functioning African-derived cults lie on the surface, to be reached by the ordinary techniques of field-work. Where the New World cults attain greater intricacy of structure, as in Cuba and Brazil, these require more sustained probing for elaborations and variants. In these countries, however, though priests and priestesses are specialized to a degree in their functions, they are far less specialized than in Africa. They can be the more readily reached, and are found to be more willing to discuss their knowledge with the student, and to instruct him in the meanings of the rituals.

Thus in Bahia, Brazil, it proved possible to obtain information concerning the months-long cycle of initiatory rites of the cult-novitiates, and of the cycle of ceremonies of the gods in such detail—and to verify at first hand much of this—that reports in hand from the related cultures of Africa stand out in new perspective, and disclose insights that the literature on Africa does not give.[1]

2. The second methodological gain to be had from applying the results of Afroamericanist research to Africanist studies is that it unfolds structural unities in African culture that touch not only tribal groups, or contiguous geographical localities within certain extra-political regions, but that it extends this horizon significantly to afford an over-all view of West African and Congo cultures in general. The theoretical or practical implications of this need not be touched upon

---

[1] Dr. Margaret Mead, in discussing this paper, pointed out how, in Java, the same methodological principle of utilizing simple outlines of ceremonies in one region to give comprehension of very complicated forms of the same rites in another region was put to use in research carried out by herself and Dr. Bateson.

here. Let us see, however, by what processes this was made evident in the New World.

In the experience of slavery, with rare exceptions, local variants could not be sustained. Differences that marked off one people from another tended to be "smoothed." The least common denominators of their cultures, however, were by this very fact forced to the surface, and where pressures were not rigid, those African elements which were incompatible with the values of the dominant groups were suppressed. The absence of the Ibo pattern of abhorrence of twins, and the practices this calls forth, is one of these. The attitude toward twins that prevails in the New World is the Dahomey-Yoruba pattern, which is not absent from certain areas of the Congo. Or again, as in Bahia, where there was no suppression of African worship, the more esthetic elements of that worship have flowered, and any deity whose dancing is too much at variance with this pattern, or whose behavior is antisocial, has been "seated," and denied the right to find expression in possession or dancing.

In any area, students tend to stress regional differences in comparing the cultures of their concern with other cultures. The importance of the local variant is in no sense lessened, however, when the value of regional unities is pointed out. It is just as necessary to differentiate the ways of a local group from those of their neighbors as it is to relate them to those of other peoples who inhabit the same area they do; but neither approach gains from undue stress. Toward a recognition of these wider affiliations, then, the Afroamerican materials can provide important leads, and thus further the study of those problems where methods requiring an overall approach must be employed.

III

A substantial number of retentions of African custom without reinterpretation—that is, in immediately recognizable form—have carried over to Afroamerican cultures. In most instances, the African character of these retentions is at once apparent because of their similarity to African cultural elements that have been observed and recorded in Africa. But an increasing number of non-European cultural elements, unrecorded in Africa or merely noted in passing, have been coming to light in the cultures of New World Negroes. These elements, when studied in Africa in the light of their New World incidence and setting, have either pointed the way to investigations that have revealed African counterparts in an autochthonous setting, where they had been overlooked, or have stimulated inquiries which have shown the corresponding elements in Africa to possess a different, sometimes a deeper significance than had previously been assigned to them.

A simple instance falling in the latter category, that has already been documented, concerns the game *wari*, or *mancala*, or *adji*, as it is variously termed. This game, played on a wooden board or using shallow holes dug in the earth, is played by distributing pebbles or seeds in these holes, in clockwise or counter-clockwise direction, until one player captures a majority of the pieces. The game itself, played over most of Africa, has been widely reported and its moves recorded. Such aspects of the game as the skill with which it is played, the frequency with which men are seen playing it, have been often commented on. Accounts of it, for the most part, are to be found under the heading "Games" in the ethnographic reports.

Work among the Bush Negroes of Dutch Guiana, however, revealed that it was much more than just a game. An intimate association with the cult of the dead explained why it was never played at night. A whole vocabulary used in playing it revealed a symbolism of war and conquest. Prestige-patterns adhering to it became evident. The fact that the Bush Negroes had four forms of the game, rather than one, was unusual in the light of the recorded data on it.

Subsequent work in West Africa demonstrated that the peoples studied all had several forms—that, in Dahomey, there was even a form of solitaire, which had been played by the King as he thought through questions of state. On a humbler level, the game functioned as an adjunct of the prestige factor. Beginners were found to play this form of solitaire to attain grace in handling the seeds, while old-timers used it to perfect their "form" in manipulating the instruments of the game. The association with the cult of the dead was found to be an aspect of the game in Africa as in the New World, while special terms comparable to those used in Guiana while playing it were also recorded. As a result of the New World findings, Driberg and others examined this cultural element and found that in East Africa and elsewhere it is much more than just a game, functioning in many more ways than as a form of recreation.

Research in Bahia, Brazil, has brought to light several highly significant aspects of West African musical and religious patterns that have been overlooked in investigations in Africa. The function of the drummer in the religious rites of the people is one such aspect. Nadel has reported a guild of drummers among the Nupe, and his account, unique in the literature of Africa, is important because it sets forth the socio-economic place of this group which, in a more general way, is matched by the informal organization of the Bahian drummers. In Bahia, as has been pointed out, the drums, which speak to the gods, are central in all public and many private rituals, while the chief drummer sets the pace of the rite and bears the responsibility that it move at a pace that pleases the gods, and, at public rites, adds prestige to the cult center.

Afroamericanist research has similarly revealed that, in this society, the drummer is the musician *par excellence,* whose virtuosity brings him coveted rewards of position and prestige. Discussion with Yoruba informants now in the United States revealed without much difficulty that here is a phase of African practice that richly merits the attention of Africanists working in the field. For the Yoruba drummer is said to play a defined role in his community. He acts as a mediator in disputes. As one who calls the gods, he should not engage in disputes himself, and his neighbors will be circumspect enough not to thwart or anger him unduly. If a drummer has not paid the school fees for his son, the boy will not be expelled. "The schoolmaster doesn't want a drummer for an enemy."

The Bahian post-possession phenomenon termed *eré*—since discovered in Trinidad by Espinet and Eduardo—is a major contribution of Afroamericanist research to Africanist studies. The phenomenon of possession is ubiquitous in West African, if not in all African religion. It has often been recorded and in these descriptions the states preceding possession, and possession itself, are invariably treated. But the experience of coming out of possession has thus far been quite overlooked. In Bahia, however, and at times in Trinidad, a person coming out of possession goes through a transitional stage wherein he is "in a state of *eré.*" That is, he does not at once recover his "self." The deity is envisaged as having withdrawn from "his head" but is replaced by that attribute of the god which is his messenger, and his childhood state. To see cult-initiates in this state—and it is not easy to do so—is a diverting experience. Some of them caricature the choreography of the ritual dancing for the gods, some feed the drummers, stuffing food in their mouths as they play their instruments, some sing children's songs or play children's games or engage in mischievous pranks. An exceptional one may be morose, or amorous, or quarrelsome. In Bahia, a troublesome *eré* would not be allowed by the cult-head to "play," but would be ritually dispatched. Quite aside from the psychological problems this phenomenon suggests, its importance in the religious complex of these two Afroamerican groups lies not only in the new data this uncovers but in its implications for a more comprehensive understanding of African religion.

Again, the Yoruba informants knew of this mode of coming out of possession. The word *eré* is Yoruba, and is part of the complex of "little creatures" known as *ijimeré, eré, egberé,* etc. And there are deeper implications, for, in the religious systems of all West African societies, and perhaps in other regions, the "little people," usually of the forest, hold a place of importance. A query in a letter to an Ashanti friend elicited a reply that the same phenomenon exists among the Ashanti, and an Ibo declared that each deity has a multitude of these creatures which he assigns to each devotee. Research on this aspect of possession should furnish new and clarifying materials concerning the association of concepts within the structure of African theology and ritual that will go far to document the inherent unity underlying the complexities of African religion.

IV

Many other instances, on all levels of generalization, and in various aspects of culture, where Afroamerican findings can be useful in Africanist research could be given if time and space permitted. A few of these are:

1. *The place of the non-initiate members of cult-groups.* In Bahia, these are given the Yoruba-Dahomean names of *ekedi* and *ogan* for the female and male members of the group, respectively, who are devotees of the gods, and perform important secular as well as religious functions, but who never themselves become possessed by the gods. Their parallels are reported to exist among the Yoruba.

2. *The symbolic importance of the three-year and seven-year ritual cycle following the death of a person holding an important office, before his successor can function in his own right.* Again, from Bahia, this interim period, when the spirit of the dead functionary is believed to have direct supervisory charge of affairs, is thus seen to be a stabilizing agent in the direction of conservatism of the first order. Its presence and role in West Africa—outside the Yoruba country—and elsewhere on the continent merits investigation.

3. *The pattern of improvisation,* especially in devising songs of praise and ridicule as a technique of social control as well as an incentive for creative expression. The fact of improvisation in Africa is well known, but the encouragement it has given to forms such as the Trinidad calypso or the Brazilian carnival songs, where it is often a medium for political satire, raises points that have not been investigated in Africa.

4. *The tendency, in all the New World, for the suppression of African religious forms to be accompanied by a compensating increase in the employment of such less public controls of the supernatural forces as magic.* Whether, under pressure of European domination, African religion goes underground, and manifests itself in an increase of magic (especially black magic), is a challenging acculturation problem.

5. On the most comprehensive level, the manner in which New World Negroes have syncretized African and European custom into a functioning culture different from either of its ancestral types points to *psychological resilience as a deep-rooted African tradition of adaptation*. In Africa itself, this suggests a study of intertribal acculturation, which has tended to be overlooked in systematic programs of investigation.

These items, then, are but a few of the leads, specific and general, that the student of African cultures can obtain from a knowledge of the Afroamerican field. They stress ethnographic manifestations of the historic relations between these cultures, and thus underscore the fact that research among the Negro peoples of Africa and the New World represents no more than work on different parts of but a single field of study.

The Present Status
and Needs of Afroamerican Research

It came to be recognized that the problem was vastly more complex than a statement drawn in terms merely of the presence or absence of Africanisms in the New World. The problem . . . was the manner in which elements of European, African, and . . . American Indian cultures had exerted mutual influences. . . . The introduction of these concepts of retention and reinterpretation reorient the entire field, raising research from the elementary level of description and comparison to that of the analysis of process. . . . They replace the initial questions, "What?" and "Where?" with the more penetrating "Why?" and "How?" With this approach we can probe beneath form to meaning. For we know today that the acceptance of new forms does not necessarily preclude the retention of an underlying value system.

❖   ❖   ❖

The field of Afroamerican studies has had an extraordinarily rapid development during the past decade. In fact, the field, as such, did

This paper is based on an address delivered on October 28, 1950, before the Annual Meeting of the Association for the Study of Negro Life and History held at Atlanta University. *Journal of Negro History*, XXXVI, no. 2 (1951), 123-47.

not exist in recognizable form as recently as twenty years ago. A review of the publications of this period makes clear that the years 1930–40 were occupied with the basic task of delimiting the scientific problem that gave work in this field its reason for being. Once this was accomplished, it was possible during the following decade to devise the conceptual and methodological tools essential for the adequate analysis of the data. Today, these requirements are well in hand. The work of consolidating gains and gathering additional data, filling in lacunae in our information and prosecuting the study of more specialized research problems can go forward.

No discussion of this development would be accurate if it did not recognize the role played by the *Journal of Negro History* and its late editor, Dr. Carter G. Woodson. The hospitality to papers wherein data have been detailed and relationships discussed is evidenced by the number of titles in the Afroamerican field published by him in the organ of the Association for the Study of Negro Life and History he founded. More important still is the fact that for years this *Journal* has been the only one devoted to the historical aspects of Afroamerican study, a fact that gains added significance when it is realized that Woodson interpreted the word "history" in its broadest sense, publishing many papers that only in their implications dealt with historical data, strictly speaking. If a review of policy of the *Journal* at this time should result in giving it the compass implicit in this broader interpretation of historical study, this would be but a logical working out of its founder's position concerning Afroamericanist research.

The Afroamericanist field covers a vast geographical area and cuts across many of the conventional academic disciplines. This is particularly striking in the joint use of historical analysis and ethnographic comparison, the technique of research known as ethnohistory. Ethnohistory has been a primary instrument in establishing the field of study as such. This technique was responsible for the expeditiousness with which the long-debated problem of the predominant African influences that helped shape the cultures of the Negro peoples of the New World was solved. Without the precise knowledge it yielded, pinpointed research in Africa, aimed at understanding the historical baseline for the African derivatives found in New World Negro cultures, could not have been carried on.

It is worth noting that today the influence of this method, growing out of the demonstrated results it has obtained in Afroamerican research, is to be seen in the field of Latin-American studies, where a baseline for cultural change is being sought in Spain and Portugal as an aid in assessing this factor in the equation of the Indian cultures of Mexico and Central America. The step which must logically follow is the re-examination of the entire Latin-American field in terms of the third component of its cultural stream, which is to say, the African. Here the ethnohistorical method may be expected to reveal, as it has done in the Afroamerican field, the reinterpretation of retained cultural elements and their reworking to bring them into the framework of the cultural orientations of the present day.

With this method, too, Afroamerican research in other disciplines than history and ethnology could go forward. A dramatic illustration of this is had in the studies of Lorenzo Turner on the speech of the Gullah Island Negroes.[1] As is well known, earlier students—Krappe,[2] Gonzales[3] and, derivatively, H. L. Mencken[4]—had caused the thesis to be widely accepted that these special features represented the inability of the Negroes to learn the language of their masters, and that their dialect represented carry-overs of the speech of Elizabethan England spoken by the early whites.

On the basis of spot studies and checks of comparative morphology made during field research in Dutch Guiana and West Africa, and drawing on text materials from various English and French-speaking West Indian Negro groups, Mrs. Herskovits and I, early in the period of exploratory research, advanced a different hypothesis.[5] This hypothesis held that, structurally, the special traits in Gullah speech, like those in other New World Negro dialects, could be ascribed to the retention of certain African grammatical forms, into the mold of which were cast English and French words pronounced by speakers whose phonemic patterns were wholly or partially African.

Turner, working as a member of the group making a study of American dialects in general, approached the problem of Gullah speech from the point of view of vocabulary and phonetics. As an Afroamericanist, he recognized the possibility of African influence as having been operative here, taking it as a problem to be investigated rather than as an *a priori* hypothesis to be rejected out of hand. As an Afroamericanist, he also familiarized himself with African linguistic patterns, turning to the historical literature to discover the relevant African tongues which could be presumed to have been ancestral to the particular forms of speech he was studying.

The results, incorporated in his work *Africanisms in the Gullah Dialect* need no detailing here. He discovered a far greater degree of retention of African words in this region than even those most alert to the carryover of Africanisms in the New World had suspected. He was able to demonstrate beyond dispute that the patterns of pronunciation, which had given rise to the earlier belief that Gullah was a mispronunciation of English, actually represent the handing on of African phonemic habits. And though his research was not directed toward problems of linguistic structure, his materials in that area elaborately document the earlier hypothesis concerning the derivations of New World Negro speech. These results likewise support the findings of linguistic research, carried on quite independently, on Haitian Créole, by Suzanne Comhaire-Sylvain,[6] a student who, also, as an Afroamericanist, had gained prior acquaintance with African speech-patterns.

II

If we turn now to the wider Afroamerican field, we can, first of all, indicate the extent of our knowledge of the cultures, African and New World, that afford the basic materials for any Afroamericanist research project. As I have pointed out, the use of the ethnohistorical method has designated the significant area of Africa for research. This is a broad band of territory that follows the great double-curve of the western coast of the continent, from Senegal on the north to Angola on the south. It is an area rich in historic association between Africa and Europe, and the documentation is ample to permit us to assess change in the African cultures as well as to describe in some detail the initial stages of the acculturative process experienced by the Africans in Africa during the earlier period of slaving generations.

One highly important part of the region of our concern, the central portion of the Guinea Coast, has by now a considerable ethnographic literature. The early works of Rattray for the Ashanti[7] and of Spieth for the Ho-Ewe of Togoland [8] laid a pattern of careful factual reporting. Somewhat later, Mrs. Herskovits and I carried on research in Nigeria and the Gold Coast, but especially in Dahomey,[9] with the dual object of achieving an ethnographic analysis of Dahomean culture, and at the same time, in all three regions, to throw light on certain problems of Afroamericanist concern, as revealed by our earlier study of the Bush Negroes of Dutch Guiana. Later Africanist research in the significant area has been carried on in the main without reference to the New World scene, but is of great value in affording comparative data in the study of Afroamericanist problems. Here one may cite the papers and monographs of Fortes on the Tallensi[10] and of Field on the Gā[11] of the Gold Coast and, for Nigeria, of Nadel on the Nupe,[12] Forde on the Yakö,[13] and Meek and of Harris on the Ibo.[14] With the continuing work of Bascom on the Yoruba,[15] a people who, like the Dahomeans and the Gold Coast Fanti and Ashanti, have left a deep imprint on New World Negro cultures, we again return to Africanist research directed toward the study of problems lying both in the African and Afroamericanist fields.

In this same class is the research of Little on the Creole culture of Sierra Leone.[16] This is a valuable addition to the materials in the field, showing how similar circumstances of contact between Africans and Europeans in this region of Africa produced cultural reorientations quite comparable to those that resulted from similar contact in the New World. Here, too, is to be placed the work of Greenberg among the Hausa.[17] This research not only provided further data on the life of this people, whose presence in Brazil, at least, is specifically recorded, but also established the principle that the mechanism of syncretism has wider applicability than just to the Negroes of Latin America. For whereas in the latter areas the tradition of identifying African deities with Catholic saints by Negro members of African cult-groups living in Catholic countries had been well established,[18] Greenberg's research demonstrated that among the Hausa the local spirits (iskoki) have been syncretized with the 'jinn of the Mohammedan belief system.

Numerous studies of the cultures of this area, most of them as yet unpublished, are now in progress. These include researches carried on under the auspices of various English universities and of the International African Institute of London, largely under grants from the Colonial Social Science Research Council. They also include studies being made by permanent staff-members of the Institut Français de l'Afrique Noire and of the various IFAN local centers in French West and Equatorial Africa and of the Musée de l'Homme, and by advanced students of French universities working under their direction. The new Belgian Institut pour la Recherche en Afrique Centrale (IRSAC) gives a prominent place to the study of indigenous cultures of the Congo. Though the ethnographic work of this Institute has thus far been confined to the eastern portion of the Belgian Congo, it is anticipated that researches in the western part, which is of particular significance for Afroamerican studies, will eventually be instituted. Students and staff members of the Department of Anthropology, Northwestern University, have been sent to West Africa as a part of the Program of African Studies of this University, on grants from the Carnegie Corporation of New York, the Social Science Research Council, and the Rockefeller Foundation, and as Fulbright Fellows and research workers. Of great promise are the programs of social science research, instituted and planned, at the new centers of higher learning in British West Africa, particularly at the University College of the Gold Coast. Here Dr. Kofi Busia, himself an anthropologist, has organized a program of studies of the present-day scene that should yield comparative data of value to Afroamericanists.

In the New World, our present knowledge of the relevant historical processes and present-day modes of behavior in which these have resulted is likewise considerable. Here, too, pioneer studies pointed the way. The real values in the work of U. B. Phillips[19] for early Afroamericanists have frequently been passed over in the heat of controversies regarding the validity of Phillips' position on the historical aspects of slavery in pre-Civil War United States. Yet, in terms of Afroamerican research, it should be recognized that it was this same scholar who continuously stressed the importance of recovering from the records all available tribal and place-names to be found in the documents. Far earlier, W. E. B. Du Bois's study of the suppression of the slave trade[20] had laid a firm factual basis for later research in the history of slaving. For richness of primary materials, however, the monumental four-volume work of Donnan,[21] published between 1930 and 1935, stands alone. All American students of the history and ethnology of the New World Negro have rightly gone to this storehouse of information for data and research leads. The publications of French and Belgian historians concerned with the slave trade out of Nantes, which supplement Donnan's work, have likewise proved of great value, especially for studies of Africans brought to the Caribbean.[22]

Studies of the history of the Negro outside the United States have in the main been set in the larger picture of developments within the various countries or regions wherein the Negro population has played a significant role. The classical study of Gilberto Freyre on the place of the Negro in the culture of northern Brazil [23] comes to mind at once here; less-well-known publications dealing with the Negroes of other Latin American and Caribbean countries are too numerous to mention. Since they have not affected the trend of Afroamericanist studies, they may be left for those whose concerns are directed elsewhere. On the other hand, such a work as the recent history of the Negroes in the United States by Franklin[24] sets the discussion of its particular field of interest firmly into its larger African and Afroamerican context, and thus continues a well-established tradition of North American students of Negro history.

Much recent historical research in the Afroamerican field has been concerned with special problems. An outstanding example of this is the study of slave revolts. This is highly important, since in documenting the reactions of the Africans and their descendants to servitude, it affords one of the few available leads toward an understanding of the psychology of the Negro under slavery, and helps us to grasp the mechanisms which made for the retention in the New World of African cultural elements and their underlying sanctions. Here the work of Carroll,[25] Aptheker[26] and Wish[27] is especially to be noted. A number of significant papers by other students of this phenomenon have also appeared in recent years, most of which are to be found in the recent volumes of this JOURNAL. As concerns the total field of Negro history, there is no doubt that the interest of historians in Afroamericanist research is growing. This is made apparent, for example, by the issuance in August, 1944, of a special number of the *Hispanic American Review*, devoted entirely to articles on the history of the Negro in Latin America.

The study of the Negro in early Mexico by Gonzalo Aguirre Beltrán[28] has demonstrated the fruitfulness of the ethnohistorical method in Afroamerican research in a region of the New World previously unstudied in these terms. His analysis of the tribal derivations of Negro slaves, with particular reference to those brought to Mexico, a translation of which appeared in the JOURNAL OF NEGRO HISTORY,[29] is almost definitive for the New World in general. Its broader significance, however, lies both in the results of the investigation, which throws a new light on the demography of Mexico, and in its demonstration of the richness of the other insights to be gained by the use of the ethnohistorical attack. For this work not only established how large was the number of Africans introduced into Mexico during the early slaving period, and their tribal origins. The mechanisms whereby this population was merged into the dominant Indian component of the Mexican people is also demonstrated, and the way made clear for a study of the means whereby these Indian modes of life were influenced by the traditions of Africa, or whereby these modes of life were retained by groups who, to the present day, as in the state of Guerrero, have maintained themselves in predominantly Negro communities.

As we turn to descriptions of Afroamerican culture, we may again indicate some of the studies that pointed the way for later research. One of these, though admittedly impressionistic, nonetheless deserves more recognition than it has been accorded. I refer here to the volume by Sir Harry H. Johnston,[30] significantly a man of long experience in Africa itself, wherein the author, without applying the name, recognized the unity of what later came to be called the Afroamericanist field. To the present time, there is no better source for historical and ethnological data—such as they are—concerning the Negroes of a number of local regions of the New World.

More generally known, among these earlier studies, are certain works on the Negro cultures of Brazil, Haiti and Cuba. Here tribute must be paid to the vigor with which the authors attacked the problem. In Brazil, the work of Nina Rodrigues,[31] of Manoel Querino[32] and of Father Ignace[33] provided a firm foundation for the work of later students of the Brazilian Negro—Arthur Ramos,[34] Mario de Andrade,[35] Gonçalves Fernandes,[36] Edison Carneiro,[37] Donald Pierson,[38] Roger Bastide,[39] Octavio Eduardo,[40] Lorenzo Turner,[41] and Mrs. Herskovits and myself.[42] In Haiti, the publications of Jean Price-Mars[43] and J. C. Dorsainvil [44] foreshadowed the activity in that country which has resulted in the establishment of the Haitian Bureau of Ethnology, devoted primarily to the study of the Haitian aspects of Afroamerican research, and the work of such Haitian students in the field as the late Jacques Roumain,[45] and Lorimer Denis and his associates.[46] Finally, in Cuba, Fernando Ortiz[47] pioneered in demonstrating the presence of strong African retentions, and provided many leads for those more recent students, both Cuban and American, who have prosecuted research in that country. One may also place in this category of early studies the research of Elsie Clews Parsons into New World Negro folklore,[48] and of Mrs. Herskovits and myself among the Bush and Town Negroes of Dutch Guiana,[49] this latter research having been followed by a considerable number of investigations in various parts of the New World and Africa.

Ramos's general study of New World Negro cultures[50] was based on the work of most of the students mentioned above, and certain later publications such as the report on our research in Haiti.[51] The outbreak of the Second World War caused field investigation to be reduced to a minimum. During the period 1937–1945, however, field research was conducted by Simpson in Haiti,[52] by Mrs. Herskovits and myself in Trinidad,[53] by Turner,[54] Frazier,[55] and ourselves in Bahia, and by Octavio Eduardo and Nunez Pereira in Maranhão, Brazil.[56] An attempt was also made during this period to form an international association of those interested in Afroamerican research; but this only resulted in the abortive establishment, in Mexico City, of an International Institute of Afroamerican Studies, with a program of publication consisting of a journal, *Afroamerica*, of which, unfortunately, only two issues appeared.

Since the war, a number of researches, none of which has as yet achieved publication, have yielded results that will materially extend our knowledge of New World Negro cultures. Concurrent studies of the Black Caribs in the Republic of Honduras by Ruy Coelho and, in British Honduras, by Douglas M. Taylor[57] have at last yielded precise knowledge of one key group among New World Negro peoples. These studies, which were projected against a well-documented historical background, are of particular importance because they give full weight to the factor of Indian-African acculturation, so difficult and so tantalizing an aspect of the New World situation. Taylor, a specialist on Carib Indian language and culture, approached the Black Caribs from the point of view of his specialty, establishing the existence of strong retentions of Island Carib speech of the seventeenth century in their language, and giving a picture of the culture of those Black Caribs living under British rule. Coelho, a Brazilian conversant with African patterns, studied the Black Caribs who live in a country where Spanish influence predominates. Trained in projective psychology as well as ethnology, he investigated the psychological orientations of this group in terms of its culture.

These findings, in turn, will be able to be compared to those resulting from the recent field work of Erika Eichhorn in Haiti, and the continuing studies of René Ribeiro, a psychiatrist with anthropological training, in Pernambuco, Brazil. Ribeiro's researches will also yield more precise information concerning another variation of Brazilian Negro culture, since studies of only certain restricted aspects of the African-like ways of life found in Recife, the city in which he has been working, have heretofore been available. This knowledge of the variations on basic African themes to be found in different localities of Brazil, already apparent in the earlier studies, is also being rendered more precise as the researches of Roger Bastide of the University of São Paulo on this particular point continue to achieve publication.[58]

Research in the Greater Antilles has likewise extended our knowledge of the Negro cultures of this part of the Caribbean, particularly as regards the strength of African linguistic, religious and musical patterns. In Cuba, Bascom, working in 1949, found that the speech of the Yoruba of West Africa has been maintained as a living linguistic entity. Because of his own first-hand knowledge of Yoruba culture, he was enabled to obtain a systematic account of the ritual and theology of these cults which, adumbrated in the earlier publications of Ortiz, now appear in full-functioning African forms, comparable to those established for Brazil, Guiana, Haiti, and for certain groups in Trinidad.[59] Musicological studies in Cuba, carried on by Waterman, especially among the ñañigo groups, indicate a provenience for this cult of the Niger Delta area of West Africa. These retentions demonstrate the complexity of the problem of Africanisms to be studied in Cuba, particularly when it is realized that the Congo and Dahomean elements in Cuban Negro life that are known to exist remain to be systematically studied.

Most recently, work done by Joseph G. Moore in the Port Morant region of eastern Jamaica has for the first time established a locality where retentions of Congo languages in the Caribbean area are to be found. Recordings of a large vocabulary and considerable grammatical materials show the strength of this carry-over in the existence of such a living language, identifiable as being derived in considerable proportion from Kikongo, and in no sense vestigial. The complexity of the cultural and historical setting in this region is further illustrated by the fact that present religious patterns encompass not only the modes of worship of these Congo derived groups, but also those of the nearby Eastern Maroons, whose culture is of Gold Coast derivation, and the Revivalists, Afro-Protestants whose worship is like that of the "shouting" sects of the United States, or of the Trinidad Shouters.

The number of field researches made among Negro groups in the United States remains small and, except for music and folklore, is restricted to the Gullah Islands and the nearby mainland. The many books and papers in the *Journal* and *Memoirs* of the American Folklore Society are a mine of information on this subject, while the albums of songs made available by the Library of Congress, especially those recorded by Alan Lomax, plus other recordings by Courlander are rich in their implications for Afroamerican research. The study of the Gullah islanders made by Bascom in 1940,[60] the only ethnographic work there carried on with knowledge of the African background in mind, has not been followed through except for recent research by Simon Ottenberg, who in 1950 carried on a study of the Negroes of a community near Savannah, Georgia.[61]

It will be noted that in sketching the present status of Afroamerican studies, no mention has been made of historical research devoted to detailed analysis of the political or economic past of the Negro, or of the many investigations and action programs touching on race relations, social and economic orientations, health, agriculture, and the like. Studies of practical problems, by official bodies, such as those conducted by UNESCO in Haiti, or by the Caribbean Commission in various West Indian islands fall in this category, as do most of the researches conducted under the auspices of the Institute of Social Science of the University College of the West Indies in Jamaica. In the same way, no mention has been made of community studies and other sociological and economic research in Trinidad, Jamaica, Puerto Rico, Brazil and continental United States. Our terms of reference cannot include these studies, for though they draw their data from the same population groups, they tend primarily to be oriented in terms of practical issues rather than of basic scholarship. Or, where basic problems of scholarship are attacked, these studies tend to be local and non-historical, leaving out of account the factors of time depth and variation, with the important insights these afford. That is, such studies tend to disregard not only the historic roots of the cultures studied, but likewise to leave to one side the wider New World manifestations of the phenomena they have under investigation.

III

If the list of projects in Afroamerican research, completed and under way, that have been sketched here is compared to the list of research needs in the field presented ten years ago,[62] it will be apparent how considerable have been the achievements of the decade. This is especially true in the case of answers to the basic questions of a demographic, historical and ethnological nature that must be antecedent to an effective approach to Afroamerican materials. Yet, by the same token, to list work accomplished reveals the nature of the work to be done, the next phase of the problem to which we address ourselves here.

The challenge to historical research is still massive. Most of the documentary collections in the European centers of slaving operations have yet to be analyzed. More pressing is the need to preserve and study the great amounts of documentary materials in various West Indian Islands and in South and Central American archives. Precious materials, often stored haphazardly for want of resources to provide proper protection, are in some cases literally disintegrating. Cataloging of the collections in Latin American countries is proceeding slowly, and is recognized by the scholars of those countries as a prior condition to significant scholarly analysis.

In Brazil, where it was felt that the destruction of documents bearing on slavery and slaving operations at the time of emancipation had irrevocably weakened historical research in this area, evidence is accumulating to show that by no means all documents were burned, especially those in the archives of local bureaus not primarily concerned with slavery.[63] The work of Ildefonso Pereda Valdes and Dante de Laytano[64] suggests, furthermore, that the history of the Negro in the Rio de la Plata region, especially in the Argentine, offers fertile fields for investigation, as does the history of the Negro in Peru in the light of the contributions and suggestions for research of Fernando Romero.[65] These areas, and still others in South America, are made even more attractive as subjects for research in the history of their Negro populations when one reads the report of Antonio Vazques de Espinosa,[66] a Carmelite friar, on the Spanish possessions in South and Central America and the Caribbean at the end of the sixteenth century, a work which only within the decade has been rediscovered and translated. Intensive historical research on the Negro in most of Central and South America, outside the obvious regions of Brazil and the Guianas, is in fact one of the most neglected major areas of Afroamerican research.[67]

Studies of the history of the slave period in the United States and elsewhere continue to be made, but principally in terms that relegate the Negro to a minor place. Yet knowledge of the modes of life of this group under slavery is essential if we are to chart the course of change in their ways of life and analyze the manner in which European customs were taken over and African beliefs and modes of behavior reinterpreted to fit into their new patterns of living.

Our information concerning the cultures of New World Negroes and of the relevant African areas from which these cultures were derived likewise still show gaps to be filled. More descriptive studies of the cultures of the sub-Saharan belt, the Niger Delta region, and especially the western Congo and Angola are urgently needed. Much research in particular aspects of the cultures of the total area from which New World Negroes were derived is likewise called for. Materials for more adequate comparative studies of basic patterns in language, music, folklore and religion—those aspects of African life most strongly retained in the New World—must be made available. Similarly, intensive studies of social institutions, particularly of family structure, of certain key tribal groups of Africa should be carried on with the particular problems of the New World in mind. For it is in this area of religious and social institutions, especially the aspect of ritual in the former and family structure in the latter, that the most far-reaching reinterpretations of African patterns in the New World are found.

As concerns descriptive studies of New World Negro cultures, we count as clear gain the fact that today we at least know where the Negro populations are. This means that certain localities, earlier not thought of as significant, now call for investigation. Outstanding in this category are the Negro communities of Mexico, in the study of which only a beginning has been made—though it is apparent from preliminary field research by Aguirre Beltrán that this beginning promises important findings. The Negroes of Panama, of Venezuela, of the interior of Brazil, of French and British Guiana present almost untouched fields. So do the Negro groups of Colombia, where it is anticipated that the proposed research of Father Arboleda, based on a preliminary historical study of the origins of Colombian Negroes, as yet unpublished, will throw much-needed light. In the Caribbean, we still lack studies of the cultures of the Negro groups who inhabit the French and Dutch islands, while the cultures of the Negroes of British portions of the entire chain of the Lesser Antilles remain to be investigated.

Above all, descriptive studies, utilizing the resources of the ethnohistorical method, are needed for the United States. The methodological problems to be faced in making such studies are formidable, since the acculturative processes that have marked the historical experience of the American Negro are more complex than anywhere else in the New World. These problems, it is to be noted, were unheeded and unmentioned in the methodological preoccupations of the study of the American Negro carried on under the direction of Gunnar Myrdal. Indeed, it is striking that this study yielded no rounded description of a single American Negro community. Earlier studies, though deficient from the point of view of Afroamericanist research in their disregard of historic depth, thus stand after a decade as our only sources.

In all the Negro New World, researches in special fields that will throw light on the processes of historical and cultural change remain to be made. Music at once comes to mind as one of the most important of these. For the patterns of musical expression, that among all peoples lodge deep beneath the level of consciousness, give us a precise instrument for probing the ways in which European and American conventions have mutually influenced each other, to say nothing of their amalgamation to produce the present-day musical phenomena of jazz and its related forms. Linguistic studies, extending the work of Turner and others by the analysis of such modes of speech as *papiamento* of Curaçao, present another attractive facet of the total field for research by specialists. Here again, we are dealing with deep-seated conditionings which, under analysis, can reveal much of process and explain resultant form.

Religion provides another aspect of New World Negro life to which particular attention is to be directed, and so, as has been indicated, does family structure. For in both of these the range of variation in the New World provides us with an opportunity to analyze the problem of retention and reinterpretation in terms of differences that, of themselves, to say nothing of their scientific implications, are highly significant in pointing that comprehension of process and form which is basic to Afroamerican research. On the same comparative level psychological studies are needed to reveal the degree to which the different cultural orientations of various New World Negro groups, representing different degrees of contact with European custom and adherence to African ways of life, are reflected in personality mechanisms of individuals living under these conditions.

IV

The researches achieved during the past decade have brought about a basic reorientation in approach, and thus represent what is undoubtedly the most important development, in the Afroamerican field to date. This reorientation can best be described if we briefly consider the point of view it replaces.

Earlier students of the field and those who initially built on their work, were occupied with establishing the *facts* concerning the historical derivations and present forms of New World Negro cultures. Emphasis was thus laid, at times almost exclusively, on the African component. This, for example, is to be seen in the work of one student who, in recording Haitian peasant songs, took only those that presumably were "pure" African in conception and mode of execution. The weight of scholarly, no less than lay, opinion held firmly to the position—as a conviction that needed no proof—that Africa had no functioning part in New World Negro culture. In the United States, in particular, this resistance to the implications of the data from South America and Caribbean Negro societies, as these multiplied with increasing first-hand research the evidence of the retention of Africanisms, and when projected against real, rather than fanciful descriptions of African cultures, forced a too emphatic stress on these African carry-overs. Inevitably, this obscured the appraisal of other historical factors that were equally operative.

As in all scholarly disputes, however, the weight of evidence decided the validity of the point at issue. And after the manner of scholarship, it came to be recognized that the problem was vastly more complex than a statement drawn in terms merely of the presence or absence of Africanisms in the New World. The problem, it came to be understood, was the determination of the manner in which elements of European, African and, to a lesser degree American Indian cultures had exerted mutual influences on one another and, in the case of New World societies, had been merged to produce their present-day ways of life.

It will have been noted, perhaps, how in the preceding pages the points raised have had to do with the processes that lead to the reinterpretation of African ways far more than they have been concerned with the problem of the presence or absence of Africanisms. African custom, in relative purity, does exist in the New World, often in unsuspected places and to an unexpected degree. This has been established in the case of music, of folklore, of language, and of religion. But, taking the entire New World into account, purity of retention is the exception, not the rule. Retentions of African behavior, it is true, are found in most New World Negro communities, but they are present principally in reinterpreted form. The degree of reinterpretation varies with the geographical and political unit studied, and from region to region. Above all, it varies with socio-economic status. In those strata of society where there has been full access to the cultural resources of the dominant group, even reinterpreted elements would be idiosyncratic, rarely patterned.

The introduction of these concepts of retention and reinterpretation reorients the entire field, raising research from the elementary level of description and comparison to that of the analysis of process.[68] And at the same time it gives research in the field this new approach, it also points the significance of the findings for the understanding of some of the basic problems in the study of human culture on the world scene. It replaces the initial questions, "What?" and "Where?" with the more penetrating, "Why?" and "How?" In historical research, the problem becomes one of assessing the ways in which Africans accommodated themselves to ways of life set by their masters, and how, in turn, these latter were influenced by contact with their slaves. It becomes one, moreover, of understanding how this process worked out in different parts of the New World, where differing ecological settings, differing basic industries, differing cultural orientations prevailed; and how, in each region, the factor of class differentials influenced the accommodation of various groups within the Negro community.

With this approach we can probe beneath form to meaning. For we know today that the acceptance of new forms does not necessarily preclude the retention of an underlying value-system that derives from an earlier kind of enculturative conditioning. The outer forms of Protestantism which mark the "shouting" churches of the lower socio-economic strata of Negro society in the United States, to cite an example, take their meaningful place as an overlay on a world-view that holds much of the non-European in its ritual, and more in its theology. In this case, we can see how such a mode of religious adaptation yields a belief-system wherein the European emphasis on guilt and punishment for guilt have been rejected in favor of African religious affirmations. This same approach helps us see, in similar manner, an artificially conceived pathology in social institutions as the reality of an accepted new outer form reinterpreted in terms of the patterns of older social structures.[69]

The Afroamerican field, then, is replete with complex and challenging problems. In its present state, the young area of research may be said to be fairly on its way, with a good store of data and useful conceptual and methodological tools in hand. Because of this, its needs —which is to say, its opportunities—appear in broader perspective and of deeper significance than they could otherwise. More documentary and field research, which will give a surer basis for generalization, is a continuing requisite. But beyond this, better integration of data will not only yield more penetrating formulations of concept and theory for basic research, but will also afford approaches of major use-fulness to those concerned with the solution of practical problems aris-ing out of the ever-increasing contacts, over the world, between peoples having different ways of life.

1. *Africanisms in the Gullah Dialect* (Chicago, 1949). See also Turner's other papers on this subject listed in the Bibliography of this same work (p. 298).

2. See, e.g., "The English of the Negro," *American Mercury*, II (1924), 190–195.

3. Ambrose E. Gonzales, *The Black Border* (Columbia, South Carolina, 1922).

4. H. L. Mencken, *The American Language* (New York, 1948).

5. M. J. and F. S. Herskovits, *Suriname Folklore* (New York, 1936), especially the section "Linguistic Notes," pp. 117–135.

6. *Le Créole Haïtien* (Port-au-Prince, Haiti and Wetteren, Belgium, 1936; author's name under Sylvain, Suzanne). See also Mme. Comhaire-Sylvain's study "Creole Tales from Haiti," *Journal of American Folklore*, L (1937), 207–295 and LI (1938), 219–346.

7. R. S. Rattray, *Ashanti* (Oxford, 1923), and succeeding works in his series of publications on this people.

8. J. Spieth, *Die Ewe-Stämme* (Berlin, 1906).

9. M. J. Herskovits, *Dahomey, an Ancient West African Kingdom* (New York, 1938).

10. M. Fortes, *The Dynamics of Clanship among the Tallensi* (London, 1945); *The Web of Kinship among the Tallensi* (London, 1949).

11. M. J. Field, *Religion and Medicine of the Gã People* (London, 1937); *Social Organization of the Gã People* (London, 1940).

12. F. S. Nadel, *A Black Byzantium, the Kingdom of Nupe in Nigeria* (London, 1942).

13. C. D. Forde, "Land and Labour in a Cross River Village, Southern Nigeria," *Geographical Journal*, XC (1937), 24–51; "Government in Umor," *Africa*, XII (1939), 129–162.

14. C. K. Meek, *Law and Authority in a Nigerian Tribe* (Oxford, 1937); J. S. Harris, "Some Aspects of Slavery in Southeastern Nigeria," *Journal of Negro History*, XXVII (1942), 37–54; "Some Aspects of the Economics of Sixteen Ibo Individuals," *Africa*, XIV (1944), 302–335.

15. W. R. Bascom, *The Sociological Role of the Yoruba Cult Group*, Memoir 46, American Anthropological Association (Menasha, Wisconsin, 1944).

16. C. K. Little, "Social Change and Social Class in the Sierra Leone Protectorate," *American Journal of Sociology*, LIV (1948), 10–21; "The Significance of the West African Creole for Africanist and Afro-American Studies," *African Affairs*, XLIX (1950), 308–319.

17. J. Greenberg, *The Influence of Islam on a Sudanese Religion* (New York, 1946).

18. See, for example, M. J. Herskovits, "African Gods and Catholic Saints in New World Negro Belief," *American Anthropologist*, XXXIX (1937), 635–643.

19. U. B. Phillips, *American Negro Slavery* (New York, 1918).

20. W. E. B. Du Bois, *The Suppression of the African Slave Trade to the United States of America* (Cambridge, 1896; third impression, 1916).

21. Elizabeth Donnan, *Documents Illustrative of the History of the Slave Trade to America* (Washington, 1930–1935).

22. Gaston-Martin, *Nantes au XVIIIᵉ Siècle; l'Ere des Négriers (1714–1744)* (Paris, 1931); D. Rinchon, *Le Trafic Négrier* (Brussels, 1938).

23. Gilberto Freyre, *Casa Grande e Senzala* (5th ed., Rio de Janeiro, 1946); translated from the 4th edition as *The Masters and the Slaves* (New York, 1946).

24. John Hope Franklin, *From Slavery to Freedom, a History of American Negroes* (New York, 1947).

25. J. C. Carroll, *Slave Insurrections in the United States, 1800–1860* (Boston, 1939).

26. Herbert Aptheker, *Negro Slave Revolts in the United States* (New York, 1939).

27. Harvey Wish, "American Slave Insurrections before 1861," *Journal of Negro History*, XXII (1937), 299–320.

28. Gonzalo Aguirre Beltrán, *La Población Negra de Mexico, 1519–1810* (Mexico, D. F., 1946).

29. *Ibid.*, "Tribal Origins of Slaves in Mexico," *Journal of Negro History*, XXXI (1946), 269–352.

30. Sir Harry H. Johnson, *The Negro in the New World* (London, 1910).

31. Nina Rodrigues, *L'animisme fétichiste des nègres de Bahia* (Paris, 1900); *Os Africanos no Brasil* (São Paulo, 1932).

32. Manoel Querino, *Costumes Africanos no Brasil* (Rio de Janeiro, 1935).

33. Abbé Etienne Ignace, "Le fétichisme des nègres du Brésil," *Anthropos*, III (1908), 881–904.

34. Arthur Ramos, *O Negro Brasileiro* (2nd ed., Rio de Janeiro, 1940); *O Folk-lore negro do Brasil* (Rio de Janeiro, 1935).

35. Mario de Andrade, *Ensaio sobre musica Brasileira* (São Paulo, 1928).

36. Gonçalves Fernandes, *Xangos do Nordeste* (Rio de Janeiro, 1937); *O folclore magico do Nordeste* (Rio de Janeiro, 1938).

37. Edison Carneiro, *Religiões Negras* (Rio de Janeiro, 1936); *Negros Bantus* (Rio de Janeiro, 1937); *Candombles da Bahia, Publicações do Museu do Estado*, no. 8 (Bahia, 1948).

38. Donald Pierson, *Negroes in Brazil, a Study of Race Contact at Bahia* (Chicago, 1942).

39. Roger Bastide, "Etat Actuel des Etudes Afro-Brésiliennes," *Revue Internationale de Sociologie*, XLVII (1939), 77-89.

40. Octavio da Costa Eduardo, *The Negro in Northern Brazil* (New York, 1948).

41. Turner, "Some Contacts of Brazilian ex-Slaves with Nigeria, West Africa," *Journal of Negro History*, XXVII (1942), 55–67.

42. M. J. and F. S. Herskovits, "The Negroes of Brazil," *Yale Review*, XXXII (1943), 263–279; M. J. Herskovits, "The Southernmost Outposts of New World Africanisms," *American Anthropologist*, XLV (1943), 495–510; "Drums and Drummers in Afro-Brazilian Cult Life," *Musical Quarterly*, XXX (1944), 477–492.

43. J. Price-Mars, *Ainsi Parla l'Oncle* (Port-au-Prince, 1928); *Une Etape de l'Evolution Haïtienne* (Port-au-Prince, n.d.).

44. J. C. Dorsainvil, *Vodou et Nevrose* (Port-au-Prince, 1931).

45. Jacques Roumain, *Le Sacrifice du Tambour-Assoto(r)*, Bulletin, no. 1, Bureau d'Éthnologie de la République d'Haïti, 1942.

46. Lorimer Denis and Emmanuel C. Paul, *Essai d'Organographie Haïtienne*, Publications of the Bureau d'Ethnologie de la République d'Haïti (Port-au-Prince, n.d.); Lorimer Denis and François Duvalier, *L'Evolution Stadiale de Vodou*, Bulletin, no. 3, Bureau d'Ethnologie (1944), pp. 9–32.

47. Fernando Ortiz, *Los Negros Brujos* (Madrid, 1917); *Glosario de Afro-negrismos* (Havana, 1924).

48. E. C. Parsons, *Folk-tales of Andros Island, Bahamas*, Memoirs of the American Folklore Society, XIII (1918); *Folk-lore of the Sea Islands of South Carolina, ibid.*, XVI (1923); *Folk-lore of the Antilles, French and English, ibid.*, XXVI, Parts 1–3 (1936–1943); among many others.

49. M. J. and F. S. Herskovits, *Rebel Destiny (among the Bush Negroes of Dutch Guiana)* (New York, 1934); *Suriname Folk-lore*, as in note 5 above.

50. Arthur Ramos, *As Culturas Negras no Novo Mundo* (Rio de Janeiro, 1937).

51. M. J. Herskovits, *Life in a Haitian Valley* (New York, 1937).

52. George Simpson, "Haitian Peasant Economy," *Journal of Negro History*, XXV (1940), 498–519; "The Vodun Service in Northern Haiti," *American Anthropologist*, XLII (1940), 236–254; "Sexual and Familial Institutions in Northern Haiti," *ibid.*, XLIV (1942), 655–674; "The Belief System of Haitian Vodun," *ibid.*, XLVII (1945), 35–59.

53. M. J. and F. S. Herskovits, *Trinidad Village* (New York, 1947).

54. Turner, as in note 41 above.

55. E. Franklin Frazier, "The Negro in Bahia, Brazil," *American Sociological Review*, VII (1942), 465–478. See also, on this paper, M. J. Herskovits, "The Negro in Bahia, Brazil: a Problem in Method," *ibid.*, VIII (1943), 394–402; and René Ribeiro, "On the *Amasiado* Relationship, and other Aspects of the Family in Recife (Brazil)," *ibid.*, X (1945), 44–51.

56. Octavio Eduardo, as in note 40; Nunes Pereira, *A Casa das Minas*, Publicações, Sociedade Brasileira de Antropologia e Etnologia (1947), no. 1.

57. Douglas M. Taylor, *The Black Carib of British Honduras*, forthcoming in the Viking Fund Publications in Anthropology.

58. Roger Bastide, "Contribuição ao Estudo do Sincretismo Catolico-fetichista," *Estudos Afro-Brasileiros* (Sociología No. 1), XLIX (1946), Faculdade de Filosofia, Ciéncias e Letras, Universidad de São Paulo, pp. 11–14.

59. W. R. Bascom, "The Focus of Cuban Santeria," *Southwestern Journal of Anthropology*, VI (1950), 64–68; Bascom, "Two Forms of Afro-Cuban Divination," in *Proceedings*, XXIX International Congress of Americanists (forthcoming).

60. Bascom, "Acculturation among the Gullah Negroes," *American Anthropologist*, XLIII (1941), 43–50.

61. Since it is impossible to know all research in progress or awaiting publication in the field of Afroamerican studies, those named here are, with a few exceptions, restricted to those that have been carried on under the auspices of Northwestern University. The question may be raised whether the *Journal of Negro History* might not extend the considerable service it

has rendered Afroamerican research by periodically noting work in progress, either by listing research topics or, when these had been completed, carrying preliminary reports of findings.

62. M. J. Herskovits, *The Myth of the Negro Past* (New York, 1941), "Directives for Further Studies," pp. 326–340.

63. Octavio Eduardo, *op. cit.*, pp. 8–18. See also the recently completed study of slavery in the Parahyba Valley of Brazil by Stanley J. Stein, *Vassouras, a Plantation Society, 1850–1950* (Ph.D. Thesis, Department of History, Harvard University, 1951).

64. Ildefonso Pereda Valdes, *El Negro Rioplatense y Otros Ensayos* (Montevideo, 1937) and *Negros Esclavos y Negros Livros* (Montevideo, 1941); Dante de Laytano, "Os Africanismos do Dialeto Gaucho," *Revisto do Instituto Historico e Geografico do Rio Grande do Sul*, XVI (1936); and *As Congadas do Municipio de Osorio* (Porto Alegre, 1945).

65. Fernando Romero, "Ubicación Cronológica de Nuestro Negro," *La Prensa* (Lima, Peru), November 3, 1935; "The Slave Trade and the Negro in South America," *Hispanic American Historical Review*, XXIV (1944), 368–386.

66. Antonio Vazquez de Espinosa, *Compendium and Description of the West Indies*, Smithsonian Miscellaneous Collections, CII (Washington, 1942). Translated by Charles Upson Clark.

67. How rewarding such research can be may be seen in the preliminary papers of James F. King on the early history of slavery in Colombia as, e.g., in his "Negro Slavery in New Granada," in *Greater America, Essays in Honor of Herbert Eugene Bolton* (Berkeley, 1945), pp. 295–318, and "The Negro in Continental Spanish America: a Select Bibliography," *Hispanic American Historical Review*, XXIV (1944), 547–559.

68. For the development of these concepts out of the New World Negro data, see M. J. Herskovits, "Problem, Method and Theory in Afroamerican Research," *Afroamerica*, I (1945), 5–24; reprinted in *Phylon*, VII (1946), 337–354, especially Table I, "Scale of Intensity of New World Africanisms," p. 15. For the wider applicability of these concepts in cultural theory, see Herskovits, *Man and His Works* (New York, 1948), ch. 36 (pp. 608–621).

69. As concerns the working out of this process in its effect on the New World Negro family, see M. J. and F. S. Herskovits, *Trinidad Village*, pp. 8–17; the point as concerns religion will be documented when the analysis of transcriptions of sermons contained in wire recordings of more than thirty hour-long broadcasts of a Chicago "shouting" church, now under study, is completed.

: II :

THEORY AND METHOD

━━
|||||||||||||||||||||||||||||||||||||||||||||||||||||||||||||||||||||||||||||||||||||||||||||||||||||||||||||||
━━

Problem, Method
and Theory in Afroamerican Studies

Afroamerican studies not only cross disciplines, but are also inter-continental, treating of peoples living in North, South, and Central America, the Caribbean, and Africa. . . . here can be prosecuted those comparative researches of mixtures of physical types, of languages and of modes of behavior in terms of known rather than of assumed past contacts. . . . it must be stressed that Afroamerican studies are not to be limited to the study of Negro populations and their cultures alone, but must follow through to assess the contributions Africa has made to the peoples among whom the Negroes live.

❋   ❋   ❋

I

This paper will discuss three elements in the scientific study of the New World Negro and his African background that, hitherto in large measure implicit in my writings on the subject, suggest their timeliness for explicit formulation. These comprise a definition and delimitation of the field, which is essential for clarity of purpose in research and for directing future effort; some of the methodological concepts and techniques that have been successfully employed; and some of the hypotheses which have guided investigation and developed out of experience in the field.

It is not always realized how recent is systematic study of the Afro-

Afroamerica, I (1945), 5–24.

american field. Little of the present substantial store of facts concerning New World cultures, or the civilizations from which they derive, or the historical circumstances of their formation were available two decades ago, so that it is apparent why the need to amass data took first place in the attention of students. This continuing emphasis was particularly relevant in view of the vastness of the area in which New World Negroes live and the variety of their cultures, the complexity of the African civilizations from which they derive, the technical difficulties in the way of studying provenience and the intricacy of the acculturative processes to which they have been exposed.

Today, the scientific importance of Afroamerican studies as a field for research is firmly established. A climate of opinion, both lay and scholarly, which encourages further research, has been created, while the body of factual materials and comparative analyses that has been amassed by those working in the field allows hypotheses and procedures to be assessed in terms of collected data and achieved results rather than of probable validity and possible return. It thus appears a logical moment for stock-taking, for the explicit statement of theoretical assumptions, and for a refinement of techniques.

II

An outstanding characteristic of the field of Afroamerican studies is its interdisciplinary nature, which must be taken into account whenever problems of definition or method are under discussion. But more than that, Afroamerican studies not only cross disciplines, but are also inter-continental, treating of peoples living in North, South and Central America, the Caribbean, and Africa. The implications of this interdisciplinary and intercontinental scope, when thought of in terms of the conventional organization of scholarly study, are many. For the field cuts across so many boundaries that it cannot be defined in terms of any commonly accepted categories—a fact that accounts for its late recognition as a definable area of scholarship and for certain practical difficulties that at one time or another have faced those who have worked on its many problems.

That the ramifications of such studies extend into the social sciences, the humanities and the biological sciences, follows from the nature of the data. In this our field is no different from any research that is concerned with obtaining a rounded view of the life of man, or of any group of men. It is nonetheless worthwhile to recall how in Afroamerican studies investigation has had to have recourse to the resources of anthropology, history and psychology to reach an understanding of the social structures, the accepted patterns of behavior, and the past development of the societies studied; how linguistics, musicology and comparative literature have had to be called upon to contribute their techniques for insight into some of the most revealing data in the field; and how such problems as the incidence and effects of race-crossing, of the dynamics of Negro population formation and the like have had to be studied in terms of the techniques and orientations of human biology and demography. Not every student can study every problem, but most students of the Negro have come to realize that their competence in the discipline of their primary affiliation gives them but a starting-point for further effort; and that their field of interest has characteristically broadened as the data have been followed where they led, even when these called for disregard of current delimitation of scholarly concern.

In similar fashion, accepted regional approaches to the ordering of research have had to be transcended. Researches restricted to Latin American problems, or to the United States, or to Africa or to an island of the Caribbean alone, of course, make their contributions to Afroamerican studies. For where data are as sparse as in this field, all contributions are welcome. But those whose perspectives have not been so circumscribed know well how much researches in these areas are enriched by a broader point of view. One of the most telling instances of this is the aid which the study of New World Negro peoples can bring toward a fuller comprehension of the cultures of Africa itself. This is striking because it reverses the customary order of thought, which focuses on African survivals in the New World. That the study of African ways of life is essential to an understanding of survivals of these customs is a truism; but what, it may be asked, can the analysis of survivals contribute to comprehension of their own sources?

Though the matter cannot be documented here, it need merely be recalled that survival is an index of tenacity, which in turn reveals general orientations in parent cultures that may at times not be given proper stress without such background. This is the case as concerns the place of religion in African cultures, whose theoretical importance will be considered in a later page. Furthermore, specific complexes of significance that have been quite overlooked in Africanist studies are to be revealed by investigation on this side of the Atlantic. A recent example of this is had in the instance of the place of drummers, not only in cult-rituals, but in the life of the community as a whole. First noted in a New World Negro culture, it required only brief questioning of Africans to reveal itself as an important facet of social organization in Africa itself, that had hitherto not been explored at all.

Though overlapping many disciplines and a number of geographical regions, the field of Afroamerican studies is distinct from all those on which it impinges, from which it follows that it is therefore often a matter of emphasis and intent just where a given piece of research is to be classified. This is the source of many practical difficulties. Papers on African cultures, deriving from studies stimulated by an interest in the New World descendants of Africa, may appear in Africanist journals where much of their usefulness to those who concentrate on New World Negro societies is lost, while reports on historical aspects of the field, often published in historical journals, are not seen by those studying Afroamerican problems whose primary affiliation is with other disciplines. Conversely Africanists who confine their work to the peoples of that continent, or historians of the Negro whose range of interest is defined by their discipline, fail to benefit from New World studies, or from work on other than historical phases of Negro life that might open new vistas to them.

This may meet with the reasonable suggestion that there is enough justification for the existence of the conventional disciplines in their achieved results to give us pause before we cross their boundaries, tested by time and experience. In the final analysis, however, the ordering of the most fruitful results can be had only when the facts are studied as they lie, without those preconceptions which, in a case such as that under discussion, lead to distortion if not considered in terms of all interrelated aspects.

This leads us to the nature of the contributions Afroamerican studies can be expected to make, for the point is basic in discussing the importance of the field for scientific research. More than anything else, it comprises data that, because of the available historic controls and the range of related materials, go far toward approximating those laboratory situations which, in the study of man, are more difficult to achieve than any other single methodological factor in the repertory of science. Thus the very fact that to conduct Afroamerican studies calls on the techniques of many disciplines, and is carried on in many different areas, gives it a special significance for the scientific study of man. For here can be prosecuted those comparative researches of mixtures of physical types, of languages and of modes of behavior in terms of known rather than of assumed past contacts. And while in this, Afroamerican research does not differ in kind from studies among other groups of differing backgrounds between whom contact has taken place or is in process, it is to be distinguished from them in degree, as expressed in the very broad variety of situations that, in this field, are to be investigated.

It is not difficult to phrase the manner in which the Afroamerican field differs from the several disciplines on which it draws. To the extent that its problems are to be comprehended within their areas of interest, such problems have an affiliation immediately recognizable. Thus a study of land-tenure in a Caribbean island might find ready reception in a journal devoted to economics, the analysis of a Negro musical style in a musicological publication, the description of the physical characteristics of a North American Negro community in an organ devoted to the problems of physical anthropology. Even where cross-disciplinary considerations have entered, publication can be achieved in journals devoted to the discipline of principal emphasis or, more often, in the subject with which the student is technically affiliated. This is one of the reasons why bibliographic problems are so difficult in Afroamerican research.

To draw the line between area fields and Afroamerican research requires somewhat more careful distinctions, for here the problem of efficient historic relationships enters. It is simple to state that study of the Negro in Latin America contributes to the Latin American field; even though, in this sense, we once again encounter overlapping. Yet it is open to question how much a detailed investigation of certain Negro social conventions or music or religious beliefs that have not significantly diffused to other population elements in a given Latin American country is to be regarded as a contribution to the Latin American field, except in a secondary sense.

In the Africanist field, the matter is somewhat different. In earlier years, before the provenience of New World Negroes was known as well as it is at present, it was held that a knowledge of African culture in general was essential to effective comparative study of the New World Negro. Today, however, one may ask why, except for general background, this is needed. Field research on the cultures of East Africa, the study of the slave trade in Zanzibar, the analysis of Bushman art, or investigation of Zulu physical types deal with peoples who are outside the range of effective historic impact on New World Negro patterns, since so few individuals from the parts of Africa where they live were brought to the New World that their influence in the formation of New World Negro types and cultures could only have been negligible.

A further point to be made in clarifying the limits of the Afroamerican field has to do with the study of those situations of everyday life in many countries which, as they affect the Negro, present practical problems of great moment that press for immediate solutions. Because the student is also the citizen, with heightened awareness of the needs engendered by these situations, the temptation is great to give over the long-term view in favor of *ad hoc* solutions of such issues. This has been especially true in the United States, where for many years an almost exclusive preoccupation with action programs discouraged the type of broad research which characterizes the Afroamerican field. This is not the place to consider the problem of applied science as against research on a long-term basis, yet it is important that the distinction be made and maintained. For even in the short view, the broader base of comprehension that the results of Afroamerican studies can give those whose task is to frame policies for practical procedures would, of itself, justify the position that such studies must be held distinct from remedial programs in the troubled field of race relations.

Finally, it must be stressed that Afroamerican studies are not to be limited to the study of Negro populations and their cultures alone, but must follow through to assess the contributions Africa has made to the peoples among whom the Negroes live. Thus when race-crossing carries Negroid elements into the genetic composition of the non-Negroid groups, this is quite as significant a subject for research as it is to determine the physical traits of the Negroid group. Parallel cultural phenomena have not been systematically studied at all, except, perhaps, in Brazil. Yet just as race-crossing invariably follows on contact between peoples of different physical types, so cultural borrowing, —two-way borrowing—also ensues. The theoretical importance of this fact is clear. Here the problem is stated to emphasize the necessity of including, in the repertory of Afroamerican research, investigation not only into the maintenance of African tradition in the New World, but also into how, and to what extent African custom was diffused to the aboriginal Indian peoples and to those of European derivation who experienced prolonged contact with Africans and their descendants.

III

To the extent that the problems of Afroamerican research fall within the compass of established disciplines, or require interdisciplinary consideration of a type already employed outside the Afroamerican field, the question of method presents no difficulty. A comparative study of Negro music utilizes the techniques of the musicologist, one of language employs the methods of the linguists, research into the present-day Negro family or of living standards of Negro populations uses the approaches of the sociologist or the economist. Overall descriptions of any of these cultures, whether in Africa or the New World, require ethnological field techniques, while analyses of psychological problems arising out of the way of life of Negro peoples utilizes the methods of social psychology. Studies of the slave trade, or of the economics of the plantation, though cross-disciplinary, find research techniques at hand in the modes of investigation employed by economic historians.

Strangely enough, the resources of ethnology and history have only recently been welded into a usable tool. Despite the fact that there are historical schools of ethnology and social historians, there has been but little contact across these disciplines. The "history" of these ethnological schools has been based on the reconstruction of events rather than on documentation; while the social historian, despite the illumination his writings have thrown on the development of the institutions with which he has dealt, has worked primarily as an historian and only rarely and recently has had recourse to the methods of the social sciences. There are, of course, some exceptions to this statement. Studies of certain Indian groups in the United States afford instances of how the use of historic sources has been able to illuminate ethnographic problems, while historians of the American frontier are more and more finding it essential to take into account the relevant ethnographic facts.

Experience is teaching us that the methods of these two disciplines, more than any other two, must be jointly called on if the varying situations that are to be studied comparatively in the Afroamerican field are to be analyzed with comprehension. It must be stressed that this field, constituting as it does, a special instance of culture contact, derives its greatest significance from the fact that it so superbly documents the problems of cultural dynamics. Now in studies of culture contact it is essential to establish the cultural base-lines from which the processes of change began, to know facts concerning the culture or cultures that have emerged, or are emerging from the contact, and to comprehend how, and under what circumstances, the phenomena as observed in the culture that has resulted from the contact actually developed. The first of these requires ethnographic study, and in some measure the second. But the second also requires historical treatment, while the third demands an attack that is essentially historical.

The *ethnohistorical method*, as this combined ethnological and historical approach is to be termed, has been basic in systematic Afroamerican research, for until the use of this method was fully established, it was found difficult to achieve perspective, and comparative studies were but elusive. It is through the use of this method, and only by its use, that it has been possible to recover the predominant regional and tribal origins of the New World Negroes and, with this information in hand, to turn to ethnographic research in Africa with a certainty that the materials gathered there would be relevant to the problems of cultural retention and cultural change met with in the New World. Similarly this method has made it possible to test the validity of the rich store of existing documentary information concerning slaves and slaving, plantation life and the responses of the Negro to it, and the like, and to realize much of the potential contribution of these materials. Most important, also, has been the continuous comparison of ethnographic facts as found on the two sides of the Atlantic; for ethnohistory, as employed in the study of Afroamerican problems, consists essentially of the application of a comparative ethnographic technique in unravelling, on the basis of written sources, the historic progression of events that led up to the establishment and functioning of New World Negro cultures as they exist at the present time.

Not only has the ethnohistorical approach been able to fix the African origins of New World Negro cultures, but it has been of great value in accounting for differences that are found between the cultures of Negroes living in different parts of the New World. Thus comparative ethnographic studies have revealed that the cultures of the Dutch Guiana Bush Negroes and of the Maroons of Jamaica manifest their Africanisms predominantly in terms of Gold Coast retentions, while those of Haiti are of Dahomean and Yoruba derivation. The documents tell us that Dutch and English planters preferred Gold Coast slaves, not only because they were more likely to find these for sale by their own nationals, but because of rationalizations that came to be set up concerning the worth of Negroes from tribes of this area compared to other kinds of Negroes. On the other hand, they make it equally clear that Latin slave owners preferred Dahomean and Yoruba slaves, for the same reasons, and thus resolve what would otherwise be a difficult problem.

Another methodological device that has proved of outstanding value in analyzing the problems of Afroamerican research is that of a scale of intensity of Africanisms over the New World. This implies a logically conceived continuum which ranges from retentions that are completely African, or almost so, to those least African and most European —the Indian elements having been so little studied that they cannot be classified. Such a continuum permits an arrangement of the data that gives insight into the processes of cultural change by allowing comparisons to be drawn between cultures whose various aspects lie at different points on it. This, in turn, facilitates analysis of the processes that have operated to bring about the cultural changes observed in the course of field research.

It must be emphasized that, as in all scientific study, a classificatory device such as the scale of intensity of Africanisms is but a means to an end rather than an end in itself. In this case, the end that is envisaged is that comprehension of process which alone can lead to valid prediction. To be revealing in terms of this end the classification must be derived through induction, and flow from the data, rather than be imposed upon it after the fashion of *a priori* categories that tend to force materials into groupings that do violence to the scientific reality. Scientific analysis is impossible without classification of data, and herein lies the importance of this series of categories; but it cannot be too strongly emphasized that classification, of itself, can tell us nothing about causes, or relationships, or the processes of change.

A *scale of intensity of Africanisms* was first established somewhat more than a decade ago. At that time, however, the data were meager compared with present resources, so that of necessity the listing was tentative, and had to be in terms of whole cultures or areas or countries. That is, places were assigned to such Negro groups as those of the Guianas or the Virgin Islands, or Haiti, on a scale ranging from most to least African. A revision of this original statement was made several years later, but still in overall terms, though additional data from various regions were utilized to amplify and rectify the listing. While preferable to the earlier statement, this revision proved to be simpler than the nature of the materials has come to demand. For overall categories of this character do not adequately illuminate the complexities of the data, and often indeed, hide relationships rather than reveal them, which is their intent.

The scale given in this paper represents an application to Afroamerican studies of certain techniques of analyzing cultures that have been increasingly employed as greater acquaintance with human ways of living have been gained. That is, we now know that the broad divisions of culture, even particular institutions, behave differently in different situations. This does not mean that a given body of tradition is to be thought of as other than a unified whole, whose elements are all closely interrelated. But it has come to be recognized that the historic forces that are operative in any given situation—forces which, by their very nature, are unique in each circumstance—will eventuate differently in different instances as far as differing aspects of culture are concerned, or where different institutions within a given cultural category are involved.

The principle of cultural focus, discussed in later pages, is helpful in this connection, since its implications for the dynamics of culture in this situation, as in all others, is that it offers an important leverage to bring about changes in certain aspects of a people's way of life as against others or, under contact, to make for differential resistance to change. Thus pressures from outside the Negro groups to give over economic patterns were far greater in the New World than those militating against the retention of folktales or secular musical forms, so that the latter two manifest far more of an African character than the former. On the other hand, inner compulsions derived from the focal concerns of Africans with the supernatural tended to resist varying pressures, in varying countries, employing the different kinds of adjustments that have been described, with the result that Africanisms figure prominently in New World Negro religious behavior everywhere.

A refinement of the earlier scale of intensity of Africanisms, not in terms of total cultures, but of aspects within each culture, such as our data now make possible, is given here. In addition, a further refinement has been achieved by subdividing the areas which earlier appeared as units, where the materials indicate that within a given region districts can be distinguished wherein the pattern and degree of African retentions differ. But since it is apparent that in every part of the New World where Negroes live, excepting only the Guiana Bush, class differences operate so as to make for variation in the number and intensity of Africanisms within each Negro group, our table will record only that degree of retention for each group which is closest to African custom.

Because this point is crucial for a proper reading of the table, and an adequate understanding of its significance, it may be amplified here. Bahia, for example, is rated as most African in language because only there have certain African tongues been retained, as against retention, at most, of no more than African words or phrases or grammatical structures elsewhere. In their daily usage, as a matter of fact, the Bahian Negroes show perhaps less African elements than elsewhere, since they speak the same Portuguese as is spoken by other Brazilians, with fewer elements of African vocabulary, pronunciation or grammar than is found in the speech of almost any other New World Negro group.

It cannot be too strongly stressed that in every area of the New World, except in the Guiana Bush, variation in African forms of behavior stretches from the point of greatest intensity indicated in our table to almost conformity with European ways of life. The problem thus becomes one of accounting for differing degrees of variability in the different populations studied. But since the variation does in almost every case extend to the limit set by the conventions of European custom, it can be seen how significant is the analysis of retentions of African convention if we are to discover how far the dis-

TABLE I*

SCALE OF INTENSITY OF NEW WORLD AFRICANISMS

(Only the greatest degree of retention is indicated for each group)

	Tech-nology	Eco-nomic	Social Organi-zation	Non-kinship Institutions	Reli-gion	Magic	Art	Folk-lore	Music	Lan-guage
Guiana (bush)	b	b	a	a	a	a	b	a	a	b
Guiana (Paramaribo)	c	c	b	c	a	a	e	a	a	c
Haiti (peasant)	c	b	b	c	a	a	d	a	a	c
Haiti (urban)	e	d	c	c	b	b	e	a	a	c
Brazil (Bahia-Recife)	d	d	b	d	a	a	b	a	a	a
Brazil (Porto Alegre)	e	e	c	d	a	b	e	a	a	c
Brazil (Maranhão-rural)	c	c	b	e	c	b	e	b	b	d
Brazil (Maranhão-urban)	e	d	c	e	a	b	e	d	a	b
Cuba	e	d	c	b	a	a	b	b	a	a
Jamaica (Maroons)	c	c	b	b	b	a	e	a	a	c
Jamaica (Morant Bay)	e	c	b	b	a	a	e	a	a	a
Jamaica (general)	e	c	d	d	b	b	e	a	b	c
Honduras (Black Caribs)**	c	c	b	b	b	a	e	b	c	e
Trinidad (Port of Spain)	e	d	c	b	a	a	e	b	a	e
Trinidad (Toco)	e	d	c	c	c	b	e	b	b	d
Mexico (Guerrero)	d	e	b	b	c	b	e	b	?	e
Colombia (Choco)	d	d	c	c	c	b	e	b	e	e
Virgin Islands	e	d	c	d	e	b	e	b	b	d
U.S. (Gullah Islands)	c	c	c	d	c	b	e	a	b	b
U.S. (rural South)	d	e	c	d	c	b	e	b	b	e
U.S. (urban North)	e	e	c	d	c	b	e	d	b	e

a: very African   b: quite African   c: somewhat African   d: a little African   e: trace of African customs, or absent   ?: no report

* Derivations of the listings in Table I are given in a note at the end of the chapter.   ** Carib Indian influences are strong in this culture.

tribution extends toward the patterns that made up the cultural endowment of the ancestors of present day Negro populations that are the central concern of Afroamerican research.

Table I presents, then, these degrees of intensities of Africanisms, listed by aspect of culture and by region in terms of the most African-like manifestation of a given cultural aspect or institution. The assignment of values in each instance has either been on the basis of my own field research in the regions listed, or on the reports of trained and competent observers in areas where I have not had first-hand contact. The weightings given the entries are broadly conceived, as is indicated by the terms used to denote the categories of intensity— "very African," "quite African," and the like. To be more specific would be merely to enlarge the area of possible disagreement between students, and to no purpose, since all classifications of such data must be subjective, at least at this point in our knowledge and with the technical resources for cultural analysis at hand. The sources are indicated in the note appended to the text of this paper.

Greater refinement in the treatment of these data might also be more revealing, but the technique of trait-analysis seems to be too mechanical, and to work too great violence to the unity of the cultural elements involved, to be profitably employed in this case. In like manner, the designations are to be regarded as having been set down for convenience only, and to consider them as anything more than useful symbols would be to introduce a note of spurious accuracy against which too great warning cannot be given.

It is apparent, from scanning the table, that the overall listings in the earlier ratings are in the main borne out by the tabulations of this more refined treatment, the principal clarification being in the direction of indicating variability of retention within a given country. Especially interesting is the indication that extension of the continuum toward the pole of African traditions can be greater in certain traits manifested in centers of population than in Brazil. Taken as a whole, however, the progression of Guiana, Haiti, Brazil, Jamaica, Trinidad, Cuba, Virgin Islands, the Gullah Islands, and southern and northern United States comprise a series wherein a decreasing intensity of Africanisms is manifest. The series will be filled in after field-work has been carried on in areas as yet unstudied, but there seems little prospect of finding New World Negro cultures more African than those of the interior of Dutch Guiana, nor, in recognizable form, less so than among certain Negro groups in the northern part of the United States.

Turning now to consider the different degree to which differing elements in each of these cultures have responded to contact with non-African ways of life, we see that the carry-over of Africanisms is anything but uniform over the individual cultures, being far greater in some aspects than in others. Certain generalizations can, however, be drawn. Music, folklore, magic and religion, on the whole, have retained more of their African character than economic life, or technology, or art, while language and social structures based on kinship or free association, tend to vary through all the degrees of intensity that are noted.

These differences are probably due to the circumstances of slave life, and confirm common sense observations made during the period of slavery. Slave owners were primarily concerned with the technological and economic aspects of the lives of their slaves, while the conditions of life as a slave also of necessity warped whatever patterns of African social structures the Negroes felt impelled to preserve. On the other hand, what tales were told or the songs that were sung made little difference to the masters, and few external blocks were placed in the way of their retention. In the case of religion, outer controls were of varying kinds and were responded to in varying degree, as is reflected in the intermediate position of this cultural element. Magic, which tends to go underground under pressure and can most easily be practised without direction—the force of the specific psychological compulsions here being of special importance—persisted in recognizable form everywhere, particularly since the similarity between African and European magic is so great that the one cultural stream must have operated to reinforce the other. The failure of African art to survive except in Guiana and to a lesser degree in Brazil is understandable when the life of the slave, which permitted little leisure and offered slight stimulus for the production of art in the aboriginal African style or, indeed, in any other style, is recalled.

One further fact which emerges from our table is the differing variability, over the New World as a whole, of the several aspects of the cultures as these have been listed. Only religion and language comprehend in maximum extension toward African patterns, all degrees of intensity. Minimum variation in this respect is shown by music, which everywhere has been retained in at least "quite African" form. The degree of variation within each of the groups is likewise interesting, since it is seen how the Bush-Negro culture, the most African, is also most homogeneous as far as the African nature of its several elements is concerned, while the cultures of the Negroes of the United States, though manifesting a comparable degree of homogeneity, expresses its homogeneous quality at the opposite end of the scale.

The facts thus shown hold both particular and general significance. To students of Afroamerican problems, differentials offer leads for further historical and ethnological analysis, since it is to be assumed that the explanation for such differentials is to be discovered in the modes of conducting slaving operations and in the circumstances of slave life, as these reacted upon the aboriginal patterns of individuals derived from the various relevant cultures of Africa. From the broader point of view of understanding culture as a whole, however, such treatment documents the concept of culture as a series of interrelated, but quasi-independent variables that undergo processes of change in accordance with the particular historical situation under which impact of new ideas and new customs has taken place, and the focal concerns of the peoples who, like the Negroes of the New World, made the cultural and psychological adjustments that were called forth by their historical experience.

IV

The hypotheses that underlie the study of African cultural survivals in the New World derive from a conception of human civilization that holds social behavior to be something learned rather than inborn and instinctive. This means that though there are as many cultures—that is, accepted modes of conduct, configurations of institutions, and systems of values and goals—as there are societies, every culture, or any of its elements, can be mastered by any individual without regard to race, or by any group that has the will and the opportunity to master it.

It follows from our concept of culture as something learned that the borrowing of traditions by one people from another is a simple matter, and research has actually established that cultural borrowing is a universal in human social experience. It is today clear that no two peoples have ever been in contact but that they have taken new ideas and new customs from each other, and this quite independently of whether that contact was friendly or hostile, whether it was between groups of the same size or of unequal size, whether differences of prestige existed between them or they met on a plane of equality.

The conception of culture on which our hypotheses are based thus envisages the operation of the principle of constant change—through borrowing and internal innovation—but at the same time assumes a high degree of stability in every culture, which is assured by the transmission of habits, customs, beliefs and institutions from one generation to the next. That is, the individual member of a society learns how to behave in a given situation, how to operate the techniques which assure his society its living, how to adapt to a given system of drives, rewards and values because he is taught or observes all these things. The resultant cultural conservatism gives to every way of life a tenaciousness, a toughness—in many writings not sufficiently recognized—which comes to be of special importance in the study of Africanisms among the Negroes of the New World.

If we assume, then, that culture is in constant change because it is learned, and not inborn, but is learned by the individuals that constitute any given society so well that the tendency of human beings to conserve tradition gives to every culture great stability, the problem next presented is to resolve this seeming paradox by studying those circumstances in which changes are instituted, or in which retention of conventions makes for successful resistance to change. It is essentially the problem of balancing the drives that induce acceptance of new customs as against the mechanisms that preserve earlier sanctioned modes of behavior. It is here that the field of Afroamerican studies can make its greatest contribution.

We may say that the basic hypothesis of culture as something learned is sharpened when it is perceived that under contact elements of a culture are the more effectively retained in the degree that they bear resemblance to newly experienced patterns of behavior or institutions. This, in turn, is further refined by references to the process of *syncretism*, the tendency to identify those elements in the new culture with similar elements in the old one, enabling the persons experiencing the contact to move from one to the other, and back again, with psychological ease. The outstanding instance of syncretism is the identification, in Catholic countries of the New World, of African deities with the saints of the Church—a phenomenon so well documented that it need but be mentioned here to make the point.

The discovery that the same principle is operative in West Africa, at the southern border of Mohammedan influence, where among the Hausa the pagan *iska* are identified with the *jinn* of the Koran extends its validity. But if we turn our analysis to Protestant countries, where syncretism of this sort is not possible, we find that though the names of African deities have been but rarely retained, syncretisms take other, more generalized forms. An example of this is the retention of the African requirement of initiation into religious groups through its syncretization with the Christian concept of sanctification achieved through preparation for baptism, or as expressed in the institution of the "mourning ground."

At this point another principle must be stated—that of *reinterpretation*. For where it is not possible to set up syncretisms, the force of cultural conservatism seeks expression in substance, rather than form, in psychological value rather than in name, if the original culture is to survive at all. Here the hypothesis of the importance of resemblance of the old element, to the new is again involved. Though to a lesser

degree than in the instance of syncretism, reinterpretation also requires that some characteristic of the new cultural element be correlated with a corresponding part of the original one by those to whom
it is presented, before the mechanism can operate effectively.

In this fashion, the pattern of polygynous family structure has come
to be reinterpreted in terms of successive, rather than of simultaneous
plural matings, something which has set in motion an entire train of
adjustments. Not the least of these has been the rejection, within the
Negro group, of the European interpretation of illegitimacy as applied
to offspring of unions not sanctioned by law, and to legal divorce,
since these laws are meaningless in terms of aboriginal conventions.
The extent to which new orientations of this kind find distribution
among Negroes everywhere in the New World demonstrates the effectiveness of the mechanism, not only to achieve cultural but also
psychological adaptation to the new setting. This could also be documented from other aspects of culture—economic life, or religion, or
music—if considerations of space permitted. Here, however, the example given suffices to illustrate the principle that has been derived.

Retention of original custom under contact, whether through syncretism or reinterpretation is, however, merely one side of the problem, the other being the acceptance of what is newly presented. Here
many imponderables enter, the most important being the degree to
which outer acceptance involves transfer of values and interpretations
in the psychological as well as in the institutional sense. This, of
course, raises one of the most difficult problems in the entire field of
cultural dynamics—whether any element of culture is ever taken over
without some degree of reinterpretation, however free the borrowing.

If this particular question be for the moment disregarded, however,
it is to be seen that just as syncretism and reinterpretation are means
by which retention of the old is achieved, they are by the same token
effective in encouraging the adoption of the new. A succession of
matings entered into by a man or woman implies an acceptance of the
monogamic principle, at the same time that it points to the method by
which, through reinterpretation, the old polygynous tradition has been
retained. Where African gods are syncretized with Catholic saints,
the significance of the fact that the Negroes, as professing Catholics,
have accepted the new religion must not be lost sight of by focusing
attention too closely on the retention of aboriginal deities.

When we press the matter, however, we find that the problem is
further complicated by the selective nature of borrowing on another
level. On the basis of a comparative analysis of African and New
World Negro cultures, it is apparent that even under the compulsions
of the dominant culture of whites, Negroes have retained African

religious beliefs and practices far more than they have retained economic patterns. But when we examine the patterns of African cultures,
we find that there is no activity of everyday living but that it is validated by supernatural sanctions. And consequently, these figure far
more in the total life of the people than does any other single facet of
the culture such as those matters having to do with making a living, or
family structure, or political institutions. This weighting of the concerns of a people constitutes the focus of their culture. *Cultural focus*
is thus seen to be that phenomenon which gives a culture its particular emphasis; which permits the outsider to sense its special distinguishing flavor and to characterize its essential orientation in a few
phrases.

The role of cultural focus is of such great importance in situations
of cultural contact that a further hypothesis may be advanced to the
effect that more elements which lie in the area of focus of a receiving
culture will be retained than those appertaining to other aspects of
the culture, acceptance being greater in those phases of culture further removed from the focal area. Where a culture is under pressure
by a dominant group who seek to induce acceptance of its traditions,
elements lying in the focal area will be retained longer than those outside it, though in this case retention will of necessity be manifested in
syncretisms and reinterpretations.

For example, in the interior of Dutch Guiana, almost the only
Europeanisms to be found are those which lie in the realm of material
culture. In Brazil, where the Negroes accept most of the dominant
European economic order, they adjust to the exigencies of the Church
by syncretizing their African deities and continuing to worship them
as they are worshipped in Africa. In the United States, where pressures have been most severe, almost no African economic patterns
have persisted, but adaptation to Protestantism has been marked by
the retention of many Africanisms through reinterpretation.

Still another point that must receive attention has to do with the
degree to which elements of a culture that may be peripheral to the
focal area, but that ride high in the consciousness of the people—
that require thought, or call for decision—are retained under contact
when compared to those which, so to speak, are carried below the
level of consciousness. These may be termed *cultural imponderables.*
Prominent among these are linguistic patterns and musical style, and
such sanctions as are comprehended in those determinants of behavior
that include types of motor habits, systems of values, or codes of etiquette. Research has demonstrated that manifestations of African culture, wherein there is little conscious awareness, have persisted in the
New World to a far greater degree than those cultural elements that

lie outside the area of cultural focus. This is not surprising when the factors involved are considered, since the cultural imponderables, being those elements in culture that intrude but slightly upon consciousness are taken for granted, and are thus far more difficult to dislodge from the thought and behavior patterns of individuals subjected to a new culture than those which must be given continuous attention.

Language and musical style may be cited here to illustrate the point. In the case of the former, the analysis of New World Negro dialects in English, French and Spanish, and their African counterparts in English and French, has shown that the underlying structure of the aboriginal tongues persists longest, and is most resistant to change, while vocabulary and pronunciation exhibit the most non-African elements. But it is just the grammatical configurations of any language that lodge deepest in linguistic habit-patterns, and that present the greatest difficulties where a new language is to be learned— far more so than either phonetics or vocabulary, though this last is easier learned than pronunciation. One does not think about the structure of his speech when he uses his own language; he need only "choose his words," as the saying goes.

Such patterns are laid down very early in life; so that, under contact, they are highly persistent. In like manner it is musical style, the "grammar" of music, that most resists change under contact, so that while music proves to be among the most African elements of Negro culture everywhere, yet in such regions as the United States, or in such a country as Peru, where the retention of Africanisms has been least extensive, the elusive elements of style remain in songs where an aspect such as melodic line has given way to a more European type of musical expression.

On the basis of the findings, then, the hypothesis can be advanced that in situations involving change, cultural imponderables are more resistant than are those elements of which persons are more conscious. It is important to stress in this connection, however, the distinction between this assumption and the hypothesis which holds that material culture is more acceptable under contact than non-material culture. All those phenomena which have been mentioned do fall within the latter category, it is true, but this is incidental to the hypothesis that has been advanced, since the principle is one that concerns process and does not concern form.

An exhaustive treatment of the theoretical basis of Afroamerican research would require the statement of still further hypotheses, dealing with such matters as the effect of population mass, of isolation, and of opportunity for acquiring a new culture, or discussion of the operation of such intangibles as pride in an original culture that is under assault, and a resulting determination to retain it against odds. It would require the evaluation, on the basis of available materials of hypotheses that have been advanced as a result of research in other cultures, or of the more *a priori*, philosophical speculations, such as the principle which correlates a supernaturalistic approach to life with a primitive or rural setting, or that which assumes a special type of mentality for non-European peoples.

Enough hypotheses which have guided Afroamerican research or have developed out of it have been indicated, however, to demonstrate how significant its contribution can be, and indeed, already has been, in furthering the wider ends of the scientific study of man. We have here been concerned with principles that can be applied to culture; we have mentioned one instance where language is to be drawn on; we could, in the same manner, document the point further with reference to the problems of human biology. But whatever the problems to be studied, the advantages presented by the field of Afroamerican studies in the way of breadth of scope and historic control of data, permit assumptions within the field to be tested adequately, before advancing them as applicable to other areas, under differing situations of historical development.

NOTE

The derivations of the listings given in Table 1 are as follows:

Guiana, Brazil (Bahia and southern Brazil), *Trinidad,* and *Haiti,* field research, and various published works bearing on the Negro peoples of these countries.

Brazil (north-urban and rural), unpublished reports of fieldwork by Octavio Eduardo in Maranhão.

Jamaica, first-hand contact with the Maroons and other Jamaican Negroes, though without opportunity for detailed field research; and for the general population, the volume "Black Roadways in Jamaica," by Martha Beckwith.

Cuba, various works by F. Ortiz, particularly his "Los Negroes Brujos," and on R. Lachetáneré's "Manuel de Santeria."

Virgin Islands, the monograph by A. A. Campbell entitled, "St. Thomas Negroes —a Study of Personality and Culture" (*Psychological Monographs,* vol. 55, no. 5, 1943), and unpublished field materials of J. C. Trevor.

Gullah Islands, field-work by W. R. Bascom, some results of which have been reported in a paper entitled, "Acculturation among the Gullah Negroes" (*American Anthropologist,* vol. 43, 1941, pp. 43–50).

United States, many works, from which materials of African derivation have been abstracted and summarized in my own work, "The Myth of the Negro Past."

The Hypothetical Situation
A TECHNIQUE OF FIELD RESEARCH

With great frequency . . . the hypothetical person turns out to be the informant himself, who is freed by the fictional quality of the approach to reveal facets of his personality he would take all pains to conceal were he speaking about himself. . . . And since . . . it brings forth responses that are in the nature of projections of the informant's experience against the background of his culture, it affords the investigator a heightened sensitivity to those relations of person to person . . . that reaches to the deepest levels of the equation of the mutual influences exerted by the individual on his culture and by culture on the individual. . . .

*   *   *

The present paper will describe a technique in ethnographic investigation that has been developed during research on the cultures of the Negro peoples of West Africa and various parts of the Caribbean area and South America. It consists, in essence, of devising, *ad hoc*, situations in the life of a people in terms of hypothetical persons, relationships, and events, which, being in accord with the prevalent patterns of the culture, are used to direct and give form to discussions with informants and other members of a group being studied. It will be of aid in considering the nature and utility of this technique to indicate something of its origin, development, and use.

The basic procedure was first employed in analyzing the proverbs of the Kru of Liberia. In 1927–8, a member of this group, resident in the United States, became available as an informant. The study was a linguistic one, but since proverbs seemed to offer good text materials, a collection of these was made. In working over the proverbs, however, it soon became apparent that the problem of meaning required a special kind of probing. At that time it was not recognized, as it is today, that the texts and translations of proverbs, without explanations,

Southwestern Journal of Anthropology, VI (1950), 32–40.

are of little utility; that only when the nuances of value-statements concealed in proverbs are analyzed, does their real meaning and the significant insight this gives into the implicit assumptions underlying much of the institutional and behavioral aspects of the cultures where they are employed, become apparent. Working with an informant far from his country, it was necessary, if the proverbs were to be made understandable, to set up hypothetical situations which revealed this meaning by reference to concrete instances of the circumstances under which these aphorisms would be employed. Informant and collector were thus continually engaged, conversationally, in aiding each other to build a canoe, or setting magic against one another's field, or preparing for a journey, or killing an animal belonging to the other—in short, going over situations of everyday life in terms of the human relations and the sanctions that would actually give rise to the use of a proverb and make it meaningful. The worth of this method, as evidenced in the manner in which these proverbs, in the published collection,[1] are embedded in a matrix of explanatory data, has been confirmed by its use in a number of studies of proverbs that have since appeared.

The value of this technique of discussing persons and events in terms of hypothetical situations again became apparent during fieldwork among the Bush Negroes of Dutch Guiana. Because of historical reasons that have been detailed elsewhere in a work where the methods of field research employed in studying this culture have been described,[2] the use of informants in the conventional sense was not possible. Information could be obtained in two ways only—by chance observation of actual happenings, and by discussing specific events as they entered into conversations with individual Bush Negroes. In these conversations, however, it was possible to move from an actual happening to a hypothetical one, especially regarding the reactions of the people to situations where supernatural power was believed to come into play. Birth-customs offer a good example of how this worked. These include provisions to cope with an entire category of events, which may be subsumed under the heading of abnormal births. Women are most reluctant, not only to discuss such births, but even to mention actual cases of them. For in the beliefs of this people, the mishaps that can and too often do mark the birth of children, especially where actual or sociologically defined abnormalities are concerned, are ascribed to powerful beings, who will visit the same ill fate on those who talk too freely about what they have done. However, much of the reluctance to discuss child-birth, especially in its abnormal aspects, disappeared when hypothetical situations were presented, and it was literally only by the use of this method of indirection that data bearing on what proved to be an important aspect of the beliefs and practices of this people could be obtained.

In Africa, though the method was found useful where there was reluctance to discuss actual events touching on the numerous fields where the supernatural enters, it also proved its worth in investigating problems lying in secular phases of the culture. Here, unlike among the Bush Negroes, it is possible to employ the more customary informant technique to establish a core of data to be checked by observation and informal conversation. Even with informant-interpreters who were sympathetic and willing aides, however, it soon became apparent, for instance, that to obtain data concerning the family and its extensions, especially the sanctions under which these groups function in the daily life of the people, presented many unsuspected difficulties. Not only is there a strongly patterned reluctance to reveal too much about one's own group, but concomitantly there is actual ignorance of the families of others about which a person might be willing to talk if he had the requisite information. Essentially, not only does convention tend to inhibit the discussion of such matters, but where sib myths are concerned, or where information is sought regarding the functioning of the characters in these myths in the everyday round, the fear of penalties exacted by these supernatural beings, on those who tell of them to unauthorized persons, imposes a very real barrier to effective probing.

The attempt was made to circumvent these sanctions by removing the discussion from the realm of reality, thus shifting it onto a plane where sanctions could not be operative, since there were none to apply. It was suggested to an informant that it might be interesting if the origin and growth of a relationship group were to be traced over the generations, beginning with a man who was merely named "A," and who, it was assumed, left his own family, migrated in the early days to another part of Dahomey, married, and founded a new line. This individual was then held to have had two sons, called "B" and "C." These, the assumption went, married and, when the founder of the group died, came in their turn to head the relationship unit.

As the discussion developed of the manner in which position was assumed and controls exercised, the entire pattern of the organization and structure of the Dahomean immediate family, extended family, and sib was revealed. Not only did the dynamics of the formation of the relationship groupings become apparent, but such matters as the inner functioning of these entities, the changing roles of their members with increase in age, and the differentials in the position and duties of men and women were made clear. It would be interesting to follow through and describe the data which this procedure brought to light, but since these have also been published,[3] they likewise need not be repeated. Suffice it to say that, after the line begun by "A" had been brought to the place where it had attained the position of a sub-sib, a situation had been reached where, the basic outlines of Da-homean social organization being in hand, further discussion could be in the nature of directed interviews—still in hypothetical terms, how-ever—calculated to obtain detail and clarify points arising from the range of sanctioned forms, wherein differences which might involve contradictions or discrepancies were revealed. More than this, the ma-terials proved to be of great utility in adding understanding to the ob-servation of overt behavior. Without these basic data, indeed, the implicit values that underlie the forms of the sib system or the various kinds of marriage or even of the ancestral cult itself could have been gathered far less adequately, if at all; and, in any event, only with the expenditure of much more time and effort than when operating in terms of the background of knowledge that had thus been obtained.

In subsequent field-trips, the method of the hypothetical situation was employed repeatedly. Sometimes it entered as routine field method. But it always remained as an available instrument for the probing of those cultural elements of which the members of the so-ciety being studied were reluctant to speak. Thus in New World Ne-gro societies, where African or African-like religious practices were banned by governments or operated under the disapproval of the le-gally sanctioned European Church, it functioned most effectively. In Haiti, many discussions of the *vodun* cult were begun, at least, by in-troducing hypothetical situations as if they were merely in the realm of possible happenings. A variant of the method was also found useful in Haiti, where local districts, bounded by ranges of hills, are distinctly set off from each other in the thinking of the inhabitants. In such cases, the community in another district could frequently be used as the locale of hypothetical incidents whose actual counterparts, the princi-pals who lived in the neighboring valley, would be named.

The subject of magic, which concerns protection against forces of evil or which brings them into play against others, is a topic that must be approached with particular delicacy. In all cultures, these things are regarded as anti-social, and thus something furtive, and to be con-cealed—covert, that is, in the accepted dictionary sense of the word. This is particularly the case in Haiti, where all forms of magic are out-lawed by the legal code. Certainly attempts to discuss its nature and functioning, in specific terms, in a country village, would meet with the greatest resistance. It is, of course, possible to talk about it in terms of abstractions and thus obtain native theories as to the nature of magic and its setting in the total system of *vodun* belief. Yet we recognize that materials lying on this plane make it difficult for the student to obtain a sense of the variability we know exists in the actual functioning of any cultural phenomenon whose theoretical form and implications he obtains in what may be termed its stylized version.

The method of the hypothetical situation provided an admirable solution for this difficulty. It had become apparent that in African and African-derived belief, good and evil are but the obverse and reverse sides of the same shield. Just as there is no dichotomy between good and evil as such, so, in the functioning of magic, a charm or spell that can aid one man or woman can harm another, or even bring evil to the same person if the setting in which the magic is to be employed is changed. In accordance with this general principle, it follows that those who work with the supernatural must know and be able to control magic; that one who works with magic in any form must be conversant with its evil as well as its benevolent manifestations. For, the argument runs, how can the specialist be expected to protect his client against evil if he does not know it well enough to track it down and set more powerful beneficent forces at work to negate its effects? Obviously, in such an atmosphere of belief, to discuss specific cases is impossible. By the use of hypothetical situations and personalities it was possible, however, to induce a worker of magic to make a charm of great potency as a demonstration—a demonstration so realistic that at the end of the session there was some difficulty in convincing him that the hypothetical situation was not merely a mask to conceal actual intent, and that it was not really desired that the charm that had been made should not be empowered. The esoteric details that were made available by the use of this method may be seen if the published account of the manufacture of this charm is consulted.[4]

With increasing use, it became ever more evident that the method of the hypothetical situation was by no means restricted in its effectiveness to those matters regarded as esoteric by the people being studied, or in analyzing complex structures of exoteric aspects of a culture. It was found to be equally valuable in bringing to light those elements of culture not mentioned because they are taken for granted. Students inevitably tend to overlook such points, which as often as not lie in the field of implicit sanctions and are thus not revealed by the observation of behavior or generalized discussion. The technique, that is, applies tellingly in those situations that were first given explicit recognition by one of the most astute field-workers American anthropology has produced, Elsie Clews Parsons, when she wrote: "In a conservative, secretive community the social detective learns much from efforts to conceal. . . . I was to learn that in social as in personal life the idea that there is nothing to conceal may result in almost complete concealment." [5]

Thus, in Trinidad and again in Brazil, the use of the method brought naturally to minds of informants and others points that they would have simply overlooked if describing a given institution in general terms rather than in the specific frame of reference this method entails. In Trinidad, for example, it was used in obtaining accounts, among other things, of the place of fishing in the life of the community—its economic role, the techniques employed in it, the modes of training fishermen, and the like. Again, it was used in studying child-care and child-rearing, and in reaching and understanding the basic meaning of the two types of marriage, particularly the system of extra-legal mating which, as in all New World Negro communities, was a puzzling element in the social organization of this group.

In Brazil, it yielded data of a type not ordinarily obtainable, not alone because of the esoteric elements involved, but also because the details of procedure entering into the situation were so numerous that in attempting to give an overall account in pattern-like terms the informant would inevitably miss many items. This concerned the economics of the situation wherein an established cult-center is reëstablished in a new locality—something that brings religious precepts and monetary considerations together in a focus where their common role is not easy to dissect and understand. It was learned that a woman, with whom good rapport had been established, was in the process of forming a new cult-center. Though it would have been a violation of accepted canons of etiquette to have questioned her about a project of this sort, it was not difficult, in discussing cult-procedure of various kinds, to lead the analysis to a point where a hypothetical cult-house was to be founded. Soon, however, the discussion moved from this hypothetical situation, first to the project in which she was actually engaged, and then, again hypothetically, to reëstablishing an older center. Here, once more, she moved to the exposition of an actual case. In both instances she cited facts that were so inclusive as even to yield budgetary figures, and in their totality to demonstrate the foresight with which developments of this sort are planned, providing a sense of how carefully financial provisions are made, as well as of the intricacy of the ritual procedures involved.

The most recent consistent use made of this method has been in connection with research carried on among the Black Caribs of the Republic of Honduras.[6] Here the pressure from the Spanish-speaking majority in the population causes the Negroes to be cautious about revealing many distinctive aspects of their system of belief, while factors of prestige which come into play make them reluctant to speak of those elements of their personal and social life which are at variance with the customs of the majority groups in the Honduran population. Observation and direct questioning seemed to have yielded everything that might be obtained, when recourse was had to the method of the hypothetical situation—in this case, in terms of a hypothetical family.

This family, as a whole, was given a name and, as it grew—for at the end it comprised a considerable number of consanguine and affinal members—each individual who entered into the discussion was also named. Once the "family" was established, the informant with whom it was initiated entered into the spirit of the discussion with far greater freedom than had been the case previously. Not only did it prove possible to obtain information concerning matters that direct questioning or suggestions of actual cases had been responded to by evasive or negative answers, but often unsuspected ramifications of a given situation were introduced into the discussion by the informant, or situations which had neither been encountered nor hinted at in previous conversations were called to mind and introduced into the overall picture. Moreover, word about this hypothetical family spread to friends of the informant with whom it was used, and they, too, entering into the spirit of the thing, would indicate still other situations in which it and its members might function. As in the instance of the Brazilian cult-member, telling of the fortunes of a hypothetical cult-house, the discussion in Honduras would frequently slip from hypothetical to actual occurrences, as confirmation of a supposed happening was given by reference to an actual event in village life in which a particular person, indicated by name, had been involved.

The method discussed here brings to mind its nearest counterpart among those techniques of field-work that have been given formal expression—the genealogical method announced four decades ago by Rivers.[7] In a manner not unlike the method of the hypothetical situation, the genealogical method was worked out in an attempt "to investigate abstract problems on a concrete basis"—that is, to obtain documentation which would assess the relation of the ideal, generalized patterns of accepted behavior in a society to the range of variation in actual behavior by a process of induction whereby the patterns flow from specific instances. Like the genealogical method, that of the hypothetical situation is a tool with which to explore relationships between members of a given society and the sanctions which cause these relationships to have meaning in the life of a people.

It is apparent that these two techniques are in no way opposed; indeed, they can, and have been combined, as in the instance given of the use of the hypothetical situation in Dahomey and among the Black Caribs. It is a simple matter, in working out a specific relationship system, to make of *Ego*, the point of reference in such work, an hypothetical individual rather than the informant himself. In many situations this may not only be profitable but essential; indeed, one wonders why such a useful way out of difficulties that Rivers himself enunciated did not occur to him. For, it will be recalled, he speaks of how, among some groups, "The existence of a taboo on the names of the dead . . . can sometimes only be overcome with difficulty." The question arises whether the recourse to secrecy he suggests as the essential way out of a difficulty of this sort might not effectively be replaced by the use of the method discussed here. This would be equally true where political tensions or religious prohibitions might operate to induce resistance to probing actual relationships, for in such cases the genealogical method would inevitably encourage evasion and invite falsification, and thus at best make the problem of verification more difficult and time-consuming where it did not lead to erroneous conclusions.

To indicate the contribution which the indirections called into play by the method of the hypothetical situation can make to efficiency and reliability in field research does not, of course, imply that it can solve all the problems or should be regarded as a substitute for those other techniques that over the years have proved their utility. It is quite conceivable that in cultures where no pattern exists to encourage a play of the imagination along the lines it calls for, the method could be used with difficulty, if at all. Again, where reticence in the face of questions posed by the ethnographer does not appear, as in certain South Sea islands, to use it would be merely to introduce an unnecessary extra step in research procedure. In such cases, it would at best be a means of objectifying and making specific the telling of rare occurrences, or those of a censured or pathological nature, or of revealing characteristic reactions and attitudes so taken for granted that they would not ordinarily be verbalized.

In essence, the method of the hypothetical situation is a novelistic technique, the utility of which arises out of its character as a kind of projective device. It has long been recognized by students of literature that the creative process feeds on experience. Even the most fantastic tale bases its fantasy on reality; even when writing most objectively about his characters, an author reveals his own beliefs, his own drives, making of his tale a reflection of his own background and of his own personality. It is a commonplace in the teaching of elementary composition that the student be continuously cautioned to write of what he knows, not of times, places, and persons far removed from his experience. In terms of ethnographic science, this principle is one on

which we constantly rely in doing field work, for we assume that no
human being has the creative resources that will permit him to fantasy
a culture, or even a part of a culture. It is for this reason that we feel
that working with a single informant, perhaps in our museums or
universities, far removed from the life of his society, is in the study of
many problems methodologically justifiable. No one can make up a
social system, a grammar, a theology; at most, he but registers the
flow of his imagination over his enculturative experience, in introducing the deviations from the common custom of his group we sometimes
find, later in checking in the field, that his account contains.

It is on the functioning of just this creative, projective mechanism
that the method of the hypothetical situation draws. Wherever the
play of the imagination can be called upon, this technique makes use
of the insights this affords, plus the solid body of fact that must come
forth because the informant is basing his discussions on specific
situations, happening to specific persons, the whole set in the matrix
of specific cultural orientations. With great frequency, as might be
expected, the hypothetical person turns out to be the informant himself, who is freed by the fictional quality of the approach to reveal
facets of his personality he would take all pains to conceal were he
speaking about himself. In similar fashion, he is released to tell of
happenings to himself or to others that, in any terms, he would be
loath to reveal were he naming "actual" persons. Thus both in the
personal and the cultural sense, he can go further, and will go further
in expressing reactions than conventions of approved conduct would
otherwise permit.[8]

We all use this method informally when we "suppose" happenings
of various sorts to have occurred when talking with persons from
whom we seek information. What the method of the hypothetical
situation does is to give to these happenings a structured form that
permits us to direct discussion toward the solution of a particular
problem in a given research project. And since, as we have seen, it
brings forth responses that are in the nature of projections of the
informant's experience against the background of his culture, it affords
the investigator a heightened sensitivity to those relations of person
to person, in the group being studied, that reaches to the deepest
levels of the equation of the mutual influences exerted by the individual on his culture, and by culture on the individual who lives in
terms of it.

1. M. J. Herskovits, *Kru Proverbs* (Journal of American Folklore, vol.
43 [1930], pp. 225–293, 1931).

2. M. J. and F. S. Herskovits, *Rebel Destiny: Among the Bush Negroes of Dutch Guiana* (New York, 1934).

3. M. J. Herskovits, *Dahomey, an Ancient West African Kingdom* (2 vols., New York), vol. 1, pp. 139–144 ff.

4. M. J. Herskovits, *Life in a Haitian Valley* (New York, 1937), pp. 230–237; cf. Chapter 12 for the broader setting.

5. E. C. Parsons, *Mitla, Town of the Souls* (Chicago, 1936), pp. 14–15.

6. By Mr Ruy Coelho. Information concerning the use of this technique among the Black Caribs was obtained through personal communication with him.

7. W. H. R. Rivers, *The Genealogical Method of Anthropological Inquiry* (Sociological Review, vol. 3, pp. 1–12, 1910).

8. I am indebted to F. Kluckhohn for the suggestion that, insofar as the projective aspect of the method of the hypothetical situation is concerned, care should be taken to distinguish two different kinds of reactions likely to be called forth by its use. The first of these is attitudinal, and would arise from its utilization in probing those experiences of the individual and aspects of culture having a heavy loading of affect. This would yield results different from those obtained when the method was used to collect descriptive ethnographic data where no particular ego-involvement might be expected.

On Some Modes of Ethnographic Comparison

> . . . *a pattern of conceiving area research in terms of conventionally delimited geographical units has acted as a deterrent to the utilization of findings of comparative studies of culture cast in frames of reference that fall outside these patterned conceptions. The suggested revision in terms of analysis of* cultures lying within a given historic stream *is thus intended to give a name to a model for comparative research that will aid us in bringing such deviations from traditionally channelled approaches more fully into the stream of anthropological concern.*

* * *

To what extent are we as anthropologists creatures of anthropological convention? To what degree does the historic factor in the development of our particular scientific sub-culture mold our ways

Bijdragen tot de Taal-land -en Volkenkunde, CXII (1956). Issue in honor of Professor J. P. B. de Josselin de Jong. Abridged.

of thought, our reactions to innovation? Do we realize, perhaps, that we ourselves provide materials for the study of the very phenomena which it is our task to investigate?[1]

These, and other questions, prompt this attempt to scrutinize a small facet of anthropological culture. We shall see that such debated factors in cultural dynamics as the weight of historic tradition, the balancing of conservatism against change, and the reinterpretation of old values in terms of new forms are all in play in the two instances of anthropological response we shall use to document our discussion. We shall see, in the first instance, how persistent is the culturally sanctioned, ideal concept in the face of the actualities of change; and in the second observe how conventional categories that frame research have made for what is analogous to social blindness concerning an entire field that contravenes the accepted limits of customary usage.

Our first example derives from certain aspects of current anthropological interest in enthnographic comparison. This interest is apparent from the impressive list of titles given by Lewis in his bibliography of works published between 1950 and 1954[2] that deal with this question. From the point of view of the ethnography of the anthropological sub-culture, the role of these studies has been to make explicit techniques and assumptions that have long remained implicit and unformulated, and thus prepare the way for a significant change in this segment of the total body of anthropological tradition. In this we see how a changing pattern permits analytical tools that have been allowed to become dull to be resharpened, and in some instances to be reshaped to meet new needs.

For our second example, we shall turn to some of the implications of the large body of findings in the Afroamerican field. Here we shall see that, though work in this field adds markedly to the documentation of the use of comparison as a frame of reference and affords controls that come as close to those of laboratory experiment as is possible in the social and humanistic disciplines, yet because its scope transcends accepted categories of time and space, it has been largely overlooked even where, as in discussions of ethnographic comparisons, it would seem to be most pertinent.

. . . In contrast to the conservatism which permitted the argument concerning the phrase "the comparative method" to continue when it had become almost meaningless, we shall see how the methodological and conceptual innovations of Afroamerican researches brought into play cultural resistances which, quite without being verbalized, operated so as to inhibit anthropologists from making the most effective use of the fresh approaches to the use of comparative data that the results of work in this field presented.

If we consider the comprehensive bibliography in the paper by Lewis, we find that Afroamerican contributions are given minimal attention. There is, for example, no entry for Ortiz' treatise on Afrocuban musical instruments, which continuously compares Cuban data to their related African forms, even though four of its five volumes appeared during the half-decade covered by the bibliography. Nor does the Memoir by Ribeiro on the Afrobrazilian cults of Recife appear, though it also continuously refers Brazilian to comparable African practices. Only one of the eight papers in the Afroamerican field that were published in the *Proceedings* of the XXIX International Americanist Congress is noted, despite the fact that four of the contributions in this section utilize comparative data. Other examples could be cited.

Another cogent example is a Memorandum on area research, prepared by Steward. Though he recognizes the importance of comparative analyses in area studies, Afroamerican researches receive no mention, despite the fact that his discussion is based in considerable measure on his own work in Puerto Rico, a very substantial component of whose population is of African ancestry.

These instances, and those others that could be cited from numerous earlier publications, give us our starting-point for this phase of our investigation into the dynamics of the anthropological sub-culture.

It is important to enquire into the causes that have made for this inertia. There are four that come to mind, all being related to the fact that the Afroamerican field, in its development, has struck out in ways that have reached outside customary practices, or initiated a realignment of interests, or introduced methodological innovations.

For one thing, anthropology, more even than is perhaps recognized, is still apprehended by anthropologists in traditional terms as the study of "primitive" peoples—and this is true even in the United States, where the argument that the study of man must not draw the line at literacy, if it is to fulfil its scientific mandate, is most often advanced and most ardently argued. But Afroamerican societies are not only aggregates where literacy is present, but where the languages employed are the written tongues of European derivation. In these societies, moreover, whatever of aboriginal custom remains from Africa is in considerable measure shot through with reinterpreted innovations, taken over from the traditional modes of behavior of the dominant white population, or that of the Indian groups with whom the Africans came into contact.

Again, the Afroamerican field, in its geographical definition, cannot be compassed in any of the areas which anthropologists customarily envisage as framing the physical limits of their research interests. It lies both in the Americanist and the Africanist fields—in both, that is, but in the conventional sense in neither. It is, in essence, a field whose bounds have been set by the need to pursue data relevant to a problem, and this is a delimitation rare in anthropology, and one that many anthropologists still find difficult to fit into their conceptual framework. We have but to consider, in this connection, how long it took Americanists devoted to the study of the *mestizo* culture of Latin America to initiate field research in Spain. Or consider, again, the richness of opportunity for systematic investigation presented by a project which would be based on comparative research into the detailed relationship between the cultures of Madagascar and Indonesia; or the challenge, on a larger scale, offered by the systematic study of the actual similarities and differences that mark the cultures of Melanesia and Africa. Yet these areas of research, potentially of enormous significance in their implications for the analysis of historic relationships and of cultural dynamics, with the generalizations that would be expected to flow from such studies, have remained to all practical purposes untouched.

Two other reasons also seem to enter. Afroamerican societies, for the most part, do not stand alone, clearly separable, as do the tribal aggregates customarily studied by anthropologists; and this holds whether we consider them on the geographical, the social or the cultural level. Such groupings as the Bush Negroes of the interior of Suriname are rare in the New World. The essence of the situation with which the student of Afroamerican societies is presented involves the study of customs resulting from the constant and continuing contact which the descendants of Africans have had with peoples of different cultural antecedents and of different physical types. Moreover, the character of the integration of the cultural streams in play—African, European and American Indian—is far more complex, for example, than is true of the *mestizo* cultures of Latin America, for the principal element in our equation, the African is, of course, not autochthonous to the New World. And this obviously increases the methodological problems to be faced and the intricacy of the conceptual structure that must be employed in shaping and executing research. We shall later consider some of the implications of this fact.

Finally, we must take into account the dominant orientations in Afroamerican cultures as these play against the prevailing pattern of research interests in anthropology. There can be little question that, in general, the traditional breadth of anthropological concern has been progressively narrowed. This is most striking in England, where concentration on the study of social institutions has divorced most of the professional anthropologists from considerations of religious belief—as against ritual and magic—or of art, or folklore, or linguistics. The same process, to a lesser degree, is manifest in France and in the United States. But in Afroamerican research, belief systems, folklore and music are of fundamental importance in the range of data that bear on the essential comparative analyses. Again, research into the social aspects of Afroamerican cultures is complicated, as has been mentioned, by the fact that Afroamerican groups are integral parts of larger population aggregates. This means that to analyze them requires a firm grounding in the cultures of certain key African areas if the extensive reinterpretations that characterize these social structures are adequately to be assessed. Without this background for analysis and comparison, the investigations have tended to be sociological, which is to say analytic and ahistorical, with the historical component, indispensable in Afroamerican research, foreign to directing interest and procedures.

These considerations help us to understand why, despite the continuous interest in the method of comparison, the comparative studies of a considerable body of scholars in Spanish America, Brazil, the Caribbean, France, the Netherlands and the United States, carried on for four decades and more, have been bypassed for researches that fall into the more conventional anthropological patterns, Since, as we have indicated, the Afroamerican field has much to offer that is applicable to comparative studies elsewhere, we may now consider some of its achieved and potential contributions that can be distinguished.

Let us, first of all, reconsider the way in which modes of cultural comparison have been derived. In this, it will be remembered, the organizing factor that has been stressed in distinguishing types is a geographical one—whether comparisons are made on a global scale, or between continents or nations, or within a continent or nation, or within a culture area or a single society. Yet as we have seen, the Afroamerican field falls in none of these categories. More than this, though it is intercontinental, the fact that it comprises three continents and one great island area is incidental to the major objective of the research. But whereas in many cases where intercontinental comparisons enter—as, for example, in attempts to equate American Indian and Oceanic cultures—the geographic element is paramount, since the resolution of the problem of distance is essential to discovering the historic contacts involved, in the Afroamerican field the historic contacts are known, the ethnographic comparisons in the historic stream become ethnohistorical, and research is freed to establish the dynamics of contact rather than the fact of its occurrence. It is thus clear that a further class of comparative studies is needed to encompass it, and those others that will be suggested by the mere act of designating the category. This class we will call the *comparative study of cultures within a given historic stream.*

This work of comparing cultures in a single historic stream, which involves the welding of ethnographic to historical materials has characterized the work of students in the Afroamerican field since its inception. Early Afroamericanists, such as Nina Rodrigues in Brazil, Price-Mars in Haiti, or Fernando Ortiz in Cuba, long before the concept of ethnohistory as such had been advanced, turned consistently to historical materials to throw light on the derivation of the African ancestry of the people they studied. With these facts in hand they then drew on such African ethnographic materials as were available to them to check their own data against similar cultural aspects described as occurring among the relevant peoples of Africa. This use of the ethnohistorical method was developed further by myself,[3] and culminated in the definitive work of Beltrán,[4] whose analysis of the tribal origins of Africans brought to Mexico provides the essential data for all the New World.

Recourse to the ethnohistorical method in studying culture, and more especially of cultures undergoing acculturative change, which marks research carried on in many parts of the world, is a reaction against the inadequacies of historical reconstruction for the scientific analysis of cultural dynamics. The unique feature of the use of ethnohistory in Afroamerican research lies in the scope of this field, both as regards time-depth, population mass, and geographical spread, and the number of variables that enter. In all probability it offers the closest historical controls of any major area of research in social science. The analogy of the laboratory experiments was early employed[5] and, in broader formulation[6] has since been consistently utilized. Materials of comparable spread and depth are rare, but the applicability of the methodological devices worked out in Afroamerican research to the analysis of more restricted situations elsewhere, the scope of which permits a comparable use of historical documentation, will be apparent.

Another refinement of procedure that derives from this field is the technique that has been used to arrange ethnographic data on a continuum.[7] It is logical and useful, in classifying research materials, that the gradations in different manifestations of variables lying between two extremes be recognized. In many studies where this technique has been employed, however, the historical component is unsatisfactory and the categories have had to be reached on the basis of deduction. Not only this, but the progressions have tended to be stated in terms of total cultures. Yet, quite aside from the advantages to be gained in analyzing data from the use of categories inductively reached, work in the Afroamerican field has clearly demonstrated that to place whole cultures on a continuum masks significant intracultural differentials. In New World Negro research it has been found useful to break down the cultures whose variations in the degree of retention of Africanisms are under study into their component aspects. Experience has shown, through the use of this approach, that the degree of acceptance of non-African elements by the descendants of Africans, and of retention of African custom, varies significantly when one compares technology or economics with religion or music. More than this, the selective approach has also shown that culture-change differs in degree and intensity with the socio-economic position of the individuals that make up a given Afroamerican society, the amount of retention of Africanisms being inverse to acculturative opportunity as represented by position in the total community of a particular stratum.

As concerns the use of the method of comparison, strictly speaking, Afroamerican researches suggest further broad methodological formulations which introduce a needed corrective in the study of culture. How much overstressed the antithesis between the two can be is apparent when we consider the way in which impulses from the three American studies have been analyzed. The critical discussions of the use of the concepts of cultural trait and complex that followed on the initial realization that cultures could be broken down into these components have applied a healthy corrective to their over-use, it is true, and so have the equally critical analyses of the various functional approaches that have been advanced since the concept was first employed. In studying the acculturative history of New World Negro societies, however, we can see how the manner in which elements, such as the name and role of a deity or of a saint, or the complex of death rites, or attitudes towards twins, or the specialized use of magic as protective or aggressive self-help can be extracted from an original setting and be reworked into another. Or we can study how a whole pre-existing social complex, such as a tradition of polygyny, can be integrated into a different set of conventions which sanction monogamy, to form a new marriage pattern. These, and other instances that enter into Afroamerican studies, demonstrate the utility of a flexible approach. In this field, that is, materials of all cultural dimensions are considered where pertinent, an approach which both points the utility of analyzing cultural elements in terms of their intermeshing parts, yet adds a dynamic aspect to the essentially static nature of most analytical research.

Ascertainable time-depth enters in still further ways to offer leads for research elsewhere. Though in the New World the time involved in forming the cultures being studied varies from one region to another, there is no group of descendants of Africans, except in Brazil and Cuba, where significant contact with Africa is less than four generations away. In the case of the Bush-Negroes or of such a group as the Black Caribs of Honduras, it is more than twice that figure. In Afroamerican societies, that is, we can see how the various cultural elements which were brought together have developed their own unity; a unity which, though it can be dissected by the student into its historical components, carries for the person living in the society all the subliminal sanctions of any long established social entity. When we turn to the problem of enculturation, as this has to do with personality formation in terms of the conflicts commonly held to assail the child in cultures of multiple derivation, we find that in Afroamerican societies the enculturative process is no necessary road to disorganization. Yet the variables in degree of integration of the components found within the historic stream of Afroamerican culture permit hypotheses regarding the relation between cultural setting and personality integration in acculturated societies to be tested on a broad comparative basis difficult to find elsewhere.

This brings us to the contributions of Afroamerican research to the theory of culture. Arising out of the acculturative situation that is basic in these studies, it is apparent that generalizations will lie primarily in the field of cultural dynamics. The propensity of culture to change, however, is axiomatic in cultural theory, so that many of the generalizations that derive from Afroamerican studies will also have utility in shaping research into the problem of cultural changes in societies where the acculturative factor is not crucial. Again, any analysis of structure in which the time-factor is called on to account for the reorientation of component elements entails approaches for which the findings of Afroamerican research are pertinent.

One of the earliest concepts of students in the Afroamerican field was that of syncretism. In extended form, it was given expression by Ramos in his studies of the religious beliefs of Afrobrazilians, and was used to designate the identification, that had been previously remarked in Brazil, of African deities with Catholic saints, a mechanism that has since been found to be operative in many aspects of Afroamerican societies in all the New World. On the psychological plane, syncretism involves the internalization of an ascribed unity between similar phenomena from the cultures that have contributed to the acculturated end-product. That is, while to the student the derivation of the items identified is clear, a comparable differentiation in terms of conflicting values marks the reaction toward the unified duality only of a few of the most specialized and skeptical members of the society in which it is found. The predominant attitude recognizes, for example, in the case cited, that a saint is a Catholic concept and an orisha an African one, but in day to day behavior there is no difficulty in accepting as conviction that the same supernatural entity functions in different settings within the totality of the culture.

Another concept of broad applicability, to be regarded as a lesser degree of identification than syncretism, is that of cultural reinterpretation. In the early days of Afroamericanist research, the need to discover retentions so as to provide the ethnographic component for ethnohistorical comparisons caused students to search out the purest and least acculturated Africanisms in the New World. This was one of the greatest values derived from studying the Bush Negroes of Suriname, where African custom continues in almost unchanged form, and dominates the total gamut of their culture. This was also why, in Brazil and Cuba and Haiti, almost exclusive attention was given to the religious beliefs and rituals of the Afroamericans. Yet with time, the facts of provenience well established, the nature of the problem changed. It came to be not a search for Africanisms as such, but a study of the forms and meanings these had taken in their adaptations and transmutations within the new cultural matrix in which they had to find their place. Thus today the attempt is made to understand how the diverse cultural traditions involved are brought into consonance with the demands of psychocultural identification. In these terms, the focus is on the dual marriage systems that co-exist in the lower class sects that mark most Afroamerican communities of Protestant countries, or the transmutation of African musical idioms that analysis shows to be reworkings and recombinations of African and European traditions.

The problem of the nature and functioning of values in culture similarly enters into the comparative study of African and New World Negro cultures. Here we call not only on the concept of reinterpretation, but that of cultural focus, which was also derived from Afroamerican research. The retention of religious values, in pure or reinterpreted form, as holistic ethnographic studies of Afroamerican culture came to be made, was found to be a striking feature of these societies. The question has thus posed itself whether first in Africa, and then in cultures elsewhere, a similar concentration of interest in particular aspects of culture does not provide any way of life with the special emphasis that gives it describable synthesis.

Beyond this, however, are the data from Afroamerican societies which indicate ways in which value-systems are integrated in different cultural systems from those in which they were worked out. Much has been written of the Protestant ethic; what, we may well ask, has been the effect of this ethic where economic and social practices sanctioned by European custom have interacted with the differing value-systems of Africa? In terms of what may be termed *the ethnology of knowledge,* we may ask how attitudes toward the use of time, or toward the accumulation or spending of wealth that prevails in Europe have come to be accepted or reinterpreted by the descendants of Africans in the New World? What effect have African values of this order had on those of European cultural derivation with whom they have come into contact? To what extent are the differentials in such values among the different European groups that came to dominate various parts of the New World manifest from one New World region to another? Or, to take another example, what reconciliation of the values in interpersonal relations has occurred when those deriving from the large social structures of Africa have been brought into contact with those that are based on the more fragmented family system that dominates the structure of a society such as the United States?

A final point has to do with the tenacity of culture, and goes to the heart of theories of ethnopsychology. Though there is a tendency, in the study of cultural dynamics, to lay emphasis on the phenomenon of change, Afroamerican studies have demonstrated from the first that retentions, whether in pure or reinterpreted form, are of quite equal importance. We have but to refer to what is known about the role of learning during the earliest years of life in setting behavior patterns, to recognize the fruitfulness of this approach. Motor behavior, concepts of time and space, ethical concepts, aesthetic tastes, and many other basic cultural orientations are inculcated in these years, and shape characteristic reactions manifested during the whole of the individual's life. They form the background against which innovations are projected; they provide the basis for his evaluations of what is newly presented to him; they afford the rationale for the conclusions today generally agreed on by students that under culture-contact, those innovations that are most in consonance with pre-existing custom will be accepted. In the study of New World Negro cultures, it is possible to assess, in terms of the different historical situations that existed in various regions, what has been accepted, what reinterpreted, what rejected; we can find least common denominators of acceptance and rejection and modes of reinterpretation throughout the area on a comparative basis. We thus further document and illumine this most important problem of balancing and accounting for the constant play of conservatism and change that is basic in the dynamics of culture.

This discussion has indicated certain advantages to be gained from studying the ethnology of our own anthropological sub-culture, and applying concepts derived from cross-cultural research to the analysis of our discipline. We have seen how a failure to reconcile historic meaning with functioning reality has made for confusion in terminology and consequent difficulty in phrasing the objectives of research. Taking some of the lessons we have learned from the study of culture in general, it has been suggested that this difficulty can be resolved both on the semantic and the procedural levels by taking the historic factor into full account, restoring perspective by replacing the designation "the comparative method" by the phrase *the method of comparison* when we name techniques that are most customarily employed in comparing various kinds of data.

We have also seen how a pattern of conceiving area research in terms of conventionally delimited geographical units has acted as a deterrent to the utilization of findings of comparative studies of culture cast in frames of references that fall outside these patterned conceptions. The suggested revision in terms of the analysis of *cultures lying within a given historic stream* is thus intended to give a name to a model for comparative research that will aid us in bringing such deviations from traditionally channelled approaches more fully into the stream of anthropological concern.

1. For anthropology as a tradition or sub-culture, see Tax, S., *passim*.
2. Lewis, O., pp. 279–92.
3. Herskovits, M. J., 1941.
4. Beltrán, G. A., 1946.
5. Herskovits, M. J., 1930.
6. E.g., Ramos, A., 1937.
7. Herskovits, M. J., 1945.

REFERENCES

Ackerknecht, Erwin H., 1954. "On the Comparative Method in Anthropology," in *Method and Perspective in Anthropology* (R. F. Spencer, ed.), Minneapolis, pp. 117–125.
Beltrán, Gonzalo Aguirre, 1946. *La Poblacion Negra de México, 1519–1810. Estudio Ethnohistórico*, Mexico, D. F.
Bidney, David, 1953. "The Concept of Value in Modern Anthropology," in *Anthropology Today*, an Encyclopaedic Inventory (A. L. Kroeber, ed.), New York, pp. 682–699.
Boas, F., 1940 (1896). "The Limitations of the Comparative Method of Anthropology," in *Race, Language and Culture*, New York, pp. 270–280 (reprinted from *Science*, n.x., vol. 4, pp. 901–08).
Eggan, Fred, 1954. "Social Anthropology and the Method of Controlled Comparison." *American Anthropologist*, vol. 56, pp. 743–63.
Herskovits, M. J., 1930. "The Negro in the New World: The Statement of a Problem," *American Anthropologist*, vol. 32, pp. 145–156.
——, 1941. *The Myth of the Negro Past*. New York.

————, 1945. "Problem, Method and Theory in Afroamerican Studies," *Afroamérica* vol. 1, pp. 5–24.

Lewis, Oscar, 1955. "Comparisons in Cultural Anthropology," in *Yearbook of Anthropology*, 1955 (Wm. L. Thomas, Jr., ed.) New York, pp. 259–292.

Ortiz, Fernando, 1917. *Los Negros Brujos*, Madrid.

————, 1952–55. *Los Instrumentos de la Musica Afrocubana*, vols. I–V, Habana.

Price-Mars, J., 1928. *Ainsi Parla l'Oncle*. Port-au-Prince.

Ramos, Arthus, 1937. *As Culturas Negras no Novo Mundo*. Rio de Janeiro.

Riberio, René, 1952. "Cultos Afrobrasileiros de Recife: Um Estudo de Ajustemento Social," *Boletim do Instituto Joaquim Nabuco*, Numero Especial. Recife.

Rodrigues, Nina, 1933. *Os Africanos no Brazil*. São Paulo.

Schapera, I., 1953. "Some Comments on Comparative Method in Social Anthropology," *American Anthropologist*, vol. 55, pp. 353–362.

Singer, Milton B., 1953. "Summary of Comments and Discussion," *American Anthropologist*, vol. 55, pp. 362–66.

Steward, Julian H., 1950. "Area Research: Theory and Practice," *Social Science Research Council Bulletin*, No. 63. New York.

Tax, Sol, 1955. "The Integration of Anthropology," in *Yearbook of Anthropology*, 1955 (Wm. L. Thomas, Jr., ed.), New York. pp. 313–328.

: III :

ETHNOHISTORY

THE LABORATORY CONTROL IN STUDIES OF ACCULTURATION

A Footnote to the History of Negro Slaving

Much has been written of the Negro slave-trade—of the economic forces which caused its rise and fall, of its toll of human lives, of the humanitarian sentiments against it. Of the reverberations in Africa which this traffic caused we have only guesses: nowhere can one look for an account of how the Africans themselves regarded it. What of the Africans of to-day? Has all memory of the slave-raids vanished? We give here such answers to these questions as we were able to obtain during field-work in Nigeria, the Gold Coast, and particularly Dahomey, all of them important West African centers of slaving operations in the days of the trade.

❂　　❂　　❂

I

We met Felix in Abomey, the capital of the West African Kingdom of Dahomey. In former years, Felix, who was not a Dahomean but a Mina from Togoland, would not have been living there, for in the days of the kings Abomey was as inaccessible to foreigners, black or white, as the ancient walled cities of China. But now Felix drives an automobile in Abomey for a fellow Mina storekeeper.

Felix was driving us to a temple of the Thunder God, where we were to see a novice of the cult go through the ordeal of fire. As we drove through the city we compared notes with our interpreter on this deity's aboriginal worship in Africa and the manner in which he is worshipped in the New World—in Guiana, in Haiti, and elsewhere—

Opportunity, XI (1933), 178–81.

by the descendants of Africans who had come to the Americas and the islands of the Caribbean as slaves. To our interpreter, these Africans in the New World were an old story. He had decided some-time before, from our answers to his many questions about "our Afri-cans" that there were among them people who had come from Dahomey; and he had had his own opinion strengthened by hearing elderly Dahomeans exclaim, when we mentioned a Guiana deity, or some Haitian belief, "But you have real Dahomeans there! You have people from Abomey itself!" Felix, however, was learning of New World Negroes for the first time, and as we talked, he went slowly, that he might hear what was being said. All at once there was a rapid interchange between the two Africans, and then a long silence.

"He is crying," said the interpreter, "tears like his are good."

Later, as we came to know Felix and he to trust us, we heard from him why he had been so moved that day, and why he was so eager to hear about the Negroes on our side of the Atlantic. Like most Africans, Felix had been trained in the traditions of his family. He knew that long ago his ancestors had been decimated by slave raids. He could tell us the story of the wanderings of his family to escape from these raids—how, for example, his people had fled from the Ashanti after a war in which many of his ancestral relations had been lost in battle, either killed or carried off into captivity. He could re-count how later, when his family had established a new home, they had had to go farther to the East, and as their enemies found them, farther still, until it had not mattered where they went, for the *Aguda*, as he called the Portuguese, had continued to clamor for more and more slaves.

"People we call *Aguda*, they buy plenty. If they buy they put for ship. That time no steamer. If man go out, man who be strong catch him and go sell. My grandfather he say *Aguda* buy we people in Popo (now French Togoland), then take go 'way to place they now calls Freetown. *Aguda* make village there, then make we people born children. When children born, *Aguda* take away go sell."

The people who were taken away, Felix said, had never been heard from. His family did not know whether any of them had lived long enough to leave descendants. But these relatives, wherever they had died, were still members of the ancestral generations, and that is why today, when Felix's family in the city of Anecho in Togoland give food for the dead, they call also upon those who had died far away to come and partake of the offerings.

II

During our stay on the West Coast we had several times before come upon references to the days of slaving, and the recognition that in the country we came from lived the descendants of many Africans who had been carried away. But those who commented spoke guardedly, and such information as was given came from members of the ruling castes, never from commoners like Felix.

Earlier in Nigeria, which lies to the east of Dahomey, we had had occasion to speak with several of the native potentates about New World Negroes. The Alafin of Oyo, the Alake of Abeokuta, the Oni of Ife, with the circumlocution of African rulers, had made it apparent that in their courts living traditions of the slave-trade existed, while through the good offices of the Emir of Kano, we had obtained valuable information from four old slavers who came of families that had trafficked with the Gold Coast in slaves and merchandise from the earliest times. But Kano is far to the north of the coastal belt, and slaving operations have been a reality there as late as the beginning of the present century, whereas among the coastal peoples slaving on a large scale could only exist as a tradition.

That this tradition did exist among all classes, and that it had, moreover, been incorporated into the religious structure and ritual, we had had no intimation until the incident we have recounted occurred.

However, our conversations with Felix and the Dahomeans led us to the knowledge of how much in Dahomey, at least, the slaving operations were remembered, and led us finally to the cult of the ancestors. Ancestor worship, one of the most important cults not alone in Dahomey, but in all of West Africa, takes as its typical ceremonial form the annual "customs" for the family dead. At these customs food is given to the spirits of the recent dead, and to those of all the other ancestral generations; to those who died at home, and to those who met their end in distant lands; to those whose names are known and remembered, to those who have been forgotten, and to those whose names the family in Dahomey had never had the opportunity to hear. A family of rank offer a bullock to the known dead, and, for the souls of those who died in foreign parts, a goat is sacrificed, while a poor family kill a goat for the ancestors who are known, and a cock for the family dead whose names are not known.

Now, in itself, this ritual of giving food to the unknown dead follows a custom of very ancient times. It is a compliment to these dead— one that may not be overlooked, since they are easily angered, and are dangerous when offended—to call them by name, where the name is known, or to recall them from a definite land, if that can be done. In Dahomey today, therefore, there are designations for the countries to which the slaves had gone. They are called from the land of the Nago, the Yoruba of Nigeria to whom the Dahomeans for so many years sent their annual tribute of men and women, and from the countries of the white man. *Yovotome*, white-man's land, had been the name for the countries of the English, but today it is the designation for France. *Ame'ica* is America, *Agudatome*, the land of the Portuguese, or *Blezi*, is the name for Brazil, while *Kpanyo* is Dahomean for Spain, and *Kankanu* the lands of the Dutch.

Let us see the special form this ritual has taken from the historical fact of European slaving operations, by observing a ceremony for one of the dead kings of the Aladahonu dynasty which was in power from the early seventeenth century until the conquest of Dahomey by the French in the last decade of the nineteenth.

. . . It is early morning, the month is May, and we are at the palace of the son of King Behanzin, the last ruler of the native Dahomean kingdom. The customs for the kings are about to begin. In the center of the second courtyard, a young bullock lies with legs and head securely lashed, and to this bullock a goat is tied. In the first courtyard are the men whose rank does not entitle them to participate actively in the ceremony, and in the open sandy clearing in front of the palace are the commoners. Facing the entrance door from the first to the second countyard is a long pavilion, roofed and cool, and it is there that the son of Behanzin sits under his umbrella, while beside him are perhaps twenty of his younger and more beautiful wives. We are seated under a large umbrella to the right of the pavilion, facing the trussed animals and, beyond, the temple for the ancestors at the other end of the courtyard. There is a coming and going of men, their shoulders bared out of respect, and each one as he enters or leaves kneels before the present head of the Behanzin family. Men come with gifts for the customs, and the women receive these and walk about preparing large calabashes of food.

A large audience has assembled, when the priests enter the temple where iron standards, altars to the dead, are kept. Those whose duty it is to kill the sacrificial animals advance toward them, knives in hand, accompanied by others holding calabashes to catch the blood, the "food" of the ancestors. Skilfully these men do their work, for there is scarcely a convulsion as the throat of the bullock is slit, and the body is dragged across the clearing, or, as next the goat tethered at the fence is killed. The meat of the larger animal is for the living, but not that of the goat. None of its flesh will be touched by any member of the family, for this goat is for the unknown dead, among whom are the descendants of those sold into slavery, and the royal family in Dahomey does not have too quiet a conscience about the treatment of their relations of former years who were sent away.

From the temple a voice is heard chanting, then the responses of the kneeling figures. As the blood is being poured over the standards, a prayer is said:

"Oh, ancestors, do all in your power that princes and nobles who today rule never be sent away from here as slaves to Ame'ica, to Togbome, to Gbulu, to Kankanu, to Gbuluvia, to Rarira. We pray you to do all in your power to punish the people who bought our kinsmen whom we shall never see again. Send their vessels to Whidah harbor. When they come, drown their crews, and make all the wealth of their ships come back to Dahomey.

An old man calls out, "And is that not a just payment for what they have taken?"

All: "Yes, yes, yes! And it is not enough. The English must bring guns. The Portuguese must bring powder. The Spaniards must bring the small stones which give fire to our fire-sticks. The Americans must bring the cloths and the rum made by our kinsmen who are there, for these will permit us to smell their presence. Long live Dahomey! You who have not succumbed to slavery here, act so that those three . . .* who died for the cause of our country in Brazil be kept in the memory of all Dahomeans, and give us news of them by White strangers who come to Abomey."

III

The traditions of the slave trade are not exclusively lodged, however, in the rituals for the ancestors, but enter all phases of life that re-create the Dahomean past. When, for instance, we were discussing with old men the names and lore of the Dahomean totemic groupings, we heard of one, "You have nearly all the people of this family in your country. They knew too much magic. We sold them because they made too much trouble." Of another, they said, "This family has strong men. They are good warriors but bad enemies. When they troubled our king, they were caught and sold. You have their big men in your country." Still another time, when speaking of the indigenous inhabitants of the plateau of Abomey, they said, "When Hwegbadja became king he needed money for guns, and so he raided the country-side nightly. And anyhow, the people here made too much trouble by setting their gods against him."

* The names that are omitted here are sacred, and we promised not to publish them.

Another tradition relates to the priestly and ruling classes, and is as follows. Hwegbadja was the first king of the Aladahonu dynasty. Tradition tells that the family came first from Adja, in the west, to Alada, in the south, not far from the sea-coast, and made its way northward to the plateau of Abomey. One of the great difficulties of occupying a conquered land is that though a ruler can overcome an indigenous people, he cannot subdue the aboriginal gods, and those that have been especially troublesome in the history of Dahomey are the Earth gods, for it is the gods of the earth who punish for misdeeds by making the grains a man eats grow on his body, and when there is much evil done in the land small-pox epidemics come, and other deadly scourges. In the reign of this Hwegbadja, therefore, who ruled from about 1650 to 1680, four chief priests of the earth cult, and six of the cult of the silk-cotton tree, their families, retainers and disciples were sold to the Portuguese because of plots to incite the gods against the conquerors. In the reign of Akaba, which extended from 1680 to 1708, six chief-priests of the river cult who were suspected of a plot against the king, were sold with all their followers, and their gods were so effectively suppressed that there is no one left who knows how to worship those ancient river spirits. The Dahomeans say that these gods have been restless ever since, and this restlessness which manifests itself in drumming heard from the bottom of sacred rivers, threatens the peace of Dahomey today.

The next king, Agadja, conquered his way to the coast, and made Whydah the port of Dahomey. This port became in his reign one of the leading outlets for the slave trade on the west coast of Africa. He is said to have sold four priests of the earth cult and their followers into slavery. Tegbesu, who ruled from 1728 to 1775, sold five priestesses of the earth cult with their disciples. This king was especially troubled by plots to unseat him, so that not alone priests but many princes and their accomplices who held office in court were disposed of in the same way. Adanzan, during his reign of twenty-one years, sold, among many others, three priests of the earth cult and their disciples. This is not the whole story. With each priest or prince sold into slavery went hundreds of people, cult-followers, men of rank who because of marriage ties might be sympathetic to a pretender's cause, the offender's children, and wives and brothers, all those, in short, who might remain to organize an insurrection, or to join with other malcontents.

The climax of this account, for the natives, at least, is the story of the enslavement of the mother of Gezo. Gezo was a small boy when his father died, and the kingship went to an older brother, the Adanzan we have just mentioned. The father, before his death, had, however, predicted that Gezo would become king. Adanzan was enraged when he learned of this and proceeded to sell Gezo's mother and sixty-three of her supporters into slavery. They were taken by the Portuguese and were sent to Brazil. There, the story goes, they found many Dahomeans. Gezo's mother and eleven others were sent to America, and because she was sad and no longer young she was sold many times. She spent twenty-four years in all in America, and founded the cult of her Dahomean god there.

"When Gezo became king he was not happy. He said, 'I am a king. I can do anything I like, yet my mother is a slave.' He went to his Portuguese friend Da Souza, and Da Souza went across the seas and searched everywhere until he found her. She came back with six other Dahomeans, and from them Gezo heard what happened to Dahomeans in America. That is how we know."

This woman returned eighteen years before the death of Gezo, a time which dates her restoration to her people at about 1840. And the new name she received in honor of her return was "Knife - without - a - handle - came - back - from - White - man's - land - and - fell - into - a - dish - of - good - stew."

The Significance
of West Africa for Negro Research[1]

A unique feature of the use of ethnohistory in Afroamerican research lies in the scope of this field, both as regards time-depth, population mass, and geographical spread, and the number of variables that enter. In all probability it offers the closest historical controls of any major area of research in social science. This technique was responsible for the ex-peditiousness with which the long debated problem of the predominant African influences that helped shape the cultures of the Negro peoples of the New World was solved.

◉   ◉   ◉

In two recent papers[2] I have presented a portion of the evidence which, based on the study of historical documents and anthropological field research, indicates the preponderantly West African origin of the Negroes of the New World. In considering the significance of this

Journal of Negro History, XXI, no. 1 (1936), 15–30.

region for research on the Negro, I may, at the outset, add certain further testimony on this point, gathered by myself in the field, or which has appeared in recent historical publications, not included in these previous discussions of the subject.

I

One of the most difficult problems for students of the slave trade has been to obtain information concerning the traffic in the interior of the African continent. Current opinion stresses the vast distances which the slave caravans are supposed to have travelled to reach the coastal ports. As has been indicated in the papers cited, this opinion is to be questioned, since not only the available evidence from contemporary sources, but the logic of population distribution and the economics of the trade point toward the forested coastal belt as the locale from which the slaves were principally derived. The assumption of the derivation of slaves from tribes far inland perhaps results from the tendency to measure distance by time. The rate of progress of these caravans was very slow; yet the mere fact that the slave-coffles took a long time to reach the coast from the interior has been held sufficient to justify the assumption that they came from very far countries indeed.

The only definite first-hand statement in the literature that I have been able to discover is the description of the journey of such a caravan given by Mungo Park, who accompanied it in its travels to the sea. This account speaks of five hundred miles as the distance covered in the many weary months the slave-coffle was on its way. Undoubtedly there are other contemporary documents with which I am not familiar; in any event, human documentation concerning the latter days of the slave trade is still possible, and it is this personal testimony, obtained in the city of Kano, in northern Nigeria, in 1931, which is the first portion of the evidence I wish to lay before you today.[3]

Kano has long been an important center in the interior of West Africa. Lying some seven hundred miles from the coast, it was the capital of the Hausa Empire until its absorption into the British Colony of Nigeria, and today retains the economic importance which its strategic position as a terminus of numerous Saharan caravan routes gives it. Not so well known is the fact that it is also the terminus of an important trading route toward the southwest, connecting Kano with the territory of the Ashanti and the other peoples of the Gold Coast. And it is this trade that was carried on between Kano and the Gold Coast in human and other merchandise, with which we are concerned.

The data to be given here were obtained from four old men with whom I sat for some hours discussing the details of the trade. The oldest, a man probably well into his nineties, had made his last trip about 1880, when the slave trade was in its final stages, and, of course, had been nearly suppressed as far as supplying the New World was concerned. Yet the lateness of the date should not cause us to underestimate the importance of this evidence, for it was plain in speaking with these men that the manner in which they carried on operations was the same as that in which their forebears, traders like themselves, had also carried on theirs. The Kano slave dealers constituted an informal guild. They consulted together as occasion arose; helped one another in achieving their plans, and accepted the advice and direction of a headman. And this point, which is of significance for our argument, may be stressed at the outset; the merchants with whom I talked neither regarded themselves, nor wished to be regarded, primarily as slavers. They were merchants, who, more or less incidental to their general commerce, had slaves in their caravans as carriers and servants and drivers. If the market in the Gold Coast was good or the slaves were bad, they were sold, but it was stressed that the major portion of the slaves in the caravans were brought back to Kano, acting in the same capacities they had filled on the way to the coast.

Slaves were obtained through war, by means of raids, because of failure to pay debts, and as a result of gambling, since, under the excitement of play, men would often stake themselves when everything else had been lost. Warrior slaves were not so much liked, since often such a person had to be killed for refusing to work, or would run away when the opportunity offered and hence would have to be watched especially closely; while, of course, such men were always the centers of potential trouble. Therefore, the slaves that were taken in war or after a raid were women and children, the men being usually killed in the fighting. Often the pagan peoples among whom the raids were carried out—for the people of Kano are devout Mohammedans—attempted to destroy themselves when it was seen that resistance was useless. The brains of the children would be dashed out, wives would be killed, and, setting fire to their homes, the men would commit suicide. In some cases, a village would be captured by surprise, and the people would be allowed to remain in their homes on condition they pay tribute. This was true of the Bauchi people near Zaria, I was informed, and in such cases the tribute was given in slaves. Thus it seems likely that in a number of instances there were what might be regarded as breeding centers from which slaves were drawn.

When a sufficient number of slaves was on hand, and the amount of merchandise to be sold warranted it, a caravan, normally comprising from one thousand to two thousand persons, would be formed. The journey to the Gold Coast, a distance of some eleven hundred miles by the route taken, plus the return trip, would require two or three years. Of the personnel of a caravan of two thousand, some fourteen hundred would be slaves, the balance being traders, their wives, and their children. The reason, not difficult to see, why a large group of traders would band together in this manner concerned their safety on the march. Tribute was demanded by certain local potentates for the right to pass their countries, and this tribute would be given in kola nuts, which are much relished and not easy to get in this part of Africa, since they grow in the southern forested belt and must be imported. Raids were often attempted by the peoples through whose territory the caravan passed, and, if successful, the traders were robbed of their slaves. About one in every ten caravans was apparently thus raided, which means that about once every two years disaster came to some trading enterprise, since about five groups left Kano annually.

The principal commodities carried by the slaves were morocco leather—which, I may remark, is really Kano leather, since it has its name because it was traded into Europe from Morocco, where it was taken across the desert in camel caravans—native cloths, and a native salt called *natron*. Horses accompanied the caravan, but these were traded for more slaves as soon as the trade route turned to the northwest. Once the journey had begun, the slaves were not confined unless information was obtained from some "good" slave to the effect that a certain one might attempt to escape. If the slaves included a refractory group of men, they might be chained neck to neck even during the daytime, but this was unusual, and only done when their behavior was deemed to warrant such treatment or suspicion had been aroused concerning these men. Occasionally a slave died on the way; some of the casualties were the result of disease, but some of the deaths were due to exhaustion caused by the weight of merchandise each slave was compelled to carry. Yet the deaths were surprisingly small; my informants estimated that a loss of between fifty and seventy out of every thousand slaves in a caravan would be generous.

The two routes taken to the Gold Coast were given in great detail, and later independently checked on the map, where all the points mentioned were found. The most favored way was the northerly one which, after leaving Kano, passed through Sokoto and Dodo to Kwala, where it turned southwest to Wagadugu. From here it proceeded southeast to Tenkodogo, and then ran in a line almost due south from Tamale and Mampong to Kumasi, the capital of the Ashanti Kingdom. The other route began in a direction directly westward from Kano, passing through Djega, where it turned southwest to Ilo and crossed the Niger. Continuing in the same direction through Yendi and Salaga to Mampong, it joined the other route to Kumasi. When asked whether or not trading was carried on to the south into the territory of the Yoruba peoples of Southern Nigeria, or into Dahomey, the reply was negative—for both countries it was said that "the donkey doesn't go there." One great advantage of the routes actually taken was the fact that they lay almost entirely within Hausa territory, or at least in territory where nominal protection of the Hausa empire was to be had. With the Ashanti, Kano always apparently had close relations, and Ashanti friends told me that the two peoples consider themselves related. Today Ashanti weaving is prominently displayed in the Kano market, while every Ashanti town has its "zongo," where people from the north live their lives according to their own customs, or where Hausa Mohammedan traders can stay as they pass through.

Once in the Gold Coast, slaves and merchandise were disposed of as opportunity offered, and other wares to be taken back and sold in Kano were bought. In the time of the men with whom I talked, a good male slave brought 250,000 cauries (about $25.00), a girl of twelve to thirteen years of age twice that amount, while a boy of like age was worth some 400,000 cauries, or $40.00. Incidentally, it was felt that the blacker the slave the more valuable he was, the reason given being that the darker skinned persons could better stand the sun. Therefore the reddish-colored Fulani were not prized; in addition, they were said to be more difficult to manage on the march and while in captivity. What happened to a slave after he was sold was no affair of the Hausa traders; however, it was remarked that should a slave be retained by his Ashanti master and have children, these children could not be disposed of but remained as "slaves of the land" or serfs of the descendants of their original owners.[4]

Slaves were not sold at regular markets, but wherever anyone would buy them. Often a caravan would be stopped by someone who saw a slave he fancied, and the transaction was concluded then and there. The Hausa, apparently, never sold directly to European dealers, but to the Gold Coast natives, who liked these northern slaves for themselves, employing them as workers in their fields. There were, however, Gold Coast dealers who would go through the country and buy up slaves from their local owners, and these were really middle-men working for White slavers. Slaves, according to the Kano tradition, had then to be got on board ship secretly so as to avoid the native authorities, who did not permit slaves to be exported because they felt this lessened the man-power of the country. But if the regime in the Gold Coast approached that of Dahomey, as I suspect it did, the actual reason was probably that the lucrative nature of the slave trade made it desirable

that it be concentrated in the hands of the monarch and his subordinates, and hence private dealing in slaves was discouraged. These
Hausa merchants knew also that slaves were taken to Sierra Leone
and across the water to the West Indies, of which they had vaguely
heard. Only one of them had actually got to the coast. He had never
seen a steam vessel, but spoke of slaves exported "in wooden ships,
driven by large sacks, which the wind pushed."

This, then, is the account of the interior slave trading as given by
men who themselves, and whose ancestors before them, had actually
engaged in it. Let us assess these data in the light of our problem. The
first point to be considered in this account of the operations of these
Kano merchants who, among other wares, dealt in human goods, has
to do with the number of slaves that could have reached the coast
through their hands. In their discussion of the trade we see that though
perhaps six or seven thousand slaves left Kano every year for the
Gold Coast, perhaps two-thirds or three-fourths of that number returned north as carriers, the capacity in which they had acted during
the southward journey. And though we may suppose that more than
five caravans departed from Kano each year when the slave trade was
at its height, and that a smaller proportion of slaves than that named
were returned as carriers of merchandise, even then the number who
arrived at the coastal factories could constitute but a fraction of the
enormous numbers of slaves who the records tell us were shipped
from Gold Coast ports. Another item, in the account, is the comment
on the worth of darker and lighter individuals. If the reddish Fulani
were less desirable merchandise, then it would follow that the darker
peoples, who live to the south of Kano, would be the ones particularly
marked out for raiding rather than these lighter ones to the north.[5]

This information concerning the slave trade represents only a fraction
of the data that can be obtained on this point in West Africa today, as
is indicated in part, for example, by the vivid and touching traditions
held by the peoples of the coastal belt, which have already been
presented in a previous publication.[6]

II

The hypothesis that the locale of the slave trade was the more
restricted region of West Africa, rather than the continent as a whole,
and of this region the coastal forested belt rather than the deeper interior, is substantiated then by data of the kind given in the preceding
discussion. Furthermore, the study of the customs of such New World
Negro peoples as the Bush Negroes of Dutch Guiana, the Jamaicans,

the Haitians, the Brazilian and Cuban groups[7]—the only ones who have been studied with any degree of thoroughness—shows that many of their place-names, religious rites, names of deities, and customs of a social and political nature must be referred to tribes living between Cape Three Points and the mouth of the Niger River. The inference again that this is where those slaves lived who most often succeeded in impressing their peculiar customs on the New World Negroes would seem inescapable. Why the considerable numbers of Negroes brought to this hemisphere from the northerly region of the Gambia, and from Loango and the mouth of the Congo, to the south, should have left no more traces of their customs in New World Negro cultures than they did is a difficult question, which we will consider shortly. Whatever the reason, whenever recognizable tribal customs are found in the New World—not generalized West African ones, but those which can be very specifically assigned to a given people or locality—the tribes almost invariably represented are those of the Gold Coast, Dahomey, and eastern and western Nigeria.

It will perhaps have been remarked that in all the preceding discussion, the emphasis has been on New World rather than American Negroes. This, of course, assumes that the types found in this country are the same as those of the West Indies, of the Guianas, and of Brazil. And, since all evidence tends to show that there was a great deal of commerce in slaves between the various parts of the New World (Brazil excepted), this assumption may be regarded as a truism concerning which it is not necessary to give further testimony.[8] But we must realize that in speaking of the origins of New World Negroes, we are presumably, at least, speaking of the origins of American Negroes. And, conversely, if documentary material can be obtained to show the sources from which the ships that came to the ports of the United States obtained their cargoes, this will throw further light on the question which is under analysis here by indicating the origins of New World Negroes in general.

Let us, therefore, turn to this other type of evidence. To make my point I shall draw on the magnificent body of material which the research of Professor Elizabeth Donnan, aided by the Carnegie Institution of Washington, has recently made available to us. In documenting this approach, it would, of course, be possible also to utilize other information of the same sort that is available—work such as that carried on under the auspices of your Society, for example, or that of M. Gaston-Martin, who has analyzed the records of slaveships and slaving companies that operated from the port of Nantes in France. All this other work is given heightened significance by the data contained in the four great volumes of Miss Donnan,[9] but since her study is comparatively new—the final volume, which deals with the trade to southern American ports, having appeared only this year —I shall confine myself solely to it.

In this last volume, Miss Donnan devotes many pages to tables summarizing the manifests of ships arriving at the ports of Maryland, Virginia, South Carolina, and Georgia. Here one finds, among other data, the numbers of slaves carried by each vessel, and the ports from which this human cargo had been obtained. The materials for Maryland and Georgia are fragmentary, but those for Virginia and especially for South Carolina are extremely full, and I have therefore tabulated these data in calculating totals for the various areas from which the slaves were derived. For Virginia, the following results are found:

SLAVES IMPORTED INTO VIRGINIA, 1710–1769 [10]

Source of origin given as "Africa"	20,564	
Gambia (including Senegal and Goree)	3,652	
"Guinea" (from sources indicated as Gold Coast, Cabocorso Castle, Bande, Bance Island, and Windward Coast)	6,777	
Calabar (Old Calabar, New Calabar, and Bonny)	9,224	
Angola	3,860	
Madagascar	1,011	
Slaves brought direct from Africa		45,088
Slaves imported from the West Indies		7,046
Slaves from other North American ports		370
TOTAL		52,504

Certain comments may be made on these figures before proceeding to the table summarizing the South Carolina data. It will be noticed that aside from ships arriving from "Africa"—a designation that helps us not at all—the regions most prominently represented are "Guinea" —which, in all contemporary documents, stands for the West Coast from the Ivory Coast to the mouth of the Niger[11]—, Calabar, which represents this latter district, and Angola. The 1,011 slaves imported from Madagascar constitute an interesting item. They comprised six shipments, and came only during the earlier days of the period included in the above table—one in 1718, one in 1720, and four in 1721, two of them being transported in the same vessel, the "Prince Eugene" of Bristol.

We may now consider the derivation of slaves imported into South Carolina, as given by Miss Donnan:[12]

SLAVES IMPORTED INTO SOUTH CAROLINA, 1752–1808 [13]

Source of origin given as "Africa"	4,146	
From the Gambia to Sierra Leone	12,441	
Sierra Leone	3,906	
Liberia and the Ivory Coast (i.e., Rice and Grain Coasts)	3,851	
"Guinea Coast" (Gold Coast to Calabar)	18,240	
Angola	11,485	
Congo	10,924	
Mozambique	243	
East Africa	230	
Slaves brought direct from Africa		65,466
Slaves imported from the West Indies		2,303
TOTAL		67,769

It can be seen from the above tabulations how, once more, these data corroborate the evidence gathered in comparative studies of the customs of New World Negro groups and West African peoples. For instance, one can understand why it is not surprising that the drum to be seen in the British Museum, collected from the Negroes of Virginia during the latter portion of the eighteenth century, should be similar even in detail to those used today by the Ashanti and Fanti of the Gold Coast. Furthermore, the figures given for the number of Negroes brought either from or via the West Indian Islands (there is not sufficient time or space to detail this in the tables as presented here, but in many instances such designations as "Gold Coast and Jamaica," or "Jamaica [Gambia]" are indicated), also tend to point the assumption that the stocks represented in the United States are no different than those found in the islands.[14] Unfortunately, published data of this richness are not available for the West Indies. However, Mr. J. G. Cruickshank, Archivist of British Guiana, has very kindly furnished me with information he has found in the files of the *Essequibo and Demerary Gazette* for the years 1803–1807. Here the advertisements of sales of "new" Negroes show much the same origins, where identifications are possible, as Miss Donnan's ship manifests. Classified according to the regions given in the preceding tables, the figures are:

Angola	1,051
Windward Coast	3,014
Gold Coast	3,593
Ebo (Nigeria)	820
Others	1,029

Let us now consider further the failure to find in the New World Negro culture where Africanisms are to be discovered, such as those of the Guianas, or Haiti, or Jamaica, more than the slightest trace of either Senegalese or Congo traditions. The most likely explanation is that the peoples strongly represented in the days of the height of the slave traffic established their own tribal customs so that those in the minority, or those who came later, would have to adapt themselves to the patterns of behavior they found in vogue. Miss Donnan's tables indicate this in the case of the Congo Negroes, for in the lists of South Carolina importations of slaves, except for a few very early cargoes, by far the greater number of Congo Negroes figure in manifests dating toward the end of the trade, after the Guinea Coast was patrolled by the warships of Britain and France, while the numbers of Angola importations likewise increase materially in the later lists. This theory is also substantiated by the following quotation from a letter just received from Mr. Cruickshank:

. . . from what I have learned from old Negroes here [i.e., British Guiana] it would appear that the three or four African Nations who were brought here in predominant numbers imposed their language, beliefs, &c., gradually on the others. In course of time there were not enough of the minority tribes on an estate to take part in customs, dances, and the like, or even to carry on the language. There was nobody left to talk to! Children growing up heard another African language far oftener than their own; they were even laughed at when they said some of their mother's words—when they 'cut country,' as it was said—and so the language of the minority tribes, and much else—though probably never all—died out.

III

I have presented the material contained in this paper to point the fact of the great significance of West Africa for Negro research. If it is true, as I think must be apparent from the evidence which other workers in the field of Negro studies have discovered, and other data such as those which I have placed before you today, that New World Negroes are descended mainly from West African stocks, then the paramount importance of having adequate knowledge of the physical types, the customs, and beliefs, and the languages of the peoples of this region, is not difficult to see. It is not necessary to detail here the many questions which are raised whose answers may perhaps be obtained from an attack that emphasizes, on the African side, this forested belt of the West Coast as the principal locale for study. Thus, the problem of racial crossing is not only of paramount scientific importance, but of practical concern as well. Yet to study Negro-White crossing we must have much more knowledge of the physical types of West Africa than the fragmentary information that is now available. Or, there is the matter of the origins of American Negro speech, or the music of New World Negroes that has been so eagerly debated. Most statements on these points are obviously *ex cathedra*. Though the persons who have analyzed these phenomena have been familiar with European speech or music, they have obviously not been acquainted with the African material that is richly available, either at first-hand or through the literature. In the matter of speech, it is hoped that future research, which will include intensive work in the many grammars and dictionaries of African tongues, will help resolve the question; at the present time, the analysis and transcription by Dr. M. Kolinski, an expert in the study of primitive music, of songs recorded by myself in various field-trips to Dutch Guiana, West Africa, and Haiti, already shows results which assure us that their publication will alter profoundly our theories of the derivation of the spirituals.

Similar questions are posed in the field of culture. The traditions of African origin peculiar to New World Negroes persist in those portions of the United States even where the strongest acculturation to European patterns of behavior has taken place. Equipped with an understanding of African and West Indian Negro cultures, the resemblances are not at all difficult to discern.[15] They invade all fields of Negro life, and, as I have recently had occasion to observe, have invaded the life of White Americans—to say nothing of White West Indians—as well.[16] And the practical importance of recognizing the complex and advanced character of the West African civilizations from which New World Negroes came, and thus removing the unfortunate and undeserved stigma of the "savage" character of the African which, I regret to say, exists as strongly in the thinking of American Negroes as it does in the minds of American Whites, should be patent.

One final question may be asked. Is not this insistence on concentrated study of West Africa one of those obvious points with which everyone agrees? Why should the point be argued at all? The answer lies in the fact that American students of the Negro have, with a few noteworthy exceptions, almost utterly failed to do more than lip service to the necessity for West African study. To go to West Africa is costly, and, from certain points of view, dangerous. But it is no less costly, though somewhat less dangerous, to go to South Africa, or East Africa, or North Africa, as American students of the scientific problems of the Negro have done and are doing at this moment. I do not wish to decry the importance of study in these other regions. But it seems that with the knowledge that we have of the West African derivation of the American Negroes, and of their affiliation with the Negroes of the New World in general, studies in the scientific problems of the Negro made by those coming from this side of the Atlantic should be concentrated, for purposes of scientific strategy, on the peoples of West Africa. We know relatively little of their manner of living; we know even less of their history. This material is to be had for the seeking, and, when we have it, and compare it with the data to be gained from more intensive scientific study of the Negroes in America and the rest of the New World than has heretofore been undertaken, facts will be at hand not only of inestimable value in giving basic information to those concerned with the practical problems of race relations, but also for the study of one of the most important scientific problems known at the present time—the study of the processes and results of cultural and physical contacts between peoples of different races and differing traditions. In the final analysis, experience has taught us that in matters requiring scientific study, the longest way around is most often the shortest route to a given point. And it is thus likely that more preoccupation with the background of Negro life, and fewer conclusions drawn from insufficient knowledge of fundamentals may be the way to achieve happier results in the practical problems of race and racial relations with which we are all, as citizens, concerned.

1. An address delivered on the occasion of the celebration of the Twentieth Anniversary of the Association for the Study of Negro Life and History in Chicago, Illinois, September 10, 1935.

2. "On the Provenience of New World Negroes," *Journal of Social Forces*, vol. xii (1933), pp. 247–262, and "The Social History of the Negro," in *A Handbook of Social Psychology* (C. Murchison, Editor), Clark University Press, 1935, pp. 207–267.

3. It is a pleasure to acknowledge the cooperation and aid given me by the Emir of Kano, and by Mr. M. V. Backhouse, then Assistant District Officer in the Nigerian Political Service. Without their help, not only would it have been impossible to obtain the information given here, but I would not even have known of its existence.

4. This would seem to be a general West African custom, since exactly the same status was accorded the descendants of slaves in Dahomey, and, indeed, persists today despite French rule, these serfs giving a half of each day's work to the descendants of their masters.

5. A point of some importance as indicating the reason why the Hausa did so much raiding for slaves when such a relatively small number were taken to the Gold Coast involves the returns accruing to the Kano dealers from the slave trade to the north. Just as leather and other commodities were carried across the Sahara desert to Tunis, Algiers, Morocco and Egypt, so was human merchandise; and it was stated by my informants that the

bulk of the slaves exported from Kano went in this direction, rather than toward the coast of the Atlantic Ocean for eventual shipment to the New World.

6. M. J. and F. S. Herskovits, "A Footnote to the History of Negro Slaving," Opportunity, XI (1933), pp. 178–181.

7. Numerous references to the literature on these cultures will be found in the papers cited at the beginning of this article.

8. See, however, the two tables cited below for some figures on Negroes imported into the South from West Indian ports.

9. Elizabeth Donnan, "Documents Illustrative of the History of the Slave Trade to America" (Carnegie Institution Publication No. 409), Washington, The Carnegie Institution of America, 1930–1935, I, pp. x, 495; II, pp. xii, 731; III, pp. xiii, 477; IV, pp. xv, 719.

10. E. Donnan, op. cit., IV, pp. 175–234, passim.

11. See, for example, the map given in Bosman's "New and Accurate Description of the Coast of Guinea, divided into the Gold, the Slave and the Ivory Coast" (London, second ed., Engl. transl., 1721), or in William Snelgrave's "A New Account of some parts of Guinea, and the Slave Trade" (London, 1734), where though "Guinea" is defined in the "Introduction" as including the entire west coast from Cape Verde to Angola on the map, the region under consideration is denoted as "Upper Guinea or Proper Guinea."

12. Op. cit., IV, pp. 310, passim.

13. Where, in the tables of Miss Donnan's book, two African sources are given for a cargo of slaves, the number in the cargo has been divided equally between the two regions for the purposes of computation.

14. In the tables in Miss Donnan's "Documents" giving the sources of slaves imported into the ports of New York and New Jersey during the years 1715–1765 (III, pp. 462–512), of a total of 4,457, only 930, or 21 per cent, came directly from Africa.

15. The extent to which there has been a reluctance to admit, or inability to discern the African character of many of these traditions and modes of behavior is not without psychological interest as indicating how deep-seated patterns of thought can invade scientific research.

16. "What Has Africa Given America?", p. 168.

What the Slaves Found in Haiti

> *Certain questions . . . must be asked about this white ele-
> ment in the population. . . . What were the patterns of fam-
> ily life, of religion, of economic organization, of morals, which
> the whites presented to Negro eyes? . . . it is necessary to
> consider the types of Frenchmen whose modes of living were
> to influence the behavior which the descendants of their
> slaves were to perpetuate when these had attained their free-
> dom as individuals and their independence as a nation.*

❊   ❊   ❊

Though by the time of the French Revolution "the immense army of
slavery had increased to such proportions that in the face of it the
white world seemed reduced to a mere handful of men," [1] this was by
no means the case in the earliest days of the colony of Santo Domingo.
As late as 1681 the whites outnumbered the Negroes almost three to
one,[2] and it is not until a hundred years later that, in the words of St.
Mery, there were "eleven and three tenths slaves for one white." [3]

Yet in the fashioning of the present-day culture of the Haitian
peasants, this "mere handful" exerted an influence out of all proportion to its size. That this should have occurred is not strange in view
of the relationship between Negroes and whites, which was that between slaves and masters; that it did occur is amply shown in the
contemporary accounts of Haitian and West Indian life, which tell us
how the Negroes everywhere made conscious efforts to achieve the
standards of those who to them represented power, wealth, and position. But while the prestige of the master-class must be acknowledged,
care must be taken not to accept uncritically an assumption that has
colored many accounts of the lives of primitive peoples who have come
into contact with European cultures—namely, that the traditions and
beliefs of these groups cannot withstand the impact of what is termed
"civilization." What invariably seems to follow when peoples having
differing customs, beliefs, and cultural heritages come into continuous
contact is that both give, and each takes. What aspects of the new
culture a given people will take, and what in turn they will give, must

vary according to the particular historical situation under which the contact occurs. But both processes do go on, and, as will be shown in the case of Haiti, though the Negroes retained much of their African culture, they also freely took over and adapted the customs and behavior of the Europeans among whom they lived.

Certain questions, therefore, must be asked about this white element in the population. To what extent was it a unit in its derivation and in its special customs—did its members come from a single social class of the home country, or were all elements of French society represented? What were the patterns of family life, of religion, of economic organization, of morals, which the whites presented to Negro eyes? These are matters of great significance, for one telling factor in the mingling of cultures is the type of carrier through whom contact between civilizations is effected. If, for example, European missionaries or traders or administrators on short tenure and without their families are introduced into an area, a far different picture of European life will be presented to the native from that were immigrant settlers to come among them with their wives and children; and this result, moreover, to seek finer distinctions, will show additional divergencies according to the social position of these migrants. Therefore it is necessary to consider the types of Frenchmen whose modes of living were to influence the behavior which the descendants of their slaves were to perpetuate when these had attained their freedom as individuals and their independence as a nation.

The "Corps of Adventurers" who in 1632 comprised the dominant element in the population of Haiti included four groups: the buccaneers "who were occupied with the hunt," the filibusters "who cruised the seas," the *habitants*, "who cultivated the land," and the bondsmen "who, for the most part, lived with the *habitants* and the buccaneers." [4] Letters of the period permit a somewhat more detailed description of the social groupings of pre-Revolutionary Haiti than that just given— a matter of some importance, since it must have been at this time that the merging of African and European civilizations was at a stage when the basic outlines of its eventual structure were being formed. The early population seems to have been made up in large part of the flotsam and jetsam of Paris; "a sort of obligatory enrollment of colonists, an enforced recruiting of emigrants from those elements of the metropolitan population judged unassimilable" [5]—those who were without means of support or under suspicion of crime, insolvent debtors, "adventurers," and those for whom emigration represented the sole existence open to them.

The *engagés*, or bondsmen, were those who, lacking the funds to pay their passage, pledged themselves to planters for a period of three

years. During this time they were treated like the Negro slaves, and at
the expiration of their terms were turned into the world with little
enough to show for their hard labor.[6] The Protestants who migrated to
Haiti were a far different type of settler, but these were few in number, and some, such as the fifty-eight who came to the island in 1687,
traveled in the very ships which brought convicts condemned to hard
labor for life. Ex-convicts and escaped criminals, discharged soldiers
and deserters were also found. In many instances, however, persons
of these types seemed by their achievements to have proved themselves not undesirable additions to the population. "I have had 300 of
them whom I have placed," wrote one M. de Cussy in 1686; "they are
industrious folk, and the planters are very pleased with them." One
escaped criminal, who was not discovered as such until many years
after he had come to the colony, was permitted to buy his freedom
for ten thousand *livres*, "which," an official report stated, "will be used
to build prisons in the Cul-de-Sac." Another did so well in his new
home that, though his past was known, he was never molested and
died the owner of twenty-two Negro slaves.[7] Others who came to Haiti
were sent there for reasons of waywardness, or because they had been
involved in escapades that threatened trouble for them or their families, or because, showing no aptitude for gainful employment, their
relations chose to send them to the colony rather than to be burdened
with their support. Of these early colonists de Vassière says, with apparent justification: "In truth the morale and the manners of this population were what they might be supposed to have been, execrable." [8]

These categories, however, do not give the full tale of the non-
Negro peoples who eventually contributed of their blood to the present-day Haitian population. In the earliest times the Spaniards sold
white as well as Negro slaves to the New World, as numerous *assientos*
testify. Before the time of French control of the western portion of
the island, Haiti must have received her proportion of these unfortunates.[9] French women, many of them women of the streets, some mere
girls who had come from convents, were imported in the early days to
encourage the buccaneers and the filibusters to lead a more settled
life.[10] In 1696, when the French abandoned the island of St. Croix, its
inhabitants, both masters and slaves, were transported to Haiti, there
to re-establish themselves on land allotted to them by the government.[11] Acadians from Newfoundland were landed at the Mole St.
Nicholas in 1764, and, as has been mentioned, some of them were
eventually settled in the valley of Mirebalais, there to disappear after
a few years.[12] At about the same time, in accordance with a policy of
increasing the white population, 2,470 Germans were brought to the
island. Unlike the Acadians, these people thrived and developed an ex-

tensive cultivation of coffee, and their colony was in a healthy state at the time of the French Revolution.[13] St. Mery also records the importation and sale in 1730 of more than five hundred Natchez Indians from New France (Louisiana) "as well as others at a later date, both from Louisiana and Canada." [14]

A final class of settler must be mentioned, whose coming is reported to have given a better tone to the drab picture of Haitian life. This class was composed of members of the French nobility, who in their new home attempted to maintain the standards which characterized and regulated their lives in France. Unlike many of the earlier inhabitants, to whom the difficult life of the planter did not appeal, the nobles tended to continue their status as country gentlemen in their new environment, and, by establishing plantations, to reproduce in so far as was possible, their situation in France as a group of landed proprietors. As a result, there soon grew up between these planters living on their estates and the population of the cities and towns the same distinctions of caste and the same blind rivalry which, before the Revolution, separated the French country squires and the city dwellers in France itself.[15]

The existence of these two classes within the white population of the colony, which is commented upon by many writers of the period, must have presented to the Negro slaves strikingly different views of the life of the whites. In a manuscript of Moreau de St. Mery, at present in the archives of the Ministry of Colonies in Paris, a group of some two hundred of these gentlefolk who in 1763 lived in the region of what today is Cap-Haitien, in northern Haiti, is spoken of as that of a special class, and their existence is contrasted with that of the city folk. Living on their plantations, with the cultivation of which they were exclusively occupied, their mode of life was different from that of the inhabitants of the cities and towns, where were found dealers in wholesale produce, officers of the crown, lawyers, solicitors, and merchants. Some forty years later another writer, writing from the point of view of the planters and expressing their contempt for the townspeople, speaks of the towns as existing primarily to serve the needs of these country squires as centers for the storage and disposal of their produce: "There are found merchants, artisans, judges, recorders, solicitors, notaries, bailiffs, doctors. But one finds neither nobles, men of property, nor persons of wit and perception." [16]

The physical aspect of the cities had little to recommend them, especially since the utter lack of sanitation made for extreme uncleanliness in all Haitian centers. This fact is of special interest in the light of the frequent references to this trait of Haitian cities in the writings of those Europeans who described the life of independent Haiti. Invariably in such accounts the littered state of the streets, even in the capital, is stressed, and tendered as evidence of the absence of civilization in this Negro Republic.[17] Even though occasional mention is made that this state of affairs existed before the Revolution, nowhere, whether in St. John or in the later writers who date from the time of the occupation of the country by the United States Marine Corps, is there any realization that this condition antedates the independence of Haiti. The cleanliness of Africans in Africa wherever the natives have ready access to water has been well attested, and is still true in those regions from which the ancestors of the people of Haiti principally derive.

Yet some aspects of life in the towns livened the picture of Haitian colonial existence. Outstanding were the opportunities offered by these centers for social intercourse, and even for intellectual and artistic stimulation of a kind, such as was afforded by the famous *Cercle des Philadelphes* of Cap Française, dedicated to literary, philosophical, and, above all, to political discussions.[18] Masonic lodges, later taken over by the Negroes and today of appreciable importance in Haiti, were also instituted by the French, the first having been founded at the Cap in 1740.[19] Purely social meeting-places, such as public baths or public halls, were in operation, while in the towns of Cap Français, Port-au-Prince, Leogane, Saint-Marc, and Cayes, theaters were established which produced "the latest plays from Paris" and attracted large audiences.[20]

Despite all this, the canker of homesickness constantly gnawed at the colonists even in the towns—the feeling that a stay in the colony was only for the interval needed to allow a man to escape to the mother country with a fortune. On the estates the loneliness and isolation of plantation life are commented upon repeatedly. A letter of the period, without place or date, found in the family papers of the historian de Vassière, discusses this with poignancy:

Have pity for an existence which must be eked out far from the world of our own people. We here number five whites, my father, my mother, my two brothers, and myself, surrounded by more than two hundred slaves, the number of our negroes who are domestics alone coming almost to thirty. From morning to night, wherever we turn, their faces meet our eyes. No matter how early we awaken, they are at our bedsides, and the custom which obtains here not to make the least move without the help of one of these Negro servants brings it about not only that we live in their society the greater portion of the day, but also that they are involved in the least important events of our daily life. Should we go outside our house to the workshops, we are still subject to this strange propinquity. Add to this the fact that our conversation has almost entirely to do with the health of our slaves, their needs which must be cared for, the manner in which they are to be distributed about the estate, or their attempts at revolt, and you will come to understand that our entire life is so closely identified with that of these unfortunates that, in the end, it is the same as theirs. And despite whatever pleasure may come from that almost absolute dominance which it is given us to exercise over them, what regrets do not assail us daily because of our inability to have contact and correspondence with others than these unfortunates, so far removed from us in point of view, customs, and education.[21]

This letter speaks of the presence of five whites. The psychological state of the planter who, unmarried and alone, spent his days without the companionship of a fellow-being who as much as shared a common language with him may well be imagined. Even where there were white overseers, the prevailing sense of caste was so strong that while these ate with the head of the estate, they did not live under the same roof, for they were subordinates and were treated as such. For his most constant companions the owner had his house-servants, unless he maintained a mulatto concubine who cooked his food and looked after his personal wants, shared his confidences, and reported to him any disaffection on the part of the Negro slaves. It is understandable that, having made his fortune, the planter did not delay his return to France, where, once back in Paris, he lived lavishly on the revenues from his estates; and letters in the Ministry of Colonies show the extent to which this phenomenon of absentee ownership characterized pre-Revolutionary Santo Domingo.[22]

Haiti being thought of as but an interlude in a man's life, the loosening of moral tone so complained of in contemporary works resulted, and with this went the many forms of display in which these colonists indulged and those other aspects of colonial custom which were so often ridiculed by European travelers of the period. The distance of Haiti from Paris, or, in a later period, the time which had elapsed since the French loss of Haiti, has, however, lent an enchantment to "Créole life" which is reflected in an idealized portrayal of this existence, much in the manner of the effusions on the graciousness and glamour of life in what is termed "the old South." [23] One cannot read the extended narrative of the young Comte de C * * *, reprinted by de Vassière, without questioning this myth of the idyllic life of the Haitian Créole, even though allowing for the disdain with which an exiled Parisian dandy of 1730 would regard the inhabitants of outlying possessions, and allowing also for the savory wit of the man, which undoubtedly led him to underscore the more diverting situations which he encountered.[24]

Mention must be made at this point of the two great divisions of the white population which, as the colonizing period continued, were

created by the distinction between those born on the island and those
who had migrated there. These divisions cut across the two categories
of urban and country dwellers, both of which numbered Haitian-born
and native European members. At the time of the French Revolution
about three quarters of the whites on the island had been born outside
the colony, while of those born in the colony, women comprised the
major portion.[25] Haitian-born persons were known by the designation
Créole, which, according to a definition of the period, included all
those "who have first seen the light of day in Santo Domingo" and
was, as it is today, a term employed in all the West Indies and in
Louisiana.[26] This designation was by no means restricted to the whites,
however, for there were Créole Negroes as well as Créole whites; at
the present time in Haiti a distinction is even drawn between locally
grown "créole" rice and that which is imported!

It is common knowledge that slavery not only affects those who are
held in bondage, but deeply influences the master-class as well. In
Haiti the role played by the institution of slavery in the formation of
the character and personalities of Créole children brought up in a
setting of servility, cupidity, brutality, and terror must have been of
the utmost importance. The bad temper and domineering nature of
Créole youths is commented on again and again by writers of the
period. Owing to the unhealthy climate and the failure to maintain
adequate hygienic conditions, the health of these children was usually
poor, so that from earliest infancy they were spoiled by their parents
and servants; their least wishes were gratified, and their least com-
plaints immediately rectified so as to make them petty tyrants in their
households. This tyranny was most often exercised over the family
slaves. Regardless of the assiduous care these young despots received,
and despite the adulation lavished upon their young charges, the
Negro servants were seldom sufficiently prompt or adequate in their
attentiveness to escape the punishments, often severe, that were
meted out to them at the behest of their young masters. This tyranny
extended to the play-life of the young Haitian-born white. Surrounded
only by the slave children of the plantation, he commanded his con-
temporaries even more imperiously than his parents commanded the
grown slaves.

Whatever he saw, he wanted, whatever was shown him he demanded; and
if some fatality brought it about that one of his small companions resisted
him and he became irritated, they would hurry from all sides in response to
his cries and those of the young unfortunate, who, his color having destined
him for submission, learned soon enough that he would be forced to give
way, perhaps even being meted some punishment to penalize the disobedi-
ence of one who had not yet the instinct for servitude.[27]

Grown to manhood, the young Créole continued to act as master of all he surveyed. Imperious, quick-tempered, spoiled, his life lived in large part among slaves, when his sex drive stirred, he took what slave women pleased him. Eventually he married, to be tormented with the thoughts of the possible infidelity of his wife; the more tortured because of his extreme vanity and because, while demanding faithfulness from his spouse, he was continuing his affairs with his Negro women. Yet he had some excellences of character, as well. "Frank, affable, generous perhaps to the point of ostentation, confident, brave, a sure friend and a good father" [28]—such are his good points as set down by one who was perhaps surer-eyed than others in seeing his deficiencies, though these traits seem to have concerned more his relations with his fellow-whites than those which affected his bearing toward his Negro slaves.

The young Créole women of this same environment were destined for early marriage—too early for their best development, whether physical or mental. Given to exacting the fulfillment of their slightest caprices, they were, like their men, creatures of passion. If they survived their first pregnancies, which as a result of too early marriages often came before they were physically in condition to support the rigors of childbirth, they soon lost their youthful allure and became the unattractive women of the type so maliciously described by the Comte de C * * *.[29] In such cases they frequently survived not one but several husbands. Their associations were chiefly with their Negro women slaves, who were full confidantes, sleeping in the same chamber with their mistresses and on occasion sharing informal meals with them, though they never ate at the same table. And because, by a fine turn of irony, these Negro women were often at the same time the concubines of the husbands, brothers, or sons of their mistresses, they were as often as not treated alternately with the greatest tenderness and the harshest brutality.[30]

Whatever the inner life of white Haitians, native-born or Créole, outward ostentation was the rule. In the cities poorly furnished houses were cared for by a numerous retinue of uniformed retainers; "the supreme achievement for a European being to have himself served, he hires slaves while he waits for the time when he can own them." [31] In the country, too, life was lived on as lavish a scale as possible. This is not the place to describe the houses of masters and slaves, or the buildings needed for working sugar-cane or indigo or preparing coffee, or their distribution over the plantation, for numerous contemporary accounts, and most present-day works, give both texts and illustrations which make the economy of the plantation clear.[32] Though many stories of the magnificence of plantation life are found in current works, writers of the period seem to agree that but little attention was paid to convenience. Inventories of the contents of houses show that furnishings were at a minimum; a few chairs and small tables in the sitting- and reception-rooms, beds and minor accessories in the way of furniture in the bedrooms, dining-room tables and chairs and a cabinet for dishes. These pieces were usually built in the colony and made of native hard woods; substantial, they were essentially plain. As Baron Wimpffen remarked, "Taste, Sir, is still Creolian at Saint Domingo; and, unfortunately, the Creolian is not the right taste,—it smells too much of the *Boucan*." [33]

The table set was not distinguished. Meat, though the most important dish at the principal meals, was poor, but, on the other hand, fish, game, and wild fowl were excellent, and the best of French wines were available.[34] Whatever the fare, however, it was served in the grand manner, often on plate rather than chinaware, and by the many liveried house-servants which every great establishment could boast. An account of the mode of service has been preserved in the reminiscences of one who, writing some years later of a repast served him in 1787, says: "There were many more of these domestics of both sexes than there were diners. I could but admire their attention to the smallest details of the service, the whiteness of their clothing, and the beautiful kerchiefs in the Créole manner elegantly arranged about the heads of the women. . . . But all of them moved about on bare feet; this was the distinctive sign of slavery." [35]

As portrayed in contemporary works, Haitian white life is seen to have been lived entirely in terms of material goods and of display. Just as there was little intellectual life, so religion was but a matter of form. One M. de Larnage, writing from Petit-Goave on 25 June 1743, complains that it is unbelievable "what indifference the people of these districts have toward spiritual matters." [36] So little attention was paid to the rites of the Church that when the baptism of an infant was to be performed, it often proved difficult to find a godfather who had taken the sacrament, and many children were therefore never baptized. As might be expected, the churches were in a bad state, often having no more than earthen walls and floors, roofed with thatch, and being used as threshing-floors as well as places of worship. The description which Père Labat has given us of a church at Cap Français,[37] and of the manner in which the communicants conducted themselves during such services as were held, shows the decadence of the one religion that had any place among the white inhabitants. The clergy, too, reflected this same decadence. For though the early libertines who posed as priests were later replaced by members of such orders as the Jacobins, the Jesuits, and the Capucins, even this did not end the scandals that, from the first days of the establishment of the Catholic Church on the island, marked its ministrations.

What impression must the Negroes have obtained from their opportunities to observe the life of their masters? What patterns of behavior, what moral codes, what concepts of the way in which the Europeans regulated their own lives and, as officials, regulated the lives of others, must have been stamped on the minds of these Africans? That the present emphasis on the importance of wealth, or that a love of and demand for display, should characterize Haitian life of the cities today is not strange. Nor is it difficult to comprehend how certain other aspects of Haitian life that have so been underscored in the last half-century by those who have written of the Haitians should have developed from this initial stimulus—not to the extent to which this emphasis would lead one to believe, to be sure, but enough to give a basis for the exaggerations which have been published.[38]

Some of these charges may be reviewed. One, frequently met with and already mentioned, concerns the general lack of cleanliness and sanitation that marks the cities. As has been shown, this stems directly from the patterns of life which prevailed under French control. The matter of personal morals is also often discussed with anything but praise for Haitian custom. Quite aside from the polygamous tradition of Africa, the influence of which will be discussed later, it is only necessary to recall the example set for these slaves by the sex customs of the Créoles and other Europeans with whom they came into contact to see how the ideal of monogamic union would not be entirely convincing as one to be followed in all its implications. The failure of the Catholic Church to stamp out the African cults in Haiti, and the skepticism with which, as will be pointed out, the motivation of the priests is regarded by the Haitians must have been strengthened by the tradition of the misbehavior of those who were in charge of the religion into which baptism was mandatory, before the days of freedom.

The instability of Haitian political life, and the venality of judges and other officials have been stressed again and again in the writings of those who have passed judgment on Haiti. Yet one need but read of the readiness of the white colonists to revolt against the authority set over them by the mother country,[39] and of the manner in which during the French Revolution attempts to alleviate the position of the colored and Negro portions of the population were thwarted by the illegal political activities of the plantation slave-owners,[40] to understand at least some of the sources from which direct political action derives its sanctions. One need similarly but read comments in letters and books of the time concerning the corruption of the officials of the colony[41] to conclude that, since her independence, Haiti has in such respects but continued a tradition set by the rulers who governed the country before the Republic was established. Thus if the life of the Haitian Negro peasant of today presents aspects of harshness or instability, it would seem proper to ask how much of this might be ascribed to the examples which these Negroes were set by their masters, rather than unequivocally to assume inherent racial tendencies to account for them, as is so often done.

This, of course, is far from the whole story. For just as there were large numbers of colonists who were men of integrity and lived in accordance with the best traditions of their French heritage, so among the Negroes were many who sensed these deficiencies in the regime to which they had been enslaved, and held tenaciously to their African traditions, not only in religion, but in social, economic, and political phases, so that, when the time was ripe, these might in some measure be re-established. To approach the matter realistically, it must be recognized that just as the Africans in the islands represented numerous tribes having varying customs, and individual members of these groups possessed varying degrees of integrity and worth, so the French who came to live there and whose slaves learned of French culture from them represented not necessarily the flower of that culture, but were in the main derived from the extremes of French society, the unadjusted and maladjusted lower classes and the aristocrats. What was bequeathed by them to the Haitians, therefore, were those aspects of French civilization which, to the extent that they were accepted by the Negroes, are partially responsible not only for the graciousness, the hospitality, and the generosity of the Haitian of today, but also for the less pleasant aspects of the culture that have resulted from his historical development since independence.

1. De Vassière, 153–4.
2. Ibid., 20, note 2.
3. St. Mery, i, 5.
4. Charlevoix, ii, 9.
5. De Vassière, 45.
6. Ibid., 52; St. Mery, i, 24–5.
7. De Vassière, 52–3.
8. Ibid., 55.
9. Scelle, i, 218–20.
10. De Vassière, 21; Wimpffen, 82–83.
11. Labat, i, Book II, 73–4.
12. St. Mery, ii, 25 ff.
13. Ibid., ii, 27–8, 47–50.
14. Ibid., i, 80–1.

15. De Vassière, 104–5.
16. Quoted by de Vassière, 105.
17. Compare, for example, de Vassière, 330 ff., with St. John, 4–7.
18. St. Mery, i, 348 ff.
19. De Vassière, 333.
20. Ibid., 333–4.
21. Ibid., 280–1.
22. Letter of Mm. de Lamotte and Lalanne from Port-au-Prince, 25 October 1752; quoted by de Vassière, 300–1.
23. Stoddard, 34–6.
24. De Vassière, 255–75.
25. St. Mery, i, 9.
26. Ibid., i, 12.
27. Ibid., i, 12–13.
28. Ibid., i, 16.
29. Ibid., i, 21; de Vassière, 267 ff.
30. St. Mery, i, 22; de Vassière, 314–15.
31. St. Mery, i, 11.
32. Labat, i, Book II, plate opp. p. 245; de Vassière, opp. 289.
33. Wimpffen, 103.
34. Ibid., 103–5; de Vassière, 295–6.
35. De Vassière, 297, quoting Laujon, i, 135.
36. Quoted by de Vassière, 80.
37. Labat: *Nouveau Voyage*, vii, 125, 130, quoted by de Vassière, 81–2.
38. Bellegarde, 53 ff., comments interestingly on this fact.
39. De Vassière, 56 ff.
40. Dorsainvil (II), 83 ff.; Stoddard, *passim*.
41. Summarized in de Vassière, 89 ff.

REFERENCES

Bellegarde, Dantès. *Pages d'histoire*. I. L'esclavage et le trafic des Noirs dans l'île d'Haiti: II. La Société Française de Saint-Domingue en 1789. Port-au-Prince, 1925.
Charlevoix, P. F. X. de. *Histoire de l'Isle Espagnole ou de S. Domingue* (2 volumes). Paris, 1730 and 1731.
Dorsainvil, J. C. (II). *Manuel d'histoire d'Haiti*. Port-au-Prince, 1934.
Labat, Père J. B. *Nouveau voyage aux isles d'Amérique* (2 volumes). The Hague, 1724.
St. John, Sir Spenser. *Hayti or the Black Republic*. 2nd edition, London, 1889.
St. Mery, M. L. E. Moreau de. *Description topographique, physique, civile, et historique de la partie française de l'Isle Saint-Domingue*. 2 volumes. Philadelphia, 1797 and 1798.
Schelle, Georges. *La Traite nègrière aux Indes de Castille, contrats et traités d'assiento*. 2 volumes. Paris, 1906.
Stoddard, T. Lothrop. *The French Revolution in San Domingo*. Boston and New York, 1914.
Vassière, Pierre de. *Saint-Domingue (1629–1789), la société et la vie créoles sous l'ancien régime*. Paris, 1909.
Wimpffen, Baron F. A. S. de. *A Voyage to Saint Domingo, in the years 1788, 1789, and 1790*, translated by J. Wright. London, 1797.

The Ancestry of the American Negro

I have long been convinced that in studying the origins of the Negroes of the United States constant reference must be made to other Negro populations of the New World. For the United States was only one portion of the great slave-receiving area which also included the islands of the Caribbean and certain portions of northern and eastern South America, notably Brazil and the Guianas. The slaves were, indeed, often sent to continental United States only after a preliminary conditioning period elsewhere.

*   *   *

To understand interracial problems in the United States we must know as much as we can concerning the background of our minority groups. The most important aspects of this background material are summarized in the answers to three questions: What were the origins of a given folk? What elements in the population from which they came do they represent? What of their traditions have they retained?

So far as European or Oriental immigrants are concerned, or others who have come from historic cultures, the answers to these questions, though not completely worked out, are at least fairly well known in their broad outlines. Only in the case of the Negro, the most numerous of the minority groups, is this kind of knowledge not generally available. And here it is not only curious but potentially dangerous, especially where programs of action are concerned, that it is held either to be impossible or unnecessary were it possible to recover such facts.

The reasons for this attitude are two-fold. In the first place the idea that the Negro slaves came to the New World as savages, with nothing to give their masters, has been so deeply implanted in the minds of Americans, White and Negro alike, that it seems futile to give the time and energy needed for the difficult task of historical dissection which alone can establish the facts. In the second place it is not deemed worth while in the case of the Negro to assume this task, because there is a persistent tradition that even had the Negro brought with him a civilization worthy of the name, the cultures of Africa are

American Scholar, VIII, no. 1 (1938–39), 84–94.

so diverse and the policy of the slaveholders was so directed toward the extinction of aboriginal tradition that nothing African of any social significance remains in the present-day behavior of American Negroes. The question of their origin is thus dismissed as something that at best can be considered an academic one.

Setting aside for the moment the question of the validity of these assumptions we may ask what is actually known of the African derivation of the Negroes of this country. Before presenting the facts, however, I must emphasize an essential point almost invariably disregarded when the answer to this problem of African origins is sought as it concerns some aspect or other of American Negro life. I have long been convinced that in studying the origins of the Negroes of the United States constant reference must be made to other Negro populations of the New World. For the United States was only one portion of the great slave-receiving area which also included the islands of the Caribbean and certain portions of northern and eastern South America, notably Brazil and the Guianas. The slaves were, indeed, often sent to continental United States only after a preliminary conditioning period elsewhere. Hence it follows that whatever can be established for the rest of the New World is applicable to the United States and cannot be disregarded.

I have found it impossible, further, to study the problems of Negro origins unless both documentary and ethnological evidence is used. Contemporary historical facts of the first importance, which give direct information about the tribal affiliations of the slaves, can be found in considerable bulk once one is alive to their value and looks for them. The significance of evidence even of such direct character can only be fully realized, however, when it is correlated with a knowledge of the present-day life of New World Negroes and with what is today known of the tribes of Africa itself and of their cultures. One knows where to look because in the interior of Guiana, Haiti and Brazil (and to a lesser degree in Jamaica, Trinidad and other Caribbean islands) there are Negroes whose African personal names, place-names, names of deities, ritual practices, social organization and local economy all point toward specific areas and definite tribes of West Africa. When, in addition, such works as the report of C. G. A. Oldendorps, Inspector-General of the Moravian Missions in the Virgin Islands in 1770–1775, or the volumes of John Gabriel Stedman on Dutch Guiana, published in 1796, or the great collection of documents appertaining to the slave-trade assembled in recent years by Professor Elizabeth Donnan name the same areas and the same tribes again and again as the sources of slaves, it is apparent that the lines of attack are converging on very definite points. Finally, with the discovery that today in those very areas of Africa substantial correspondences to present-day New World

Negro behavior exist, the problem in its broad outlines is well on the way to solution.

Applying both historical and ethnological techniques, then, it becomes apparent that the significant locale of slaving operations to the New World was the western coastal belt of Africa from the Senegal River in the north, around the Great Bend to the Guinea Coast, along the Bight of Benin and southwards beyond the Congo to the Portuguese territory of Angola. Relatively few slaves came from any great distance inland and most of them were brought from the narrow forested region that follows the coast at a depth varying from two to three hundred miles. The interior of the Congo, which has appealed to those inclined to take Negro origins as a literary theme, was apparently not an area of intensive slaving. The economics of slaving would be sufficient to explain why slaves were not sent from Madagascar and eastern Africa, even if Miss Donnan's list of the slaves imported into Virginia between 1710 and 1769 did not show that of a total of 52,-504 only 1,011 were from Madagascar, and that of 67,769 imported into South Carolina between 1752 and 1808, only 473 were brought from East Africa and Madagascar.

The areas that apparently furnished the greatest number of slaves were the basin of the Senegal River, the "Guinea Coast" (including especially the southern portions of what are today known as the Gold Coast and Dahomey) and the Niger delta, or the "Bight of Benin." Later, toward the end of the slaving period, numerous cargoes were shipped from the region about the mouth of the Congo. In the central portion of the area—the Guinea Coast and the Bight of Benin—the tribes of the Gold Coast, of Dahomey and of the southern portion of the present British Colony of Nigeria are most often encountered in the literature about slave trading. Two examples of sales of slaves advertised in the *Cornwall and Jamaica General Advertiser* as cited by MacInnes in his book *England and Slavery* indicate how tribal names from these regions appear in the documents:

Martha Brae, January 27th, 1783
For Sale
On Wednesday the 4th
of February
On Board the Ship
THARP
Captain Fisher
(From Annamaboe)
440 Choice, Young Fantee, Ashantee, and Akim
Negroes
By Thorpe and Campbell

A second announcement reads:

Montega Bay, January 2nd, 1789
For Sale
On Tuesday next, the 6th instant,
On Board the Ship
VULTURE
James Brown, Master,
Five hundred and ninety-eight choice
young Eboe
Slaves
by James Wedderburn Co.

Anamabo is a coastal village of the Gold Coast, an area inhabited by the populous Fanti, Ashanti and Akim tribes; and Bonny, in the Niger Delta, was an outlet for this vast hinterland where one of the most important native groups is the Ibo. Other tribal designations that frequently appeared were those of the Nago—another name for the Yoruba peoples of southwestern Nigeria, who figured importantly in the slave contingents which came to Cuba, and whose name and the names of whose deities still persist there and in Brazil. The Ardras, the Mahis, the Popos, the Fidas and the other tribes mentioned as having been brought in great numbers to Haiti are from Dahomey. In American documents—as would be expected—we find the same tribal designations and place-names, Whydah, Fantee, Eboe and many others, representing the peoples from which the North American Negroes, like those taken to the West Indies and South America, were derived.

Knowing the region from which the slaves came we are in a position to learn something of the cultures which these people brought with them. In discussing this point I shall confine myself to the heart of the slaving area—those southern parts of the present colonies of the Gold Coast, Dahomey and Nigeria where, as has been pointed out, existed the civilizations which were dominant and therefore most significant in the formation of the patterns of New World Negro behavior.

In this general area we find native cultures so complex that they can be called "primitive" only in the technical sense of the word— that is, of a folk who have never developed a written language. Here the kingdoms of the Ashanti, of the Fanti and Akim peoples, of Dahomey, of the Oyo, Egba and other Yoruba folk and of Benin flourished, bringing to their inhabitants an ordered life regulated by stable dynasties. The continuous growth of these West African political entities through the steady conquest of neighboring states developed a marked military ability which persisted as a factor of importance in the slave areas of America. In this region, too, we find highly developed arts and crafts. The wood-carving of much of this part of Africa is today well known by all who are abreast of modern currents in art; the bronzes of Benin, the brass figures of Dahomey and the metal gold-weights of the Ashanti also enjoy a deserved reputation. Weaving of high quality is found everywhere in this area, but most notably on the Gold Coast, as well as the manufacture of pottery and of iron implements.

Obviously to support the degree of specialization necessary for cultures of this kind large populations living under efficient economic systems are needed. From the days of the earliest travellers the density of these populations has been such that most of the available land has had to be farmed to produce the requisite crops. The importance of having competent systems of exchange is also evident. A currency consisting of cowry-shells has long been in use, and has only recently begun to give way before European money. On the basis of this currency an adequate system of distribution has existed since the earliest days of European contact, and commodities circulated in numerous markets, both wholesale and retail.

Religion, like other aspects of these cultures, shows a high degree of complexity. With an economic base capable of supporting specialists in the supernatural, it is understandable how the priesthoods developed complex philosophies of the universe in terms of interrelated groups of deities, each with their specialized functions, integrated into a comprehensible and well-working whole. Together with this involved religious system goes a belief in magic, here incorporated as an integral part into the total range of beliefs and practices, while, as elsewhere in Africa, there are in addition divining cults administered by still other specialists.

Given thus the areas from which the slaves were derived and the civilizations represented in them what can be learned concerning the respective contributions to the body of slaves of the social classes which existed, and still exist within these populations? Though answers to this question can be given only in tentative form they can nevertheless be given, for a beginning has been made in analyzing the available information from this point of view.

It must, first of all, be recognized that slavery was nothing new to the slaves brought to the Americas. The institution was deep-rooted throughout all West Africa, where it took not only the mild form of household slavery but the much harsher form of plantation slavery. There, too, as in the New World, absentee ownership made for an increase in the brutality of supervision. By no means all the available human material was exported, as is apparent from such testimony as that of Captain William Snelgrave who recounts how in 1725 he was forced to wait a considerable time to complete his cargo because the King of Dahomey was unwilling to deplete the stock of slaves on hand in order to satisfy his demand. The slaves were principally obtained in raids—locally called wars—made by the more powerful kingdoms against their weaker neighbors. And here a point of significance enters: there was no distinction between combatants and non-combatants. All who fell into the hands of the hostile army lost their liberty. It must therefore be concluded that the slaves represented an adequate cross-section of the entire West African population, with neither the deficient—"who wouldn't have let themselves be enslaved if they had been any good" as it has been expressed—nor the upper-class warriors unduly weighting the scale.

Yet it is just possible that a slight weighting resulted from the internal politics of the West African kingdoms and the circumstances of their growth. Here I must be even more tentative, for I can only cite material which I myself gathered in Dahomey since no other data are to my knowledge available. In Dahomey two factors made for the enslavement of a somewhat larger number of upper-class persons—nobles, priests and diviners—than commoners. Occasionally the accession of a new king was disputed by a brother. Enslavement of the loser, his supporters and the families of those concerned was at once a simple and profitable means of resolving the situation. That nobles from other kingdoms were also sold—though whether or not for similar reasons cannot be said—is apparent from this quotation from Moreau de St. Mery:

> The Mina Negroes have even been seen to recognize the princes of their country . . . prostrating themselves at their feet and rendering them that homage whose contrast to the state of servitude to which these princes have been reduced . . . offers a striking enough instance of the instability of human greatness.

When small political units were conquered by larger ones, a larger proportion of priests was deported than their numbers in the general population might justify. Again, according to Dahomean tradition as handed down from generation to generation of official court "remembrancers," the conquest of such minor groups usually found the priests of the local cults the most intransigent members of the community. Since these priests most often refused to submit to the superior force of the conquering power they were as a rule sold. In Dahomey the sale of priests was so common that the knowledge of how to worship the river-spirits, to which these priests as heads of the local river cults usually ministered, has been quite lost. This may be the reason why baptism in a living body of water is as important among American

Negroes as it is, since this widespread custom could hardly be accidental. For may it not have been the influence of these priests, as slaves, that transmuted aboriginal river-worship into its only possible form under Christianity—baptism?

The presence, among the New-World slaves, of these members of the ruling class and of the priests is of some moment for an understanding of the development of the patterns of New-World Negro life. It is admitted by students of Negro culture that it is in religion above all that Africanisms are most often to be found. African magical practices are readily identifiable even in the United States; and though such behavior as the violent spirit-possessions which characterize worship in certain Negro churches is not so readily recognizable as of African origin it is nonetheless a manifestation of the carry-over of aboriginal customs. Elsewhere in the New World, where the accommodation to European custom has not been as far-reaching as in the United States, Africanisms in religious beliefs and practices have persisted almost unchanged. They may be seen in the religion of the Bush Negroes of Dutch Guiana, in the "fetish" cults of Brazil and Cuba and in the "voodoo" rites of the Haitians—to cite the outstanding instances. The persistence of Africanisms in song and dance in connection with worship is to be generally observed, even in the United States. This has a direct bearing on the origin of those Negro contributions to our American civilization, a problem which has aroused great general interest.

The practice of enslaving leaders as well as rank-and-file members of African communities had far-reaching consequences. The concept of the Negro as a "born slave" lodges deep in American tradition, yet nothing could be more false. From the moment of their enslavement the Negroes did not stop resisting; in the slave barracoons of the West Coast, on shipboard and on the plantations there was a persistent danger of revolt that made life a nightmare to those in charge of these Negroes. Captains of slave-ships often lost their vessels because of slave uprisings and those who were wise—and these were numerous —took out "revolt insurance." The first Negro slaves to be brought to the New World were shipped in 1510; the first slave revolt occurred just twelve years later, while eleven other revolts of Negro slaves have been recorded for Spanish America between 1522 and 1553. Recent historical research has shown that the revolts, small and large, in the United States are to be numbered by the dozens. In Brazil, in Dutch Guiana, in Jamaica, in Haiti, slaves were constantly escaping to the freedom of the bush and were there organized by men who had been leaders in the areas from which the slaves had originally come. With supernatural sanctions assured by their African priests, those who had escaped raided the plantations and rescued still more slaves, so that the little communities of "maroons" became constantly larger and more powerful. In Brazil the most important of these groups was finally subdued, but in the other three regions the operations of these bands of revolters met with a success whose implications have almost never been recognized. Today Haiti is free, the Bush Negroes of Dutch Guiana acknowledge but the nominal suzerainty of the Netherlands Government and the Maroons of Jamaica live as a self-contained community, paying no taxes and holding their own courts.

We may now return to the significance of knowing the tribal origins of the Negroes of America, their cultural endowment and the strata of the population from which they were derived. Can we justify anything more than an academic interest in findings of this sort? I am convinced that such knowledge, quite aside from its importance in furthering our understanding of cultural processes in general, is also essential both as an aid in pointing studies of the race problem and in molding practical policies.

For granting that current social and economic forces are predominant in shaping race relations, it must never be forgotten that psychological imponderables are also of first importance in sanctioning action on any level. And it is such imponderables as have been referred to in the opening paragraphs of this paper that, for all their fallaciousness, are now being strengthened by the findings of studies that ignore the only valid point of departure in social investigation—the historical background of the phenomenon being studied and those factors which make for its existence and perpetuation. When, for instance, one sees vast programs of Negro education undertaken without the slightest consideration given even to the possibility of some retention of African habits of thought and speech that might influence the Negroes' reception of the instruction thus offered, one cannot but ask how we hope to reach the desired objectives. When we are confronted with psychological studies of race relations made in utter ignorance of characteristic African patterns of motivation and behavior, or with sociological analyses of Negro family life which make not the slightest attempt to take into account even the chance that the phenomenon being studied might in some way have been influenced by the carry-over of certain African traditions; when we contemplate accounts of the history of slavery which make of plantation life a kind of paradise by ignoring or distorting the essential fact that the institution persisted only through constant precautions taken against slave uprisings, we can but wonder about the value of such work.

It is, therefore, of no small importance that the historical past of the Negro be ascertained as fully as possible. The further we can carry this investigation and the more we can learn of this African background the better the understanding we shall have of those aspects of the ancestral culture that, in the case of the Negro as of all our other minority folk, has not been entirely lost but continues in some measure to function significantly. If this be the case, then in making the studies on which much of future opinion will rest, or in developing programs of action to meet the practical problems of the present day, we shall be building on a foundation of fact far firmer than we have hitherto been able to build on and shall thus, in direct proportion, be likely to achieve more satisfactory results in understanding and solving the race problem than have thus far been vouchsafed us.

The Ahistorical Approach to Afroamerican Studies

A CRITIQUE

> In the Afroamerican field, debate over the utility of the historical dimension in the analysis of anthropological findings seems particularly futile, since here the need for the hypothetical reconstruction of contact has been reduced to a minimum. . . . I must make it clear that I am not drawing a critique of ahistoricism in the Afroamerican—or, for that matter, in any other—field, by recourse to an all-or-none fallacy. There are problems that call for the use of a structuralist approach. But when . . . the question of the significance, or even presence of African retentions becomes a matter of establishing . . . a given trait in pure form . . . ahistoricism can at best only yield limited insight and low-level generalization.

❋   ❋   ❋

As the history of anthropology goes, the need to take the factor of time into account has only recently been questioned, nor do more than a minority of anthropologists today reject the historical portion of their scientific heritage. In part, this questioning was a reaction to the ex-

A paper presented at the 58th Annual Meeting of the American Anthropological Association, Mexico, D.F., Dec. 30, 1959. *American Anthropologist*, LXII, no. 4 (1960), 559–68.

cesses of those whose desire to reconstruct the past took them beyond the bounds of acceptable method. This was evidenced in a refusal to continue the ordering of research in accordance with naive propositions of social or cultural evolutionism, or with equally naive assumptions of the extreme diffusionists of the Graebnerian or Elliot-Smith or later varieties. It can only be regarded as unfortunate that the swing of the pendulum carried some anthropologists to the other extreme, so that for the naivetes of pseudo-history were substituted the naivetes of antihistory.

The reaction to methodological excess, however, was not the only reason for the swing. Another reason was a response to a broader current in our intellectual history. Rejection of the factor of time in the search for scientific generalizations regarding human social life came into anthropology as a part of what might be termed the scientism of recent decades. The dramatic contributions of the exact and natural sciences, and the gains that had been derived from the use of methods instrumental in achieving these results, seemed to indicate the most effective kind of model for other disciplines. The acceptance of this model by social scientists was accompanied by an uncritical use of quantitative methods, plus a tendency to argue social theory by reference to analogies derived from the usages and findings of the exact and natural sciences.

Social scientists were particularly impressed by the ability of those disciplines to reach generalizations concerning the phenomena they studied, and to discern and utilize regularities in these phenomena to propound scientific "laws" which were applicable without regard to place or time. This, then, became for many social scientists the end which all disciplines seeking scientific status must strive to attain. The syllogism ran something like this: Science discovers "laws" applicable without regard to time or place; social science is science; hence social science must discover "laws" which, like their counterparts in the exact and natural sciences, must be applicable regardless of time or place.

The reality of this syllogism is documented by many developments during the past few decades. It is exemplified in the limited importance assigned the time factor in experimental psychology, in the use of mathematical models for the analysis of economic phenomena, in structural linguistics, in the search for "high-level" sociological and political theories. In the case of anthropology, the corresponding development is to be seen in the stress that came to be laid on the synchronic study of social structures and social institutions.

II

In the Afroamerican field, debate over the utility of the historical dimension in the analysis of anthropological findings seems particularly futile, since here the need for an hypothetical reconstruction of contact has been reduced to a minimum. The historical components in the New World situation of Indian-African-European acculturation are known, or can be discovered, with a degree of accuracy rarely met with in anthropological research. We need only consult the definitive work of Aguirre Beltrán (1946) to see how specifically African tribal origins of New World Negroes can be delineated. Where the Indians significantly influenced a resultant cultural synthesis there are requisite ethnographic and linguistic data for controlled analysis, as in the case of the Black Caribs of Honduras (Taylor 1951; Coelho 1955; Solien 1959).

The Europeans speak for themselves (cf. Curtin 1955).

Two subtly related factors which enter into Afroamerican research offer an instructive opportunity to study swings from an historical to an ahistorical point of view. The first is the recency of the field. Systematic scientific research among New World Negro peoples is barely three decades old, so that the process is highlighted by being compressed into so short a period. The second factor is that this field has been peculiarly sensitive to ascriptions of relative values to the several cultures that have entered into shaping the ways of life of the peoples under study, with resulting strong affect overtones that have dictated research procedures and influenced conclusions drawn from the findings. In consequence, despite much written historical documentation, Africa has been persistently denied any significant role in shaping present New World Negro cultures. With the development of ahistoricism in anthropology, this has been given a new rationale, phrased in terms of scientific method.

Afroamerican research thus has a dual utility for students of cultural dynamics. Not only does this field, by its very nature, provide a laboratory for the scientifically controlled study of cultural dynamics, but quite unwittingly it also gives us an equally useful laboratory for the study of change and resistance to change in the theory and practice of anthropology itself. I have had occasion in an earlier paper (Herskovits 1956) to show how anthropologists, taking for granted the continental and hemispherical boundaries that conventionally limit their areas of specialization, and uncritically identifying an outworn definition of the comparative method with all methods of comparison, have in their own work exemplified the very principles they have been concerned to study. Let us see how another concept, equally classical in anthropology, that of the *survival*, may be called on to help us understand certain recent anthropological developments in the field of Afroamerican studies.

Some background is essential here. Thirty years ago, when I became attracted by the potentialities of comparative ethnographic and historical studies of African and New World Negro peoples, the field— if it can be said to have existed at all—was quite unstructured. To the degree its existence was recognized as a valid area of research, it was negatively structured, in the sense that such rudimentary structuring as it possessed inhibited rather than encouraged investigation. This negative structuring blocked research because such hypotheses as had been developed concerning the nature and functioning of New World Negro societies were based on assumptions that denied any significant role to one of the historically involved components, the African. Here the factor of affect entered strongly. The unanimity with which this negative principle was accepted, that is, was deeply rooted in the biases of the time. These biases, however, when made explicit, turned out to be no more than a series of myths, albeit myths which made up a system that functioned significantly to validate a substantial segment of thought concerned with the nature of racial and cultural differences (cf. Herskovits 1941, 1958, *passim*).

It is not necessary here to repeat the proofs that destroyed the arguments of those who, scholars of repute, not only accepted myth as fact, but also gave these myths the support of seemingly tenable documentation through analyses that were couched in the terminology of science. As with any system of this kind, the arguments collapsed when put to the test of the facts. The work of these scholars remains an intellectual curiosity, data for the historian concerned with the thought of their day.

What is interesting to the anthropologist who turns the searchlight of anthropological theory on his own discipline is the survival of this position in the ahistoricism of our day. Despite the mass of specific documentary and comparative ethnographic data accumulated during the past two decades (cf. Herskovits 1958, "Supplementary Bibliography," pp. 344–349) and the development of a far more precise theoretical framework to order these data, denial of any significant African contribution to New World Negro cultures continues. As might be anticipated, the denial lies on a more sophisticated theoretical level, since scientism, as manifest in the search for "laws" without regard to historical relationships, also enters. The problem of analysis in these terms is thus one of evaluation and selection rather than overall repudiation, as was the case with the earlier hypotheses.

Let us consider one or two examples that illuminate the way in which the influence of a factor, already acknowledged and historically proved, in shaping a situation under study, can be minimized. For this we may initially turn to a symposium on Caribbean studies (Rubin 1957) where the concept of "Plantation-America" was detailed (Wagley 1957). In principle, there is no reason why the plantation system of the New World should not be studied. On the contrary, there is every reason it should be; I know of no exponent of the broad historical approach to Afroamerican studies who has rejected the problem as a problem. What is of interest to us, in the present context, is the bias apparent in the denomination of the concept, affording as it does semantic evidence of a survival that, again becoming operative, has produced serious lacunae in research.

The inconsistencies in the classification of New World cultures, of which "Plantation-America" was one class, are apparent in this initial statement: "The purpose of this paper is to delimit three cultural spheres of the New World which can serve as a frame of reference for our own studies of the contemporary societies and cultures of the Americas. These three American culture-spheres, here to be called Euro-America, Indo-America and Plantation-America, are set off one from the other by a series of interdependent and interrelated differences deriving mainly from the New World context itself" (Wagley 1957:3). Now it is quite true that in naming "the factors which seemed to have brought about the formation of these cultural spheres," the statement includes "the process of historical events as they unfolded in the New World"; yet Africa is nowhere mentioned. On the contrary; the omission becomes the more pointed when, after specifying that the classification embraces entities marked by political and geographical differences, we are told, "the concept of a New World cultural sphere used in this paper is not based upon (but also does not deny) the importance of cultural influences stemming from European countries responsible for colonizing or administering different areas."

The word "Africa," as a matter of fact, first appears on the third page of this discussion, and then only as the source of the labor needed by the Europeans. In the first five "similarities in the basic features of the Plantation-America culture sphere" that are given, the word appears once. This is when the nature of the family structure that characterizes it is considered, and here it is merely stated that "the case for African origins . . . has been . . . argued" (p. 9). No argument, however, seems to be regarded as necessary to establish European influence. Other "traits or cultural complexes" are recognized as having come under African influence, such as certain dishes or religious cult-practices or folklore (p. 10), but from the context these are obviously regarded as antiquarian and incidental.

What is significant in this refusal to consider an African component in the formation of these cultures is the demonstration it gives of how a mode of thinking that derives from a survival in our scientific methodology can becloud the processes of logical thought. Consider these three categories: In the broad sense, two are historical and cultural—*Euro*-America, *Indo*-America. The third class, however, violates a fundamental principle in that it shifts the basis of classification. Were the first two categories called "urban" or "industrial," for example, the classes would lie on the same phenomenological plane as the concept "plantation." Frazier puts the point well: "Since the other cultural spheres are described in ethnic terms, . . . the reader may ask why 'Plantation-America' was not designated 'Negro-America'" (1957:4).

Let us recall that we are here concerned with the logic of this division primarily as it reveals the operation of cultural processes in influencing anthropological thought on the problems of Afroamerican studies. In these terms, what we have is a clear example of how a survival, in this case of an earlier conception which held Africa to be a negligible factor in shaping the cultures of the New World Negro descendants of Africans, has functioned so as to force a scientifically inadmissible classification of the data. Nor is it only because the procedure contravenes a first principle of scientific logic that the classification is inadmissible; even more important is the fact that it goes contrary to the methodological axiom of science which holds that in studying any problem, no possible contributory factor can a priori be neglected.

A further instance of how the force of an earlier, outmoded tradition can shape analysis can be taken from another contribution to this same symposium (M. G. Smith 1957:34–46). This paper is particularly interesting for our present purpose, since it followed by about two years a more extended discussion by the same author that was also very largely concerned with the study of African elements in New World Negro cultures (*ibid.*:1954?). The earlier paper critically reviewed various approaches, considering them in the light of possible research techniques and types of conceptual apparatus that could be called on to extend the scientific potentialities of the field. Included in this first paper were suggestions for new directions in research that, with increasing personnel, the continuous growth in the amount of available data, and the concomitant revision of theoretical propositions underlying research carried the conviction of any soundly based proposal.

In the symposium paper, however, the position taken by the author has undergone a subtle metamorphosis. There is still no denial of the functioning of the African component. It is rather a kind of oblique response to the demands of an earlier pattern of thought, phrased in affirmative terms by setting methodological requirements that would render it futile to record as African any but the most obvious, unchanged New World retentions. Space does not permit the reproduction here of all the criteria set down as essential for the "fruitful study of African cultural persistence," but a sampling of them will indicate their character and intent.

The initial prescript is that "where specific tribal prototypes cannot be established, the items of African attribution must be demonstrable features of all the principal African cultures contributing to the area in which they are reported." This obvious loading reaches its most extreme form in the fifth requirement: "Traits regarded as evidence of the persistence of African cultural forms must be formally peculiar and distinct from the customs or institutions of all other cultural groups within the society of their location." Finally, we are instructed that "even where formal identities and historical continuities can be demonstrated, traits which reflect necessary functional adjustments to New World conditions must be distinguished from others for which functional values have not been established" (p. 45).

The comments made on this paper when it was presented (Simpson and Hammond 1957) render it unnecessary to analyze here this list of requirements. They make it clear that, if such requirements were to guide investigation, they would effectively inhibit research in the field and discourage the formulation of further theoretical postulates such as might arise from historical comparisons made between African and New World data. For us, it is the assumptions that creep out from under these prescriptions that are important; assumptions that are implicit in this attempt to place a quite unreasonable burden of proof on those who would study the functioning of an African component in New World Negro cultures. Because once again, however deeply it may lie beneath the surface of the argument, we discern a carry-over of the familiar position. This, when considered as a datum of the processes of anthropological change, can thus only be seen as another instance, in almost the classical sense, of what the earlier practitioners of our discipline called a survival.

IV

Let us now examine how the pattern of scientism has manifested itself in research on the New World Negro. In this we will be concerned with some of the recent applications of the theory and methods of social anthropology, whose ahistorical position stands in contrast to those attempts to understand present Afroamerican cultures which take the historic dimension into account.

Here the relations between the point of view that takes culture as its organizing concept, and the one which orders its propositions by reference to the concept of society, are critical. Because debate is more dramatic than agreement, argument concerning points of difference between these two positions has overshadowed the more sober fact that the areas of concordance between them are considerable, and that these are to be kept in mind when discussing methods or theories where there is divergence. Thus both cultural and social anthropologists recognize that a comparative approach is essential for arriving at valid generalizations in the study of man. Both insist on the need for first-hand observation in the field in gathering primary research data. Both reject the apriorisms of earlier schools and have reacted strongly to research and theories not based on data obtained by the use of rigorously controlled methods.

The differences between the two approaches can be categorized under three principal headings. Cultural anthropology, it can be said, is *holistic*, in that it is concerned with all aspects of human belief and behavior; *historical*, in its stress on the factor of time as relevant to an understanding of human experience; and *humanistic*, in that its point of reference includes the individual, who shapes his institutions even as he is being shaped by them. Social anthropology, in contrast, is *specialized*, in that it concentrates on the sociological aspects of group life; *synchronic*, since its aim is the analysis of relationships within a given group on a single time plane; and *structural*, in that it is primarily concerned with institutional arrangements, and tends to disregard or blur factors that lead to alternate modes of behavior, and give to any social system a degree of variation that its table of organization fails to indicate.

The most extended application of this latter position to the field of New World Negro research is in a study of the family in British Guiana (R. T. Smith 1956). The position taken concerning the factor of time is clearly put in the opening pages: "As social anthropologists, we are interested in the study of social structures as they exist over a limited timespan, usually broad enough to enable us to discern regu-

larities in cyclical processes as well as to allow us to observe and
record regular customary modes of social action" (p. 8). Later in the
same section, the dissociation of anthropology from history is underscored: "The whole picture of the establishment of the free Negro
villages is an exceedingly complex one and its detailed documentation
in the wider context of the social, economic and political movements
of the time remains as a task for the historian" (p. 13).

The history of the founding and subsequent development of the
three villages is quite effectively sketched. This allows the author
to state that, "We have no reason to believe that the 'culture' of the
Negro villages has changed substantially over the last hundred years
or so despite the continued 'culture contact' situation, and it will be a
part of our thesis that the peculiar 'culture' of the Negro villages is
correlated with their structural position in the Guianese social system"
(p. 22). Except for the fact that the word "culture" is placed in quotation marks, no historically oriented Afroamericanist would disagree
with the thesis. Granting the unities in any way of life that is a going
concern, particularly one that has been stable over a century or more,
there must be a correlation between the social organization and other
aspects of the culture, or, if it is a small segment of a total society that
is being studied, between that segment and the society as a whole.

In reality, this analysis of Guianese family structure, insofar as its
formal aspects are concerned, does little more than document relationships that have been long recognized, by adducing quantitative data
that support prevailing generalizations. But insistence that all conclusions must flow from statistical data must be followed through or the
proponent is left vulnerable to an effective *tu quoque*. What, in terms
of strict quantitative methodological reference, are we to say of a
statement such as this: "We have already discussed the major produc-
tive activities of village inhabitants and indicate that they tend to
be followed by everyone to some extent"? (p. 41).

Statistical findings, and the synchronic analysis of structure, can tell
us *what* a given system of relationships is at a given moment. They
cannot, however, answer the question *why* they take their observed
form. The ahistorical character of the structural approach makes it
inevitable that at least one element in the "why" equations, the time
factor, is relegated to a minor place, if it is considered at all. In
Afroamerican research, this means that components from Europe,
Africa, and aboriginal America are neglected. When, for instance, we
ask why the father holds the special place he has in the matrifocal
Afroamerican family, we are at a loss for an answer except by reference
to other than structural elements in the total society. One who would
understand the nature and social functioning of this role must exam-

ine the supernatural sanctions that, in retained or reinterpreted form, are conventions of spiritual as against secular patrifiliation which can be traced to specific African cultures.

The very nature of ahistoricism can cause the student to neglect relevant earlier materials. For instance, we cannot read without astonishment, in the "Foreword" to the work under discussion, written by a distinguished social anthropologist, that the discovery of the fact that "the question whether marital unions are proper or improper, legal or casual, and its legalistic corollary as to whether the children are legitimate or illegitimate, is a secondary one," had been achieved "by asking questions and following procedures that only a social anthropologist—and perhaps only one trained in the contemporary so-called British School of social anthropology—would think of" (p. xiii). This "discovery" has been a commonplace in New World Negro studies for decades. To document at random, Frazier, writing in 1939, asserted of the United States Negro family: "Our account, so far, of illegitimacy in the rural communities in the South would seem to indicate that neither the families of the women nor the community express any moral disapproval of this type of behavior" (1939:119). And Powdermaker, at about the same time, writing of the people of the Southern community she studied, stated that in terms of its age-class structure, the older lower- and middle-class group showed "a fairly complete acceptance of illegitimate children, with no feeling that they are branded or disgraced" (1939:204).

Ahistoricism also leads to insensitivity in employing the terminology of one's own science. Thus, I should scarcely call myself a follower of the *Kulturhistorische Schule*, yet in this work on the Guianese family I find myself labelled as taking a "culture-historical approach" to New World studies. This is confusion indeed. To group as culture-historians all those who take the time-factor into account in the study of man is to misread badly the variety of approaches in anthropology that accept, or have accepted, the historical point of view as relevant to the study of the traditions and beliefs of human social groups.

A more serious methodological defect is the explanation of the nature of the Guianese family by reference to kinship structures in societies that have no historical connection with it, but which present social orientations that are presumably of comparable form and functioning—Yucatan, Peru, Scotland, Malabar, Arizona. No criteria of quantity or form are suggested for these comparisons; the terms of reference, as far as can be seen, are subjective and therefore not susceptible to independent control. If one wished to make a methodological comparison, one might look on this as a structuralist, ahistorical variant of the *ferninterpretation* of the German-Austrian diffusionists.

There can be little question that the methodological inelegance of the procedure is to be ascribed to awkwardness in handling what is essentially an historical problem by means of a method of comparison that needs skill if certain of its well-recognized pitfalls are to be avoided.

V

I must make it clear that I am not drawing a critique of ahistoricism in the Afroamerican—or, for that matter, in any other—field, by recourse to an all-or-none fallacy. There are problems that call for the use of a structuralist approach. But when, as in the case of ahistorically oriented studies, whether by plantationists or structuralists, the question of the significance, or even presence of African retentions becomes a matter of establishing the presence or absence of a given trait in pure form, instead of searching out such multiple factors as class difference, historical opportunity, and the mechanisms of reinterpretation of tradition, ahistoricism can at best only yield limited insight and low-level generalizations (cf. Herskovits 1945, *passim*). In 1955, addressing myself to the need for holistic studies of New World Negro cultures, I called for more attention to the social and economic organization of New World Negro societies and for a less exclusive emphasis on detailing Africanisms in their religious life. In the face of the insistence on the study of the social structures of these societies as affording the primary, if not the sole means of understanding them, are we now to have to demonstrate again how necessary it is to continue studying New World Negro religion, folklore, art, music, values and the other nonsociological aspects of Afroamerican cultures?

Two quotations would here seem to be to the point. The first is from Frazier's Introduction to the symposium to which I have referred: "The problem of African survivals among Negroes in the United States was once the subject of much controversy on the part of anthropologists and sociologists. It seems fair to say that as a result of this controversy the sociologists gained a deeper knowledge of the persistence of certain phases of African culture traits among Negroes and the anthropologists gained a knowledge of the social history of Negroes which restricted their speculation concerning African survivals" (Rubin 1957:vii). We may profit as well from listening again to the words of one of the founders of our discipline, E. B. Tylor, who so many years ago wrote: "There are people so intent on the separate life of individuals that they cannot grasp a notion of the action of a community as a whole. . . . On the other hand, the philosopher may be so intent upon his general laws of society as to neglect the individual actors of whom that society is made up. . . . But seeing that collective action is the mere resultant of many individual actions, it is clear that these two methods of inquiry, if rightly followed, must be absolutely consistent" (1874. I:13).

REFERENCES

AGUIRRE BELTRÁN, GONZALO
   1946   La población Negra de México, 1519–1810. Estudio etnohistórica. Mexico, D.F., Ediciones Fuente Cultural.
COELHO, RUY
   1955   The Black Carib of Honduras. Unpublished Ph.D. dissertation. Northwestern University.
CURTIN, PHILIP
   1955   Two Jamaicas; the role of ideas in a tropical colony, 1830–1865. Cambridge, Harvard University Press.
FRAZIER, E. F.
   1939   The Negro family in the United States. Chicago, University of Chicago Press.
   1957   Introduction. In Caribbean studies; a symposium, Vera Rubin, ed. Jamaica, Institute of Social and Economic Research, University College of the West Indies.
HERSKOVITS, M. J.
   1941, 1958   The myth of the Negro past. New York, Harper & Brothers. (Reprinted: Boston, Beacon Press.)
   1945   Problem, method and theory in Afroamerican studies. Afroamérica 1:5–24. (Reprinted in Phylon 7:337–354.)
   1955   The social organization of the Candomble. Anais do XXXI Congresso Internacional de Americanistas 1:505–532.
   1956   On some modes of ethnographic comparison. Bijdragen tot de Taal-, Land-, en Volkenkunde 112:129–142.
POWDERMAKER, HORTENSE
   1939   After freedom; a cultural study in the deep South. New York, The Viking Press.
RUBIN, VERA, ed.
   1957   Caribbean studies; a symposium. Jamaica, Institute of Social and Economic Research, University College of the West Indies.
SIMPSON, GEORGE and PETER HAMMOND
   1957   Discussion (of paper by M. G. Smith). In Caribbean studies; a symposium, Vera Rubin, ed. Jamaica, Institute of Social and Economic Research, University College of the West Indies.
SMITH, M. G.
   1954(?)   A framework for Caribbean studies. Caribbean Affairs. University College of the West Indies, Jamaica.
   1957   The African heritage in the Caribbean. In Caribbean studies; a symposium, Vera Rubin, ed. Jamaica, Institute of Social and Economic Research, University College of the West Indies.
SMITH, R. T.
   1956   The Negro family in British Guiana. London, Routledge and Kegan Paul, Ltd.

SOLIEN, NANCIE
  1959 West Indian characteristics of the Black Carib. Southwestern
        Journal of Anthropology 15:300–307.
TAYLOR, DOUGLAS
  1951 The Black Carib of British Honduras. Viking Fund Publications
        in Anthropology 17. New York, Wenner-Gren Foundation for
        Anthropological Research.
TYLOR, E. B.
  1874 Primitive culture; researches into the development of mythology,
        philosophy, religion, language, art and custom. 2 vols. New York,
        Henry Holt and Co.
WAGLEY, CHARLES
  1957 Plantation-America: a culture sphere. In Caribbean studies; a
        symposium, Vera Rubin, ed. Jamaica, Institute of Social and
        Economic Research, University College of the West Indies.

:IV:

ETHNOPSYCHOLOGY

‖‖‖

Freudian Mechanisms in Negro Psychology

Among the most widely employed concepts of psycho-analysis are those of repression and compensation. Together with the associated concept of the unconscious, it may be said that the mechanisms implied by these two words are basic to psychoanalytic theory. It is, therefore, not without interest that we find numerous examples of these mechanisms in Negro cultures; not only this, but there exists both a recognition of the nature of the neuroses as induced by repression, and of the therapeutic value of bringing a repressed thought into the open, though the explanation . . . is usually given in terms of the working of supernatural forces.

❈   ❈   ❈

The analysis of the drives which actuate the behavior of primitive folk presents one of the most difficult problems confronting the cultural anthropologist, since it necessitates a comprehension of traditional values entirely foreign to the observer's own background. Among the non-literate Negro peoples of West Africa and the New World, this same problem is heightened in interest by the widely spread distribution of patterns of behaviour that reflect a characteristic psychological "set." An example, taken at random from the travel literature of the West Indies, will serve to illustrate the point. The account tells of a "Danse Congo" held on a small island off the coast of Haiti. This dance was given by the richest man on the island, one Polynice, and host

E. E. Evans-Pritchard, R. Firth, B. Malinowski, and I. Schapera, eds., *Essays Presented to C. G. Seligman* (London: Kegan Paul, Trench, Trubner & Co., 1934), pp. 75–84.

and guests were having a fine time of it; yet one of the songs sung by a guest was:—

Polynice is the tax-collector. He comes riding at night on his white horse to rob us; we will drive him away with stones, and a misfortune will happen to him.

The observer, commenting on this song, states that Polynice "accepted it without malice," and "doubtless would have felt hurt and neglected if they hadn't sung it." [1]

Investigators, seeking understanding of the significance of occurrences such as this, have turned to the concepts of the various schools of psychology for aid, and anthropological literature does contain numerous psychological interpretations. However, analyses of primitive behavior based on the Freudian postulates are seldom encountered. The reasons for this are not difficult to see. The method of the Freudians themselves has been one of clinical analysis, and when the psychoanalysts have stepped out of their clinics to apply their theories to society as a whole, and particularly to primitive man, their disregard of anthropological methodology has carried its own conviction of insufficiency. Like all other disciplines, anthropology has special techniques to cope with its problems. Those unacquainted with cultures other than their own, except through an outdated literature that persists in the concept of the primitive man as a child, are easily captivated by the speciously convincing character of deductions as to "origins" drawn by the use of a methodology that is now discredited. As a result, one witnesses such scientifically unacceptable conclusions as those presented by Freud in *Totem and Taboo*, to cite one of the earliest examples or, to cite one of the latest instances, the arguments of Rank in his volume *Art and Artist*.[2]

It is not necessary to do more than to state these facts, however, since both the dangers to the anthropologist in too fervent a devotion to the Freudian system, and the gains which should accrue from a realization of its significance as a technique to be used with other methods, have recently been fully assessed.[3] As has been suggested, anthropological recognition of the availability of psychoanalysis as a tool to be tested, and, if valid, applied in the study of primitive social behavior, together with the recognition by at least one psychoanalyst of the necessity of studying primitive cultures at first-hand through field investigation,[4] gives hope that the question of its degree of applicability to the problems of anthropology may soon be resolved.

In this paper it is proposed merely to indicate certain aspects of the psychology of primitive Negro cultural behavior which may be the better understood when some of the broader, simpler concepts of psychoanalysis are applied to their interpretation. It is not intended to do more than to present and point out the definite material contained here. Thus, we will not be concerned with the question whether or not the fact that the dream-interpretation of the Dutch Guiana Negroes, "if a person dreams he sees snakes, that means he has enemies," is of significance for the Freudian theory of dream-symbolism; whether or not "when you dream of monkeys, it is Obia Winti[5] that is seeking to come to you" derives from sex-symbolism or from the historic fact that, in West Africa, it is the supernatural monkey-like "little people" of the bush who are believed to have given magic to men. Nor will we concern ourselves with the validity of conclusions such as expressed by the student who, having drunk deep at the Freudian fountain, remarked that the slouching gait of American Negroes is due to a castration complex, for it was obvious that he had not observed the motor behavior of Africans, or for that matter, of New World Negroes, carrying head-burdens. What is to be reported here are field data, with native interpretations of them which suggest the availability of psychoanalytic concepts as an aid to understanding primitive psychology.

Among the most widely employed concepts of psychoanalysis are those of repression and compensation. Together with the associated concept of the unconscious, it may be said that the mechanisms implied by these two words are basic to psychoanalytic theory. It is, therefore, not without interest that we find numerous examples of these mechanisms in Negro cultures; not only this, but that there exists both a recognition of the nature of the neuroses as induced by repression, and of the therapeutic value of bringing a repressed thought into the open, though the explanation of the phenomenon is usually given in terms of the working of supernatural forces. It seems valid to assume that this sanctioned release of inhibited feelings was at the basis of the Haitian performance recounted at the beginning of this paper, and this conclusion becomes inescapable when knowledge of the historical derivation of the practice of singing songs which state grievances against those in power is available to reinforce the psychological explanation. For socially institutionalized release constitutes an outstanding characteristic of the Negro cultures of West Africa and of the New World. That this is the case among the Ashanti is testified by Captain Rattray. Thus, during the *apo* and similar ceremonies, to revile those in power or about to assume power is not only permitted but urged, the reason being given that this is done so that the soul of the one who rules will not be sickened by the evil thoughts held against him by those whom he may have angered.[6] Similarly, in explaining the broadness of the action in many Ashanti folk-tales, Captain Rattray gives the native explanation of how it is held to be "good" for people to discuss and laugh at things otherwise forbidden. He concludes that "West Africans had discovered for themselves the truth of the psycho-analysts' theory of 'repression,' and that in these ways they sought an outlet for what might otherwise have become a dangerous complex." [7]

In Dahomey, the institution of the *avogan*, the dance in the market-place, is similarly recognized by the natives as affording release for suppressed emotions. At stated periods the people of each of the quarters of the city of Abomey have in turn their opportunity to stage such a dance. Crowds come to see the display and to watch the dancing, but, most of all, to listen to the songs and to laugh at the ridicule to which are held those who have offended members of the quarter giving the dance. Names are ordinarily not mentioned, for then fighting may result. In any event, the African relishes innuendo and circumlocution too well to be satisfied with bald, direct statement. However, everyone who is present already knows to whom reference is being made. Thus the song might be:

> Woman, thy soul is misshapen.
> In haste was it made, in haste.
> So fleshless a face speaks, telling
> Thy soul was formed without care.
> The ancestral clay for thy making
> Was moulded in haste, in haste.
> A thing of no beauty art thou,
> Thy face unsuited to be a face,
> Thy feet unsuited for feet.[8]

A name may be used, but usually it is one given for the occasion, and employed as a symbol of baseness or treachery:

> Call Adjevu to me, I would insult her . . .

This same release through song is accorded co-wives. Nothing could have offered more striking testimony of the manner in which songs of this kind have a welcome place in domestic Dahomean life than the reaction of the wives of a chief who were asked to sing some of them. The first response was shocked amazement that anyone not a Dahomean suspected the existence of such songs; when, however, they were convinced that this was more than a shot in the dark, their amazement gave way to peals of laughter before and after the singing. In the following song, which may serve as an example, the recrimination of one co-wife against another—a princess—is masked by the reference to her as a "man of rank"; the singing takes place while the women work together in a court-yard of their husband's compound:—

> O son of King Hwegbadja
> To you I bring news
> With you I leave word
> That a man of rank who kills and then steals is here.
> Something has been lost in this house
> And the owner has not found it.
> The man of rank who kills and then steals
> Has been here.

Even the play of fancy in a language unknown to outsiders is not scorned by the West Africans to get release from repressed grievances, and this is especially true where their impotence against European control is concerned. The experience of companies who have recorded West African songs sung by Africans in European ports which, when offered for sale in West Africa, were found to have their popularity rest especially on the fact that many of them made sport of the Whites, is a case in point.

As in West Africa, so in the New World this channelling of emotional release takes characteristic forms. Among the most picturesque of these is the *lobi singi* of the Negroes of the coastal region of Dutch Guiana, especially of Paramaribo. This socially recognized form of ridicule is most often directed against a woman who has taken a man away from another. Less ritualized, the *lobi singi* may take place between two women who have quarrelled if, while the two are both working in a compound-yard, one of them sings songs which, though traditional in words and melody, have a reference that everyone present recognizes as applicable to the other. In the ritualized form, however, the ceremony of recrimination is one which takes preparation and must be carefully staged. A musical accompaniment is provided, and the friends of the aggrieved woman, dressed in their best, come to assist her in shaming her rival. The locale of the performance is the yard of the compound where the offender lives, and this woman, at the appointed time, barricades herself in her cabin and gives no sign. The occasion has been well advertised, and many spectators are present when the injured woman arrives with her friends and the music.

The players arrange themselves before the tightly-shut house; the music to one side, the audience making a cleared space for the dancing. The songs are all of leader-and-chorus type, and the phrase ending the chorus is sung with a few dancing steps, accompanied by a disdainful lifting in back of the voluminous skirts of the traditional dress of the Paramaribo Negro women. As the steps are executed, the exclamation "Ha! Ha!" is heard. The words of the songs are to-day no longer as pointed as they were before recourse to the Dutch courts on charges of slander made watchfulness necessary. But the songs sung at the present are still adequately suggestive, as examples demonstrate:—

> What can an ant do
> With a cow's head?
> Ha! Ha!
> She must eat the meat,
> And leave the bones.
> Ha! Ha!

Again the injured woman may sing:—

> You are handsomer than I
> You are fatter than I
> But I am sweeter than you.
> Ha! Ha!
> That is why, my treasure,
> My treasure, cannot bear,
> To leave a sweet rose
> To come to the house of a crab.
> Ha! Ha!

Or, she may tell how the man who has jilted her was worthless until she took him up:—

> When I bought my cow, my cow,
> When I bought my cow,
> When I bought my cow, my cow,
> My cow did not even have horns!

It must be recognized that the Negro sees in the *lobi singi* a twofold purpose—to make the woman who has been wronged "feel better" and also to castigate the offender with ridicule. And those who have worked with Negroes know that ordinarily they prefer a blow to ridicule.

There is, however, still another type of *lobi singi*, which affords the release that comes through public confession and public proclamation of the intention to turn to a new and better way of life. A girl who has been promiscuous and who later desires a respected place in the community, herself leads the singing, and the songs dwell on her past mode of life; the young men she has led astray, the women she has wronged, her intention to reform. Whatever the lines, the members of the chorus do not fail to end with the dancing steps and the exclamation "Ha! Ha!". The following is an example of the songs sung at a *lobi singi* given by a young woman for herself:—

If I were a rich man
I would buy a large farm.
And what would I plant in it?
And what would I plant in it?
I would plant experience in it
So that when I went out
Experience would be a perfume for my body.
Ha! Ha!

That repression is a cause of neurosis is an elementary tenet of psychoanalysis; the fact, explained in different terms, has been recognized by Negroes in even more explicit fashion than in the instances which have been quoted. Often the explanation of the importance of release takes the form of assuming supernatural vengeance as a cause of the ills that follow on repression. Instances from the beliefs of both African and New World Negroes which demonstrate this are to be found; however, it will suffice to restrict examples to certain institutions studied in Guiana. The most explicit statement, one that would be instantly recognized as valid by any psychologist, has to do with the cause of insanity. The Paramaribo Negroes see it as bound up with the *winti*, as the African spirits worshipped by the coastal Negroes of Guiana are named. These spirits, which are inherited, are thought to come to an individual at about the age of puberty, after which active worship in the form of dancing to drums takes place. Everywhere in the New World, before and after emancipation of the slaves, pressure has been used by European officials to discourage the worship of these pagan deities. This has driven the worship of African gods— in this instance the *winti*—more and more into secret ritual. Yet the forbidden dances do take place. In Paramaribo dancing is permitted several times during the year, and then the adherents of the *winti* worship them openly. But there are some *winti* who drive their followers to more frequent worship with an urgency that cannot be denied; and at such times a basin, overturned in a larger container of water, is struck to simulate the drums ordinarily employed and the devotees dance. Were they to inhibit the call of the gods to dance and persist in their refusal over an extended period of time, the Negroes say they would go insane. Indeed, the *winti*-worshippers insist that the insanity found among the Christian Negroes of Paramaribo is due to this cause. It is believed that these persons have inherited spirits, and because their new religion prohibits dancing for them, the resistance to doing the bidding of the inherited gods robs them of their reason— that is, the spirits which "possess" them drive them mad.

An even clearer appreciation of the consequences of repressing emotions—in this case, anger, bitterness, or hatred—is seen in the Guiana concept of *fiofio*. Historically, this can be related to that same *apo* ceremony which Rattray has described among the Ashanti, that period of release from the ordinary social controls that marked the time when a man might make free with anyone, even the King himself. In Suriname, however, the form of the belief is different from the institutionalized license that marks the African periods of freedom from restraint. *Fiofio* is primarily the name of an insect. However, it is also conceived as a spirit which, taking the form of this insect, enters the body, causing illness and even death. This deadly presence is brought on when a quarrel between intimates has not been followed by a reconciliation, and when some gesture of affection occurs between such participants to a quarrel at a later date; in a phrase, when hypocrisy, conscious or unconscious, is practised, the souls of those concerned are resentful, and their owners sicken and die. An example will make clear the concept and the behavior resulting from it. We may suppose that two close friends, or two relatives, or two persons who are members of the same household have quarrelled, and no reconciliation has been effected. Time passes, the incident loses its importance, and gradually the two may no longer even consciously remember that it had taken place, so that a normal friendly relationship is resumed. Then one of them accepts something from the other. Since the inner hurt has never been healed, ill-luck—bad crops, illness, children stillborn—befalls one or the other of them, or both. Diviners are consulted, and if it is the long-standing difference that is shown to be the cause of the trouble, the ceremonial retraction known as *puru mofo*—literally, "withdraw from the mouth"—takes place. The one who has wronged the other calls on the soul of the wronged one, saying:

"*Akra Kwami*,[9] I did not mean to offend you. I was hasty. Do not avenge yourself on me, or on my wife, or our children. I beg you, overlook what I said and do not bear me any ill-will." He takes water in his mouth, and spurts it over his doorway three times, repeating the formula each time. The retraction is preceded and followed by ceremonial washing—"to wash *fiofio*" is the native phrase—when the parties to the quarrel pronounce this formula:—

"Just as this broom sweeps heaviness away, so, too, must your heaviness go away. Just as the mother hen carries her child until it breaks the egg,[10] so everything that you carry must break and come into the open." Should the ceremonial retraction not take place, it is believed death will ensue. To have honest dislikes is natural enough and, says the native, these do a man no harm; it is only when quarrels are masked in surface friendliness and an ancient grudge is harbored that it is dangerous to make an exchange of belongings or accept any gesture of affection.

The discussion thus far has had to do with socially sanctioned mechanisms which permit of release from inhibitions and conflicts of various sorts. What has been shown is that among the primitive Negroes, both in Africa and the New World, patterned types of psychic purges are recognized as valid; what is important for a psychoanalytic approach to the understanding of these social data is the fact that, in every case, the native explanation of the particular type of behavior, though ordinarily couched in terms of the supernatural, can be restated in terms of the unconscious.

Less sharply pointed toward Freudian mechanisms, but nevertheless intelligible in terms of compensation through rationalization, are the following attitudes from Dahomey. Among a people where the worship of gods and ancestors plays as prominent a rôle as it does there, it is necessary to explain national mishaps on grounds other than the powerlessness of these beings who rule the destiny of the living, for it is clear that doubt in their power would rob the Dahomean of the security he feels in the structure of his world. Rationalizations of such mishaps, therefore, are not lacking. A small-pox scourge or a locust plague is a punishment meted out for the misdeeds of the living, for a breach against supernatural decrees. Defeat in a battle comes as punishment for violating the edict of an ancient ancestor that there be peace; the conquest by the French is accounted for by the fact that King Glele, the father of that Behanzin who was the reigning monarch when the French took Dahomey, had advised his son against war, and especially against war with the Whites who were the makers of implements of war—guns and gunpowder. Because, therefore, Behanzin followed his own headstrong course, the ancestors would not support him, and Dahomey fell. Since it is not always convenient to comply with the non-worldly edicts of the ancestors—for some of them were short-sighted humans, and the Dahomean laughs as he tells of these rulings—it is the letter of the law which is often obeyed to cope with such taboos, but not the spirit. Thus for the ancestor who enjoined peace, a village has been selected and ordered to remain forever at peace. When King Tegbesu found it tiresome to have the marks of the leopard's claws cicatrized on his forehead, as the ancestors commanded, and in consequence remain inaccessible to all other humans, he designated a man to act as his substitute for the observance of this, and himself took all the prerogatives of kingship, and the freedom to enjoy them as well. Since it was felt that there were spiritual dangers in warring against other kingdoms who had powerful gods of their own, it was not the King of Dahomey who declared war, who directed the campaign, and who took the slaves. The Minister of War did the first two, and the soldiers did the last. During a war the King's tall stool was occupied by the commanding general, and the King himself sat on a low stool, and nominally he was under this officer. When slaves were captured, each soldier received from the King's hand a few cowries—admittedly a ceremonial gesture —and thus "sold" each of the captives to the King, on whom no vengeance could then fall, for he was only engaging in barter. It is significant that this payment was called "washing the hands."

Another instance of behavior immediately available for Freudian analysis may be given. This trait differs somewhat from those heretofore discussed, and is taken from the customs of the Bush-Negroes of Suriname, a people whose isolation in the bush has largely protected their African culture from European influence. The example to be cited contributes material for the consideration of the extent to which the Oedipus complex may be variously shaped in different cultures. Malinowski has shown that among the strongly matrilineal people of the Trobriand Islands, the Oedipus complex in its classic form is not found, but that the unconscious hatreds are transferred to the maternal uncle, the incest-wish to the sister.[11] The social organization of the Bush-Negroes is legally matrilineal, spiritually partrilineal, resembling in its double exogamic features the principal outlines of the Gold Coast type from which it derives.[12] What, then, is the form this "nuclear complex" takes in such a society?

It was not in an investigation of Bush-Negro psychological processes, but during an attempt to obtain as much detail as possible regarding death-customs, that the answer came in terms of an Oedipus reaction as "correct" psychoanalytically as though it had been stated by Freud himself. The question which had been asked was, "When a man dies, do they destroy his house?" And the reply: "Not unless he has done black magic. If it is an ordinary man, his widow lives there with his daughters." "What happens to his sons?" "They are sent away for a long time." "Why?" "Because the soul of a man loves his daughters but hates his sons, and if they remained in his house, his ghost would kill them." "And if a woman dies?" "Then the husband continues to live there with his sons, for if it is a woman's ghost, she will destroy her daughters. But her sons, she loves them and watches over them."

1. W. B. Seabrook, *The Magic Island*, pp. 225–6.

2. For example, on p. 170 of the English translation Rank provides us with the following, which is only one of the many statements of its kind that might be quoted: "The primitive precursor of this head-gathered pillar-man of Greece may be found in the wooden house-pillar of art in the South Seas . . ."

3. C. G. Seligman, "Anthropological Perspective and Psychological Theory," *Journal of the Royal Anthropological Institute*, vol. lxii (1932), pp. 193–228.

4. Geza Róheim, "Psychoanalytic Technique and Field Anthropology," *International Journal of Psychoanalysis*, vol. xiii (1932), pp. 6–22. However, the exaggerated field-technique of Róheim, as revealed in this and other papers, and his unquestioning acceptance of Freudian terminology, coupled with his undisguisedly emotional strictures on the acceptability of Malinowski's study of the Oedipus complex among the Trobriand Islanders, make one fear that this grain of acceptable material will be so far overshadowed by the faults of the work that its chief result will be further to prejudice anthropologists against psychoanalysis as a working technique.

5. An Obia spirit.

6. R. S. Rattray, *Ashanti*, pp. 151–171. See especially the songs quoted on pp. 156–7.

7. R. S. Rattray, *Akan-Ashanti Folk-Tales*, pp. ix–xii.

8. I am indebted to Mrs. Herskovits for this translation.

9. That is, "Saturday soul."

10. The imagery here is somewhat confusing; the meaning is "Just as the chick emerges from the egg-shell, so the sickness must leave the person who is ill."

11. Cf. *Sex and Repression in Savage Society, passim.*

12. Cf. M. J. Herskovits, "The Social Organization of the Bush-Negroes of Suriname," *Proceedings of the XXIII International Congress of Americanists,* 1928 (New York, 1930), pp. 713–727.

Some Psychological Implications of Afroamerican Studies

A culture . . . is to be thought of as the summation of the forms of behavior, both overt and implicit, manifest by a given people, and the sanctions underlying these forms of behavior. . . . Except in a sense so broad as to be without significance for the analysis of the nature and mechanisms of culture, they do not arise from any special innate capacity . . . but are learned. It becomes self-evident, therefore, that the study of those problems we subsume under the category of the psychology of culture is especially critical for an understanding of the processes that constitute the dynamics of cultural change, the analysis of which, in terms of the ethnohistoric study of acculturation, forms the very core of Afroamerican research.

*   *   *

Sol Tax, ed., *Acculturation in the Americas*, II. Proceedings of the 29th International Congress of Americanists (Chicago: University of Chicago Press), 152–60.

Most generalizations from the analysis of Afroamerican data fall into the broad category of anthropological theory designated as cultural dynamics. Because of the relatively precise nature of the historic controls which Afroamericanists can command, it has been increasingly apparent that materials are here at hand for the investigation of some of the most debated propositions in the repertory of anthropological assumptions concerning the nature and mechanisms of culture. Such questions as the tenaciousness of institutions or the nature of cultural change, as concerns both cultural elements and whole cultures, have offered a logical starting point for the study of data concerning the range of variation in the ways of life of the descendants of Africans who were transported to the New World. Studies of this kind have made it apparent that the differences in the aboriginal cultures of the areas of Africa from which Africans were derived tended to be suppressed in favor of basic patterns common to all these ways of life— a finding whose significance for the analysis of cultural change in general far transcends its obvious importance for the Afroamerican field. Further investigation along these lines has revealed another form of cultural variation that likewise has wide implications. For not only the differences between the cultures of different New World Negro groups, arising out of their contact with Europeans and Indians of varied cultural background, have been recorded but also the range of variation in sanctioned behavior manifest within each given Negro society. The bearing of such findings on the question of the nature and functioning of sub-cultures is self-evident.

In addition to these approaches to the study of Afroamerican cultures are those which follow from a recognition of the essentially psychological nature of culture itself. A culture, in these terms, is to be thought of as the summation of the forms of behavior, both overt and implicit, manifest by a given people, and the sanctions underlying these forms of behavior. It is assumed, in terms of this hypothesis, that, except in a sense so broad as to be without significance for the analysis of the nature and mechanisms of culture, they do not arise from any special innate capacity of the members of any particular society, but are learned. It becomes self-evident, therefore, that the study of those problems we subsume under the category of the psychology of culture is especially critical for an understanding of the processes that constitute the dynamics of cultural change, the analysis of which, in terms of the ethnohistoric study of acculturation, forms the very core of Afroamerican research.

These are terms of reference, however, that call for an extension of the psychological concerns of anthropologists beyond those that have come to occupy their attention in recent years. This interest has tended to be directed almost exclusively toward what may be termed the psychiatric or psychoanalytic analysis of the relation between the personalities of members of a given society and the conventions which order their lives, especially as early enculturation molds their characteristic reaction patterns through the experiences of early childhood. The rewards of this approach are apparent to all who are conversant with the recent literature of our science. It will be indicated later how the gains of this approach to problems of the relation between culture and personality can be extended by more adequate use of the controls yielded by the comparative study of Afroamerican and African cultures. At the moment, however, let us direct our attention to the phase of the over-all field of psychology and culture that has received relatively less attention from anthropologists.

II

If we assume that culture is learned, it becomes apparent that the enculturative experience, the cultural expression of the learning-conditioning process, is so effective in shaping thought and behavior that the major portion of the response-patterns of the individual tend to be automatic rather than reasoned. In this sense, then, cultural stability derives from the fact that so much of socially sanctioned behavior lodges on a psychological plane that lies *below the level of consciousness*. It is only when these automatic responses—which, it should be recognized, may include either overt or implicit reactions—are challenged, that emotional and thought processes are called into play. In terms of cultural dynamics, the analysis of these deeply rooted, automatic, enculturated behavior patterns affords a relatively neglected lead to an understanding of cultural change. It is precisely here that the broad historic controls of the Afroamerican field have the greatest significance. For they permit the assessment of data in terms that make it possible to determine not only which aspects of culture run most deeply beneath the level of consciousness, but how deviations from behavior patterns of earlier historic periods are the reflection of differing degrees of intensity of exposure and reconditioning—in this case, to various types of non-African cultural conventions.

Motor habits of all kinds must be placed high on the list of cultural elements that can be profitably studied from this point of view. As has been pointed out elsewhere, such humble aspects of behavior as patterns of walking, or of the use of gesture to accompany speech, can be analyzed through the techniques of the psychologists concerned with such matters, particularly if motion pictures are employed to obtain the basic data. Work habits afford valuable clues to the study of this problem. Thus, while it might be chance that in the Gullah Islands basketry made by the Negroes is of the coiled, sewed variety, as it is in so much of West Africa, the element of chance is considerably diminished when we find that in these islands, as in West Africa, the coiling goes in a clockwise direction. Again, though the strip weaving of Africa has not survived in the New World, it is worthy of note that hats made by the Haitian peasants consist of narrow strips of woven straw, sewed together in a manner quite analogous to that in which the cloths of the West Africans are made, and quite in contrast to the hat-weaving techniques of the Indians of Central America. That the aesthetic implications of this particular retention are also to be taken into account is apparent when we consider the cloths of the Bush Negroes, which are made of strips cut from bolts of striped cloth, across the design, and similarly sewed edge to edge to make an African-like covering.

These aesthetic patterns are similarly found to lodge deep beneath the level of consciousness, and underscore the contribution that studies in the field of the humanities can make to our understanding of human social and cultural behavior. Though the New World Negro has preserved little of the graphic and plastic art that is the most distinctive contribution of Africa to the aesthetic resources of the world, he has preserved much of the musical, dance, and literary patterns of Africa. As in the case of linguistic modalities, the manner in which such aspects of musical conditioning as are to be inferred from historic continuity, not only of rhythmic structure and tonal progressions of New World Negro music but also of such subtle factors as skips, modes of attack in singing, tessitura, and inner structure of melodic line, all offer valuable documentation of how cultural items, whose existence is scarcely realized by those who behave in accordance with them, exhibit great tenaciousness under conditions of cultural change. The comparative study of the dance is in its infancy, and no controlled analyses of patterns of Negro dancing in Africa and the New World are available. Yet non-technical observations of such a choreographic item as the fact that in West Africa, South America, the West Indies, and the United States the religious dances of the Negroes almost without exception move in a counterclockwise direction are significant. So, too, is the manner in which the arms and legs are employed, and the complex "foot-work" that is so characteristic a feature of Negro dancing everywhere.

Value systems, which form the basic sanctions of the way of life of any group, ordinarily fall into this category of cultural elements that run beneath the level of consciousness. In the case of the New World Negroes, the psychological problem of retention and reinterpretation of African values assumes a greater significance than in undisturbed cultures, because of the very fact that they are systems which for generations have been under continuous questioning. The analysis of which values of aboriginal Africa have been retained and which values and traditional ways of thinking of non-African peoples with whom the New World Negroes have been in contact have been taken over will tell us much not only of the nature and functioning of culture but of the character of the learning-conditioning system. The resilience of the learned patterns of African thought in the face of new situations need not be considered again, since it is well recognized today as a real factor in making for the successful adaptation of the New World Negro to the cultures of the societies in which he now lives, either numerically or psychologically, as a minority group. Research must rather take the form of detailed analyses, on as broad a comparative basis as possible, of the actual nature of the value systems and world views of given Negro groups. From this, the investigation must move to the study of the modes of learning and conditioning that, induced by the changing historical stream which has provided the setting of a given system of values, can be held to comprise the factor that has caused a given value system to take the form in which we find it today.

A research project now under way can be briefly described as contributing one approach to the problem of how underlying values can be retained in reintegrated form. Perhaps the last places where one would expect to find relevant data are the Negro radio churches, whose broadcasts are to be heard each Sunday, often late at night, over obscure stations of the metropolitan districts of northern United States. Yet consistent attention to such services over a period of years has forced the conclusion not only that they represent an important factor in the life of the urban Negroes of this area, but also that they afford valuable data which, objectively analyzed, will yield much insight into the question of the retention of values under extreme conditions of acculturation.

Because the services are broadcast, their preservation for study presented a relatively simple methodological problem. By connecting a wire recorder to an ordinary receiving set, it was possible to record the services, week after week, of hour-long broadcasts of a particular church in Chicago. As a result, there is now in hand over thirty hours of these programs, covering a selection from services heard over about fifteen months. The general pattern of these services, with their songs, announcements of activities for the days ahead, and, above all, their sermons, has been established. Comparison with urban and rural "shouting" churches that do not have radio outlets, as well as with the broadcasts of other radio churches in the New York metropolitan district and in other cities, has demonstrated the typicalness of the church whose broadcast services have been recorded.

Preliminary analyses of transcriptions of some of the services reveal unsuspected aspects of these forms of worship. Thus, though the independence of religious groups of this type has been stressed, a web of close inter-church relationships is revealed in the announcements. The music of the songs, which represent what may be termed the "spirituals" of the present day, show how enculturation to basic musical patterns finds expression in forms that are common to church and to dance-hall—jazz, "blues," and "boogie" rhythms and singing-styles all being present in this religious music. But, above all, the sermons indicate how tenaciously values and world view, no matter how strongly reinterpreted, have maintained themselves.

It will be remembered that these are Protestant churches of unaffiliated Baptist denomination. Those who will recall the stress on sin and punishment for sin that characterizes the world view of evangelical Christian sects will at once recognize the degree of deviation represented in the sermons of this Negro church when it is pointed out that only rarely in the broadcast, or in broadcasts of services of other churches of this sort, are the words "hell," "damnation," "punishment," and the like to be heard. The religious attitude here is one of affirmation. God, Jesus, the characters of the Bible are close to man, affording him a support that can be relied on for practical aid in time of need. "Can't give a man religion on an empty stomach," cries the preacher; or "Jesus is in the folks, and when you feed the folks, you feed Jesus." "My God is a right-now God!" he exclaims again and again. Jesus moves from sickbed to sickbed, bringing his healing power at the behest of the preacher; the ill are instructed "Turn your face to the wall and pray" as the voice of the preacher, over the radio, summons the healing hand of Jesus.

Nor do these sermons, when written out and analyzed, show the kind of free association they have been asserted to manifest. Fully structured, their striking imagery is skilfully directed toward inducing in the worshipers that particular kind of identification with the power of the universe which may be recognized as a common element in the religion of most New World and West African Negroes. This identification has been enculturated so powerfully that it is to be regarded as a supreme factor in making for the psychological reintegration that marks the stage of adjustment of the Negro to the difficulties he has had, and still has, to face in living his daily life. In the hard-headed approach to the universe, the determination shown to harness its power, here and now, for the use of man, and in the immediacy of the relationships between these powers and men, we find in this area of life further instances of the persistence of elements of value system and world view that have been preserved, reinterpreted in new form, through the strength of the enculturative learning-conditioning process.

III

Let us now briefly consider some of the implications and opportunities which the Afroamerican field holds for research into the relationships between culture and personality, in terms of the psychiatric-psychoanalytic approaches which predominate in the study of the psychology of culture at the present time.

The methodological implications of Afroamerican data for the study of this problem must receive our attention initially. The vastness of the canvas on which the history and present cultural status of the Negro is painted and the historic controls that permit precision in assigning provenience and recovering the cultural base-line from which acculturative change is to be assessed are especially significant for this area of research. A few instances will make the point of how hypotheses can be treated by reference to these data. Thus, we may consider what has come to be thought of as the "national character" approach to the problem of the relation between culture and personality, which lays stress on the patterns of infant training in accounting for differences between the personality types which characterize different societies.

If we consider the conventions of infant care of two West African peoples, the Ashanti and the Dahomeans, we find the resemblances between them in this element of their culture are such that, on the face of it, the security constellations held to be of primary importance in determining the adult personality structure would be expected to yield quite similar types. Children are nursed over a long period, and at their desire; the bodily contact between infant and mother is continuous, intimate, and protective; hygienic training is not such as to give rise to traumatic experiences; children are taught to walk and to talk by being praised for success rather than by punishment for failure. Yet no precision instruments are needed to force the recognition of striking personality differences between adult Ashanti and

Dahomeans. The latter are characterized by strong and pervasive patterns of competition for prestige and power that give a harshness to interpersonal relations which are merely brought into relief by the institutionalized sentimentalism of such a convention as that of the best friend. Among the Ashanti, however, such emphases are of minor import.

This is in Africa. Let us now consider two related New World cultures, those of the Bush Negroes of Dutch Guiana and of the peasants of Haiti. In the former, Ashanti patterns predominate and in the latter, Dahomean. The differences between them as regards those characteristic reactions to human situations that reflect personality are likewise those that mark off the peoples whose cultures are ancestral to each. Yet, again, if we turn to the patterns of infant care in these New World settings, we find no differences so striking between the two, or between them and the related African ones, that would account for the difference in personality type one immediately recognizes. It is quite true that punishment in childhood and during adolescence are much more severe in Dahomey and among the Haitian peasants than is the case among the Ashanti or in the interior of Dutch Guiana. Yet these later experiences of individual socialization are not now at issue, since it is on the factor of infant training that we are focusing our attention. Here we see methodological implications, even in this single instance drawn from the Afroamerican field, that are obvious in their potential contribution to a much debated problem.

For another example, let us turn to the utilization of projective techniques for the determination of the modal personality structure of a people. The problem of the validity of such tests, either as a whole or when considered individually, for purposes of cross-cultural analysis, is still, in the best tradition of scientific method, being explored. A number of studies of American Indian, Pacific island, and Far Eastern peoples form the basis for the discussion of this question. From the point of view of established principles of investigation, however, it would scarcely seem that the problem could be resolved as long as samples from one entire major group of mankind were lacking. Moreover, data gathered from different groups within the single historic stream of African and Afroamerican cultures would afford a further test, on a far-broader scale than has heretofore been attempted, of the degree to which characteristic responses found in African and European behavior are to be encountered in altered form in the New World concomitantly with the degree of acculturation manifest by a given society at a given place on the historical continuum. Field experience forces the conclusion that the tenaciousness of African cultural elements, even in the face of the most severe attack—in social organization, in language, in religion, and in the arts—are but cultural correlates of the tenaciousness with which certain personality characteristics of Africans have held over in their New World descendants, even where acculturation to Euroamerican patterns has been extensive.

Not only this, but certain researches suggest that the problems of the influence of culturally established reactions to projective tests themselves can advantageously be studied by the use of data from the Afroamerican field. Coelho, in unpublished preliminary analyses of Rorschach tests given to Black Caribs of the Republic of Honduras, was struck by the absence of attention to fine detail, and the relation of this fact to the cultural tradition of divination by the interpretation of the configurations of various objects used in divining, a widely spread convention among the Negroes of Africa and the New World. The religious significance of the bat, and the relation of tones of gray to concepts of magic, also were found to enter into the reactions of Black Caribs to the forms presented to them for interpretation. One fact worthy of note in this connection, whose relevance will be immediately apparent to those conversant with the Rorschach cards, is the practice of the Black Caribs of pressing a certain insect between the pages of a book and then divining by interpreting the resulting unstructured form.

Certain data which throw light on the role of culture in providing mechanisms of adjustment for the individual in later life, especially as regards those situations where Freudian types of responses come into play, have been pointed out in an earlier paper (III). With more research, new data that further document the nature and extensiveness of these mechanisms have become available. A few examples can be given here. The characteristic phenomenon of spirit possession will afford us a good instance of what is meant, especially data from the Afrobrazilian cults of Bahia. In these cults, as in other Afroamerican religious groupings manifesting various degrees of reinterpretation of Africanisms, possession of the individual devotee by a supernatural spirit, in which there is a displacement of personality that causes the worshiper to behave in accordance with the patterned concept of the nature of this being, is the rule. It has often been noted that the individual who has been possessed, despite the fact that the experience often entails strenuous muscular exertion in dancing, comes out of his possession manifesting far less fatigue than might be expected.

Underlying this fact is that of the psychological catharsis yielded by such experiences, something that affords a fresh lead for the understanding of the phenomenon. In many instances recorded in Brazil, this catharsis takes the form of the resolution of a guilt feeling or other personality conflict, especially through the confession compelled of a devotee, while under possession by his deity. The confession most frequently calls into play the father, or mother image, represented by the cult head, a person in whose hands the spiritual well-being of the initiate lies and who is actually accorded the title of "father" or "mother" when addressed.

Examples range from the trivial to the tragic, but all have in common this fact that the compulsion toward confession of conduct not socially sanctioned is projected onto the god and is thus achieved without distortion of the individual's ego-image or the destruction of those rationalizations which soften a sense of guilt at his misconduct. Thus, one cult-initiate, because of curiosity about spiritualism, a belief system that has spread widely among New World Negroes (offering another problem for study which, unfortunately, we cannot consider here), visited one of their sessions. This is contrary to a rule of the cults, because of the belief that the gods and the dead—to which they are exposed when the medium calls his control—should not mix. Arriving at the session, this woman sat until the voice of the control was heard. Then, her god coming to her, she ran out of the session and across the city to her own cult-house. Here she knelt before the priestess and, speaking as the god, denounced herself for what she had done, imposing the proper penalty on herself.

Another instance concerns a young priest who had never married because, as he said, his deity, a goddess, was jealous of him. In actuality he represented a case of inversion, though he had no lack of temporary alliances with women, for whom he appeared to hold considerable attraction. On one occasion he contemplated entering into a continued but illicit relationship with the daughter of a friend of his father, a girl who had been protected against such adventures by her parents, whose standards were of the sanctioned European type. Shortly before the two were to go off together, the priest became possessed by his patron goddess and informed the girl's father fully as to their plans. His reaction to the situation he faced when he emerged from his state of possession to learn that what he proposed to do was known was a striking demonstration of the effectiveness with which this mechanism had operated to resolve what in this case was a potential personality conflict.

In broadest terms, then, the adjustment of the Negro to his New World setting offer these and numerous other leads toward insight into the interplay between the individual as a member of society and the body of custom that dictates the characteristic modes of behavior of his group. The fact that in Brazil men and women can successfully compartmentalize their mental processes so as to live simultaneously in terms of the economic, technological, and political patterns of Euroamerican culture, and yet maintain a belief system that is based on the sanctions of a non-mechanistic order, points toward generalizations of the broadest scientific, no less than practical, importance. The suggestions contained in this paper thus indicate but one of the lines along which studies lying in the Afroamerican field, both in hand and in prospect, are making and will continue to make their contribution.

: V :

THE ARTS

Bush-Negro Art

What is it that has made for the flourishing of the Bush-Negro's art in his South American isolation? . . . When we reflect that the slave owned or had access to few material possessions, that escape from his master was perilous, that for tools with which to build his bush civilization he had practically only his machete, so that he may be said to have wrested his livelihood from the jungle with his bare hands, is it not astonishing that he should have found the psychic need for these painstaking and beautiful carvings, and the leisure to satisfy that need in an existence which allowed so little leisure?

*   *   *

Within recent years the attention of artists and those interested in the study of art has been increasingly directed toward the art forms of primitive peoples. One of the first questions which arose in the consideration of primitive art was concerning the nature of the "primitive" in art. Is primitive art the result of a naive playing with form and mass, a crude but happy groping for that which we today call self-expression, the satisfaction of the æsthetic impulse? Or is primitive art merely the manifestation of adherence to traditional forms, the beginnings of which it is impossible to trace, and therefore to analyze?

Both of these answers are given. The adherents of the position that the primitive artist is a sublime child did not encourage this probing, but there were those, who, though not students of primitive culture,

Arts, XVII, no. 51 (1930), 25–37, 48–49. Illustrations are from the Herskovits Collection owned by the author's daughter, Jean Herskovits Kopytoff.

perceived that there might be a definite interrelation between the art of a people and the cultural matrix within which it is set. What is the "primitive" in art? they persisted to ask. What is the comparative primitiveness of symbolic as against representational art styles? Of decorative as against "pure" art forms? What is the role of the artist amongst a non-literate people? What is the artist's own attitude toward his work? How does his group's participation in his art influence the primitive artist? Does the genius of the individual succeed in breaking through the mould of tradition? To what extent is felicitous grouping of form and mass haphazard? To what extent is it objective, devoid of psychological or magico-religious implications?

Most of these questions have yet to be answered, but it has become clear to many students of art that they can never be answered by means of an objective consideration of art objects alone, for the resulting commentary is but made in terms of our own psychological and æsthetic idiom. It is becoming more and more widely felt that students of art, in order fully to evaluate an art form, must go to the people who create it, so that the art may be seen in its cultural setting, and insight may be gained into the inner significances of that art form in the life of the society where it is found. That there is such inner significance for primitive peoples in their art, those who have had work in the field among Indians, Africans, or South Sea Islanders will emphasize.

Let us restate this in another way. In our own society the psychological setting, or, for that matter, the entire cultural setting of any given work of art is in the majority of cases implicit. A painting of a Madonna and Child, or a bust of Minerva, a prize-fight by Bellows, or a dancer by Degas needs no particular elaboration of its setting, but in discussing an African piece of woodcarving, it is of value to know that the rigid angle of arms and knees in the modelled figure is not felicitous distortion, but the realistic treatment of the figure of a dancer in many of the traditional dances.

I

The discussion which follows concerns the art of the Bush-Negroes of the Dutch colony of Suriname, in South America. These people may be said to have evolved an art form that, in many respects, may be considered to be a new one, for the Africanists who have seen the specimens to be described could not identify them with the art products of any definite area, though, to be sure, parallels in detail may be found on the West Coast of Africa, and particularly in the

Kingdom of Ashanti, among certain Nigerian tribes, and the Benin bronzes.

The tools of the Bush-Negro are few. He uses a small knife, of the type of a small kitchen knife, and his machete, which serves him equally in felling trees, hollowing out the trunks of massive logs for his dugouts, clearing the jungle, building his houses, cutting his nails, and picking his teeth. The fine polished surface he achieves principally by the use of sand, while the artist who desires to darken an object carved of a lighter wood will use palm oil and smoke to attain his end. The Bush-Negro knows the compass and dividers, which his ancestors learned to use during their slave days in the colony, and which the African does not utilize. A wealth of detail is lavished on their combs, which are not used as hair ornaments, but for actual hair combing, and the same exuberance of design may be noted in the decoration of the house front, whether of dwelling, or man's "treasure" house, and on stools, trays, food stirrers, and other kinds of utensils which these people ornament. As in Africa, the wood-carving is done by men only. *"Tembe no muye sundi,"* says the Bush-Negro tersely. "Wood-carving is not a woman's affair."

Woman, however, is not deprived of an opportunity to show her skill in ornamentation. It is she who decorates the calabash dishes, often with designs as striking as those which appear on the very fine stools; she cuts the trade cloth obtained from merchants of the distant city into African strip-weaving patterns, and she sees to the cicatrization of the young girls' bodies and faces in designs which follow in outline and symbolism some of those appearing on the wood-carvings.

What of the symbolism of the art of the Bush-Negro to which we have made reference?

Bush-Negro art may be said to be extremely stylized. Analysis of it is impossible without the assistance of the natives, and the natives have an engaging way of evading the questions of the investigator when appealed to for the meanings of the carvings. Some of this evasion may be traced to the African's love of strategy though, in the main, there is a more direct factor. These carvings given to women by men have a sex symbolism which dominates most of the art, and, since this symbolism is related to the concept of fertility not alone of the women, but also of the fields and of the forest and the game animals which inhabit it, it is dangerous to offend the spirits by speaking too freely of these matters.

Whatever the psychological motives, the Bush-Negro is ingenious in eluding his questioner. He will say that the carving is of wood; he will name the wood it is made of; he will say it is beautiful; that it is an "in and out" design; he will say it is carpentry, or that it is done with a knife, or that it is decoration, to name a few of the recurrent answers. The fact is that we were entirely unsuccessful in obtaining a single explanation of design during our first visit to these people, and we count it sheer good fortune that brought to our camp early during our second expedition a young man with one of the crudest stools we had seen on the river. We bought the stool and it is from him that we learned enough to guide our future questioning.

The description of the pieces figured in this article must, in the nature of the case, be brief, but we will attempt to give something of the background of these people wherever a knowledge of it will contribute towards a fuller understanding of the pieces illustrated, and the art as a whole.

II

The Bush-Negroes of Dutch Guiana whose art, for two summers, it has been our privilege to study[1] are the descendants of escaped slaves, who as early as 1650 began running away into the jungle behind the coastal region, and who, having remained faithful to their African traditions, present the unique phenomenon of an autonomous civilization of one continent—Africa—transplanted to another—South America. Life in the interior of Dutch Guiana is difficult. It yields little more than bare sustenance, which, in the main, means that in good years there is enough to eat, while in bad years, the natives know hunger. But the meagerness of their material existence is more than balanced by the complexity of their social organization, their intricate religious life, and their deep æsthetic response, as it is manifested in song, dance, and the art-forms to be described here.

In the Bush-Negro village the native men carve boat and paddle, door-frame and house posts, mortar and pestle, comb and clothes-beater, food-stirrer and tray and peanut pounding board, drums and gods, while the women, as we have mentioned, incise designs on gourds, and sew their picturesque cloths. Indeed, this love of ornamentation may be said to be an outstanding aspect of the civilization of the Bush-Negro. It is, of course, true among these Negroes, as it is among ourselves, that artistic excellence is not achieved by all those who attempt artistic production. For example, every Bush-Negro man must know how to carve, for among the gifts which he must be prepared to make the woman whom he seeks to marry are the articles

[1] Our field trips, the Northwestern University Expeditions for the study of the Negro, were made possible by the generous support of Dr. Elsie Clews Parsons to whom it is a pleasure to here acknowledge our gratitude.

we have enumerated, and the amount of skill in beautifying them with his designs will influence appreciably the extent to which he will be acceptable as a suitor to the most desirable of the young girls. For such a girl must be wooed not alone with anklets and cloths, but with many carved pieces whose artistry will make her the more envied in her village.

The natives have undoubted standards of artistic merit. An impressive comment on this point is the manner in which they came to our camp to view the pieces we had collected. Their critical examination of the pieces, and their enthusiasm for rare ones differed in no important detail from the behavior of an art connoisseur in our own culture before a work of art of excellence. Perhaps as fine a piece of carving as is found among these people is the peanut pounding board figured and described in these pages. It was acquired from a woman who lived in the village of the chief of the tribe, far in the interior. The board was hanging on the outside of the hut obviously there to be admired. While she was pleased at our proposal to buy it, and flattered by the valuation we set upon it, it proved to be difficult to induce her to part with it. It took many hours of tactful bidding, and a family council, to break down the woman's resistance. She loved it; it was beautiful; she could do without the several pangis (cloths) the money we offered for it would buy, she had continued to repeat.

This woman's attitude was by no means exceptional, as the following incident, which may serve to throw light on another aspect of the Bush-Negro's attitude towards the art of his people, shows. The carvings are not made to be sold. Near the railhead, however, some of the natives have discovered that there is some demand for their woodcarving in the city, and this production has lowered the quality of the work. At the village of Kadju we were shown these market carvings, and when we rejected them, and went into a hut and came out with several well carved old pieces, we heard a murmur, and then the voiced comment of an old native, "They want carving, not timber!"

III

A Bush-Negro village, as one enters it after tramping up a path from the river, presents to the eye a clean sandy clearing about which houses are grouped much as appears in the opening illustration. The larger huts are for dwelling purposes, while the very small ones shelter shrines to various spirits, or house communal fetishes. The dwellings are made of palm fronds woven so as to make a pleasing design. The decorative emphasis, however, is given to the door-frame. The one which is shown is not only an unusually good example of the structure of this frame, but it is noteworthy because it affords us one of the clearest examples of the survival and adaptation of the West African mask. In the center of the cross-piece above the door is a human head, and in the outlines surrounding the head the artist gives the conventionalization of a woman's body. The studded design is achieved by brass nails acquired in trade, and represents the cicatrized patterns on body and face.

The trays figured measure about thirty inches in diameter, and are used for carrying produce from the field to the village, and for winnowing rice. The carving is often done on both sides, but it is the inner surface which receives the more elaborate treatment. The one first illustrated represents two human couples and a pair of twins. The balance achieved by the artist in utilizing his surface is particularly interesting, as is the breaking up of the outer rim, but it is not so much our purpose here to point out to the reader the effectiveness of the art of the Bush-Negro, as to analyze the pieces as the Bush-Negro himself sees them, believing that the objects themselves make the former point. The design is symmetrical, and each half of the tray holds a *"manu ko muye"* (man and woman) figure, so stylized that only the limbs are shown. The two smaller outlines near the center of the outer rim, facing each other, represent the male and female child to be born of the matings, and the Bush-Negro artist has distinguished the male child by repeating the line of the inner design of one of the symbols for the children. The breaking up of the rim is also an integral part of the symbolism, for the sections containing the alternating squares represent the hair of the two women, while the cross-hatching represents the hair of the children. To synthesize the symbolism of this and succeeding specimens, we must call attention again to the importance of the concept of fertility among these people —a concept which makes twins the object of worship. We must also refer in passing to their belief in sympathetic magic which makes the portrayal of these symbols of fertility significant to the Bush-Negro. This tray was collected from a village about one day's travel by corial above the railroad.

The tray which follows was acquired at a village about ten days' travel farther in the interior, and is given here to show the essential unity of the culture and its art. Although so much richer in detail, the symbolism is relatively the same, the chief difference being that of more realistic treatment of the two female figures, which are shown with head, arms and body. We found the brass-headed nails, as seen here, consistently used to a greater extent in the deep interior. On the

Baikutu, Upper Suriname River, Dutch Guiana

Carved Door-Frame, Manlobbi, Upper Suriname River

Village God

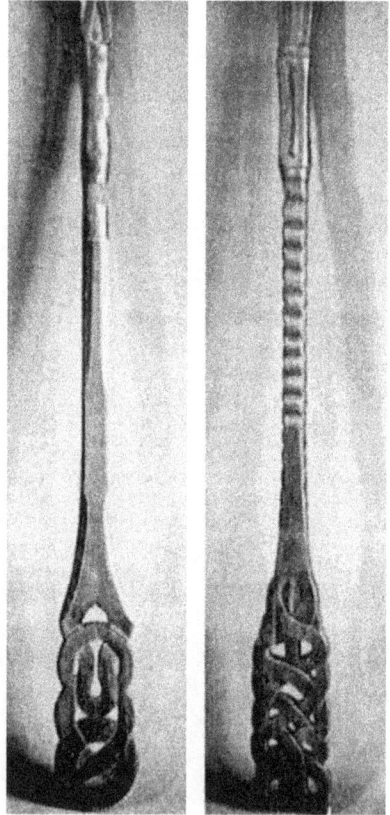

Canoe Paddles, Saramacca Tribe

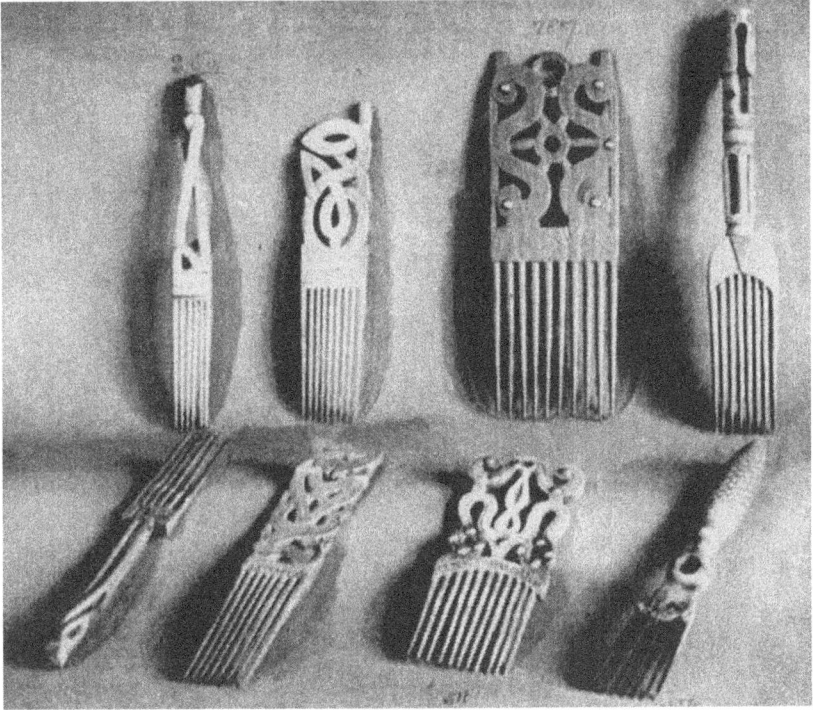

Bush-Negro Combs

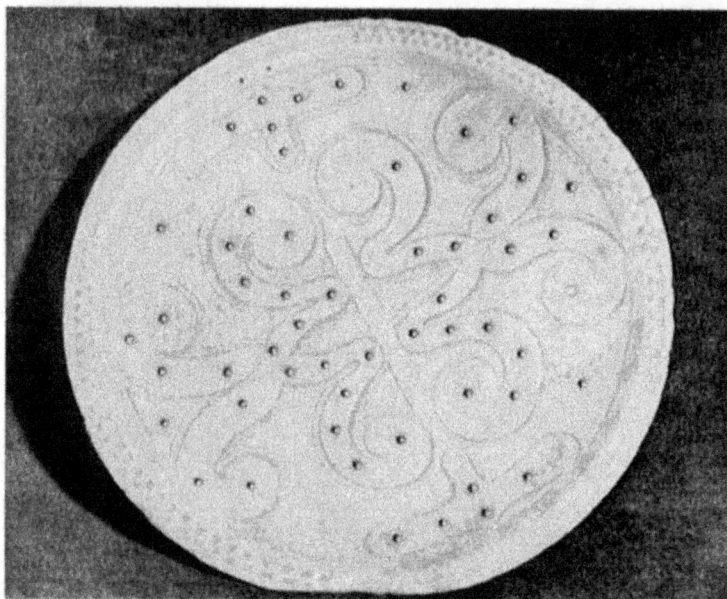

THYLLI RAMMING

Carved Tray, Saramacca Tribe

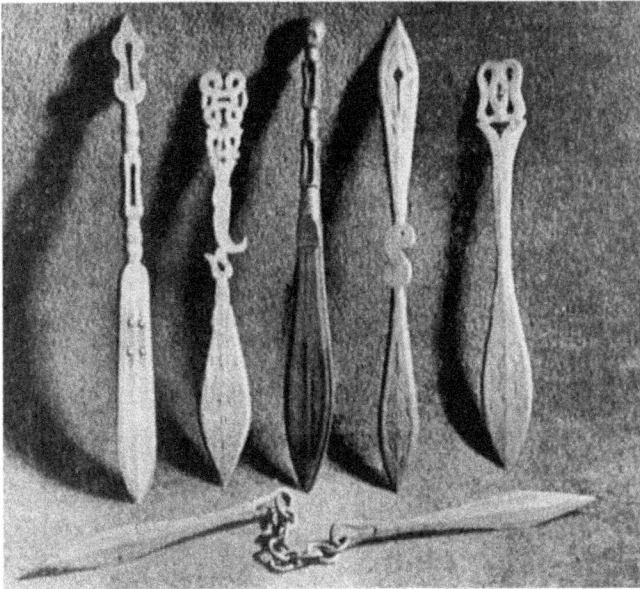

Bush-Negro Carved Food-Stirrers

Woodcarvings, Saramacca Tribe

JOHN D. JONES

Carved Wooden Tray, Saramacca Tribe

ROBERT BUCHBINDER

Peanut-Pounding Board, Saramacca Tribe

Bush-Negro Carved Stools

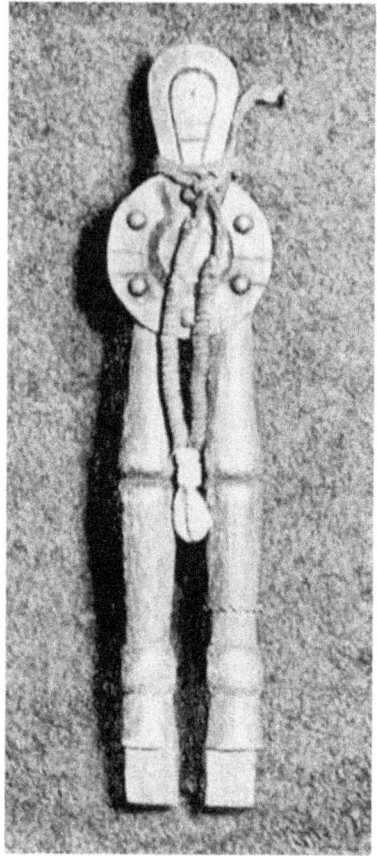

THYLLI RAMMING

Fetich against Evil Eye

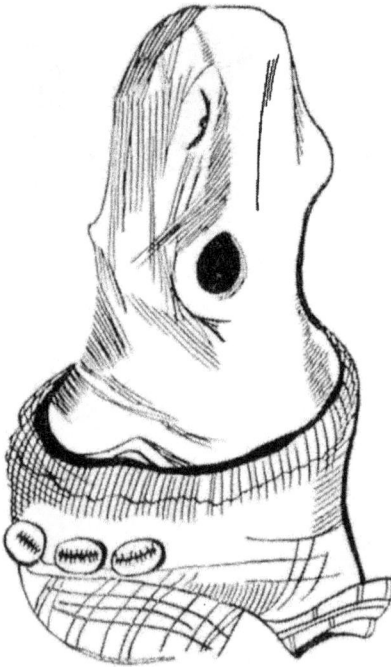

"Kromanti Mama," Guard of
Saramacca Secret Society

surface this appears to be an anomaly, since the African knowledge of the working of metals has been completely lost by the Negroes in the Suriname bush. Why is it then that on the lower river there is less use of these nails? The answers appear to be that the use of nails is the survival of the African ornamentation of woodwork with iron, and where the African elements have been most faithfully retained, we find the use of metal on the carvings.

The third tray is figured to give some concept of the manner in which the artist plays with his technique, and to show that primitive man also knows how to ignore function when he plays with form, for trays, as has been mentioned, have two functions; they serve for carrying produce from the provision grounds, and for winnowing rice, after it had been pounded in the mortar. Obviously this last tray is useless for winnowing. The carver in his abandon has here gone to extremes in demonstrating his craftsmanship, and the way in which this craftsmanship was admired by the natives down the river who saw it was striking. The symbolism is involved, but, in the main, the tray may be said to represent the heads of eight women, whose common womb contained in the inner inlaid square is penetrated by representations of the male symbol.

In the foreground of the same illustration is a clothes-beater. It is carved out of hard wood and is about two inches thick at the base, tapering to its rounded end some eighteen inches removed. The body of the instrument represents a male *Vodu* god—one type of snake which is sacred to these people—and the handle is that of a female. The decorative circles are made by a process generally called "poker work" which is extensively used in Africa. The use of the brass nails on the body of the snake deserves comment, for, since this studding with nails represents to the native the cicatrization of the body, it becomes evident that the intention is to give the snake human attributes.

The comb in the same illustration is one of a large series we collected, for combs and food-stirring paddles are the two most common objects carved. This comb, measuring about eighteen inches in height, is unusually large, although larger ones are met with occasionally. The average size, however, is from eight to ten inches. Again the symbolism is that of man and woman, but this time the man is more fully represented, the outer border representing his head-dress, the center cross-hatching his body cicatrization, while the lower cross-hatching represents the ornamented stool upon which the woman is seated.

In the photograph of combs, from left to right, in the background, are first a realistic representation of the human form, then a con-

ventionalization of the snake, while in the cross-piece above the tines
of the third, a stylized coffin with the characteristic "coffin-eye," which
appears on every coffin, may be seen.

IV

The next illustration figures food-stirring implements. Since it is
not possible to trace here the probable African provenience of this art,
we will not discuss the stylistic differences between the two Bush-
Negro tribes, the Saramacca and the Auka peoples, whose work is
represented. The symbolism remains basically the same. Attention may
be called to the center paddle, the handle of which ends in a recognizable human head.* This is modeled in the round, and resembles
more nearly than any other piece collected by us, the treatment of the
head in certain regions of West Africa. The paddle to its left, elaborately carved, is from the Auka tribe, figuring on handle and blade
two women, a snake and four birds. The pair of chained paddles in
the foreground present a technical *tour de force,* for both paddles
and chain are carved out of one piece of wood, and when it is considered that the delicate "lizard's tooth" design has been done with
the same crude knife, their beauty is the more to be admired.

The stools among these people are principally of three types, the
crescential, resembling in shape the Ashanti stools of West Africa, the
oblong, and the circular stool. The decorative and symbolic emphasis
may be associated or not, may appear on top, or sides, or both. The
stools in ordinary use are often but little decorated, sometimes having
only the emblems of the clan graven on the sides, or at times some
sacred symbol of inlaid wood on top, as in the case of the ones used
at council meetings, or the yet plainer stools used about the house
and village.

In the illustration, one bench rests upon the other, and these have
been placed as they are to be seen, for example, in the council house
of the chief of the tribe. These more highly ornamented stools are
but little used, and so placed as to be admired for their craftsmanship,
and to exert whatever magic powers they have been endowed with.
The crescential stools are to be distinguished from the others in several
respects. They represent the most readily identifiable West African
form of stool, are invariably carved out of a single block of wood,
and are least decorated. The natives call them *libba bangi*—moon, or
high stools, but we have been unable to establish ceremonial use for
them.

* Compare this representation of a human head with that in plates 14 and 15
in Carl Einstein's "Neger-plastik."

The two stools in the center are an example of the most favored general design. The natives call it *"pau-pau-dindu,"*—wood within wood. This design both in bas-relief, as in the lower stool, and in full relief as in the upper one is to be found on paddles, and house fronts, on trays and stools, and, in fact, on all objects which the Bush-Negro decorates, and it is perhaps owing to this intertwining of line that so frequently the casual observer will ascribe all the designs to snake worship. In some instances, this interpretation is correct. The upper stool, for example, contains two representations, male and female, of what the natives call *"gran-tetei,"* the great boa constrictor. The side of the lower stool, however, figures four headless human forms with their bodies intertwined. The circular stool shows in the carved design of the top the sacred *Vodu* snake realistically treated.

We have already spoken of the difficulty with which the peanut-pounding board, which is figured, was obtained. We have mentioned the feeling for its beauty which the natives everywhere on the river showed. But perhaps another reason why the woman who owned it was so loath to part with it was its symbolism. The piece itself is of a reddish brown wood, with purple-heart inlay. The handle and upper decorated portion represent a female bird which the natives term *"auko,"*—the English equivalent for which we do not know,—and a man. The bird is visualized as human, for while the wings are at once apparent, the artist has conceived her as possessing hair on her head, and human breasts. As is so often the case, the man is represented merely by the male symbol. It is also interesting that the artist has conceived the bird's thighs as cicatrized, this being indicated by the cross-hatching. Below the unornamented space are a male snake and a woman. Here the usual pattern is ignored, for the snake is fully represented, while, of the woman, we have only those portions of the body which have to do with reproduction. In addition, the new moon, a symbol of fertility, is present.

One of the most important factors of the Bush-Negro's existence is the river. The Bush-Negro worships it for its beauty and its terror. The name of the spirit which actuates it will never be spoken by the native while in a boat, except in prayer, when the euphemism "Mother of the River" or "Great Ancestress" is employed. Like all of the South American rivers, the rapids in it are many and dangerous. Yet it is to these rapids the Bush-Negro owes his freedom, and he has built his villages each above a dangerous passage. The river is navigated in heavy dugout canoes, and everyone,—man, woman, or even a very young child,—is at home in them. We illustrate here two paddles, both of which are carved out of hardwood, brown-heart in the instance of the one to the right. The blade, which could not be shown, is of the same shape as that of the food-stirrers. The one to the left is a man's paddle, the other a woman's. The familiar motif of man and woman appears in both, and the female figure in the woman's paddle is again treated in detail. The name for the chain-like portion of the handle is called by the natives, "*Moni moro muye*," "Wealth is more than woman," and shows that the native artist does not despise humor.

Many students of art have remarked on the difference between the styles of secular and religious art. The magico-religious elements in the Bush-Negro wood-carving have already been mentioned in the discussion of the pieces we have figured, although none of them is primarily religious, and all are in everyday use. Yet the Bush-Negro does have a sacred art, distinguished by its striking crudity of technique when compared with the craftsmanship of the pieces heretofore described. Not many examples of village gods and other sacred objects could be obtained, for the reason that when a village fetish such as the larger one figured here is set up, it may not be removed. (It is left to decay, for it is conceived by the Bush-Negro to be the potential habitat of the spirit to which it is dedicated, and to remove it would mean to expel the beneficent spirit from the village, and lose to its inhabitants the protection it affords them against invading evil.

Indeed, the *obiaman* (priest) who consented to make this new figure for us, came to us, ill, a few days after he had turned it over to us. He explained that his spirit had taken offense at his deed, and was plaguing him. Only after we had given him our assurance that the figure would be placed in a great house where white men might come and respectfully look at it, did we allay his fears, and the next day he came back, once more well, telling us that our assurances had satisfied the deity. The crude anthropomorphic figure which we show is about thirty inches high, and is heavily coated with a white clay, which these people hold sacred. About the neck is a charm, and it is in this that the power resides, for it must not be felt that this figure is itself worshipped, or that it is anything more to the native himself than a repository of magic strength. The fibre about the body of the figure is the grass skirt worn by priests in certain especially sacred and esoteric rituals. The small figure at the left is a personal fetish, and was given to us by the owner to put up over our outer door to render impotent the evil which might enter with an ill-intentioned visitor.

Figures of the type just discussed are to be seen in any village, but the figure pictured in our next illustration may be looked upon only by members of what we believe to be the warriors' secret society, and our native friends who made its acquisition possible assured us that no one outside the tribe even knew of its existence. It illustrates an entirely different medium, for it is modelled out of the sacred clay. It represents the Kromanti guardian spirit. In the secret houses of the Kromanti group, the inside of which we were not permitted to see, though we had been allowed to enter the closed shrines to the gods, it rests on a stool, not elaborately carved, but heavily covered with the same sacred white clay. The figure, which is called *"Kromanti Mama,"* —mother of the Kromantis—has a bit of cloth about it to represent the native woman's *pangi* (skirt), while about its breasts is an iron armlet decorated with white clay in which are embedded a number of cowrie shells. This figurine, as it rests on the bench, has modelled about it a realistic snake, also in the same medium. The native belief holds that when danger threatens, the figure, magically sensing it, transmits the alarm to the snake, which thereupon turns the color of blood and thus warns the members of the Society.

v

Bush-Negro art in all its ramifications is, in the final analysis, Bush-Negro life, and a more intensive study of Bush-Negro art may well serve to cast some light on the more fundamental problems of the processes of culture and cultural survivals and adaptations. What has made for the vigor of the Bush-Negro's civilization? What is it that has made for the flourishing of the Bush-Negro's art in his South American isolation? The question is one we do not pretend to be able to answer. Yet, when we reflect that the slave owned or had access to few material possessions, that escape from his master was perilous, that for tools with which to build his bush civilization he had practically only his machete, so that he may be said to have wrested his livelihood from the jungle with his bare hands, is it not astonishing that he should have found the psychic need for these painstaking and beautiful carvings, and the leisure to satisfy that need in an existence which allowed so little leisure?

What of the art style itself? To what extent is it unique and indigenous? What African elements have been retained? What of the influences of the Portuguese and English and Dutch in this art? These are some of the questions that must be added to those already posed, for much further study is needed both in Africa and in Suriname. But whether this art represents a new art form, or is a faithful record of a type of African art which had become decadent in the country of its origin; whether it has been perpetuated by the passion of the slave ancestors for freedom which to them was synonymous with African magic and tradition, or by the vision of individual genius, no student living among these people can fail to recognize that the thriving Bush-Negro civilization owes its vitality to survivals such as these.

What Has Africa Given America?

On the basis of our present knowledge, what can we trace in the complex pattern of our American cultural fabric to African influences? Can we find anything African not only in our music and our speech . . . but also in such aspects of our culture as our manners, cooking, religious expression?

❋   ❋   ❋

It has long been understood that contacts between groups representing different customs, practices and beliefs result in mutual borrowings. In the instance of contacts with Negroes in the United States, however, this principle is either blandly overlooked or emotionally denied. Why is the proposition that the Negro contributed nothing of his aboriginal African heritage to American life so firmly rooted in American thought? The answer is not difficult to find, if it be sought in terms of those social and economic forces that lodge deep in the historical past of our country; and, more directly, in the institution of slavery, within which the slaves were marked off from the rest of the population not alone by social status, but by a striking difference in skin color. With this in mind, we can understand why it is generally believed that the Africans brought to this country had neither innate capabilities nor cultural endowments that they could transmit to their white masters.

An impartial investigation of the facts, however, will show, first, that those who were brought not only to the United States, but to the much larger area in the New World where Negro slavery prevailed, came preponderantly from regions of West Africa where the high and complex civilizations of the continent are found; that, therefore, they brought with them a culture that provided much they might offer in exchange for the European tradition of their masters. And in the second place, those Negroes who were enslaved constituted at least an adequate cross-section of the human resources of the region from which they were taken. Indeed it is quite possible that they represented more than the expected proportion of those from the upper end of the scale. Is it not possible that the enslaved New World Negroes had cultural traits of their own that were handed on to their masters?

If this is the case, it should be possible to find that Africanisms, in however modified a form, are present in at least some aspects of the life of the predominant white population of this country. It must be evident from what has been said above that this field is one as yet largely unexplored, though even such a preliminary review of the evidence as I have been able to make has disclosed some suggestive material for more intensive study. The task presents large difficulties, however. Thus, to trace Africanisms in the behavior of American Negroes, let alone of American whites, comparison with the customs of the Negroes of the Caribbean must be made before we can think of correlation with the complexities of West African civilizations. As a result, in attempting to indicate certain phases of our culture that are marked by Africanisms, it is essential that the mutations undergone by these traditions be kept in mind. On the basis of our present knowledge, what can we trace in the complex pattern of our American cultural fabric to African influences? Can we find anything African not only in our music and our speech, where this element has sometimes been felt to be present, but also in such aspects of our culture as our "manners," cooking, religious expression?

Two distinct types of American music generally recognized as Negro are the spirituals and jazz, though to admit they are of Negro derivation does not necessarily mean that they are African. This, indeed, has been denied most strongly in the case of the spirituals, which, while held to be the product of the Negro's musical gift, are claimed merely to be songs based on themes learned from the white masters. I myself, some years ago, accepted the propositions that the element of syncopation, a trite African rhythmic form, in the spirituals has been inspired by the "Scotch snap"; that part singing is unknown to primitive Africans; that the pentatonic scale is Celtic, not Negro; and that major-and-minor singing is entirely foreign to Africa.

Since that time, field work has shown me that these conclusions do not hold. The Ashanti who sang into my recording phonograph could not refrain from part singing, while I have heard and recorded many songs in the minor key in Dahomey, in some of which the pentatonic scale was regularly employed. It is impossible to speak of "an" African music, just as it is impossible to speak of "an" African language. There are as many musical idioms as there are dialects, and more, for each culture has various forms of song. Some of those songs, among certain West African tribes, sound not at all unlike spirituals, even though our spirituals have become so refined and over-refined as they are sung in the concert hall or white churches that the difficulty in recognizing their parentage is quite understandable.

We are prone to overlook the important fact that the spirituals comprise only a small portion of American Negro music. Even religious music itself varies strikingly; those who have heard Negroes sing in some of the "shouting" churches will understand how different from the spiritual, as conventionally conceived, these songs can be. In addition, there are work songs and songs of derision, love songs and dance songs. It is these less known forms of music that have come down into American life as jazz, rather than the spirituals; it is in their rhythms, their melodic progressions, their seeming cacophonies, that we must look for the heritage that has been given musical America by the Africans who sang and, singing, inspired those to whom their song eventually passed down.

One need only play phonograph records of African music to a group of young people of dancing age—to a class of college students, let us say—and watch their unconscious bodily movements and the expressions on their faces, or listen to their comments after the record is finished, and contrast with this the manner in which they react to another primitive musical idiom—such as that of the American Indian—to realize that the latter is entirely foreign to them, while the African song is received with the recognition that is accorded something pleasurably familiar. Jazz is uniquely American, as anyone can testify who has heard a group of French or British or German musicians trying to play it—but in its derivation and its spirit it is African. And by the same token, those experiments in "serious" music that have attempted to utilize this form owe their inspiration, all unknowingly and unadmittedly, to the African sources from which this "American" musical form came.

Certain aspects of American speech, particularly the pronunciation of English by Southerners, whether Negro or white, must also be referred to Africa. This fact, like the provenience of the spirituals, has been asserted by some, but, as with the spirituals, recent thought has swung away from such an explanation. Southern speech is now most generally accounted for by reference to the various dialects of English that were current during Elizabethan and post-Elizabethan times. Quite aside from the difficulties present in attempting to reconstruct the pronunciation of English dialects of that period, the logic of the explanations put forward to bolster the validity of this hypothesis fails to carry conviction. Thus, it is pointed out that there are a variety of southern dialects, and that this precludes any acceptance of an "African" origin of these modes of pronunciation. Yet a person unskilled in differentiating a Virginian from a Georgian accent would have no difficulty in distinguishing the speech of either from that of a New Englander, though New England speech is derived from types of English pronunciation not too dissimilar to that which marked the speech of the ancestors of present-day Southern whites. Furthermore, it cannot be overlooked that those who maintain the Elizabethan origin of Southern speech have had little or no contact, either at first hand or through an analysis of the published literature, with the structure and phonetics of the West African tongues.

In this case the argument runs something in this fashion: that the Negroes brought to the New World came from peoples having entirely different cultures and mutually unintelligible languages; that it was the policy of slave owners to separate the slaves who came from the same tribe; that the slaves, therefore, being unable to speak to each other, lost their aboriginal speech and adopted the language of their masters. Yet the first of these propositions shows lack of knowledge concerning the cultural and linguistic situation in West Africa, while to maintain the last indicates a high degree of linguistic naïveté. Actually, though each of the cultures and languages of West Africa displays a superficial individuality—I cannot here give the evidence that proves a preponderantly West African origin of New World Negroes —a closer study shows that underneath the surface dissimilarities there exists a basic resemblance. In the field of language this takes the form of mutually unintelligible dialects, which, however, have very similar structural and idiomatic organization; while the phonetics of all these tongues is about the same.

What happened, then, when the Negroes came to the New World? They learned new words—in English, Spanish, Portuguese or French —but they spoke these words with a West African pronunciation, and poured their new vocabulary into the mold of West African grammatical and idiomatic forms. And, having done this, many of them were entrusted with raising the children of their masters. From whom, then, did these white children learn to speak? Obviously from their Negro nurses, as many Southerners acknowledge.

Yet it is not only phonetically that Southern speech has been influenced by the Negro. It is trite to point out how "musical" is Southern speech. Cadenced more than any other American dialect, it may almost be said to have melodic line, and it is not insignificant in this connection that a basic aspect of West African speech is the presence of what linguists call "significant tone." This is a characteristic that we most frequently associate with Chinese, but it is true of many other languages, such as those of numerous American Indian tribes, and means that to pronounce a word—a phonetic combination—in different tonal registers gives it different meanings. In the United States, significant tone has not persisted, but its survival as modulation may well have given Southern speech its distinctive musical quality. There remains the matter of idiom, and certain survivals of African idioms can be detected in American speech. One example may make the point —that of the word "hot" used in the sense of "exciting." "Now you're getting hot!" someone says to a jazz player, never dreaming that he is repeating an African turn of phrase also found in Negro French.

Another distinctive quality in the life of the South is the important role assigned to the art of proper behavior. "Mind your manners" is a fundamental tenet there, and the graciousness of life in the South is due in no small measure to these values. Now it is indeed a commonplace that all peoples have their codes of behavior, and that, as population increases and allows of the development of a leisure class, these codes become more and more involved. Is there nevertheless something especially African here? It is, in all probability, more a matter of emphasis than anything else. We know that Africans place the greatest of emphasis on good manners; that proper behavior—in the sense of an ability to observe the minutiae of a code of politeness—is a first requirement in any social intercourse. It is an attitude seen in the tale of the Ashanti nobleman who committed suicide because he had been guilty of a breach of decorum; and in the fighting reaction of a Haitian when called "mal élevé," to use two extreme examples.

Respect for elders, the soft voice before one who is a power in his community, the excessive employment of terms of endearment or kinship in neighborly contacts—these partake of the essence of African behavior, and are familiar to us as elements in the Southern-white code of politeness. The forms themselves are in the main those of European derivation, and are particularly referable to the codes of chivalry. Yet again, it is the spirit of African politeness that has been borrowed, and, in this case as in that of speech, it has given a flavor to the specific social phenomenon so distinctive that it cannot be mistaken by those who have experienced African politeness in its native home.

As far as I know, no one has attempted to account for the distinction of the Southern cuisine. This development of a special series of dishes marks the cooking not only of the southern United States, but the Caribbean Islands as well. Of course, it may be objected that there is no such thing as a Southern cuisine—that the dishes of New Orleans are not those of Charleston. Yet fried chicken, like gumbo, or the extensive and particularized use of yams, okra, rice, is fairly general throughout the South; and even though one grants the differences in local cooking traditions, it must nevertheless be realized that the cuisine of Richmond is no more merely a modification and adaptation of that of England than the dishes served at New Orleans are those of France. Yet the ancestry of the master class in the first region is English, and in the second French.

It is instructive to compare the cooking of the southeastern United States with that of New England. Both these traditions are held by people—white people—of British descent. It is almost self-evident, however, that New England cooking is closer to the ancestral tradition than is that of Charleston or Savannah. May not the unknown element in the equation be the Negro? I can cite one case of a family whose cook, in slavery times, was for some reason incapacitated. They were forced to put a newly arrived slave girl, fresh from Africa, in the kitchen and found her cooking quite acceptable. This is not surprising to one who has visited Africa, learned something of West African cooking, and has seen the cooked foods for sale in every market. Cooking in deep fat is one of the most important African methods of preparing food, and fried foods are standard there. The very word "gumbo" is African in its origin. Of a similar character is the high seasoning found in most Southern cooking. The African and Caribbean Island Negro cook of a white visitor finds it difficult not to season his employer's food too highly, for even though it may seem insipid to him, there is still too much pepper in it. Hence once again, influence of an African tradition on at least certain regional aspects of American cooking should not be neglected, nor, in the extent to which these have spread, its general influence on American cuisine.

As a final instance, we may turn to the field of religious behavior, particularly to that of sects where worship through possession takes its more violent, unrestrained forms. Here it is important to ask how similar sects in Europe—if, indeed, they have any counterparts there —conduct their worship; for possession, as such, is a world-wide phenomenon. When the forms that possession takes in Europe are investigated, however, these socialized types of auto-hypnosis that characterize our American churches are found to be absent. In Europe possession is more personal, resulting from individual hallucination rather than from the group excitation superinduced by a monotony of rhythm and the exhortations of a preacher. On the other hand, numerous similarities are found between the services in Negro "shouting" churches and those of the white cults where possession occurs. Often the same sect includes white as well as Negro congregations; thus, the Church of God, most of whose members are Negro, has its headquarters in the North, and most of its leaders (though not its preachers) are white men.

When it is observed how similar is the behavior of the whites and Negroes in these hysterical sects, the problem once again poses itself —did the Negroes take their tradition from the whites, or did the whites borrow from the Negroes? Those who hold to the former position point out that white churches of this type exist in the West, or in the mountainous regions of the South, far from any Negro influence. They also point to the traditional camp meeting, with its hysterical forms of worship. Yet once more, one who is acquainted with the African forms of possession seen in Africa itself, and, no less, in the West Indies and in certain American Negro churches, and who recognizes the ease with which the diffusion of culture can take place, is led to ask why the possibility of worship of this type having come from the African side of the contact is left out of account.

In religious practices, therefore, as in those several secular aspects of life that have been mentioned, it would seem that reasonable indications of revamped survivals of African traditions are not lacking. Much further investigation along these lines is desirable, and necessary if we are to have an undistorted concept of the roots from which our culture has grown. Enough has been said to indicate that, in this country, both whites and Negroes took, both gave. Just how much was taken from the Negroes remains to be determined.

Some Next Steps in the Study of Negro Folklore*

A point today which is rarely considered, but which is pertinent to the study of Negro folklore, has to do with the difference between folklore as folk literature, and folklore as folk custom. The divergence between the two points of view implied in this distinction is fundamental.

*   *   *

The contributions of Elsie Clews Parsons to the study of Negro folklore are so extensive as to comprise, in themselves, the bulk of the available materials in this field; they are so important that no significant work can be done in the future without using them as a base. The volumes of folktales published over her signature, and the other materials that appeared as articles in this JOURNAL, and elsewhere, are the more notable since they represent one of the first applications of modern field method to the study of Negro folklore.

It is difficult, without going back through the files of the relevant

Journal of American Folklore, LVI, no. 219 (1943) 1–7.
* Because this paper is written while in the field, no citations to literature can be given.

journals, to realize today how fragmentary most of the earlier materials were, or, where they represented systematic work, how different the criteria employed from those now in common use. The tales themselves are principally abstracts; when given in full, sequence and dialect were frequently distorted. Moreover, even where Negro tales were carefully gathered and presented with due attention to dialect, they were rarely unselected. Animal tales predominated, with the result that Negro lore was, and still is, largely looked upon as the epitome of primitive naïveté.

That such approaches and such techniques no longer mark scholarly work in the field of Negro folklore is due in very considerable measure to the influence of Parsons. The principle of collecting tales without selection based on preconceived categories, which she introduced into the study of Negro lore, is today universally accepted; that the story should be set down as narrated insofar as this is possible, is another commonplace of present procedure. Careful notation of time and place of collecting and, where feasible, the name of the storyteller and such facts about him as indicate his competence are today accepted by students as normal practice. The application of the catch-phrase to the presentation of Negro tales was a further methodological advance, which even today is not used as much as it might profitably be, despite its demonstrated usefulness to students in the comparative analysis of folktales from other peoples, notably the North American Indians.

An important aspect of Parsons' work in the field of Negro folklore was the conceptual framework she held—an aspect not often recognized, since it was rarely stated explicitly in her publications. The anthropological point of view dominated her research. The study of folklore was for her important always in terms of the larger problems of cultural form and cultural dynamics. Negro lore was of special and specific significance to her because, as she phrased it in conversation, it permitted the study of diffusion in process. And since she held that in working with scientific materials conclusions could be regarded as valid only when based on rigorously controlled data, it followed that the conventions of field-method and form of publication outlined above developed as an integral part of her approach.

To these conventions then, we owe the tales, proverbs, and riddles collected by Parsons in the Sea Islands, Georgia and other regions in the south of the United States; from the Bahama Islands; among the Cape Verde folk who migrated to the New World; and, finally, her most recently published work in the field, on the folklore of the Antilles—two volumes of data in print, the third, which includes abstracts, bibliographic data and comparative analyses, now in press. To this body of Parsons' own work, we must also add the collections from

Nova Scotia and Santo Domingo, from Dutch Guiana and West Africa, gathered with her encouragement and support. If to these materials we further add those other collections of scholarly significance made in the United States, Jamaica, Haiti, the Virgin Islands, Brazil, and West and Central Africa, we have almost the entire tale of our present resources in Negro folklore.

What, may we ask, are some of the next steps to be taken in the study of this field that will carry forward the work already done? Phrased in terms of the most urgent needs of the field, they are as follows:

1) The need for definitions in organizing and orienting field research;

2) The need for additional data, especially from certain key areas;

3) The need for a re-analysis of existing materials on the basis of underlying similarities and regional differences;

4) The need to understand more fully the social setting of the tales.

The need for definitions is peculiarly pressing in the study of Negro folklore, though it exists as well in other divisions of the total field. For while it is understandable why folklorists, in recent years, have been so largely occupied with gathering and organizing data, it is, nevertheless, to be deplored that discussions of ultimate aims in the study of folklore, or attempts to define more sharply the terminology employed, are so generally lacking. We have but to page through files of any folklore journal, contrasting the amount of space devoted to data with that given over to theory to realize the extent to which this is true. Folklorists have their own convictions as to why they are concerned with making their collections, or their comparative analyses, and any folklorist can explain the meaning of the terms he uses. But these matters are rarely made explicit, either in books, in folklore journals, or at the meetings of professional societies of folklorists.

A point today which is rarely considered, but which is pertinent to the study of Negro folklore, has to do with the difference between folklore as folk literature, and folklore as folk custom. The divergence between the two points of view implied in this distinction, is fundamental and, if probed, goes far to explain why some groups of folklorists understand with difficulty what other groups of equal professional competence are about, and why. For these differing points of view reflect divergences in method no less than in ultimate aims. How deeply they lodge can be grasped when it is recalled that they derive from the historical fact that, in the earliest days of the discipline, folklore was understood and defined almost exclusively as the study of survivals of earlier custom—survivals, that is, represented even more by the folk-beliefs and the folk traditions of such groups as the peasant populations of Europe than by their folktales, proverbs, riddles and songs.

With the development in recent times of research among non-literate peoples, and with more intensive study of these European peasant groups, it was increasingly apparent that to draw a distinction between the literary aspects of folk life and other manifestations of the culture of a people was essential. Thus there was worked out the distinction between folk literature, accepted today by the majority of professional folklorists as the special field of folklore; and ethnography, the study of custom, whether among nonliterate folk of the far reaches of the earth or among groups who, because of historical factors, had in Europe and the Americas developed characteristic ways of cultural behavior.

In the instance of research among African peoples, this distinction has been accepted as a truism. There, as with any nonliterate group, the methodological problem is that of studying all the various aspects of the culture, and it follows that collections of African tales, proverbs, riddles and songs are normally regarded as falling within the field of folklore, as against other aspects of the lives of these people, which are studied as ethnography. In the New World, however, the situation is quite different. Here, except in a few regions such as the interior of Dutch Guiana, the Negroes merely constitute more or less well differentiated groups in general populations, where conventions of behavior are more or less in accord with overall patterns. Such divergences as the Negro groups exhibit can thus properly be regarded as survivals of pre-American, African traditions.

With this historical factor before us, it is understandable why, in many parts of the New World, including the United States, Negro folklore has so often been regarded as incorporating the study of Negro custom no less than Negro folk literature. This approach has had two results, both of which have stood in the way of attaining the clarity essential to scientific investigation. In the first place, it has had the effect of emphasizing the study of folk custom to the neglect of folk literature. The tales, proverbs and riddles which in many regions are today the most purely African aspects of the life of the Negroes, have been put aside by students of the Negro for the study of other phases of Negro life more difficult of access and less amenable to identification and interpretation. Again, though this approach has provided materials of value for comparative analyses of New and Old World Negro custom, it has almost always carried with it the attitude that the survivals thus studied are in the nature of cultural curiosities. Yet modern ethnographic research has demonstrated that African survivals in the New World, whether these be folktales or other bodies of custom, are rarely cultural curiosities. The most valuable results obtained from the study of these materials has come from the fact that they are living, functioning realities in the lives of the people. Therefore any approach that evaluates them as cultural exotics distorts the findings—a point that can be richly documented with instances from many parts of the New World.

Thus, in brief, can be described the need in Negro studies to define more sharply the very word "folklore," in terms of the distinction between folk literature and folk custom. With this also goes the need to clarify the aims of folkloristic research in this field; the analysis of the various approaches used at the present time in terms of their applicability to the specific problems encountered by workers in this special area; and the sharpening of definitions, already more or less well agreed on, of such terms as "myth" and "folktale" in the light of the materials encountered in Africa and among New World Negroes. Since the mere posing of these questions should be sufficient to point out many of the problems implied, this can be expected at once to clarify objectives in terms of the planning and organization of future studies.

Though in this, as in other areas of folkloristic study, data can never be full enough, the field of Negro folklore is in especial need of additional materials from certain key areas. As with all other aspects of the comparative analysis of Negro cultures, folklore is useful here primarily for the study of cultural dynamics. The historic controls that are so important can be effectively applied, however, only to the extent that the data represent all regions from which New World Negroes were derived, and all the areas to which they were taken.

Despite the amount of materials in hand, the lacunae to be filled are large. In Africa itself, tales and other data from various tribal groups of Senegal, Sierra Leone, Liberia, the Ivory Coast, the Gold Coast, Dahomey and Nigeria have been published, as well as from inland peoples well to the north of the West Coast. Yet the materials, for many of these tribes, are only fragmentary, while the tribal coverage is decidedly spotty. Furthermore, many of the collections from these areas were gathered by the use of methods today held to be faulty— the tales are obviously selected, and are rarely more than abstracts. Certainly there are few tribes whose myths, tales, proverbs and riddles have been given anything approaching a representative sampling of the wide range of resources in folklore we know these people possess, with the consequence that while the data from this area are relatively good, actually a real need for much fuller collections exists.

This need is not as great, however, as it is in other parts of Africa, even if we limit our discussion here to those portions of the continent from which materials are required to make valid comparisons between the historically connected African and New World Negro folklore systems. From Nigeria southeastward, around the bend of the continent and into the Congo, existing collections are rare indeed. Except for one early group of stories published as a Memoir of this Society, journal articles giving two or three tales, or a few animal stories appended to a travel book, are the rule. An important collection of proverbs from the southeastern Congo is available, but of the tales, proverbs, riddles and songs of the numerous tribes in the Congo basin and in Angola, we have almost nothing.

In the New World, the collections of Parsons and other field workers provide data of a richness excelled only by the materials on the American Indian. These data make it possible to predict, with considerable confidence, what will be encountered elsewhere when future studies are undertaken. Prediction, however, is not verification, and these other studies are needed to test such hypotheses as that which holds for the tenaciousness of folklore under contact in comparison with other elements of culture; an hypothesis which, on the basis of facts already gathered among Negro groups, may prove to be of far wider applicability. Such collections will be most economically made in connection with the field study of other aspects of the lives of these folk, though if necessary they can be restricted to folklore, since such materials can profitably be studied as a unit, awaiting the time when it will be possible to analyze them in terms of their social setting.

The need for comparative data from Latin America is most pressing. Two collections, both restricted to animal tales, are all that exist for Brazil, except for a few volumes of stories for children which suggest opportunities for study, but do not offer materials of aid in solving problems of scientific folklore. Yet in Brazil, Negro folklore of all kinds is to be found in as rich assortment as anywhere in the New World—African myths, animal tales of the conventional kind, tales of human beings, proverbs and riddles, to say nothing of songs. The problem here, furthermore, calls for an intensive collecting program among the Indians, since Indian-Negro contact in certain regions has been great, and, in discussions of folklore, there has been a tendency *a priori* to ascribe Indian origins to Negro tales which appear to an Africanist as of African provenience. In Venezuela and Colombia and Peru, as well as in Central America, collections are needed for similar analyses of African survivals and Indian influences. Materials from British and French Guiana are desirable to compare with those from the islands of the Caribbean, and from Suriname, but such collections may await convenient opportunity. Additional data from Negroes of the United States, and from islands in the Caribbean not intensively studied are likewise desirable, though such data are indispensable only for the solution of points of detail.

It is as important to rework existing collections as it is to gather new materials. For the data in hand, whether collected in recent times in accordance with the techniques of modern scholarship, or earlier by more casual methods, can be made to yield far more information concerning fundamental similarities and regional differences in Negro folklore than they have thus far. For this, an adequate critical bibliography of Negro folklore is the first essential, and the second, a concordance of Negro folklore on the basis of this knowledge of the sources.

These older data at times prove to be surprisingly good. Selection rarely went so far that some tales of types other than those which constituted the basis of selection did not find their way into a collection. Close scrutiny of such materials can thus give the student hints of real value in planning future research, or in assessing the variation in the resources of a given area, or in suggesting comparisons that might otherwise be overlooked. Sometimes only two or three stories from an African tribe otherwise not represented in the literature, or from a New World area where no systematic collecting has been done, can confirm for the alert student the existence of relationships that could otherwise only be surmised.

Scattered materials of this kind, however, are not readily found, and it is to be doubted whether any worker in the field can unearth even an appreciable proportion of data in this category without adequate bibliographic aid. Certainly these materials have not been uncovered to any considerable degree in the course of investigations made while analyzing any particular collection thus far published—when, indeed, such bibliographic searches have been made at all. This is presumably why, in the field of Negro studies, so many published collections lack comparative references, and are offered as no more than raw, unworked source material.

Folklorists confronted with the task of finding comparative data are understandably appalled at the magnitude of the task. Short ethnographic papers in anthropological journals often carry a few tales as appendices, which in their totality bulk large. Articles in geographical and other journals, even in popular travel magazines, give many stories that can be used. When we turn to books, it is necessary to scrutinize almost all of the vast literature of African travel to insure adequate coverage of the field. In the New World, we are faced with a similar bibliographic problem. In the older travel reports, a tale, usually in an abstract, will creep into the text of an author's account of slave life, while even as concerns modern collections, it is suggestive to call to mind that the best collection of Negro stories from Brazil is to be found as an appendix to an annual report of an historical and geographical society.

At the present time, the only published bibliography is a general one on the Negro which allots to folklore only a short section; the titles listed there are the standard items that are, or should be, known to every professional folklorist even casually concerned with the field. Wieschhoff's bibliography of African ethnology, when published, will be of considerable aid, especially since it will provide a series of maps showing tribal locations, the inadequate knowledge of which has so often handicapped those who work with African data. But even in this bibliography, folklore is only incidental, while New World materials do not enter at all.

A bibliography of the type suggested would, as stated, be an essential first step in compiling a concordance of Negro folklore. Such a concordance would greatly accelerate the comparative study of existing and new materials in terms of such problems as the diffusion of motifs and plots within the African continent, their retention or change when carried to the New World, and the effect in this latter area of contact with non-Negro peoples. Here, again, a beginning has been made. Klipple's motif-index of African tales, developed along the lines of the standard general work of Thompson, in accordance with the principles of the Finnish school of folklorists, will be of great use. It is desirable, however, that this study be supplemented by the use of motif-designations that derive more directly from the folklore system which is being studied rather than from the more generalized orientations of the Finnish school; similar work will have to be carried on in the materials from the New World, as well as for both African and New World proverbs and riddles.

The social setting of folklore is of particular importance for the scientific analysis of materials from Negro societies. In Africa and among New World Negroes, the entire configuration of folktale telling —by whom certain tales are told, when they may be told, the formularies employed, the significance of the *double entendre* so characteristic of them, their association with divining and curing, the educational role of the tales—is so closely connected with the tales themselves that it must be thought of as an integral part of any collection. For comparative work, such information is as valuable as are the stories themselves, and the other materials more conventionally regarded as falling within the province of folklore. This is especially true when we are concerned with understanding the depth to which these patterns strike in the story-telling complex of Negro folk.

In illustration of this complex of beliefs the following may be cited.

In many parts of Africa and the New World, it is said, to tell stories in the daytime is dangerous because spirits of the dead will come and take away the soul of the teller. This, in turn, derives from the use of folktales during wakes, where the tales fulfill the role of amusing the dead. Under contact, this idea that tales are not to be told before nightfall is so tenacious that even where the historically valid reason has disappeared, it persists. The incident of the Afro-Brazilian nurse who refused to tell her young charge stories until it became dark is to the point. For, in this culture where tales are not commonly told at wakes, she feared that if she violated the traditional precept, she would grow a tail!

Such supplementary materials are as significant in understanding other aspects of Negro folklore—proverbs, riddles and songs—as they are of the stories. The essence of the proverb is the particular meaning it conveys among the people by whom it is used, and unless this meaning is analyzed in terms of the cultural setting out of which it grows, the value of the proverb for scientific study will be greatly lessened. It is a simple matter to record several hundred proverbs from almost any Negro group, and it does not require much time to collect them. But to answer whether, in two different cultures, proverbs that appear similar in phrasing are of the same connotation cannot be determined except with a knowledge of the meaning of the sayings in the cultures where they are employed. The same is true of riddles and, to an even greater degree, of the analysis and comparative study of songs, whether it be of their music or of their words.

As we see it, then, future steps in the study of Negro folklore should follow from the needs that have been discussed above. They are especially relevant in this field because of the kind of materials available in Negro societies, and the kind of problem susceptible to study on the basis of these materials. Other needs in this field could be named, but they are either not as urgent, or less practicable to include in a program of work, than those listed here. But it is safe to say that such a program, when achieved, will go far in making available the potential contributions of the field of Negro studies in folklore both to the study of folklore in general, and to our knowledge of human social behavior as a whole.

Drums and Drummers in Afrobrazilian Cult Life

Instruments that normally do not fall into the percussion group at all may be employed in it by the Afro-Bahians, for both religious and secular purposes. The guitar (Portuguese violão) is used thus more than any other instrument. In the cults termed "Caboclo," in which the so-called "Indian" deities are worshipped, a guitar, rattles, and calabashes often accompany the singing; the rhythms are strummed on the guitar in accordance with drumming patterns.

*   *   *

The patterns of musical training and the canons of musical competence in Afro-Brazilian society, as in other Afro-American and West African groups, make of the drummer the musician *par excellence*. Nothing better demonstrates the standing of the good drummer in the community than to observe him at public rituals. He moves about the scene, assured, confident, respected. His place, when he himself is not playing, is usually near the platform on which the drummers sit; and at a ceremony when the gods, in the persons of those possessed by them, greet and bless those among cult members and spectators whom they wish to favor, they invariably single him out. During intermissions, when the "gods" are being robed, he goes into the cult house, or stands about, chatting with friends or fellow musicians, until it is time to resume his place.

At the drums his manner radiates confidence, in himself and in the power of his instruments. Relaxed, the drum between his legs, he allows the complex rhythms to flow from his sure, agile fingers. It is he who brings on possession through his manipulation of these rhythmic intricacies, yet he himself never becomes possessed; though to one unfamiliar with the usages of this religion he often seems to be on the verge of possession. As the music becomes "hotter," he bends to his instrument; and the swelling volume of the chorus, the movements of the dancers, respond to the deep notes of the large drum, whose voice commands the gods themselves. Spectators may give their attention to

Music Quarterly (1944), XXX, no. 4, 477–92.

the dancers and listen to the singing; yet the drummer knows that, without him, the gods would not come and worship could not go on. He is the mainspring of the ritual, its focal point, and he bears himself as one fully conscious of his importance.

Investigation into this culture of African derivation, outside Africa, has provided materials that shed light particularly on the value of studying drums and drummers as elements of cult life. To be sure, the place of rhythm in African and New World Negro music has long been recognized, and we do have a certain amount of information concerning drum-types and the manner in which the instruments are made, as well as descriptions of how they are headed, and similar data; yet the cultural setting of this form of musical expression is rarely indicated, and we know almost nothing about the musicians themselves—their training, organization, and standards of performance.[1]

The facts here presented, bearing on these points, were obtained in Bahia, Brazil, in the course of research carried on during 1941–1942 in that city.[2] As in all West African cultures and their New World derivatives—Bahian Negro culture stems principally from Western Nigeria and Dahomey, and from the southwestern part of the Congo—religion is a primary point of cultural focus; and in this intricately organized aspect of life music bulks large. One objective of the research was the recording of Bahian Negro songs,[3] and this afforded an opportunity for close contact with certain of the more prominent Afro-Bahian drummers. Conversations about drums, drummers, and the rôle of music in this society, confirmed by first-hand observation, yielded a large part of the materials that will be considered.

It must be made clear that the music under discussion, which is associated with worship of the African gods, by no means represents the whole of Afro-Bahian music; for the place of song in all aspects of life is as important here as elsewhere among Negroes of the New World and in Africa itself. The *samba*, *batuque*, and *capoeira*, work songs, lullabies, and other forms, whether for solo voices or chorus, with or without percussion accompaniment, mark the daily round from childhood on. Yet the most consistent and integrated body of music this people possesses is undoubtedly that associated with the religion their ancestors brought from West Africa and the Congo.

This religious setting has received considerable attention.[4] The drums play their most important rôle in the public rites, which all persons may attend and at which large numbers gather to enjoy the dancing and listen to the songs that mark the coming of the gods "to the heads" of their devotees. They also figure in certain more private rituals. Rhythm is so important in African music that it is never absent; and there are many ways of marking it in addition to those that require drums. Handclapping suffices for most songs that accompany the sacrificial offerings given the gods in their shrines; while at death-rites a pottery jar struck with a doubled fire-fan and calabashes beaten with sticks are mandatory.

Instruments that normally do not fall into the percussion group at all may be employed in it by the Afro-Bahians, for both religious and secular purposes. The guitar (Portuguese, *violão*) is used thus more than any other instrument. In the cults termed "Caboclo," in which the so-called "Indian" deities are worshipped, a guitar, rattles, and calabashes often accompany the singing; the rhythms are strummed on the guitar in accordance with drumming patterns. At rituals of the Caboclo cult, one sometimes even encounters an ordinary jazz-band taking the place of the customary African-like percussion group. All this would seem to be of significance in suggesting why the guitar and banjo have attracted Negroes in the United States, as well as why the music of the Negro church, conserving aboriginal rhythmic patterns, should have slipped over readily into prevalent secular jazz and swing styles.

The most African use of percussion is in those cults termed Gêge, Ketu, and Jeshá. The first of these stems from the West African culture of Dahomey, the latter two from the Nago-speaking Yoruba folk of Nigeria. The second is at present the most important, and, while the other two have smaller followings now than in earlier years, they still function significantly. Moreover, being held in great respect by all cult members, they exert considerable influence on the cult life as a whole.

The membership of a cult group consists of priests and priestesses, initiates who have undergone specialized training, and associated members. Most of the initiates are women, though there also is an appreciable number of men in this category. Most men who are affiliated with the cult fall in the third class, and among them are those termed *ogans*; drummers may be *ogans* or initiates. Some drummers are closely identified with their own groups; others go from cult house to cult house, welcome in any if they are good players. Every house has a chief drummer, the principal *alabe*, who has a definite place in the hierarchy of officials that controls, to the last detail, the direction of cult affairs and assures ritual correctness in every step of the intricate ceremonial.

The public rituals—which is where drums are most in evidence—are held in large open or partially opened rooms, brilliantly lighted, centering about a rectangular dancing space. Spectators occupy bleacher-like seats on either side of this space, women separated from men. Those who cannot find seats peer through the windows or crowd about the open end of the rectangle when they are permitted to do this. At the center of the other end, opposite the door through which, in most cult houses, the gods and those they possess make their entrances and exits, is a small platform, often with a railing about it. Here the drummers sit, playing the rhythms that call the gods, bring on possession, control the choreography of the dance, and, at times, represent the voice of the god who is being worshipped.

This platform is the focal point of the action on the dance-floor. The priest in charge and his assistants, when they are not occupied in the shrines, sit on low stools at its side, and honored guests are given chairs as near it as space permits. The dancers face the drums except in the introductory section of the rite, when they circle about the dance-floor; and no one under possession may turn his back to the drums when dancing. A rhythm to which special importance is attributed welcomes the entrance of a distinguished visitor, who walks directly to the platform before greeting any persons present, acknowledging the honor by touching, with the tips of his fingers, the three drumheads and, on occasion, the iron gong. Any well known drummer is accorded this salute—it is his right, and must be given him.

The drums employed in the cult rituals are termed *hū* ("the largest"), *hūnpri* ("the medium-sized one"), and *le* ("the smallest"). For the Ketu and Gêge rhythms, played with sticks, the drums should be headed *de torno*, that is, with the head held in place and tuned by means of pegs, inserted in the body of the drum near the top. For the music of the Angola, Congo, and Caboclo cults, whose rhythms are produced with the hands, the heading is of the *cunha* type, in which the cords are attached half-way down the body of the drum to a skin-covered cord or hoop, held in place and tuned by wedges forced between it and the wood. This type of fastening withstands the heavier battering from the impact of the player's hand better than does the closer heading, which, when played by hand, tends to "soften" and lose pitch.[5]

The preferred material for the head of the large drum is deer-skin or calf-skin; for the other two, goat-hide. The skins of sacrificial animals are employed for this purpose, and the visitor to a cult house will frequently see skins pegged against the wall, drying. In at least one cult center, these skins when dry are kept in the room where the drummers have their paraphernalia, and the men appropriate them as opportunity offers and sell them. "Many's the skin I've swiped and sold," one

drummer, identified with this house, said with a laugh. A priest does
not sell surplus skins. Even so, he may run out of stock, and, if he
has none to head a drum himself, a friendly colleague may supply him
or he may have one bought at the market.

Once the drum is headed, the hair is shaved off the top, if it has
not already been removed from the entire skin. The head is moistened
to permit its being stretched to the proper degree of tautness; it can
be played as soon as it is dry. Drums are kept in a cool, dark room,
the heads relaxed. Palm-oil is rubbed into the skins, and they are
thoroughly aired before use, the pegs being tightened to attain the
desired pitch. The instruments are never placed in direct sunlight, however, since this is believed to damage the head.

Drums are called 'tabaques (or atabaques, the term usually encountered in the literature), and a set is called a terno, a "trio." They
are of the customary West African hollow-log type; but drums actually
made of hollowed logs are rare. Ordinarily staves are used, the drums
being made by a cooper. The cost varies with the size and kind of
wood used. Drums of patumujú or jaqueira, the preferred hardwoods,
are the most expensive; when they are made of a somewhat softer
wood and are slightly smaller, the prices are about one-half to two-
thirds lower; while the cheapest type, of even softer wood, costs still
less. The cooper is given part of the agreed price when the bargain
is struck, the balance when the purchaser comes to take the instruments, after he has checked for imperfections and seen to it that the
openings at the bottom are of the proper size. This is the most important single feature to be watched, since, if they are too large, the drums
will not give the proper sound—the smaller the opening, the greater
the volume.

Next, the drums are taken to a cabinet-maker or painter. Here a
point of particular interest arises; for, while all hollow-log drums and
many drums made with barrel-staves are painted, it is felt that, for
the best results, instruments of the latter type should be varnished.
The principle here is exactly that which applies to the violin; varnish,
it was explained, makes the tone of a drum brilliant. A possible
rationalization of this is the belief that varnished drums are more
beautiful than those having painted designs. They are less frequently
encountered than painted sets; and the best drummers, who are highly
sensitive to the tone-qualities of the instruments they play, take particular delight in attending the ceremonies of cult houses that have
sets of varnished drums.

Pegs for the torno type of heading are made by a cabinet-maker out
of hard, strong wood. They vary in number, the largest drum having
seven, the middle one of the set, six, and the smallest, five. A special

kind of rope must be used. This is about the thickness of the little finger and is called *corda de linha*.

Drums are headed in the house in which they are to be used by the *alabes*. "An *alabe* who cannot head a drum, or take it apart when it must be repaired, isn't worthy of being a drummer," observed the man who had admitted filching skins; and often, at ceremonies, one may see a drum, completely dismembered, being worked over to restore its tone, the rhythms being carried on by the two remaining instruments. An *alabe* can destroy a drum-head as effectively as he can repair a drum. A pointed thumb-nail is pressed hard against the head, a sharp stroke is given with the other hand near the rim, and the small hole that is made grows larger with later playing until the head becomes useless. A drummer who explained this technique, in the course of the field work on which this article is based, told about one excellent player whose propensity for ruining drum-heads on the slightest provocation is well known; chief drummers see to it that he is permitted to play only such rhythms as are produced with drum-sticks.

To head a drum, the skin is put over the large opening and a strip of wood, like a hoop, is placed about the body of the drum, over the skin, the leftover portion, hanging below the strip, is then doubled back and cut off. The strip prevents the head from tearing when the cord is passed through the holes that are cut in it and is pulled tight. The cord is knotted to prevent slipping, brought through the first hole, over the strip and back under the peg; then up and through the skin and along the strip to the next peg; then under, over, and along, this process being repeated until the ends of the cord meet, when they are firmly tied. Pegs are relaxed when the drum is headed, and then are very gradually pounded in, so that pressure on the head will be equalized all round. This operation can take several days if the drums are not immediately needed, though it can be greatly accelerated if they must be used at once.

The drum-sticks (*agidavi*) are ordinarily made of hard-wood (*pitanga* or *ingá*); if softer wood (such as *arassa*) is used, the sticks fray rapidly. Any competent drummer can make sticks, and those made with care will last from three to five years. The twigs are first denuded, and are then rubbed with fat, after which they are heated over a fire so that the fat will thoroughly impregnate the wood. The sticks are left for some days in the sun or in the smoke of the kitchen fire, and are then placed in a shrine "at the feet of the god" where they remain until the next rite requiring drums, when the head of the house turns them over to the head drummer.

The same "power" believed to exist in the drums is believed to reside also in the sticks. Sticks are provided by each cult house, and a visiting drummer bringing his own is at once under suspicion. A drummer who bears a grudge against a house will secrete on his person a stick that has been "put at the feet of Eshu," the trickster-deity, who is credited with malicious power, able, if properly directed, to interfere sadly with the progress of events. When such a stick is surreptitiously brought into play, it is expected that the ceremony will be completely disorganized.

The "power" of the drums is conferred upon them by means of painstakingly performed rituals; it is prolonged and assured by an annual ceremony, when the drums are "fed." The first essential element in the initial rite is the "baptism" of the instruments, this being an example of the striking quality possessed by such African cults as have survived in New World Catholic countries, a quality by means of which African and Catholic elements are harmoniously combined.[6] Unbaptized drums, called "pagan," and those that have not been fed should not be played, because of the danger that they may not properly perform their functions—that they may, for instance, call the wrong god.

A drum is baptized shortly after its completion. It must have a godfather and a godmother (a *padrinho* and a *madrinha*), selected by the head of the house from among its personnel. If the new drum, or new set, is the gift of an individual, he will be designated for one of these rôles. With the godparents standing on either side, the priest or priestess takes holy water, obtained from a Catholic church, and, speaking entirely in the African tongue employed by the group in its rituals, blesses the drums while sprinkling them with the sacred liquid. A candle, held by the godmother, is then placed on the floor in front of the drums, where it is allowed to burn out; each drum is decorated with a bouquet of paper flowers, allowed to remain in place for a while.

The act of naming is carried out at this time also. Only the great drum is given a name. The "real" designation of such a drum is in the African tongue of the group, though the one by which it is known is the Portuguese equivalent of the African term. Drum names are of two types. First are the day-names, the drum being called after the week-day on which it is first played in a ceremony. The second is one that happens to strike the fancy of the priest or the donor: *Ca te espera* ("You will wait here") or *Vencedor* ("The Conqueror"), to cite two actual names. Or the donor may honor his own ruling spirit in naming a drum: "I will call this drum 'Slave of Oshossi,'" he may say, if his deity is the African god of the hunt.

Drums may or may not be "dressed" on this occasion—that is, encircled with a cloth. This is called an *oja* and is the equivalent of the cloth tied about the breasts of a possessed initiate. The dressing is optional at baptism, because the drums are still pagan; observation did not show the corollary—that baptized drums must be dressed when in ceremonial use—to be in force. It would seem, actually, that the person who directs a given ceremony may say whether or not the drums are to be dressed, though the feeling that an unbaptized drum should not be so decorated is very strong.

Baptism alone will not give drums power, since to be strong they must be fed. Offerings to the drums consist of blood, palm-oil, honey, and holy water. The head of a chicken is first severed, the blood being allowed to flow over the bodies of the drums, which are in a slanting position. Care is taken that no blood falls on the heads. Then the oil, the honey, and the water are poured over them, and they are left in place until the following day, when the first ceremony at which they are to be used is held.

As the chicken is killed, the priest says, "The drums will eat today." After the blood and other offerings have been made, the head, intestines, wings, and feet are cooked with palm-oil, shrimps, and onion, but without salt, after the manner of most sacred foods. This dish, together with beans (*feijão fradinho*), a bit of *acassá*, white flour, and popcorn, is placed before the drums to remain the entire day; a candle is lighted, placed with the food, and allowed to burn out. Should the head of the cult group decide to make this initial feeding of the drums the occasion for a ceremony, the offerings must be presented during the morning, to allow the drums time to eat before the night ritual.[7]

The annual feeding of the drums, which renews their power, is the rite of the *alabes*, and is a joyous event. When it occurs, all the percussion instruments are fed, since drum-sticks, irons, calabashes, and rattles must likewise be strengthened. The food is the same as that given at the initial rites. The drums are dressed in their *ojas*, and, while the sacrificial cock is being killed, ritual songs that accompany the offering of a feathered creature (a *bicho de penna*, as distinguished from a "four-footed animal") are sung. The feet, head, and intestines, prepared as described above, are placed in a pottery vessel, while the other foodstuffs to be offered are put on plates. Now the members of the cult group, singing, bring the offerings, holding the plates upraised before the drums while a candle is lighted. Then the round of songs of the *shiré* is sung—three songs for each deity worshipped by the group—, the singing being accompanied by hand-clapping.

After the offerings have remained an entire day before the drums, they are taken to the shrines of the gods who "live" out-of-doors—the

gods of the hunt and of the bush—and are thrown away in the ceremonial "forest" that each cult house possesses. The remainder of the
food is served to the members of the cult group, and there is eating
and drinking, but no dancing. The head of the group provides a bottle
of rum (*cachaça*), while the drummers furnish wine and beer. A
kind of game is played by the drummers, who hide bottles of rum in
the woods. Others watch them and later put the bottles elsewhere, to
bring them out as the supply runs low.

The spiritual attributes of the drums and of other percussion instruments may be further considered. As shown by the discussion of
drum-sticks, any element in the percussion group, if given the proper
spiritual treatment, may be endowed with the power of disrupting a
ceremony. It is this susceptibility to magic, rather than any inherent
magical qualities of the drums and other instruments themselves, that
makes it necessary for them to be handled so carefully. Their own
power, of a different order, is derived from the tones they give out
when played—sounds so potent that the gods themselves must respond.
Being thus at the very heart of supernatural power, they constitute a
strong-point at which an enemy might well decide to strike.

It is thus understandable why the greatest care is taken to prevent
access by outsiders to the musical instruments of a group. A new
drum-body, before it is allowed to join the property of a cult group,
let alone enter the cult house or a shrine of the gods, must be spiritually
disinfected; so must a new skin acquired outside, and so must a new
iron gong. Similar care is observed concerning nonritual objects
brought to a cult center; but, as regards the musical instruments among
these objects, the priest, as an added precaution, divines so as to
make doubly sure that nothing has been "put in them."

The fear of magic explains why drums and other instruments are
seldom borrowed in Bahia, even when badly needed. Certainly the
loan of drums or other instruments is an expression of great friendship
and trust. At only one of the numerous public rituals that the writer
attended were borrowed drums used. In this instance, not only had the
priestess been in long professional association with the head of the
house who had loaned her his drums, but this head was of sufficient
age and possessed of great enough power to cope with any attempt to
utilize evil against him, his group, or the rituals of his house.

When drums are loaned, it is possible that they may not be accepted
on their return. Understandably, not to receive them is an act of
open hostility, and the resulting breach is not easy to heal. The fact
that the priest or priestess accompanies drums that are loaned does
not alter the situation. A case in point was that of an initiate, about

to celebrate the important fourteenth anniversary of her initiation. The head of her cult group being no longer alive, she was holding the rite at a private dwelling outside the city, specially rented for the purpose. Yet the priestess who was to direct the ceremony for her refused to bring her own drums, apparently fearing that they might be useless to her thereafter, so that the woman giving the *festa* was required to order a new set just for the occasion.

When drums are loaned, the priest or priestess performs a secret rite, an *obrigação*, within the shrine of the principal deity of the house, while the instruments wait to be taken away. On their return, another rite is performed inside the shrine, and *abo*-water, used ritually on all occasions in cult practice to cleanse, purify, and strengthen, is sprinkled over them. To make triply certain that evil will not result, the drums are left in the unused dancing-space outside the shrines for some days before they are put in place again.

In certain New World Negro societies—in Haiti, for example—a set of drums is regarded as an indivisible unit. This is not so in Bahia. One drummer, who was courting the favor of the head of an important house, spoke of offering this priest, as a gift, a large drum to replace the one he was using, which had a tone less brilliant than the best standards would require. There would be no difficulty, he said, in incorporating the new drum into the *terno* employed by the house; and he pointed out that at recent rites two drums had for a time been played in place of the three ordinarily used. This is musically permissible since, most often, the two smaller drums play either identical rhythms or rhythms so similar that for one of them to be lacking does not change the total effect.

The sale of drums is not permitted. The African fiction of "exchange"[8] is resorted to instead. Should someone wish to acquire from a cult group a baptized set that is in use, the head of the group, by divination, consults the deities to ascertain their wishes. Should any of these beings "object"—that is, if the lots should fall unfavorably—the matter ordinarily goes no farther. If considerable inducement is offered, however, divination may again be used, until a bargain is struck with the deity. Should none of the house pantheon object, new drums are ordered, and after they have been received, both sets are fed and disinfected spiritually, and the new ones are baptized. The cost of such a transaction includes expenditures for the drums themselves and for sacrifices, fees to officiants, and a gift to the priest from whom the old drums are obtained.

All this, as well as the precautions taken when acquiring or lending drums, contrasts strongly with the almost casual way in which old drums are discarded. When no longer usable, they have no more power, and, since they hold no further threat, they are merely thrown away. A drum is reheaded without ceremony also. Unless the old skin can be used to head a smaller drum, it is merely discarded. "The drum-head is only a hat," it was explained.

As in all African and African-derived cultures, drumming is for men. The taboo against the playing of drums by women, however, is not as strong in Bahia as elsewhere; in the interior of Dutch Guiana, for example, a woman is inhibited from even simulating drum-rhythms by the belief that, if she breaks the rule, her breasts will lengthen until they drag on the ground. One Bahian woman, at least, is a very good drummer; but she is a distinct exception and would never presume to play at a rite unless in an emergency when no male drummer was available. It is significant, moreover, that the god of this woman is a male deity.

The best drummers have a background of life-long, close association with the cults. Many of them belong to families of distinction within their groups, with parents and grandparents who were renowned priests and priestesses. Often their fathers, and sometimes their grandfathers, were drummers of repute. They are anxious that their own technique should, in turn, be handed on to their sons; several drummers boasted of their sons' ability, one complained of a son's lack of interest in drumming, while a grown but not very musical cult-member related how severe his father had been with him in the vain attempt to transmit to him the family aptitude.

Boys are encouraged by tradition to learn the drum-rhythms, and are often to be seen thumping boxes or calabashes. At ceremonies, before the skilled drummers take over, the older boys and young men of the house begin beating out rhythms. At one important cult-center, two small chairs placed in front of the platform were regularly occupied by their owners, a youngster aged two and another aged five. Each had a calabash, which he struck in time with the drums behind him. One of the writer's pleasantest recollections of the dances at this center is that of seeing the younger boy gradually relax into sleep, until an especially loud stroke of the drums roused him, when, with a start, he would resume for a few moments, almost automatically, the rhythms he had left off.

Wherever drums are played, a group of boys is invariably found standing close by, listening, watching, learning. A youth who shows talent is sometimes permitted to play a smaller drum, but this requires unusual ability—and courage as well. For not only is he put to public test before the gods themselves, but any deviation from the strict rhythm will be punished by a sharp rap over the knuckles, administered by the player of the large drum, who uses his drum-stick for the purpose. "Many's the time I've gone home with aching fingers," said one drummer, whose reminiscences were touched off when a novice failed to hold the beat.

Drummers form a group of their own, and regard each other with the friendly respect of professionals who acknowledge one another's competence. They have their special names within the cult, and one may ask cult members for a particular drummer almost in vain if one uses only the name by which he is known in the secular world.

These men have their own games. At one ceremony, during an interlude, a particularly fast rhythm accompanied a dance by a young man who had earlier been at one of the drums. He faced the great drum, whose player, from time to time, would tauntingly extend the drum-stick towards him for an instant, or would touch it to the ground, when the dancer would lunge for it. If he got it, he was the winner; if he stopped before getting the stick, he was the loser. If he won, he took over the drum, and the drummer, in addition, had to treat him to beer; if he gave up too soon, it was he who paid the penalty.

Another even more difficult game involves a drummers' dance termed *kungu*, after the name of the special rhythm consecrated to those who play the drums. The challenger dances facing the drum, kerchief in each hand, and his steps follow the initial basic fast beat. Then the dancer breaks step, introducing variant figures, which involve a change in rhythm. If the player of the large drum follows the irregularities in the dance with his beat until the dancer is exhausted, he is the winner; if not, the dancer wins.

All this, understandably, promotes a feeling of unity among the Bahian Negroes; historically, it represents the survival of a West African pattern. The position of the drummer has been but little studied in Africa, and the subject has thus almost gone by default. Yet conversation with certain Africans resident in the United States has made clear how important drummers are in West Africa. Among the Yoruba of Nigeria, drummers constitute a group apart, with their own names and their own traditions. When disputes break out in a village, they act as arbiters; similarly, they may not become parties to a feud. Among the Ibo of the Niger delta, also, drummers are important people; it is they who know what god is to come to a person, and how and when to call the god to the head of his future devotee.

When we consider the musical resources drummers must command, we can see why a feeling of group identity and pride of place exists among them. The range of their knowledge is varied. For each deity worshipped by the members of a given cult-group—and the group may serve twenty or twenty-five gods—there are songs to which there is at least one rhythmic accompaniment and many for which there are alternative accompaniments also. In addition, it is necessary to master certain drum-rhythms that do not accompany songs and are played at special points in the ritual, such as the *adahun,* the exciting piece that brings on possessions in great number. This, however, is but the beginning. The Afro-Bahian "nations," the groupings descended from various tribes of West Africa, have different rhythms for the deities they hold in common, in addition to the rhythms they have for such deities as each "nation" may worship by itself. Finally, the songs for the Congo and Angola spirits and for those of the Caboclo cult—which, according to the members, is devoted to the worship of aboriginal Indian gods—possess their own special rhythmic accompaniments.

Any good drummer, as leader of the *terno,* must be able to come in with the proper beat for any song for any deity of any "nation" as soon as the first phrase of the leader-and-chorus pattern has been sung. Quite aside from the fact that this means knowing an enormous number of rhythms, which may differ from each other only in subtle detail, the tune, as sung, is often enunciated in such a manner that one wonders how it can be identified. For the criteria of a good singer have but little to do with voice quality. A good singing voice is appreciated, but in these rigorously disciplined cults it is "liturgical" knowledge that counts in the musical as in the other aspects of cult procedure. An elderly priest or priestess, with a voice almost completely destroyed by long years of throat-wracking efforts to make it heard over drums and against the chorus, is nevertheless accounted a fine singer if able to sing without hesitation the proper song for a given deity of no matter what "nation." This was made strikingly clear, just before a recording, when a well informed soloist appeared with a cold so bad that he could barely make himself heard, yet who, with the approval of the chorus and drummers present, insisted that the session could go on as usual!

The greatest musician is the drummer who knows the songs and can relieve the priest of seeing to it that the proper one is sung at the proper time. Such a person is not only *alabe,* "drummer," but *alabe huntor,* "drummer-singer." His knowledge is superb. He must, of course, know the *shiré*—the cycle of songs for the gods of the house—, which opens every rite. He is able to sing and drum the round of Data, in honor of the thunder-god, one of the most difficult of the many song-cycles of the cult. After the house deities have been sung for, the gods of visiting initiates from other houses and of other "nations" must be honored by the rendition of music belonging to their cult, while at any time during a ritual someone may become possessed and the possessing spirit, on announcing himself, may have to be similarly honored; and the *alabe huntor* must be prepared for all such contingencies.

Most difficult of all is meeting the test presented by visitors who have been cult initiates for more than seven years. Such a person, when possessed by his god, has the right to ask for a song believed to be of the god's choosing, and if the musicians of the house giving the ceremony do not know it, their prestige is lessened, while that of the visitor's cult group is enhanced. The problem this situation poses is of the first order when the visitor is from another town; it is amazing, however, how the good musician will listen to an obscure enunciation of an unfamiliar song by a possessed person and after a few repetitions will have drums and chorus giving a full, vigorous rendition of it, to which the visiting deity can dance with complete satisfaction.

Add to all this that every rhythm has two parts (in the polyphonic sense), and that some have three, depending on whether or not the smaller drums play in unison, and it may be seen why the musical competence of the drummer commands respect. Acquaintance with these patterns of disciplined musicianship destroys completely any idea one may have had regarding the fortuitous or casual nature of primitive music, or any conception of African rhythm as spontaneous improvisation.

1. The only African data of this kind available are to be found in F. S. Nadel's recent work on the Nupe, "A Black Byzantium," pp. 301–3.

2. This field-work was done under a grant from the Rockefeller Foundation.

3. These recordings are to be found in the collections of the Folksong Archive of the Library of Congress, of the Division of Music of the Pan-American Union, and of the Department of Anthropology, Northwestern University.

4. Earlier descriptions, in Portuguese, are those of Nina Rodrigues, *Os Africanos no Brasil,* and of Manoel Querino, *Costumes Africanos no Brasil.* The most recent comprehensive work is Arthur Ramos, *O Negro Brasileiro* (2nd ed., 1940). In English, the relevant passages in a book by this same author, "The Negro in Brazil," may be consulted. A summary of the data in the Brazilian works on the subject is available in a volume entitled "Negroes in Brazil" by Donald Pierson (Ch. IX and X); while a brief résumé of the cult, in terms of its place in the total culture of the Afro-Bahians, may be found in an article "The Negroes of Brazil," by M. J. and F. S. Herskovits, in *The Yale Review,* Vol. 32 (Winter, 1943), pp. 263–279.

5. This discussion, summarizing that of an expert drummer, is a statement of theory rather than of practice.

6. *Cf.* M. J. Herskovits, "African Gods and Catholic Saints in New World Negro Belief," in the "American Anthropologist," XXXIX (1937), 635–643.

7. For details of comparable rites in the Haitian *vodun* cult, *cf.* M. J. Herskovits, "Life in a Haitian Valley," pp. 273–277, where an account of the making of drums will also be found.

8. For exchange as applied to the acquisition of wood-carvings in Dahomey, West Africa, see M. J. Herskovits, "Dahomey," Vol. II, p. 368.

: VI :

CULT LIFE IN BRAZIL

The Southernmost
Outposts of New World Africanisms[1]

*Yet African culture, it must be repeated—perhaps all cul-
ture—does not give ground as readily as had been supposed.
Many variants of African traditions and beliefs already
studied in the New World have aided us to understand how
custom can adapt itself to new institutions; how the modes of
behavior of a people, altered in outer form if necessary, can
be retained when they lodge deeply enough in the patterns of
a culture. . . . Aspects of the African patterns of plural
marriage with supernatural sanctions derived from the ancestral cult have been retained by the Brazilian Negroes,
despite the pressures of majority patterns in favor of the European monogamic tradition.*

* * *

The ethnographic materials presented in this paper were obtained in
the city of Porto Alegre, capital of the state of Rio Grande do Sul,
Brazil, in July, 1942. These data, which sketch certain little known aspects of the life of the Negroes in southern Brazil, point the richness
of the materials available in this area and their promise for future
study, particularly when considered in conjunction with the known
historic facts concerning the Negro in Uruguay and the Argentine.
This is especially seen to be the case when it is realized that the data
were gathered during a short visit, whose primary purpose was other
than research.

Census figures concerning the numerical strength of the various

American Anthropologist, New Series, XLV, no. 4, pt. 1 (1943), 495–510.

ethnic groups in Porto Alegre are not available, since no questions
bearing on racial affiliation are included in the Brazilian census tracts.
However, estimates made by persons intimately acquainted with the
city make it apparent that this center has a Negro population[2] that is
quite adequate to provide the numerical base for the preservation and
maintenance of African customs there. These estimates agreed that
the Negroes form between 15% and 20% of the total population; which,
if we accept the most conservative figures, means that the city includes
more than 50,000 persons of predominantly African ancestry. The base
becomes broadened, furthermore, if the remainder of the state, particularly the southern coastal belt, and the towns lying southwest and
west of the capital, are taken into account. Though it was not possible
to visit these districts, information volunteered by those familiar with
the area indicated that a comparable density of Negro population can
safely be assumed to exist there.

II

As in northern Brazil, the Negroes of Porto Alegre count descent
from certain well recognized, specific West African tribal and sub-
tribal groups, termed *nações*. According to one cult-head, the principal
"nations" in Porto Alegre are the Oba (Yoruba), Gêge (Dahomean),
and Jesha (Yoruba), though a second cult-head named the Oyo, of
the Yoruba city of this same name, and did not include the Oba group.
This latter informant stated explicitly that there were almost no
Congo Negroes in Porto Alegre; however, several persons encountered
claimed Congo ancestry. The differences in traditions of descent held
by the Negroes in Porto Alegre and the North are striking. In Bahia,
for example, no Oyo group exists, and few persons who called themselves Oba were encountered there among the many who named their
ancestral affiliation. The strongest group in Bahia, the Ketu, derived
from persons originating in this southwestern Nigerian town was, on
the other hand, completely absent from accounts of the "nations" of
the southern center.

The position of the Gêge (Dahomean) group in the two areas calls
for comment. In Bahia, though few Gêge cult-houses exist, this "nation," always held in high esteem, continues its prestige. The situation
is somewhat similar in the South. The Gêge were included in both
lists of "nations" collected, while knowledge of Dahomean names of
deities seemed actually to be greater than in the North. The names of
Mawu, the great god of the Dahomeans, rarely heard or recognized in
the North, is well known in Porto Alegre, as is Aida Wedo, the rainbow
serpent. Sogbo, encountered in the North, and *vodun*, the Dahomean

term for the deity, are also found in the South. Linguistic survivals of this group would seem to be quite extensive. Certain songs heard in Porto Alegre were in the striking Dahomean musical style seldom encountered in the North. The outstanding characteristic of Dahomean music is its use of the falsetto, and this was specifically named as such by one singer, who, contrasting it with Oyo music said that while Dahomean songs are more easily remembered, they are harder to sing; that is, while they are "without the cadenzas" the Oyo songs have, their falsetto "tears the throat."

It was somewhat surprising to find that the well developed *caboclo* cult of the North—the cult which worships deities held to derive from the aboriginal Indians—seems to be almost entirely absent in the South. One priestess manifested lively interest in this cult, which she knew of. She stated that, on occasion, a *caboclo* deity would possess a devotee; in this case, the person possessed would only be initiated if the spirit manifested an obstinate demand for this, otherwise it would be "turned away" and "seated"—that is, satisfied with offerings and restrained from returning to trouble the one to whom it had come.

An idea of the strength of the cult may be had from the registration figures in the Statistical Department of the municipality of Porto Alegre.[3] The forty-two "Centers of African Religion" noted for 1941 may be compared with thirty-seven registered in 1940, twenty-seven in 1939, twenty-three in 1938, and thirteen in 1937. The larger numbers in more recent years represent an increasingly efficient administration of the registration program, rather than growth of the cults. The thirty-seven centers registered in 1940 had forty-two altars in their shrines. Membership on the first of January of that year totaled 510 men and 675 women; 79 men and 42 women joining during the year to make a total of 1,356 cult-affiliates at the beginning of 1941. The 37 cult-centers held 891 ceremonies during the year. To what extent these figures are complete is not known, but even taken at their face value, they clearly demonstrate the vitality of the African cults and indicate that, as in the North, they may on closer investigation prove to be merely one facet of a well-rounded, well-integrated and distinguishable Afro-Brazilian way of life.

African survivals in Porto Alegre are of particular interest because the Negroes of this city and the surrounding area have apparently lived for many years isolated from other Afro-Brazilian communities. This is quite unlike the situation elsewhere. Many of the Negroes of São Paulo migrated there from the state of Minas Geraes, whole villages of Negroes in the states of Rio de Janeiro and Espirito Santo were imported from Maranhão, while Bahian Negroes go everywhere, there being a whole colony of them in the Federal District who retain their identity through the maintenance of distinctive Bahian traditions in the city of Rio de Janeiro itself. But Bahian or Minas or Perambuco Negroes are almost never encountered in Porto Alegre, nor could the informants tell of any existing tradition of migrations from these other states. It would go beyond the dictates of scientific caution to assert that the many similarities between South and North are the result of an independent, but parallel working out of identical aboriginal African cultural impulses. But this should be held to as a working hypothesis, which, as soon as possible must be tested through an examination of the relevant historical documents bearing on Negro migration within Brazil, and the African tribal provenience of the Negroes imported into the southern part of the country.[4]

III

As elsewhere in Brazil, cult-life in Porto Alegre centers about the cult-house, the residence of the priest or priestess who heads the group. Here the shrines of the gods are installed, and here the cult rituals are carried on. The word used by cult-members to designate these centers and their rituals is *pará*, though *batuque*, employed by outsiders[5] is more often encountered. These terms are the equivalents of the better-known *macumba* of Rio de Janeiro, the *candomblé* of Bahia, and the *xango* (shango) of Pernambuco. Certain of these centers are of considerable age; some of them have traditions going back three or four generations, evidenced by the ability of their heads to tell those who preceded and trained them.

Physically, cult-houses are small and, in comparison to those of Bahia and Pernambuco, unimpressive. Those visited were nothing more than the typical small dwellings of working-class districts, outwardly differing not at all from the structures that jostle them on both sides. One such cult-house was somewhat removed from the city—a matter of a twenty-minute walk from the end of the car line. It was one of a row of small homes situated on a hillside, and had a yard large enough to permit placing a few shrines there. Several other centers are located nearby, on the same street. Cult-houses are customarily constructed of wood (32 out of the 37 registered in 1940 were built of this material) and are completely enclosed; in this, as well as in their size and location, they stand in contrast to the semi-open structures with spacious grounds of the Bahian and Recife cult-groups. It must be remembered, however, that Porto Alegre is well below the tropical belt, often experiencing freezing temperature and having occasional snowstorms. Therefore, while the smallness of the cult-house is probably due to economic reasons, its form must be considered as an adaptation to the climatic conditions of the temperate zone.

As a person enters one of these houses, he finds himself in its largest room, where ceremonies are customarily held. As would be anticipated from the size of the structure, this room is quite small indeed, and while no rites were witnessed, it is apparent that they must be relatively quiet affairs when compared to the great gatherings that mark the worship of African gods in the North. As elsewhere in Brazil, the rooms are decorated with brightly colored paper streamers suspended from the roof, or strung from wall to wall. Altars to the Catholic saints identified with the principal African deities worshipped are to be seen, and a door leads to the *pegí*, where the altars of the gods are placed. In Porto Alegre, these altars seem always to occupy a single room, instead of the two or more devoted to them in the cult-houses of certain "nations" in the North.

The cult-house is marked by a brass plate affixed to the outer wall facing the street, which indicates that the group has official recognition. In the list of the forty-two cult-groups licensed in 1941, only one was designated by the name of an African deity, two being simply termed "African Society" and "African Religious Society." Twenty-two were called by the names of Catholic saints—the "Santa Barbara Society," the "Religious Society of St. George," the "Benevolent Society of the Divine Holy Spirit," the "Benevolent and Religious Society of St. Jerome," and the like. These names, however, represent an adaptation to local patterns of the well-known tendency of New World Negroes living in Catholic countries to identify African gods with Catholic saints. Thus, a society which takes the name of Santa Barbara is likely to be one whose ruling *santo* is the African deity Yansan, one which is called St. George may well have been founded by a priest whose principal deity was Ogun, and the like. The "public" name of such a group is thus the Catholic equivalent of the African spirit believed to "rule" the house—the *dono da cabeça* or "master of the head" of the first to head the group.

The shrines are less elaborate than those of the North. In both areas, the objects sacred to the gods are covered with cloths in the appropriate colors, vessels filled with the water sacred to the spirit stand before the altars, while food offerings of various kinds are on the floor. Every shrine visited had oranges before the altars, something that was never encountered in the North. It is quite possible that these were in the nature of first-fruit offerings, since the period when these observations were made coincided with the orange harvest.

Most sacred on any altar is the stone dedicated to the god. Here, as elsewhere, the stone is the seat of power, the sacred object to which the spirit comes. The attitude toward these stones expressed by one priestess was affection and pride as well as respect. She exhibited one newly-acquired, exclaiming at its beauty; during a second visit, she drew back the cloth behind which the stones lay in their containers, with the exclamation, "Here are all my fathers."

In Porto Alegre, certain deities have shrines apart from the others. This is everywhere mandatory, for the shrine of Eshu, guardian of the cross-roads and entrances, must always be at the entrance to a cult center, to a cult-house, and in some cases, to the shrine of another deity as well. Here Eshu receives special sacrifices, and is always worshipped at the outset of any ceremony so that he may "open the path" for the other gods and, appeased, will not "overturn" the ceremony to follow. In the North the other gods who characteristically live outdoors—Omolu and Oshossi, for example—in Porto Alegre, are housed in the common *pegi*. One priest exhibited a special outdoor shrine for Shapana (Omolu) in the restricted space available behind his house, while at another center an attempt had been made to "seat" Oshossi in a small tree, growing near the entrance-gate. "City life is difficult for us," said the priestess, "but we try as well as we can."

"Why don't you get a place in the country?"

"It wouldn't do any good. You would be off by yourself, and people would talk. Anyway, land is too valuable down here."

The priests and priestesses who head these groups see to it that the gods are properly worshipped, direct the rituals, divine, and initiate into their cult those of their group to whom the gods come. These cult-heads are dignified, assured personages. They rigorously exact the discipline that characterizes African cult-life. Their word is given profound respect, their commands obeyed without delay. Their position depends on their knowledge of the theology and ritual of the cult and, as in the northern Brazilian centers of African survivals, they impress one as individuals of great intelligence.

Comparative figures of the number of priests and priestesses could not be obtained, but the impression was gained that women substantially outnumber men in this calling. When engaged in ritual work, cult-heads wear distinctive clothing and ritual paraphernalia. One priest was encountered immediately after he had concluded a divining session. He wore a colored sash about his waist, a small round cap in the color of his god, Shapana, was atop his head, and his long, vari-colored strands of beads went over one shoulder and under the opposite arm. The priestesses visited in their homes wore nothing distinctive. Except that the prevailing colors of their dresses were those of their principal gods, no one unaccustomed to associating colors and deities would realize that there was anything of cult significance in their dress. Priests and priestesses, like all cult-members, however, wear the beads of the *santo* to which they have been vowed, under their outer clothing and carry *figas*, mediaeval charms widely used by Afro-Brazilians against the evil eye, carved in the shape of a clenched hand. Beads and *figas* are both to be purchased in the public markets of the city.

Divination is an important function of the cult-head. The divining session mentioned in the preceding paragraph was for the benefit of a client who was about to go on a journey. Sitting in the large room of this cult-house, separated only by a half-wall from the shrine where the divination was taking place, it was possible to hear the throw of the *kpele* or chain of shells used to foretell the dictates of fate and reveal the wishes of the gods. The prescription of the priest-diviner, that for a safe and profitable journey, the client should bring a cock and hen, white and red cloth, and other ingredients was carefully and, from an African or northern Brazilian point of view, correctly given. Techniques of divination vary, the throwing of cowry-shells and water gazing being among those mentioned, in addition to the *kpele*. One cult-head knew, by name at least, of the Yoruba-Dahomean system of Afa.

In Porto Alegre priestesses may kill the sacrifices for most gods. In this, they are unique in Brazil. This is perhaps because the cult group, in certain respects, itself seems to be differently structured here than in the North. In Bahia, Rio, and Recife, initiates are principally women, and in most cases, a man who affiliates with the cult becomes what is known as an *ogan*. The only male initiates one encounters there are those whose mothers gave birth to them during initiation, thus automatically "making" their offspring, born in the cult-house; or men who, because of professional reasons, have been put through the initiatory rites individually instead of with a "class"—an expensive proceeding—or who were inducted into the cult because of the insistence of their gods.

In the South, however, no distinction is apparently made between men and women as far as candidacy for initiation is concerned, while the very word *ogan* seems to be unknown. The matter may conceivably refer back to a kind of puritanical reluctance found in the North to initiate mixed classes, since there the initiatory process involves a stay of three to twelve months at the cult-center, the initiates living in the most intimate relationship with each other, being, indeed, confined to one room for considerable periods. In the South, where cult-groups are smaller and resources less, candidates cannot give so long a time and cult-houses cannot afford the long rites prevalent in the North, and initiation by "classes" seems to be unknown. It is possible, of course, that individual initiations were common in the North until recent times, as is evidenced by the description given by Nina Rodrigues of the ceremonies witnessed by him, before the turn of the century, when a single candidate, one Olympia, was inducted into cult-membership.[6]

Since initiation in the South is an individual matter, the rites are relatively brief. One priestess volunteered the information that she was planning to spend two weeks of the next months in a town in the interior of the state, to initiate a woman who had been possessed by a god and whose family had called her to perform the necessary rituals. The entire ceremony, which would be entirely carried out at the home of the novitiate, would not take more than a week. All expenses would be borne by the candidate's family, and it was made clear that all essentials of initiation would be included in the intensive, individual training compressed in this period. Specifically mentioned was the giving of the cult-name and the making of the sacred cuts at the top of the novitiate's head, two of the most important items in the longer cycle of ceremonies in the North. That initiations in Porto Alegre itself are short (the maximum period indicated by anyone was three weeks) is further shown by the fact that the heads of the candidates are not completely shaven, but the hair is merely cut at certain indicated points.

IV

The best known aspect of New World African cults is the names of the deities worshipped, the African supernatural beings known everywhere in Brazil as *santos*. The identification of saints of the Church with such African deities is likewise a well-established phenomenon, resulting from the acculturative process in all New World Catholic countries.[7] Since the names of African deities give some of the most definite leads to African provenience, the collection of such a list from Porto Alegre was indicated as offering one of the few opportunities possible in a short visit for systematic analysis of local survivals and their adjustment to this setting.

The African deities named below follow an order of precedence known as the *'shiré;* that is, they are named in the order for which they are sung during the initial rites of ceremonies. The only exception to this is in the case of the first named *santo*, Eshu, since in Porto Alegre, as in all Brazil, this deity is evoked, "fed," and "sent away" before the ceremony proper is begun. That certain of the deities named have various "qualities" may also be pointed out as characteristic. In some cases, these "qualities" are expressed in terms of "older" and "younger" aspects of a given deity. In other instances, differing names are given to the several "qualities" of a god. Since the nice theological problem involved in this series of distinctions can only be resolved through further study, particularly in West Africa from whence these names have come to the New World, only the names themselves are given.

The list of deities, as obtained from a priestess of the Oyo "nation," and various members of her group who participated in the discussion during which they were gathered, follows:

Eshu (Leba, Elebara)	St. Peter (Eshu the elder)
	St. Anthony (Eshu the younger)
Ogun	St. George
Ogun olira	
Ogun meji	
Ogun medye	
Oya (Iyansan)	St. Barbara
Aganju (Shango the younger)	St. Michael the Archangel
Ogodo (Shango the elder)	St. Jerome
Shango Dada	St. John
Ode	St. Onofré
Osain	St. Emmanuel
Shapana (Omolu)	Nosso Senhor de Bomfim (Christ)
Oba	St. Catherine
Oshun Panda	Nossa Senhora de Conceição
Beji	Sts. Comas and Damien
Oshun Doko	Our Lady of the Rosary
Yemanja	Nossa Senhora dos Navegantes
Oshala	The Holy Ghost ("Divino Espirito Santo")
Orunmila[8]	St. Joseph

The order of precedence in this list may be compared with the typical 'shiré of the Ketu cult-houses of Bahia, the most numerous West African sect there. The Ketu, though of the same Yoruba stock as the Oyo, are derived from a town 150 miles away. After Eshu has been "sent away," the songs of the 'shiré are sung in the following order: Ogun, Oshossi (the equivalent of the Porto Alegre Ode), Osain, Oshunmare (correlated by the Porto Alegre priestess with Oshun Panda), Omolu (the equivalent of Shapana), Nana, Yemanja, Oshun, Oba, Eowa, Yansan, Shango, and Oshala. Identical gods begin and end both sequences, but Orunmila is omitted in Bahian practice, the 'shiré ending with Oshala. The theory behind both endings is, however, the same, for in the North, Oshala, as father of all the gods, comes last as a token of the reverence in which his children hold him. In the

South, to Oshala is added Orunmila, his father, who is thus likewise accorded the place his relationship to the other gods merits. The comment of the informant concerning Orunmila may be noted: that he is "god of all, father of all"; that he "has 'daughters' (i.e., initiates), but doesn't 'come down'"—that is, does not possess them. It is worth noting that Olofin, perhaps the equivalent of the Nigerian being Olorun, invoked in the North, has no cult in Porto Alegre. He, too, was described as "father of all," but it was pointed out that he is a being who lives in "the spheres," does not concern himself with man, and has no initiates. "He is the true god," remarked the informant.

The concept of Eshu (Leba) held in Porto Alegre is like that in the North (where, however, it is revealed only on close acquaintance with the cult); both these conceptions differ from the manner in which he is customarily presented in the literature. As in Africa itself, Eshu, Elebara, or Leba, the divine trickster, is held by writers on the subject to be correlated with the Christian Devil, and northern Afro-Brazilians, like Africans, give this identification unless the matter is probed further. The priestess in Porto Alegre who gave this list, however, described Leba as the one who "opens the roads," and went on to tell how, if his demands are not carefully met, he will harm the negligent one just as he will reward the one who cares for his wants. When the identification of this spirit with the saints of the Church was brought up, she named St. Peter. That Leba could be correlated with the Devil was a new idea to her, rejected with the remark that while it was interesting, and she could see how some misinformed persons could make this "wrong" identification, yet since Leba performs good as well as evil, the correspondence was obviously invalid and the result of misunderstanding.

The absence of Oshossi from the Porto Alegre 'shiré is striking, until it is pointed out that the Ode of this series is the Oyo name for this god of the hunt. The name Oshossi, as a matter of fact, is well known in Porto Alegre, and is identified with St. Michael and the Souls of the Dead (S. Miguel e Almas). The omission of Oshunmare and Nana, both of whom are prominent in Bahia, is due to the fact that they are recognized by the members of this group who gave the list above as Gêge (Dahomean) gods and are, therefore, not worshipped by these Oyo folk. The play of inter-African syncretisms is manifest here, however, since Oshunmare is recognized, and was specifically stated to be the same goddess as Oshun Panda. The use of Shapana for Omolu is also worth noting. Both are Yoruba terms, but the former predominates in the North. Ogodo is known in Bahia, where certain Ketu informants stated that this being is the "thunderer" of the Tapa people, a "quality" of Shango, the thunder-god of the Yoruba.

The significance of its use by the Oyo priestess in Porto Alegre lies in the fact that the Nigerian city of Oyo is in the Northern Yoruba territory, close to the country of the Nupe, and the Yoruba name for the Nupe is Tapa (Takpa).[9]

The identification of Yemanja, the Yoruba goddess of the sea, with Nossa Senhora dos Navegantes, is in line with the practice of northern Afro-Brazilian groups for whom she is the "mother of the waters," likewise identified with the Virgin Mary in various other of her manifestations. Outstanding in the accounts of rituals of the North is the giving of "presents" to this being to insure good fortune not only to those whose life takes them to sea, but to all who worship the goddess. This is paralleled by the importance of the Catholic festivals in the South for Nossa Senhora dos Navegantes, in the course of which, to quote the Porto Alegre informant, "We give presents to Yemanja so she will help us."

Since no ceromonies were witnessed while these materials were being collected, it is impossible to give any details of ritual practices. Descriptions of rites of various kinds thus remain for the future, as does an account of the paraphernalia used in the worship of the gods, the colors sacred to them, and the like. Yet discussions with cult-heads suggested that ritual procedures here do not deviate too greatly from those of the North. Understandably, these discussions were carried on with much in the way of a knowledge of cult procedure taken for granted on both sides, so that major divergences, at least, would have become immediately apparent—as they did become apparent, for example, in the instance of differences in custom such as the initiation of men, or the absence of the *ogan* in the southern cult-groups. Another divergence concerns the number of songs sung for each god in the *'shiré*. In Bahia, Recife, and Rio de Janeiro, at least three songs sacred to each deity worshipped by members of the cult-house giving a ceremony must be sung before the rite can proceed. In Porto Alegre, however, while three songs are sung for Eshu, Ogun, Oya, Aganju, Ogodo, Shango, Ode, Osain, and Shapana, each of the others receives four songs.

A devotee inherits his gods from a member of his family. They can be passed down on either side, a child customarily taking the parent's god which is stronger. However, unlike "orthodox" practice in the Yoruba-Dahomean cults of the North, a person may actively worship and become possessed by several deities. In this respect, indeed, Porto Alegre is more like Haiti and Guiana than northern Brazil. In the latter area, while a number of deities may "descend on the head" of a devotee, all but one will be "seated"—that is, sent away so they will not trouble him by possessing him. In the South, while a cult member is initiated for his principal god, the "master of his head," he can be possessed by any of the other gods who come to him, and will dance for all who do possess him at any given ceremony.

As everywhere in New World African societies, possession is the supreme expression of worship. The theory of possession in Porto Alegre is the same as elsewhere; the god "descends" to the head of his devotee, replacing him and thus rendering him unconscious of what transpires until the deity departs. During the visitation of the god, which comes in a ritually prescribed manner, usually during a ceremony when the songs and drum rhythms sacred to the god are heard, the devotee dances, sings, prophesies, or manifests other characteristic behavior of the deity. As has been indicated elsewhere, some of the most revealing findings of this period of field work in northern Brazil include details of the way in which a possessed person returns to his normal state. He does this by passing through a condition called *eré*, a type of semi-possession described as "the childishness that goes with every god." That this phenomenon is also known in Porto Alegre, whose cult-groups have had so little contact with other centers where it is found, points emphatically to the need for a re-analysis of the possession-experience in West Africa itself.

As is customary among Negro groups, the drums are the most important musical instruments. Several sets of drums were inspected. None of the hollow-log variety was seen; the body is characteristically barrel-like, headed at both ends, the heads being held in place by strips of leather laced diagonally the length of the drum. No pegs are used in these drums. One house had a set of three, another had two and in a third only one was seen. There was no opportunity to hear them played, nor to find out how many comprise the orchestra. Rattles and gongs are used but for what deities, of what "nations," and on what occasions, remains to be determined.

v

Despite the importance of the problem, the integration of religious and non-religious aspects of life could only be explored briefly. As has been found in northern Brazil,[10] the religious customs of the Afro-Brazilians are only one facet of a well-integrated, smoothly functioning way of life. As such, religion carries over into other aspects of daily existence; but it is of particular importance in orienting family relationships. Aspects of the African patterns of plural marriage with supernatural sanctions derived from the ancestral cult have been retained by the Brazilian Negroes, despite the pressures of majority patterns in favor of the European monogamic tradition. Just as in other localities of the New World, this monogamic tradition has prevailed as far as outer form goes, the mechanism for carrying on the patterns of plural mating being found in the accepted forms of common-law marriage. In Brazil, the system of forming extra-legal alliances, more or less permanent, is termed *amasiada*.

This system is operative among the Negroes of Porto Alegre, and reactions to it in terms of its relation to the legally approved monogamic form of union are those encountered in other parts of Brazil. For while the socially most desirable type of mating is the one which has legal sanction and the blessing of the Church, the custom whereby a man or woman may take on other mates is also recognized by the group as constituting a valid form of union. In certain instances, this actually results in the maintenance of what to all intents and purposes is a series of polygynous households. That is, men set up and maintain continuous relationships with more than one woman over a given period of time. It must be pointed out, however, that neither in Porto Alegre nor in the North does this mean that women party to such an arrangement grant the rights of the others to the common mate; wisdom, indeed, dictates that a man maintain such plural relationships as discreetly as possible.

The supernatural sanctions of the system become apparent when we consider the manner in which a man's legal wife, his common-law wife or wives and their children regard his spirit after his death. As in the North, widows and children stand in fear of an offended ghost of their dead husband and father; as in the North also, all the children of a man, whether by wife or *amasiada*, must join in providing the required sacrifices to the spirit of the dead on pain of severe retribution. The story of an elderly woman of Gêge descent was recounted to illustrate how terrible the vengeance of a dissatisfied spouse can be. Despite the fact that her late husband, before his death, had forbidden her to remarry, and though she was of an age when, to quote the informant, "She should not be thinking about men any more," she had become infatuated with a much younger man and preparations for her remarriage were fully under way when she was stricken with paralysis. "She should have known better, but people are often foolish about such things." Her death was anticipated shortly and there was no doubt in the mind of the teller of this tale why this woman had been thus afflicted.

African beliefs are integrated with family life in still other ways. It has already been stated that gods are inherited. Certain of these beings, as is the case in the North, can be "sent away" by a parent who fears that a child will not serve them properly and therefore will be liable to the penalties that are exacted for neglect. In both parts of

Brazil, however, the one god to whom this cannot be done is Shango. He leaves a devotee when death approaches, but goes immediately to another member of the same family.

It was also stated that food taboos are inherited in family lines, though on which side of the family these prohibitions are handed down was not made explicit. The point needs further confirmation, however, since it is a survival of African totemic belief rarely encountered in the New World. More common, and as characteristically African, is the belief held by the Porto Alegre Negroes that violation of a food taboo, whether pertaining to one's family or given by the gods, brings on skin disease as a punishment.

The cult of the dead, whose importance in Brazil has gone largely unrecognized, is subsumed under the Yoruba term *egun*, the word used in Brazil to designate the dead. In the North, every cult-house has its shrine for the *egun*, where sacrifices are offered periodically by male members of the group, most women being excluded from the practice of this cult. In the South, while it cannot be said whether or not special shrines for the *egun* are erected, the information gathered concerning the rituals of the cult of the dead, when projected against the much more extensive data gathered during field work in the North, was sufficient to indicate the likelihood that future research in Porto Alegre would show this phase of cult-life well developed.

A series of rituals called *acheché*, which endure for seven nights after death and separate the dead cult-initiate from his cult-group and his family, is held when a member of one of the Porto Alegre cult-groups dies. At one house where this cult was discussed, it was described how a "four-footed animal"—an important sacrifice in terms of what is given in this cult—is offered to the spirits of the dead on the last night of the *acheché*, in the manner customary in other parts of Brazil. As in the North, the spirit of the dead is interrogated, and through divination the wishes of the deceased are determined regarding the disposition of the ritual paraphernalia he used during his lifetime. If the god so wills it, those objects, and the stone sacred to his god, are made up into a bundle, the *carrega*, which is taken to a beach to be carried away by current or tide.

In addition to the sacrifices offered when a cult-initiate dies, the *egun* are "fed" annually. The important offerings for the soul of any cult-member are made on the first, third, fifth, and seventh anniversaries of his death. Of these, the seventh year offering has the greatest significance, since the spirit of the dead is then definitively "sent away." After this time, the surviving members of the family have no further obligations toward the spirit of the dead relative which participates casually in offerings given in connection with the observances decreed by the cult of the dead.

VI

The position most commonly taken by students of Africanist problems in the southern hemisphere is that the distribution of African survivals, to say nothing of the Negro population itself, has its southernmost significant extension at about the latitude of Rio de Janeiro or São Paulo. It is a commentary on this prevailing point of view that when the trip on which these data were gathered was projected, the reaction almost invariably encountered was that while it would round out a knowledge of Brazil to visit the South, nothing was to be gained if research objectives in the field of Negro studies were envisaged.

Exceptions to the common point of view are, of course, found. The excerpts from Ramos' work on the Brazilian Negro already cited [11] are to the point. In Porto Alegre itself, the existence of the cult is more or less taken for granted. A substantial proportion of the data presented in this paper was gathered from cult-heads to whom introductions were arranged by Professor Elpidio Paes, Director of the Faculty of Law of the University of Porto Alegre, and his colleagues, Professors Euclydes Castro and Dario Bittencourt.[12] Moreover, a considerable amount of work on African survivals in Porto Alegre, as yet unpublished, has been done by Dr. Dante de Laytano and Dr. Leopoldo Bethiol.[13]

Such studies of Africanist problems in southern South America as have been made to date are principally historical, perhaps because of the assumption that south of Rio de Janeiro it is pointless to attempt ethnographic research. Yet the two papers by Dr. de Laytano[14] in the publications of the Institute of History and Geography of the State of Rio Grande do Sul not only show how considerable was the influence of the Negro in this state during the period of slavery, but also demonstrate that this African influence was sufficiently strong to impose itself on local speech, as is evidenced by the considerable number of African words he gives in Gaucho dialect.

The discovery, in 1940, in the city of Rio Grande do Sul, some hundred miles south of Porto Alegre, of a specimen of African-type wood-carving is to the point here. This statuette, a female figure of artistic distinction in terms of West African patterns, was found[15] buried beneath the foundation-stones of the altar to the Virgin in the parish church of São Pedro in that city. One can only conjecture why the slave who perhaps carved this figure placed it there. That

such a carving was found where it was points to the existence of living African beliefs and techniques at the beginning of the last century
and, what is more, hints that at least the basis for the Afro-Catholic
syncretisms existing at the present time had already been laid down
during that period.

The vitality of Africanisms in the region where the data in this
paper were obtained raises the question whether survivals may not
also be found to exist in the republics to the south of Brazil, Uruguay
and the Argentine. The writings of Dr. Ildefonso Pereda Valdés[16]
note the many African influences in present-day Uruguayan Spanish
and, as an historical justification for these findings, give the numbers
and types of Negroes imported into the country during slavery. How
large a proportion of the Uruguayan population were Negroes is indicated by a census of Montevideo taken in 1803, in which, out of a
total population of 4,726, 899 slaves and 141 free Negroes, or 1,040 individuals of African origin or descent were reported, this comprising
one-quarter of the entire population.[17]

The number of Negroes imported into the Argentine, and their influence in the development of Argentinian culture is rarely discussed;
yet in a volume of reminiscences concerning life in Buenos Aires about
1850,[18] many details as to the types of Negroes found in the city at
that time, and valuable information as to their customs, are encountered. One item which, in the light of the discussion in this paper of
the various "nations" into which the Negroes of Porto Alegre and
northern Brazil divide themselves, is particularly suggestive, can be
given:

Estaban perfectamente organizados por nacionalidades, congos, mozam-
biques, minas, mandingas, banguelas, etc., etc. Tenía cada nación su rey y
sua reina; sus comisiones, con president, tesorero y demás empleados sub-
alternos.[19]

Early nineteenth century sources give further information concerning these societies, which were mutual-aid groupings to help worthy
fellow-Africans acquire their freedom and, among other objectives
"held an annual mass for the souls of the dead." The names given in
one of these sources confirm and amplify the list given above: Ca-
bunda, Bangala, la sociedad de Moros, Rubolo, Angola, Conga and
Mina.[20] Such documents as these force the conclusion that systematic
research on the Negro in these southernmost countries, based on a
comparative knowledge of the African background and its manifestations elsewhere in the New World, offers a lead as promising as it is
important.

As regards the data from Porto Alegre, they teach how tenacious

African custom can be under contact. In demonstrating how cult-adaptations can be made in the face of the most diverse conditions of life, these materials further contravene the assumptions of those students in the Africanist field who, in underscoring the presumably ephemeral character of African institutions in the New World, find ground for predictions as to the extinction of these ways of life. Yet African culture, it must be repeated—perhaps all culture—does not give ground as readily as has been supposed. Many variants of African traditions and beliefs already studied in the New World have aided us to understand how custom can adapt itself to new institutions; how the modes of behavior of a people, altered in outer form if necessary, can be retained when they lodge deeply enough in the patterns of a culture. This additional variant from Porto Alegre carries the tale, and the lessons to be learned from it, one step further.

1. This paper incorporates a portion of the results of a field trip to study the Negroes of Brazil, made during 1941–1942 with the aid of a grant from the Rockefeller Foundation.

2. The word "Negro" is used here in its Brazilian sense—a person of African descent whose physical traits indicate little or no European mixture.

3. These data were recently forwarded by Professor Elpidio Paes, whose kindness in doing this is greatly appreciated.

4. It is for this reason that the descriptive materials from Porto Alegre are, whenever possible, projected against the background of contemporary Afro-Brazilian ways of life in northern Brazil which have been extensively described in many publications, some of which follow: Arthur Ramos, *O Negro Brasileiro* (2nd ed., Rio de Janeiro, 1940); Gilberto Freyre, *Casa Grande e Senzala* (3rd ed., Rio de Janeiro, 1938); Gonçalves Fernandes, *Xangôs de Nordeste* (Rio de Janeiro, 1937); Nina Rodrigues, *Os Africanos no Brasil* (São Paulo, 1932), and *O Animismo Fetichista dos Negros Bahianos* (Rio de Janeiro, 1935); and João do Rio, *As Religiões no Rio* (Rio de Janeiro and Paris, n.d. pp. 1–57). In English, A. Ramos, *The Negro in Brazil* (Washington, 1939), Donald Pierson, *Negroes in Brazil* (Chicago, 1942), and M. and F. Herskovits, "The Negroes of Brazil" (*Yale Review*, vol. 32, 1943, pp. 263–279), may be consulted.

5. The newspaper account of a ceremony quoted by Arthur Ramos (*O Negro Brasileiro*, pp. 169–174) is headlined as a description of a *batuque*, while Ramos himself states (*loc. cit.*), "As macumbas se chamam lá batuque."

6. *O Animismo Fetichista dos Negros Bahianos*, pp. 76 ff.

7. For a summary of the data on New World Afro-Catholic syncretisms published up to 1936, see M. J. Herskovits, *African Gods and Catholic Saints in New World Negro Belief*. Ramos has further extended the list of Brazilian syncretisms in *O Negro Brasileiro*, pp. 165–168; more data on Cuba have been made available by R. Lachetañeré, *Manual de Santeria* (Havana, 1942), while similar materials from Louisiana have been published in M. J. Herskovits, *The Myth of the Negro Past*, pp. 245–261.

8. Similarities and differences between this list of syncretisms and those published by Ramos for Porto Alegre (*op. cit.*, pp. 165–168), may be noted: Eshu is not given for Porto Alegre but Bará, a Porto Alegre term for Leba (Elebara) is correlated with St. Peter; Ogun, as in this list, is given as St. George; Shango is identified with St. Michael the Archangel (though Aganju and Ogodo are not mentioned); St. Onofré is identified with Osain instead of Ode, and St. Emmanuel is not listed, while Ode in Ramos' list is identified with St. Sebastian. In both lists, Oba is identified with St. Catherine, and Oshun with Nossa Senhora de Conceição; similarly, the twins, listed by Ramos with a query, as "Beifes," an obvious distortion of Beji, are identified with Comas and Damien. It is to be noted that the above comparisons concern only the items in Ramos' list that deal with Porto Alegre. The variation over all Brazil is considerably greater and, in many cases, Porto Alegre identifications given in this paper are listed by Ramos for other Brazilian centers.

9. F. S. Nadel, *A Black Byzantium* (Oxford, 1941), p. 10.

10. M. and F. Herskovits, *op. cit., passim.*

11. A. Ramos, *O Negro Brasileiro, loc. cit.*

12. It is a privilege to acknowledge with gratitude the warm cooperation of all these in this research effort.

13. It was a great advantage to have been able to discuss the problems considered in this paper with both these students.

14. *Os Africanismos do Dialeto Gaucho* (Rev. do Inst. Historica e Geografia do Rio Grande do Sul, 2º trim, an. XVI, 1936); and *O Negro e o Espírito Guerreiro nas Origens do Rio Grande do Sul* (*ibid.*, 1º trim, an. XVII, 1937).

15. By officials of the Servico do Patrimônio Histórico e Aristico Nacional. The courtesy of Dr. Rodrigues Mello Franco de Andrade, Director of the Service, and his associate, Dr. Luis Jardim, in making it possible to examine this important find and to obtain information as to the circumstances of its discovery, is gratefully acknowledged.

16. *El Negro Rioplatense y Otros Ensayos* (Montevidio, 1937), pp. 47–78; and *Negros Esclavos y Negroes Livros* (Montevidio, 1941).

17. *Revista Historica* (Uruguay, vol. 4, 1911), p. 583. Dr. James F. King has been most kind in making available this table, as well as the other materials bearing on the Negroes of Uruguay and the Argentine quoted below.

18. José Antonio Wilde, *Buenos Aires desde Setenta Anos Atrás* (Buenos Aires, 1917), pp. 126 ff.

19. *Ibid.*, p. 135.

20. Fac. de Fil. y Letras, *Documentos para la Historia Argentina*, t. vii, "Comercio de Indias Consulado, Comercio de Negros y de Extranjeros (1791–1809)," con introducción de Diego Luis Molinari. Buenos Aires, 1916, p. lxxvii.

The Panan,
an Afrobahian Religious Rite of Transition

[The panan] *in its relaxation, its humor, its quality as theater, . . . helps us understand some of the intangible reasons why African cult practices have been retained so tenaciously in this portion of the New World.*

＊   ＊   ＊

The rite to be described here is one of a cycle that marks the emergence of novitiates (*yawo,* Yoruba "junior wife") in the Ketu sect of Afrobahian cult-groups (*candomblé*) after a period of seclusion wherein they are ritually dedicated to the worship of the gods (*orisha*) by whom they have been chosen. As such, it functions as a mechanism of social reintegration, assuring the initiates that on their return to the daily round they will not be spiritually or physically beset by the dangers arising out of intercourse with the secular world from which they have been withdrawn, and which they are soon to re-enter with new names, as new personalities.

Descriptions of the "public" ceremonies of these cult-groups, especially of the Ketu variety are numerous and, on the whole, give adequate knowledge of their manifest forms of worship. We have relatively little information, however, as to their integral organization, and less on their complex theology, their inner rituals or their social functioning. As we probe more deeply into their working, we see emerge a well-defined system of belief that is based on the substantial knowledge of African lore, language and ritual by officials of the various cult-groups, whose role is accurately described in the local idiom as the *estado-maior,* the "general staff," and on the discipline they enforce in administering the affairs of the group and regulating the behavior of its members. This presence of a clear-cut system is further found in the reasoned understanding and controlled ritual expression of worship on the part of the cult-initiates and other affiliates with various degrees of "understanding" who make up the cult-group.

Les Afro-Américains (Mémoires de l'Insitut Français d'Afrique Noire, no. 27) (Dakar: 1953), 133–40.

For cult-affiliation, it becomes clear, responds to an hierarchical pattern, stratified on two levels. The first distinguishes the degree of
sanctioned participation according to the ritual experience, including
the type of offerings, of the individual in relation to his personal god
(*eleda*). The second is in accordance with the powers and role assigned to the individual by his *orisha*. The first category determines
priorities in participation, the second in direction.

In broadest outline, theology and ritual of all the Afrobahian cult-
groups in Bahia, as elsewhere in Brazil, represent well-defined retentions of African worship. A person may become a member in various
ways, but can acquire the right of active worship only through initiation. The only exception is the individual who is born in a cult-house
while his mother is undergoing training, and becomes an initiate by
virtue of having shared the mystic experience *in utero*. The need for
initiation—the ultimate degree of participation in cult life—is signal-
ized by the possession of an individual by a deity, who "mounts the
head" of the one thus marked as his devotee, and by subsequent divination to determine the name, nature and wishes of the god. Urgency is
demonstrated by an act of possession by the god, known as "falling"
and "rolling," during the progress of a ceremony at a cult-center.
This is directed toward the feet of the priest or priestess of the cult-
house (*pai-* or *mãe-de-santo*, or Yoruba *babalorisha* or *iyalorisha*),
and toward the quarters which house the novitiates when they are
undergoing initiation, the *camarinha*, known by the Gêge (Dahomean)
terms *hunko* or *hundemi*, or the Nago (Yoruba) *yara ashe*. In most
cases, however, the deity is less exigent and the candidate is permitted to amass the considerable amount of goods and money—considerable, that is, in terms of the prevalent standard of living—that
must be in hand to defray the expenses of induction into the cult.

The many cult-groups found in Bahia, and elsewhere in Brazilian
centers with an appreciable population of African descent, differ in
the degree of their adherence to African religious custom. The most
rigorous—"orthodox," in the African sense—are the Gêge, of Dahomean derivation. Most numerous today among those who hold
closest to African procedures are the Ketu, who take their designation
from the town of the same name lying on the Yoruba-Dahomean border in West Africa. They are essentially Yoruba in derivation and
linguistic expression. Another smaller group, the 'Jesha cult, is to be
traced to the Yoruba political group of the same name (Ijesha). It
may be regarded as a local variation of the generalized Yoruba religious culture that was continued in Bahia. The Nupe, called Tapa,
the name even today given them in Africa by the Yoruba, and rem-

nants of the Hausa and their northern and westerly neighbours are incorporated largely into the Ketu group. The Congo-Angola sect, as its name indicates, comes from the more southerly portion of western Africa; its linguistic usages have been traced to Kimbundu, but intensive research, in Brazil, Angola and the western Congo will be necessary before precise provenience can be determined.

The Congo-Angola groups provide the link to the less "orthodox" Caboclo cults, wherein Indian and Portuguese names of deities abound, wherein Portuguese words are sung to many of the songs, wherein initiatory periods are truncated to a few days or weeks, and wherein the most diverse African and non-African innovations are present. Finally the continuum moves to the Spiritualist groups, and to full-blown European beliefs and practices, many of which are syncretized into even the most "orthodox" aggregates. In a sense, this completes the circle, and makes for the cultural integration of Afrobahian religious life that is the outer form of the inner unities of belief and value systems that give the Afrobahian the psychological adjustment seen in his relations with his fellows, with those of other social classes, and with the universe in which he lives his life.

The *panan* (or *pana*, without nasalization), essentially comprises a series of major rituals, each of which symbolically reproduces some act which the emergent initiate will perform in daily life. Because, as in West Africa, these initiates are in great majority women—in the rite described here, there were no male initiates—most of the acts symbolized pertain to the woman's sphere of life. In performing these acts, the initiate brings into play a protective force that comes from anticipating unwitting transgression of ritual prescription, while at the same time re-introducing this newly-born personality—in a spiritual sense—to the world in which life must be lived.

Unlike the great "public" ceremonies, the *panan* is a quiet, almost intimate ritual. At the one to be described there were no more than twenty-five or thirty spectators, many of them officiating members of the cult-group holding the rite, the others relatives of the initiates. The contrast of this with the elaborate ceremony of name-giving, shortly before, marking the initial emergence of these same initiates from their seclusion, publicly demonstrating their skill in dancing for their gods, and showing their rich ceremonial paraphernalia, could not have been greater. No general announcement of smaller rituals of this sort is made, as is done for the "public" dances. For while the *panan* is in no way to be regarded as one of the esoteric elements of the initiatory cycle, of which there are many, an outsider, unless he were a friend of the priest or of the family of an initiate, and his interest in these matters was recognized, would never know of its occurrence. Yet in its relaxation, its humor, its quality as theater, it helps us understand some of the intangible reasons why African cult practices have been retained so tenaciously in this portion of the New World.

The particular ceremony now to be considered had been scheduled for six o'clock[1] in the evening; but actually it was well toward 10 o'clock before the rite was to begin, since there was an unexpected interruption of the sort that helps us understand the flexibility of this belief-system in meeting unforeseen contingencies. A sailor, presumably in a state of possession, announcing himself as the Deity Eshu-of-the-crossroads, entered the establishment, demanding offerings of money—for the cult-house—and rum for himself. He proceeded to upbraid those who were not adequately deferential, calling for songs in his honor, and in general making difficulties for the priest and the *ogans,* the men whose duty, on occasions such as this, is to see that cult practices go on without disturbance. Finally, after an hour, the head *ogan* of the cult-house, with the aid of the priest, induced him to leave.

There was some question whether the sailor's behaviour was an actual manifestation of this powerful, feared god, or of a man the worse for drink, and some speculation whether the priest would order the postponement of the *panan.* But whether divination dictated otherwise, or considerations of accepted practice entered, it soon became apparent that the ritual was to go on. For the spectators, this occasioned further waiting while the newly initiated *yawos* were being dressed; not, this time, in ceremonial finery such as they had worn at their initial appearance at the public dance, but in the distinctive costume made famous by the Bahian Negro woman, the *Bahiana.*

At 9.45, all being in readiness, the *yawos* filed in and stood, heads bent, in a row before a bench that had been placed along the wall of the *barracão,* the large room where the public ceremonies take place. The priest, holding each in turn by the shoulders, lowered and raised her three times before finally seating her. Then first the priest, and after him in turn the assistant priestess, (the *mãe pequena;* Yoruba *iyakekere*) and a younger woman, wearing a plain white dress, later identified as the named successor of the *mãe pequena,* first took up a switch lying at hand for the purpose, then a *palmatória*—an instrument of wood with holes bored in its flat surface that was used to chastise slaves by striking them on the palm of the hands—and a broken china dish. With the switch, each of the *yawos* was symbolically whipped on shoulders, arms and legs; her hands were struck twice with the *palmatória;* and from the dish some dust was scraped off with a stone and made to fall on her head. The significance of the whip, called *atori de Oshala,* was explained by the priest in a short homily. If in the future, he said, these initiates do not obey those who rank them, saying when they are called on to perform a task for their *orisha* that they will not do it, that they are too busy, or that they cannot, then they will be punished by Oshala who, as father of the gods, is the one who more than any of the other African deities chastises those who disobey. And when the *mãe pequena* used the whip on the two initiates for Yansan, the goddess of the wind, she prefaced her statement about the need for obedience to one of them with the phrase ". . . . . as you know already." The *palmatória* similarly signified that punishment would be meted out to those who disobeyed; but the significance of the grains of dust from the broken dish was not indicated. However, it was thrown, crashing, to the ground after it had been used.

When this episode was finished, the priest called the senior initiate of the cult-group, an elderly woman, who repeated the symbolic whipping and palmstriking on each of the *yawos,* and after her all other women who were present were summoned to perform the same acts. As each woman went forward, she put a coin in a plate placed on the ground for the purpose; in one case, where a woman had no money, the priest himself gave her a coin to put in it. The *mãe pequena* then concluded with a quick repetition of the two ritual acts in the name of five women who could not themselves perform them. One wore a black skirt, and hence could not approach the newly initiated *yawos* whose spiritual condition was still precarious, wearing the color of death, while the others were caring for infants and could not be disturbed. It was then the turn of the men. First the chief *ogan* of the group performed the symbolic acts, then a man, an *ogan* of another center, his guest, then an elderly white-haired man, the father of one of the *yawos,* and then some ten or twelve others present. This concluded the first episode, which took just under an hour to complete.

The second part, which began at 10.40, symbolized the re-entry of the initiates into activities of everyday life. The priest again pointed the lesson of the symbolism—that each initiate must perform each of these tasks since, if this were not done, harm might come to her when she later had to do them. The order of the tasks, and the manner in which they were performed, follow:—

(1) Along one wall of the room stood a row of water-jars, one for each initiate. Each jar was covered with a cloth, which the *yawo* who used it made into a head-pad, putting the jar on her head. Then, in a line, the group went outside the *barracão* "to get water." In several minutes they returned with the pots upright; each "poured" the imaginary water into a tin container, and put the jar down.

(2) Each took the broom that was standing ready, and swept a part of the floor.

(3) Each went through the pantomime of "pouring water" from the container into a basin, and then "washed" the cloth that had been used for head-pad.

(4) At the center of the hall was a table, an iron standing ready on the floor nearby. Each woman, in turn, went to the table and, taking up the iron, which was cold, went through the pantomime of "ironing" her cloth. It was a commentary on the differing personalities of the *yawos* to see how differently each went about the task in hand. All of them, however, gave a creditable performance, in a light, humorous vein, but without exaggerated caricature or exhibitionism.

(5) A coal-pot, some coals, a grate and a fire-fan were brought forward. Each *yawo* lighted a match, applied it to the coals, and fanned the "fire."

(6) A pot was then put on the "fire," and each initiate, using the stirring spoon in it, proceeded to "cook" and "season" her dish.

(7) A mortar and pestle was used by each. The pounded "meal" of cassava or beans, was placed in a woven sifter and "sifted" into a basin.

(8) Each initiate worked at a grinding stone.

(9) A basin of water was placed on the table, containing two leaves, each leaf symbolizing a fish. The *yawos,* in turn, using the knife ready at hand, "cleaned" the "fish." One of them, with a sense of theatre, added a realistic touch by snipping off the "tail"—that is, by cutting off the stem of the leaf. All this went on to the accompaniment of much laughter from the audience, and an impassive seriousness of the *yawo.*

It was now 11.05, and the *yawos* were again seated on their bench. The next two episodes represented acts that are taboo for an initiate, and for which immunity must be had if later done, even unknowingly.

(10) A candle was lighted, and after it had been passed behind the head of each initiate, she blew it out.

(11) Lighting a cigarette, a young man blew smoke in the face of each *yawo.*

The women then arose from their places, and, forming a line, filed outside the *barracão.* The following items were next enacted:—

(12) As each initiate re-entered the hall, she simulated buying at a market.

(13) She took an incense-burner, and went about the room with it, making motions as though to distribute the smoke in the manner of purifying the hall with incense,

(14) A tray of fruit was brought in, and each *yawo* put it on her head, going out of the door and back and about the hall, hawking her wares. This was a further source of great amusement, since each initiate tried to be as imaginative as possible in naming what she had to "sell."

(15) In the meantime, on the other side of the room, the *yawos* went to grate leaves on a grater—this was "grating coconuts."

(16) Simultaneously, nearby, others were now mashing leaves in a basin, representing the preparation of the seasoning for dishes to be cooked.

(17) A ladder was placed near a window. Each *yawo* climbed it to call to an imaginary trader outside to come and bring his wares— again, with imagination in what was said, and much laughter from the audience.

(18) The initiates then went outside once more, and, despite the full skirts that each wore, climbed over the window-sill and into the hall. One or two of the women had to be helped in this, an incident that the spectators punctuated with comment and laughter.

(19) Now they made themselves ready to go out. On the settee were comb, brush, powder, mirror and other feminine accessories, and each took her turn at using them.

(20) Next each woman went over to the dish in which offerings of coins had been placed, and "counted" what was there. Each announced her "findings" in fantastic figures, with simulated high seriousness, to the delight of the spectators.

The time was now 11.20, which gives some indication of the celerity and smoothness with which the items in the program of events succeeded each other. The next group of episodes, that continued without pause, concerned still other phases of life:—

(21) The shoes of the initiates had been brought into the hall some time previously, and each *yawo* now got into hers. This proved to be somewhat difficult, since, as the priest remarked, "Your feet are large," and in actuality must have spread during the period of seclusion, when none had been worn. This was a part of a series of preparatory acts that symbolized getting ready to go to Mass[2] and continued with gestures putting on of bracelets and other ornaments. A woman came out holding three comic looking hats, which three of the initiates put on; then she handed them three books which represented missals. There was great laughter again as the three, caricaturing elegance at every step, walked a short disance out of the door on their "way to mass," to be followed by the remaining group of initiates who repeated the act—three *yawos*, then three more, then the remaining two.

(22) The next episode to be "experienced" was "getting married." The priest went off to a small chapel, of the type found in all cult-centers, which in this case was then in a nearby house of the complex of cult buildings. These chapels, in appearance at least, do not differ from any private Catholic altar, with a small figure of the patron saint of the establishment—in this case, Saint Anthony, syncretized with the African deity Ogun, the *orisha* of the founder of the cult-house. This episode had as its aim to ensure that the *yawos* would find happiness in the relationships that had been interrupted when they went into seclusion, and were to be re-entered, or that were later to be formed. The episode, it should be indicated, not only included the taking of the vows but simulated the performance of the sexual act, the "groom" in each case being represented by a male infant. It is to be noted that when a small boy of about five years of age was brought forward to act in this capacity, he was rejected by those in charge as being "too old." The *yawos* went off to the chapel two at a time, and the bell could be heard ringing to "celebrate" the "marriage." When they returned, each "groom" was carried by his mother, while each "bride" had flowers. The "couple" then lay down on a sleeping-mat that had been placed for the purpose, and were covered with a cloth for a moment before the *yawo* got up and the infant was taken away. The audience was especially diverted by the first "groom," aged perhaps two years, who disliked the entire performance and made vocal his protest.

The "marriage" over, the succeeding episodes concerned behavior inside the home, where the initiate was presumably mistress of a prosperous house.

(23) Each initiate took her turn at hammering a nail.

(24) Each took a small piece of cloth, cut it a bit and sewed a few stitches.

(25) A meat-grinder was given a few turns by each.

(26) Each turned a few pages of a cheap magazine as though reading it.

(27) A dust cloth was used.

(28) Each put up an umbrella.

(29) Each brushed her clothes.

(30) The radio was turned on and, as the *yawos* listened for a moment, some short-wave station was heard.

It was now 11.45, and from the interior of the building adjoining the *barracão* came the sound of voices, and some music. The *yawos* stood about, waiting until the table was set for the final episode.

(31) The senior initiate of the cult-house, acting as hostess, cut the

meat that had been brought, and put a piece on each plate. The *yawos* then took their places, to simulate partaking of a "formal" meal. They ate the meat; then bread was passed. Their manners were excellent, and their comportment was watched with interest by all those present. A young man, as "waiter," poured a little wine for each, which each drank, first holding up her glass and pronouncing the polite "Licença" before drinking. Each drank a little water, and then partook of dessert, which consisted of small cakes. Finally all arose, and once more took their places on the bench.

At midnight a five minute interval ensued, after which the priest announced that they would proceed to the ceremony of "purchasing" the *yawos*. He pointed to each, asking who would "buy" them. One had a father, one a husband as "purchasers"; one was named as a "slave of Ogun." This may have had one of two meanings—that she had been "purchased" by an *ogan*, a member of the cult-group, for the deity, or that she "redeemed" herself. The other initiates seemed to have no one to "purchase" them; whereupon the priest asked "How much are the *yawos* worth?" and forthwith announced prices, which would either have to be paid by a future "purchaser," or paid by the initiate herself over a period of time. Though actual money passes when these "purchases" are made, the obligations assumed in the ensuing relationship between the "purchaser" and the *yawo* make for a complex of reciprocal obligations, much of which is ritual in character. The prices announced for devotees of the various deities were as follows; for those vowed to Yansan, the god of the wind, 400$000,[3] for those of Ogun, Oshala and Oshosi, the gods of iron and war, the sky and the hunt, respectively, 350$000, those for Oshun and Omolu, the deities of fresh water and of the earth, 300$000.

Without waiting for further bidding or permitting conversation, the priest went on to the closing episode, the benediction. A mat was put down and, beginning with the "slave" of Ogun, each *yawo* prostrated herself individually in turn before him, kissing his hands, and then the hands of the younger woman who was to be the future *mãe pequena*. The mat was then transferred to the opposite side of the hall, near the spectators, so that all might receive blessings. The collection plate was put down at the head of the line which the new initiates now formed, and as each spectator passed down this line to receive the blessings bestowed, he placed a contribution in it. The chief *ogun* was first to be blessed, after putting a note for 100$000 in the upturned hands of the first initiate; then two other *ogans;* the other male spectators, followed by the women who were present, and then the children. Contributions were generous in terms of accepted values, with

more than 250$000 in the plate by the time the children went down
the line of initiates to be blessed. The blessing itself consisted in having the hand kissed by each *yawo;* and to simply make a contribution
was not regarded as sufficient, as was seen in the rebuke administered
by the priest to one spectator who hesitated at participating in this
aspect of the rite.

The ceremony ended at 12.45 a.m. The *yawos* returned to their living quarters to await the next rite that would bring them one step
nearer the resumption of everyday life as full-fledged initiates. Spectators and cult-members went about exchanging greetings. The ceremony had gone off well, and if this Eshu who had intruded had actually come with evil intentions, he had been powerless to halt the
smooth flow of the ritual, or to bring about untoward happenings during its performance in the face of the spiritual strength of the cult-
group and its priest.

1. Eighth of February, 1942. It was one of the many rituals, public and
private, attended in various cult-houses during field research carried on in
Bahia and elsewhere in Brazil, under a grant from the Rockefeller Foundation, that occupied a period of 12 months in 1941–1942.
2. As has been demonstrated by all students of these cults, the members
are simultaneously worshippers of the African gods and communicants of
the Catholic Church. It is from this fact that some of the most significant
syncretic aspects of Afrobrazilian cultural adjustments arise.
3. At the time of this research, the unit of currency in Brazil was the
milreis, now termed *cruzeiro.* One of these units (1$000) has the value of
five United States cents, or about thirty French francs.

The Social Organization of the Candomble

> . . . the candomble is to be thought of as a grouping based
> on free association that . . . is considerably influenced by
> kinship relations and African tribal derivation. . . . It is hier-
> archical in its structure. . . . The identification of members
> with the group and its activities are internalized to become a
> primary mechanism for individual adjustment by providing a
> sense of psychological security and the means of achieving

Anaais do XXXI Congresso Internacional de Americanistas, I (1954) (São
Paulo, 1955), 505–32.

social, economic and status goals. . . . belief in the efficacy
of the supernatural power of the deities worshipped by the
candomble devotees, and especially in the force of African
safeguards against hostility and frustration, goes far beyond
Afrobrazilian circles. Similarly, belief in . . . divination em-
ployed in cult worship and acceptance of the power of twins
as bearers of good fortune, reinforce these beliefs.

❉   ❉   ❉

There is no part of the New World where research into Afroamerican
culture has been carried on with greater intensity or more continuity
than in Brazil. Before the turn of the century such figures as Manoel
Querino and Nina Rodrigues, working in Bahia, and João do Rio, in
Rio de Janeiro, described African elements in Afrobrazilian life and
raised pertinent questions concerning the African provenience of this
segment of the Brazilian population. When it is remembered that
none was trained either in the techniques of their time for the study
of culture, or in the Africanist field, which is to say that their control
of the comparative data could only be rudimentary, it is all the more
remarkable that their pioneering efforts produced a sound body of fact
that revealed ethnographic and historical problems which have continued to be a challenge to students of Brazilian culture.

It is a temptation to discuss the many contributions made by Gilberto Freyre and Arthur Ramos and their associates, who in the next
decades, through the significance of their discoveries, enhanced the
investigations in the field which these pioneers ploughed, but the nature of the problem we are considering here permits us only to indicate the stages through which Afrobrazilian research as we know it
today has developed. The period from 1920–1940 witnessed a steady
growth of knowledge of Afrobrazilian life, refinement of approaches
to the field, and the placing of Afrobrazilian research in wider perspective. From 1940 to the present, research has been characterized by
further geographical extension of work in Brazil, and by greater so-
phistication in the use of techniques of investigation. Studies have
been carried on by more investigators with professional training. Results have been consolidated so that, as a part of Afroamerican studies
in general, the field has become a recognized branch of both ethnological and historical disciplines.

Among the most striking of the continuities in this development, certainly insofar as anthropological research is concerned, is the preoccupation of students with the religious aspects of Afrobrazilian life—
with the candomble, or the Shango, or the macumba, or the *casas das*
Minas, as the Afrobrazilian religious complex, in different regions, is

variously named. The results have been impressive. We know the major Afrobrazilian cult groupings, and their points of African derivation. Our knowledge of the names of the deities and their syncretisms with Catholic saints has reached a point where it is doubtful if further information about them can do more than add or correct details. We have a wealth of data concerning the paraphernalia used by the worshippers, offerings given the deities, songs sung in their honor, with admirably full textual data. We know the basic patterns of public ritual in various cult groupings, and something of their local and regional similarities and variations. Our knowledge of the theological concepts underlying these outer manifestations of Afrobrazilian religion is reasonably full, in general outline, though more is known of ritual than of theology, just as more is known of actual syncretisms than of the reasons for the identifications that result from this process.

Emphasis on Afrobrazilian religion represents a scientifically valid response to actuality in Afrobrazilian life. For this group, as is the case with other Afroamerican populations, religion is the focal aspect of their cultures. We are coming to recognize, however, that to devote disproportionate attention to one phase of the life of any group, no matter how important this phase may be, yields only partial insights. Our aim, as students of human behavior, must be to attain a rounded portrayal of life in which no element will be neglected, and each will be shown in terms of its significant interaction with the others.

Afrobrazilian traditional modes of belief and behavior comprise a sub-culture that is lodged within the matrix of Brazilian culture as a whole. It should be emphasized that in this it is no different than other sub-cultures of the country, just as Brazil, as a whole, like any other large nation, has its recognizable groupings with special characteristics based on occupation, or region, or ethnic derivation. The fact that the Afrobrazilian sub-culture has ethnic identifications simply places it in the same category as those other special modes of Brazilian life which, for example, are influenced by traits and orientations that come from Portugal, or Germany, or Italy, or Japan.

The holistic approach to culture makes it apparent that study of the social structure and economic base of the Afrobrazilian sub-culture and its setting in the total Brazilian scene must be the next major objective of Afrobrazilian research. If we take the cult-group as an outstanding social expression of the Afrobrazilian sub-culture, then a micro-ethnological analysis of its non-religious aspects would seem the logical point of attack. This paper, employing materials gathered during field research in Bahia during 1941–42, will outline the social organization of the Bahian candomble groups, and indicate some problems toward which future investigation can with profit be directed.

I

From the point of view of its social organization, the candomble is to be thought of as a grouping based on free association, that in turn is considerably influenced by kinship relations and African tribal derivation. It functions as an instrument of social adjustment and social control, which on the economic side operates as a means of furthering mutual self-aid. It is hierarchical in its structure, with well recognized lines of authority and responsibility. The seniority principle plays a major, though at times a limiting role in determining the position of the individual in the group. Though never rigidly applied, this principle is instrumental in maintaining corporate structure as an end to achieving stated religious aims, and those social and economic objectives reflected by cult organization and the patterned behavior of cult membership. Social controls are achieved through the manipulation of the supernatural sanctions at the command of those in authority. The identification of members with the group and its activities are internalized to become a primary mechanism for individual adjustment by providing a sense of psychological security and the means of achieving social, economic and status goals.

It is not necessary here to consider the physical setting of the cult-center where the activities of the cult-group are carried on. Descriptions of the more frequented centers, diagrammed to indicate the locale of the religious rites and the living-quarters of officiants dot the literature from the time of the early writings. The extent to which cult affiliation, in terms of the location of the cult-house, influences the residences of its membership is, however, not known. Thus at this initial point in our discussion we come on a basic research problem to be framed in terms of a sociometric analysis of the place of residence of the members of different cult-groups in the centers where these organizations exist. What proportion of the membership, let us say, of the Bahian or Recife cult-groups of various kinds live within one kilometre, or two, or three, or more, of the cult-house? To what degree are such historic factors as the length of time a cult-group has existed, the length of time its cult-house has occupied its present site, the particular "nation" to which it belongs, correlated with the residence patterns of the membership? There can be little doubt but that answers to questions of fact such as these would give us the data necessary to analyse the ramifications of the candomble in the community of which it is a part, and the extent to which in addition to being the focus of religious activity it is also the center about which a social community is formed.

The lines along which the candomble hierarchy are drawn and the organization of its membership are, in general terms, known. The names of the various officials and ranks necessarily move in and out of the descriptions of rituals which form the basis of most accounts of Afrobrazilian religion, though these are presented without ordering of precedence of function. A formal listing of these officers was made by Edison Carneiro in 1941 [1] in an article which, in enlarged form, later appeared as a monograph treating the candomble world of Bahia along broad lines.[2] Similar data, less formalized because the structuring is less formal, are found in the studies of Nunes Pereira[3] and Octavio da Costa Eduardo[4] for Maranhão. Most recently, the organization of the cult-groups of Recife has been excellently described by René Ribeiro.[5] The data given here represent the organization of the Ketu cults of Bahia. This is a useful type-form because it is that of the largest numerical grouping of the more orthodox African cults, and comparisons of it with other groupings will indicate something of the variations to be found in Afrobrazilian cults. Such variations reflect the fact that each cult-group is an independent social entity, and the further fact that their organization differs in accordance with the "nation" with which a given group is identified.

II

It is scarcely necessary to emphasize the dominant position of the cult-head, the *pai-de-santo* (*babalorisha*) or priest, if a man, or the *mãe-de-santo* (*iyalorisha*), if a woman. This personage exacts, and receives the respect and obedience of all functioning members of the group on the basis of authority derived from the control of supernatural power and demonstrated competence in administering its affairs and counseling its personnel. Carneiro[6] and Ruth Landes,[7] who have stressed the preponderant role of women in the cults, hold that male leadership is relatively recent. Since we are concerned with present organization rather than historic development of these groupings, we need only cite the figures adduced by Carneiro himself, which show that of 67 houses of all "nations" counted by him in Bahia, 37 were directed by priests and 30 by priestesses. It may be further remarked that the hypothesis is not supported either by the African data or the known names of priests who in earlier years attained prominence in Bahian candomble circles.

Whether male or female, the primacy of the cult-head is manifest in numerous ways. It is the priest or priestess who, in the ordinary course of events, carries on the divinatory procedures held to be essential to the successful operation of the cult-house. The post is held only by those who have manifested the spiritual and administrative capacity to fill it, and after a long period of special training. This is not the place to detail the powers and prerogatives of the cult-head. It is sufficient to indicate that it is the priest or priestess who, in the important rite of initiation, shaves the top of the head of the initiate and makes the cuts that are the seat of the deity to whom the novitiate is vowed. At the death of this officiant, the one thus initiated must have the "hand of the dead" withdrawn from his head by a colleague of the deceased of comparable rank. A most significant indication of the role of the priest or priestess is to be found in the further fact that on his death a successor does not take full title to the post until the seven-year rite for the *Egun*, which divests the dead cult-head of active control over the house which he directed, has taken place. In many cases, the candomble is dormant during this period, with the cult-house closed for all public worship, and rituals held to a minimum. Such a seven-year hiatus, or one of a multiple of seven, which has tended to be overlooked in Afrobahian studies, explains why certain houses that figure importantly in the writings on the candomble of one time tend to disappear from reports of investigations carried on in the same locality a few years later, or to be mentioned as existing in a state of desuetude.

The numerous outer symbols of authority of the cult-head are indicative of the relationships between the priest or priestess and the other members of the group. The priest or priestess presides at all public ceremonies, welcomes special guests, designates the initiates to whom the god will come and in general supervises each rite and sets its rhythm. The man or woman who heads a cult-group, especially in the case of a larger and older house, will move with great dignity, and be considered in speech and action. Initiates prostrate themselves before him, and ask his blessing. If he enters a room where initiates are seated, all rise; if he sits on a chair, they will seat themselves on the ground, on mats, since they may not sit on the same level as their superior. All instruments of initiation are under his control. Certain portions of the animals that are sacrificed are his by preemptive right. The cult-head judges disputes between the members of the group, and presides over the panel of cult officers which considers the cases of those who have been guilty of infractions of cult rules. On the death of an initiate, he officiates at the funeral, and directs the subsequent ritual of mourning, called by the Dahomean word *sihun* or the Yoruba *acheche*, that culminates in sending away the soul of the dead after its desires as to the disposal of its cult paraphernalia and other sacred objects have been obtained and executed.

The cult-head thus is the spokesman, representative and, most importantly, the symbol of the cult-group, which in turn draws its support and, in a narrower sense its membership, from the Afrobrazilian population in general. There are, of course, Afrobrazilians whose relation to the cults is tenuous or entirely non-existent, just as there are Brazilians not identified with the Afrobrazilian community who are attracted to it through curiosity or conviction, and whose interest varies from an occasional visit at public rituals to the rare instances of full membership. Public rites are well attended, sometimes by several hundred persons, though an audience of this size would be seen only at the larger candombles, where the renowned priests and priestesses are in charge. Many who come to the cult-houses do so to have "work" performed for them—for purposes of healing, or for divination, or to obtain supernatural assistance in facing hostility, or in achieving desired ends. Finally, there are those to whom the gods come unexpectedly, usually at public ceremonies, where they "fall" and, depending on the nature of the possession, are either admitted for initiation at once or after preliminary rites begin the process, often protracted, of assmbling what is needed to enable them to become full-fledged members.

III

The core of candomble support comes from those who are committed to cult membership—the initiates, properly speaking, plus candidates for full or partial initiation, and those who in Bahia are known as *ogans* and *ekedi*, and who will be discussed later. The initiates may be men or women; the *ogans* are only men, the *ekedi* only women. Various explanations of why women preponderate among the initiates have been offered, but the best hypothesis would seem to be an historical one, that reaches back into African custom and is bolstered by the comparable position of women in African and African-influenced religious groups elsewhere in the New World. The reason, under terms of this hypothesis, is economic. The initiation being a process that requires several months, and in some cases a longer time, it is less difficult to release a woman from her accustomed routine than for a man to relinquish his work and the pay that is needed for the support of a family.

Initiation lies at the very heart of the social organization of the candomble. Psychologically, it is the confirmation of the unity of the initiate with his god, and an opening of the road to control of supernatural power. Viewed sociologically, it is the major rite of aggregation, binding the individual to the group through the operation of supernatural sanctions invoked in the elaborate rituals that characterize the progress of the initiate to full membership in it. Yet initiation is only the commencement of the long process by which a member moves up the social ladder, gaining an increasing measure of the knowledge that, according to the theory of candomble worship, is essential to the proper service of the gods and of the acquisition of the rank and prestige that come with time and experience.

The organization of the initiates gives the stratification of candomble social structure its most explicit expression, especially in the position of members of the three major categories of *abian, yawo* and *vodunsi*. At the base are the *abian*, those whose tutelary deity, the African god that is the guardian angel, the *anjo da guarda* of the individual, has either revealed himself through possession or has been determined by divination. As "master of the head" of this person, the *olori* or *eleda*, as it is called, this being will be the chief of whatever other deities may later come to him. The *abian* are novitiates, properly speaking. Each will first of all have the proper beads to his *eleda* that have ritually been "washed" (the *contas lavadas*), and will have a complex of ritual objects for this deity in the shrine of the cult-house. Somewhat later, at a succeeding rite he will attain the position of a worshiper with a *santo sentado*. At the cult-house, they begin their instruction in cult ritual and behavior, helping with the everyday tasks that must be performed in the day-to-day maintenance of the house, and doing work assigned to them on the occasion of cult-rites, where they learn procedures of worship by observation and minor participation. It should be noted, however, that not all *abian* are active in the cult-house. Some go through the required rituals to satisfy the demand of a deity, and being uninterested in the candomble, perform these minimum duties and go no farther.

Those who do go on next become *yawo*, a term that is the Yoruba word meaning "Junior wife." They enter the seclusion of the cult-house for a period of instruction and spiritual preparation, in the course of which they emerge, during an impressive public ceremony, to give their new names as initiates, and to demonstrate their ability in performing the dances of their deities. Later, they go through the series of rites that reintegrate them into the world at large, such as the public *quitando*, where they sell the wares of the market, and the private *panan*, when they symbolically perform the tasks they will have to do in the society of which they newly become a part, and thus bring into play the protective force that is derived from anticipating unwitting transgressions of ritual prescription.

The initiate is now *feito*, a full-fledged though junior member of the candomble group. As such, the new *yawo* has opportunities not accorded any outsider to learn the work of the gods and to participate in public worship, though unless he is the heritor of a powerful deity the principle of seniority relegates such a man or woman to a relatively humble place in the organization of the cult. Certain rights now vest in the new initiate. The *yawo* is free to visit many parts of the candomble closed to non-members, though the shrines themselves can be entered only by the elders of the group, and during rituals inside them these junior members kneel in the corridor outside, singing the prescribed songs. When contributions are required for ceremonies, the *yawo* has the right—and it is regarded as such—to give a larger sum than the *abian* are permitted to give, and to offer certain sacrifices. When possessed at public ceremonies, the *yawo* dances in the costume of the deity each initiate must provide, and even when not possessed at such rites, can remain on the dancing floor and dance with the gods. But above all, initiation brings to the new *yawo* an assurance that the full supernatural power of the deity is behind him, something which, when to this is added the greater social and supernatural force of the group to which he now belongs, has far-reaching repercussions in his dealings with those of other houses or in the world outside candomble circles. This is clearly shown when, as a *yawo* first released from the cult-house after initiation, he or she is escorted home by senior cult-members, who detail the rules that must thereafter govern the relations of the new initiate with his kin, and describe the penalties that will supernaturally be exacted for infractions of them.

During the next seven years the *yawo* gains stature through the opportunities to learn more and more of cult lore and procedures. In accordance with the saying, "To climb the ladder of the candomble, a person mounts one rung at a time," at the end of this time, unless economic or other reasons cause a postponement, the cult-member is ritually eligible to perform the ceremonies that mark passage to the status of senior cult-member. For this the Dahomean term *vodunsi*, in literal translation "wife of the deity," is commonly employed, though in the literature *ebome*, from the Yoruba word *egbomi*, "senior" is also encountered as a designation for a member of this grade.

The *vodunsi* is a cult initiate who has arrived at that state of knowledge and supernatural power which allows full freedom of action as regards the candomble group. This means release from the control of the cult-head, if the *vodunsi* wishes, a control symbolized by the presence of a complex of objects sacred to the deity the initiate worshiped which, for the *yawo*, are retained in the shrine of the cult-house. The performance of *obrigação de sete anos*, the rite of the seventh year, with its spiritual renewal of powers, marks the attainment of full status in the cult. The *vodunsi* is now held competent to worship his deity and to guide others in this worship. If the requisite supernatural sanctions have been manifest, and the man or woman has enough followers and a "gift" for cult-headship, he may now institute a new cult-group; and in any event, he has the right to make a shrine for his god in his own dwelling where the deity is "fed" and otherwise cared for. In the majority of cases, this latter act does not mean a break with the cult-house where the *vodunsi* received training, or with its leader, who continues to retain a measure of power over all those who have been initiated there by permanently keeping in the shrine of the cult-house the tuft of hair shaved off the top of the initiate's head at the time of initiation. Whether affiliation continues or not, however, the *vodunsi* is a free agent, within the group as well as outside it, to a degree the *yawo* can never be.

The place of the *vodunsi* in the strata of cult membership is reflected in the number and importance of the rights that accrue to persons of this rank. The *vodunsi* are accorded the special greetings due superiors, by *yawos* and *abians*. With continuing activity inside the group, they may begin to work into its hierarchy of officials, and in any case will be consulted by these when major decisions affecting the group as a whole must be made. At public ceremonies, the *vodunsi* have the right to name the songs each will sing in honoring the deity he is worshipping, while at the rituals of cult-houses other than their own they will be greeted with marks of respect that can extend to a salute sounded on the drums as one of them enters the dancing-space. Cult members of this rank who gain a reputation for knowledge and supernatural power will be consulted by junior colleagues, but more importantly by non-members who experience difficulties they feel may be caused by deities, perhaps whose very identity is unknown to them, for lack of proper worship. In this and other activities, the *vodunsi* obviously functions as a source of recruitment for the cult-groups.

IV

The second large category of cult-affiliates consists of the *ogans*. Though not initiates in the technical sense of the term, they are men who play important roles as advisers, protectors and helpers of the cult-group, and participants in its activities. Those whose interest is a continuing one, and who take the required ritualistic steps may have a knowledge of cult-practice and theology as complete as any other member of the group, excepting only the priest or priestess, and may rise to high position in the executive hierarchy.

It should be made clear, however, that the institution of the *ogan*, in name if not in form, seems, as far as has been ascertained, to be restricted to Bahia and perhaps such cult-centers elsewhere as are offshoots of Bahian cult-houses. Its importance in discussions of the candomble may very likely have arisen out of an historical accident, the fact that the research which set the pattern for discussions of cult-organization and procedures was done in a relatively small number of Bahian cult-centers, and the larger ones, at that. In this context it is not without significance that in one major cult-house, special terminology has been introduced for male affiliates whose functions are comparable to those of the *ogans* elsewhere in Bahia. Here they are called "the twelve ministers of Shango," and are named *magba*, the Yoruba term for Shango priest.

The derivation of the word *ogan* is clearly Yoruba-Dahomean. The former kingdom of Ketu, which has given its name to the Bahian "nation" currently most numerous among the candomble groupings, lies on the border between these two African peoples. In both these tongues, the word *gā* signifies "chief." More specifically, we find the word *oga* in the Oxford Yoruba Dictionary[8], with the translation "a distinguished person in any sphere, chief, superior officer, headman, master," meanings which quite fit the application of the word in its Bahian candomble usage.

The absence of this category of cult-member, as such, has been specifically noted for Maranhão[9], for Recife[10], and for Porto Alegre.[11] The problem which this fact presents goes beyond the simple presence or absence of named cult-affiliates of this category. It moves rather to an analysis of basic Afrobrazilian patterns as these have to do with the functioning of the men who are affiliated with the cult-groups. To what extent, it must be asked, does the Bahian institution of the *ogan* represent anything more than a specialized version of certain functions performed by men in the operation of the cults that we know from these and other reports are to be found elsewhere? Phrased differently, we may say that it is essential to ascertain who, in the regions where the *ogan* is not found, plays the role of the Bahian *ogan*, especially as to the degree to which the position of such a person in the cults corresponds to that of the Bahian *ogan* of comparable rank, or differs from it. To this end, we may indicate the nature and functioning of the *ogan* in the social organization of those Bahian cult-groups where he exists.

In the literature, stress on the function of the *ogan* as the protector of the cult-group has tended to obscure the role he may play inside it. The nomination of an *ogan* to be a protector is obviously a useful device; it permits a cult-group to honor a friend who is an influential outsider without committing him to full affiliation with it. The one who falls in this category, however, is an *ogan de ramo*, or, as an alternate term sometimes heard has it, an *ogan figueiro*, and is quite different from the *ogan confirmado*, who is important in the internal organization of the candomble and, insofar as is in accord with the principle of seniority, participates fully in its affairs.

An *ogan de ramo* is thus an influential interested affiliate, to whom the group can turn when funds are needed for special purposes, or licenses to hold ceremonies must be obtained, or who can influence the police on occasions of tension. *Ogans* in this category are named, often without their prior knowledge, at the direction of the priest or priestess, by a cult-initiate under possession. If he accepts the nomination, he is escorted about the dancing-space of the cult-house to the acclamation of those assembled. He is seated on a special chair for *ogans*, and carried on the shoulders of other *ogans* into the shrine of the deity that, through the medium of the possessed initiate, named him. He is now *levantado;* if he goes no farther, his obligations are entirely voluntary, though he is informally regarded as the patron of the initiate who named him, and to whom he may give gifts from time to time when food must be offered to the tutelary deity whom they are to serve in common. He will be called "father" by all initiates of the house, who kiss his hand in greeting him.

Should he desire a closer affiliation, he will then be "confirmed." We are here concerned with his position in the cult-group, rather than with the details of ritual that this involves, though it is a temptation to describe these in view of their almost complete absence in the literature. It is sufficient for our purposes, however, to state that the induction may require a period of as much as three weeks to complete. Because of the demands of regular employment on a man, which rarely permit him to absent himself from work, a cult-initiate acts in his place. It is understandable that henceforth he stands in a special kind of relationship to this initiate. They will share a *bori,* the important rite in which offerings are given to the head of an individual, the seat of spiritual power and knowledge, and in other rites manifest their close spiritual relationship.

As an *ogan confirmado,* he has a special high backed arm chair, often elaborately carved, in which he takes great pride as a symbol of this position. This chair, which often has his name and the date of his confirmation on it, is the one he occupies by right at the public ceremonies given by the cult-group to which he belongs.[12] He is honored by the initiates of his and other groups, and will come to occupy a special place and receive special salutations when he visits the public ceremonies of the candomble elsewhere than in his own cult-house. He will assist in keeping order at the rites of his group to which the public are admitted. As an *ogan confirmado,* he can wield the sacrificial knife in cult rituals, if necessary. If he continues over the years to be assiduous in the affairs of the group, is generous in his donations and in meeting other demands on him, demonstrates wisdom in the advice he gives and shows increasing knowledge of cult-theology and ritual practices, he will move steadily into the upper levels of the cult hierarchy. With the passage of time, he may become chief *ogan*. As such he will be entrusted with the task of seeing that the physical properties of the cult-houses are properly maintained, and that his junior colleagues perform the duties which, at the behest of the cult-head, he assigns to them; and in some houses may be the executive head of secular affairs, as the priest or priestess is the spiritual head.

v

Between the body of initiates and affiliated cult-members and the priest or priestess who is the chief executive officer of the cult-group are the officials at times designated by members of the candomble as "the general staff." The titles of these officials given here are those used in Ketu houses, and come from the Yoruba language, or Nagô, as it is called in Brazil. The listing is given by sex, in accordance with candomble practice in differentiating the position and function of those who hold the various posts in the cult hierarchy.

Men	*Women*
Pegigan	Mãe pequena (Iyakekere)
Asoba	Adoshun
Apashogun (or Ashogun)	Adagan
Alabe	Adagansi
Alabe-huntor	Amoro
	Abase
	Ekedi

In the principal Ketu and Ijesha Bahian candomble centers, all the men in this list are *ogans*. The offices, however, held by men who are initiates and perform the same functions have been reported from the parts of Brazil where the *ogan* is not known. This must be so, for their assignments are as essential to the operation of the ritualistic and other activities of the cult as are those of the female officials who, except for the last one named, are initiates. In the case of the men, indeed, this differentiation between initiate and non-initiate does not entirely hold even for the Bahian male cult officials. Thus, for example, the drummers, who can only be men, in a number of cases were *feitos*.

It must also be understood that the list of officials given here is a maximal one, the full complement of which is to be found only in the largest and wealthiest cult-groups. The majority of the cult-houses in Bahia, as well as in other centers, have a smaller executive staff, where each member performs a number of functions, or a qualified outsider is brought in to ensure that a particular rite will be properly performed.

There is reason, indeed, to question on both ethnographical and historical grounds the typicality of the candomble which, in its various forms has served in Afrobrazilian research as the model of African carry-overs. Afrobrazilian religion has been studied almost exclusively in urban centers; the only systematic investigation of the phenomenon in a rural area, made by Eduardo in Maranhão, showed no comparable organization. The UNESCO investigation of race relations in rural Brazil, though it touched on the religion of the Afrobrazilians only in passing, specifically noted the absence of candomble groupings there.[13] This makes the historical question a fair one: Do the candombles, that have been assumed to be the only valid expression of African religious retentions in Brazil, rather represent special and restricted forms of organization found in the urban centers of Dahomey and Nigeria, transplanted to the urban centers of Brazil? This of course leaves un-answered the further question of whether intensive study of Afro-brazilian religion in the rural areas may not reveal retentions of more widely-spread African patterns organized in terms of family and lineage worship of the deities reinterpreted as saints, or under African designa-tions as well, with specialists called in to perform more complex and extensive rituals when these must be given. These points cannot be pursued further here, but the indications for the essential research that is needed are clear.

We may now return to our particular problem, the position of the "general staff" in the social organization of the candomble. It is obvious that both men and women must be persons of long experience in the cult—senior *ogans* or initiates in the case of the men, *vodunsi* in that of the women. The one exception to this last statement has to do with the *ekedi*, who in some ways may be regarded as the female counterpart of the *ogan*. She will in many cases be one whose deity "never comes to her head" as the saying goes, or as it is otherwise expressed, has "nothing in the head," and who therefore is not eligible for initiation. Her tutelary deity will be known, however, and she may have her washed beads and her *santo sentado*. Some *ekedi* go through all other steps in the preparation of an initiate except the final one, in which the head is shaved and the sacred cuts are made on it. The derivation of the word is the Yoruba *akede*, which the Dictionary translates as "public crier, proclaimer, herald" but to which a Yoruba informant added the meaning "messenger."

The position of the *ekedi* has been stated by Carneiro[14] to be that of "slaves" of the *filhas do santo,* for "being constitutionally unable to receive the deities, they are employed in subordinate roles, devoting themselves to the care of dress and ornaments" which the initiates wear in the cult rituals. The imagery evoked by the use of the word "slaves" is unfortunate, and is perhaps a fault of the translation of his article from the Portuguese, since his later discussion in that language[15] is more in accord with the actual position of this kind of cult-member. The *ekedi* does perform the services mentioned; she also bathes and dresses those possessed by the gods, gives food to the *eré,* the child-like beings that "come" as the aftermath of possession, and has "the right of the towel" with which she wipes the faces of the dancers at ceremonies. With the passage of the years, her experience and knowledge gain for her, too, a substantial measure of respect.

The *pegigan,* as the title implies, has charge of the *pegi* or altars of the cult deities and, under the direction of the cult-head, officiates at the rites held in these shrines. As the oldest and most respected of his category, he has the first "right of the knife" when sacrificial animals are to be killed, unless he cedes this right to the junior colleague, the *apashogun* or *ashogun,* who specializes in and usually performs this ritual task. The *asoba* is another high title, as the literal translation of this Yoruba word, which means "the King's guard" indicates. In some houses, indeed, the *asoba* is a kind of vice-*pegigan.* The *alabe* and the *alabe-huntor,* the leaders of the ritual songs and the drummers, are indispensable in the worship of the gods. Because of the technical musical competence these men have in common, drummers have secondary affiliations to an informal organization of their own, and when they wish, play at the rites of other cult-houses than those to which they belong. This, however, in no wise lessens the strength of their identification with their own cult-centers.[16]

Turning now to the female members of the hierarchy, it can be said that as a whole their activities are somewhat more restricted to the affairs of the cult-group, as these relate to the local Afrobrazilian population, as against the concern of their male colleagues with the relations of the candomble to the community at large. The *mãe pequena* is essential to the operation of any cult-house. She is the second in command, and must have training, experience and ability comparable to that of a priest or priestess. She has well-defined prerogatives, and is the only official of a cult-group who can fine its head for infractions of ritually prescribed behavior. She is the intermediary for the cult-head with the other members; there is, in fact, nothing the priest or priestess can do that she cannot, save to place her hand on the head of an initiate. The *adoshu*, a kind of executive assistant to the head of the cult, in some instances can be thought of as holding a post that will train her as successor to her *mãe de santo*. She alone, of the hierarchy, except the priestess, has the right to make the all important cuts on the head of the initiate. She may be a younger *vodunsi* than other members of the cult hierarchy, if divination dictates her appointment at an earlier age than that customary for members of this group.

The *adagan* and *adagansi*, who are senior members, are what might be termed spiritual aides to the cult-head and, among other important ritual obligations, care for the proper worship of his personal deity. The significance of the duties performed by the *amoro* will be apparent to all who understand the place of leaves from the forest in cult practice and theology, when it is indicated that it is she who sees to the preparation of the sacred infusions made from these leaves. Finally comes the *abase*, sometimes referred to as the cook in charge of the kitchen of the cult-house. The high place accorded her ritual function derives from the fact that as "mistress of the knife" she must see to it that the meat of the sacrificial animals is properly apportioned, and that offerings given when the gods are "fed" are prepared in accord with the complex ritual prescriptions that govern them.

VI

If we seek to understand the nature of the candomble as a cohesive social entity, we must look in two directions. We must consider both how it is set among the other elements of the society of which it is a part, and also indicate those mechanisms of interpersonal relations that are operative inside it and account for the identifications which give it continuity. In theoretical terms, we are here treating of the forces which are spoken of in the sociological literature as the play of out-group and in-group drives in maintaining the stability of a given social form.

The candomble has its widest circle of contact with the total community of which it forms a part. Here its members rub shoulders with Brazilians of all kinds, primarily on the level of social, economic and religious relationships. One of the most significant elements in these contacts has resulted from interaction of those factors that tend to derogate African religious traditions as "superstitions" and place high value on those of European derivation.[17] Such attitudes are bolstered by the association of the candomble in the minds of most Brazilians with low socio-economic status. They are, for example, at the basis of the police supervision that presents candomble devotees with the particular problems they face in carrying out the mandates of the deities they worship. This factor varies with time and place, but is often present in actuality, and always presents a potential threat to freedom of candomble action.

Despite all this, the position of the candomble in the community at large is by no means unimportant, though to obtain precise materials bearing on this point presents difficult and delicate problems of field procedure. There is no question, however, that belief in the efficacy of the supernatural power of the deities worshipped by the candomble devotees, and especially in the force of African safeguards against hostility and frustration, goes far beyond Afrobrazilian circles. Similarly, belief in the effectiveness of the methods of divination employed in cult worship, and acceptance of the power of twins as bearers of good fortune, reinforce these beliefs. The candomble also profits socially from appreciation of the aesthetic aspects of cult-rituals, of the beauty of the costuming, the intricacy of the choreography of the dances and the excellence of their performance, the skill of the drummers and the discipline of the singers.[18] This, in turn, is reinforced by the excitement engendered by what, from the point of view of European patterns, is regarded as the exotic nature of these rites, and by the knowledge that these are but outer expressions of those esoteric aspects of cult life which are the subject of much speculation and conversation outside Afrobrazilian circles.

These positive and negative factors aid powerfully in giving the candomble a definite place in the social landscape, and affording those both inside and outside it a sense of the institution as a functioning feature of the community as a whole. It is these, among many other factors space does not permit naming here, which hold it in social equilibrium and, from the point of view of its inner cohesiveness, give its members common symbols of opposition that strengthen the positive values it holds for them and thus comprise a powerful force making for its survival.

As we move from the community in general to its Afrobrazilian component, we must consider not only how the candomble fits in the general patterns of this sub-culture, but also how a network of relationships between cult-groups is maintained that gives the total structure of Afrobrazilian religious groups, whatever their derivation and particular forms of worship, a unity that has largely gone unrecognized.

The influence of the candomble within the Afrobrazilian segment goes far beyond its membership, nor can the degree of interest in it be calculated in terms of the numbers of persons in attendance at public cult ceremonies. For one thing, it must be recognized that in the family of each cult-member we have a center of influence and interest. Family members, concerned with the progress of a relative who is a novitiate and later a *yawo*, join in contributing what is needed when the rituals of the deity the kinsman worships must be performed. They share the security that comes from having a family member knowledgeable in the work of the gods, and are beneficiaries of the supernatural protection this affords. Many an Afrobahian who is not interested in being a member of the cult repairs to a priest or priestess for advice through divination when confronted with a problem to be solved, or for means to ensure the successful outcome of a new venture, or for a *despacho* that will outwit malevolent forces set against him by an enemy, or crush an adversary.

The total complex is held together by relations between independent cult-groups that are rarely mentioned in the literature. Some of these are entirely informal, as where heads of two houses, through friendship or alliance, make it logical for their followers to be in closer association than would otherwise be the case. A cult-group gives no public ceremony of importance to which priests, priestesses and senior members of other houses are not invited as guests of honor. At these ceremonies, too, initiates from other candombles come as spectators, and if they become possessed will, no matter to what "nation" they belong, be cared for like any other initiate, and furnished the proper costumes so that they can dance for their gods. This kind of relationship reaches across the categories of African sects despite the attitude of disdain one encounters on the part of those who belong to the more "orthodox" groupings toward the rituals of houses that deviate from strict African practice.

One formalized expression of this network is to be found in the institution of the *ajibona*. Like any element of candomble organization, it varies in accordance with the particular situation in which it is operative. In summary, the *ajibona* is the ritual sponsor of an initiate, and in common reference is called the *madrinha* or *padrinho do santo*, a person who stands in the familiar god-parental relation to the initiate sponsored. The *ajibona* may come from the same cult-house as the initiate; we are concerned here with the instances in which he is drawn from outside a given cult-group. This person will always hold at least the rank of *vodunsi*, and may be a priest or priestess; he must always worship the same deity as the candidate he sponsors. If a person of prestige is invited by a minor cult center, he will be honored for bringing to it his greater knowledge, and may even be asked to initiate the candidate. Conversely, the head of a minor, especially a new house, will hold it an opportunity to sponsor an initiate of an important center where he can learn much that will give him increased power, and in this case he is expected to defray substantially the costs of the initiate in return for the privilege. The *ajibona* from outside a house spends the crucial period of the initiation rites at the center to which he has been invited, and escorts the *yawo* on her return to her house. The relationship between initiate and sponsor is a continuing one, and can become of the greatest importance should the *ajibona* later establish a new cult center. In any event, it is not difficult to see that this institution provides a cross-candomble mechanism of substantial significance in unifying the candomble world and those who are affiliated with it.

Within the cult-group, position and interpersonal relations do much to knit personnel into a unified social entity. The stratification of candomble social structure that has been described in this paper is by no means complete. A group of candidates initiated at one time are members of a *barco*, a boat, and those who belong to it have in common an experience that in its emotional force and spiritual significance forges bonds of major strength, as the appellation used between these members of the same initiation-group, *irmã-do-santo*, "cult-sister," implies. These bonds are reinforced through the operation of the principle of unity through opposition. The members of a given *barco* form a group that takes its rank, as a unit, within the organization of its cult-house in terms of the length of time that has elapsed since its initiation. Inside it, however, there is a fixed order of precedence in terms of the relative place of the deity a given novitate worships, as determined by ritual grouping. This is given outer visual expression through the fact that, in forming the line for the dances of public rituals, a member of a *barco* who is vowed to Ogun, for example, will always precede the one whose god is Oshossi, or Omolu, while certain "male" deities will precede the "female" ones. On the other hand, all members of an older *barco* will take precedence over those belonging to a more recent one.

There are lines within lines. At rites such as the *lorogun* the "male" deities will in some houses contest with the "female" to determine which will "rule" during the year ahead. The relation between the *ogan* and the *vodunsi* who acted for him during induction has been mentioned; that between an *ajibona* and the initiate who is sponsored, where the two belong to the same house, is also close. Initiates who are vowed to the same gods have ties that cannot be neglected, while an older *vodunsi* who is a trader will utilize the services of younger women to assist her, and thus create another grouping.

Recruitment is from various sources. No detailed research has been conducted to ascertain the precise relationship that obtains between cult membership and kin affiliation. It has been stated that the post of priestess in the cult-groups headed by women is inherited in the maternal line, and there are enough data to establish the fact that this does occur. But there are also enough cases where a successor is chosen from the senior staff of the candomble, and may be no relation at all of a dead priestess, to prove that this is not the rule. It is clear that all candomble posts can be inherited, but the fact that divination precedes election and that this may indicate a nominee who is no relative of the holder of a given office shows that the rule, if this is one, is by no means always followed.

Membership is clearly not dictated by kin affiliation. A person born in a cult-house while his mother is undergoing initiation becomes *de facto* an initiate; this is the source from which male initiates often derive. A person may "inherit" a deity that over generations has attached itself to a given family, but this merely means that this deity must be worshipped by someone in the family, or its worship must be provided for, not that the one who inherits it must necessarily affiliate with a given cult-group. Some become members because they were promised before birth to a god, and are being troubled because the vow has not been fulfilled; some join a cult-group because they have been helped to gain some aim, or have prospered, because of the advice of its priest or priestess; some become members because of certain circumstances that may have attended their birth, which divination revealed as a sign that a deity had designated the infant as a future devotee.

In view of the fact that candomble structure is a complex whole, comprehending many lines of potential stress as well as elements that make for aggregation among its members, we may ask how its functional unity is achieved and maintained. The external pressures, in terms of the reactions to the attitudes of society outside the candomble world, has been discussed. The power of spiritual sanction, both positive and negative, and the supernatural controls over cult-members that rest in the hands of the cult-head, obviously constitute a most significant factor. The aesthetic and emotional satisfactions afforded by cult-rites also enter, in terms of the release from tension they provide, and the excitement and dramatic suspense that attends them. Psychologically, the expansion of the ego-structure that results from identification with the achievements of the candomble must not be overlooked, achievements which, in the ontological aspect of cult philosophy, are ultimately ascribable to the beneficence of the supernatural beings that rule the affairs of the group and its members. Finally, the supreme compensating device in candomble structure itself is found in its flexibility. There is no rule that does not have its exception; in all instances, situations alter cases. This tradition is basic in candomble psychology; from the point of view of candomble structure, it is one of the bequests of African tradition that has been a primary cause of the survival of this complex institution despite the historical pressures to which it has been subject.

VII

It is apparent, as we consider recent Afroamerican research that, for all its refinement in method and its improved conceptual apparatus, except in the case of certain psychological studies, it has in the main lodged on dead center. Whether in the American continents or in the Caribbean, preoccupation with the religious aspects of Afroamerican life has in most investigations continued to dominate the concern of students. As a result, research has consisted either of reworking materials from areas already studied on finer lines or, in new areas, of providing fresh factual data in the same category.

A striking parallel, of considerable consequence for Afroamerican studies, can be found in the present status of African and Afroamerican research. For if in the New World emphasis on religion has tended to relegate the study of social and economic aspects of Afroamerican life to a subsidiary place, so in Africa the stress laid on the investigation of social structure has made for a comparable restriction of research activity, in this case to the relative neglect of African religious life.

It is the thesis of this paper that a rounded approach to any culture or sub-culture is essential for an adequate scientific analysis of it. Attention to special aspects yields results whose importance must not be underrated, but from the point of view of theory and method in the study of culture, they cannot give a full understanding. No part, that is, however meticulously analyzed, can give us more than partial comprehension of the whole. For the Afroamerican field, the fact that research interests in Africa and the New World run along different lines has serious implications. The historical relationship between Afroamerican and African cultures has been fully established, together with the principle that adequate analysis of the former cannot be attained without due regard for the role of the African traditional component in setting its present configurations. Yet if the effort in New World studies is such that the excellent social and economic comparative data from Africa go unused, while the more sophisticated approaches to Afroamerican religion now in play cannot call on data derived from the use of comparable methodological techniques in Africa, it is apparent that the gears of the two intimately related fields cannot mesh.

Because religion is the focus of Afroamerican culture, the data in hand are of the utmost importance. But it is time, and more, that we take adequate cognizance of the holistic principle in the study of culture as it applies in our field, and especially in Brazil, where the materials are so rich. In taking advantage of the richer insights this approach can yield, we will broaden the contribution that has already been made, enriching the scientific potentials of these previous studies for the analysis and comprehension of the nature and functioning of human culture as a whole.

1. Edison Carneiro, "The Structure of African Cults in Bahia." *Journal of American Folklore*, vol. liii (1940), pp. 271–78.

2. *Ibid.*, "Candomblés da Bahia." *Publ. do Museu do Estado*, N.º 8, Bahia, 1948.

3. Nunes Pereira, "A Casa das Minas." *Publ. da Soc. Bras. de Antropologia e Etnologia*, N.º 1, Rio de Janeiro, 1947.

4. Octavio da Costa Eduardo, "The Negro in Northern Brazil." *Monographs of the American Ethnological Society*, vol. XV, New York, 1948.

5. René Ribeiro, "Cultos Afrobrasileiros do Recife: um Estudo de Ajustamento Social." *Bol. do Instituto Joaquim Nabuco*, Número especial, Recife, 1952, p. 41.

6. Edison Carneiro, 1940, pp. 272–3; 1948, pp. 84–88.

7. Ruth Landes, *The City of Women*. New York, 1947, pp. 34–37.

8. Oxford University Press, *A Dictionary of the Yoruba Language* (by various authors). London, second edition, 1950.

9. Octavio da Costa Eduardo, 1948, p. 47.

10. René Ribeiro, 1952, p. 42.

11. M. J. Herskovits, "The Southernmost Outposts of New World Africanisms," p. 199.

12. For a description of the ogan's chair cf. R. Bastide, "Cadeira do Ogan e o posto central." *Boletim*, Fac. de Filosofia, Ciências e Letras, Univ. de São Paulo, n.º lix (Sociologia N.º 1), pp. 44–45, São Paulo, 1946.

13. Charles Wagley (ed.), *Race and Class in Rural Brazil*, especially the chapter by H. W. Hutchinson, pp. 16–46, particularly p. 42; UNESCO, Paris, 1952.

14. Edison Carneiro, 1940, p. 275.

15. *Ibid.*, 1948, pp. 96–97.

16. This has been discussed in M. J. Herskovits, "Drums and Drummers in Afrobrazilian Cult Life," p. 183.

17. Cf. Donald Pierson, *Negroes in Brazil*, pp. 270–74, 312–13, Chicago, 1942. See also Charles Wagley, *op. cit., passim.*

18. Cf. M. J. and F. S. Herskovits, "The Negroes of Brazil." *Yale Review*, vol. xxxii (1943), pp. 263–279, esp. pp. 275–279.

Some Economic
Aspects of the Afrobahian Candomble

. . . the candomble contribution . . . to the secular econ-
omy of the city is appreciable. . . . The economic theory of
the candomble thus has implicit in it the concept of a kind
of equilibrated interplay between the command of resources
and the action of the supernatural. As concerns the individual
cult-member, this means that the degree of friendly interven-
tion, indifference or hostility on the part of the forces that
control his fate and his own personal fortune is mediated by
the extent to which he fulfils the ritualistic requirements of
worship. In candomble thinking, the degree to which he is
prepared to make economic sacrifice is an important factor
in bringing him material reward and enhanced status.

❋   ❋   ❋

Bahia is a city of almost a half-million population. Its social and
economic stratification is not unlike that of most Brazilian cities, and
its sub-groupings are in close interaction. Membership in the various
African-derived candomble cult-groups is undoubtedly weighted on
the lower social-economic levels; nevertheless, the higher strata are by
no means unrepresented. For the candombles include in their numbers
entrepreneurs who are owners of business establishments and small
manufacturing concerns, labor leaders and political figures, skilled
operatives and other minor industrial supervisory personnel as well as
manual workers and casual laborers. And when one moves out of the
category of active and acknowledged membership, those who have less
formal relations with the candomble are found to some degree in all
strata. Such relationships are to be seen in the instances where the
services of Afrobahian diviners and priests are utilized by persons who
belong to the higher social and economic levels, seeking guidance
from the powers these specialists are held to control.

Quite aside from this relation between the candomble and the
population in general as regards matters touching on the supernatural,

Paul Rivet Octogenario Dicata, II (Mexico: Universidad Autonoma de Mexico,
1958), 227–47.

its contribution to the secular economy of the city is appreciable. For one thing, an impressive amount of business is generated by its activities. In the established markets, where a large proportion of the retail trade is carried on, stalls where cult paraphernalia may be purchased are large and well-stocked. In the principal market of the lower city, indeed, these stalls are found at the entrance to the main building, where their wares will be as available for the tourist and the local non-candomble trade as for customers who are members of the cults. They offer for sale cult accoutrements of all sorts—the strings of beads of various sizes and colors prescribed for the worship of the gods, including coral, amber, crystal and imitations of them, the *ferramentos,* or metal objects used in cult ritual, and replicas of these, bracelets and armlets of silver, tin, copper and brass, and many other items. Nor can the import trade be overlooked, in this regard, for in the cults a high value is placed on certain commodities from West Africa—a *pano da costa,* or hand-loomed, strip-woven imported cloth, is worth much more than one locally hand-loomed, while cowry-shells from "the coast"—the African Coast—are so valued that certain deities will not countenance the use of non-African imitations. Other items imported for cult use are West African peppers and soap, kola nuts and herbs, and the raffia that is used, especially in making the costumes for Omolu, the earth deity. Though trade with Africa had been suspended during World War II when this research was conducted,[1] the resulting scarcities merely enhanced the prices demanded and paid for them. Those, like the Lagos Trading Company, with an office in the lower city, who had been engaged in this important trade, were waiting for the cessation of hostilities to resume it.

In gross, the stimulus given by cult worship to economic production in the city and its surrounding areas is thus by no means insignificant, though no figures are available, and an attempt to reduce this to quantitative terms having any degree of precision would present technical methodological difficulties of major proportions. Yet, for example, we need but consider the amount of cloth used in the elaborate, ample dresses worn by women initiates at ceremonies, or the even more costly costuming of those possessed by the gods, to see how this one item cannot be overlooked as a factor affecting the textile market.

Drums are a case in point. They are made in sets of three, the cost varying according to size, type and kind of wood. An average figure for a set would be about 1000$000 [1,000 milreis]. The more traditional hollow-log drums, of the hardest wood, cost about 700$000 a set; those made by a barrel-maker, of staves, about 270$000.[2] The single and two-toned gongs that fix the basic rhythms which the drummers beat out are made by iron-workers, and cost about 30$000 a set. In addition is the cost of the drum-heads—deer or calf-skin being used for the smallest, cow-hide for the larger two—the paint or varnish for the bodies, and the pegs and the cord used to fasten the drum-head to the body. Only the poorest and smallest cult-centers lack their own drums, since these instruments are held to possess spiritual powers that might be "spoiled" through use outside the cult-house where they belong, and this means that probably over a hundred cult-houses possess them, with many having several sets. And while the bodies of drums last for a long time, heads must be changed fairly frequently under the battering of hands and drum-sticks.

Any important ceremony entails offering sacrifices of fowl, goats, and sheep, and, on rarer occasions, a bullock must also be provided. In the surrounding *reconcavo,* the area lying inland on the bay, there are markets where animals of the particular color, and in adequate quantity are to be bought for the major rituals. Most cult-initiates must have a *pedra,* a stone of a particular shape and marking sacred to the deity to which an initiate is vowed. Sometimes one comes on them, but they are more frequently purchased, often from a man who makes his living diving for them in the sea. The price varies according to the deity concerned, but amounts ranging from 60$000 to 200$000 per stone were cited. The metal objects used in cult worship are made by specialists, and pottery vessels, of particular sizes and forms, are also made especially for cult use. In addition, there are the materials, time and labor consumed in the construction and maintenance of the buildings and shrines in the cult-centers themselves. Nor can we overlook the role of the consumption patterns associated with the more general religious festivals, such as the annual *presentes* for the goddesses of lake and sea, which call for the purchase of expensive large vases, of perfumes, silks, mirrors and other costly items; or the festival for twins, Comas and Damien, with the necessary provision of food-stuffs these rites entail; or the substantial expenditures made in connection with ceremonies for the dead.

Another way in which the candomble impinges on the general economy of Bahia is in the vending of cooked foods. These vendors, for the most part, are *Bahianas,* as the picturesquely dressed Afrobahian women are termed, and though they are not seen in costume on the streets of the city as often as they were in earlier times, they are still to be encountered. The point here is that these women are nearly all cult-initiates, and the foods they sell are African foods. Each has her place, and at lunch-time those who work in offices and shops or on the docks come to buy their lunches where these women sit outside a cafe, or at a street-corner.

The trade is well-organized, and each vendor has her helpers, usually younger cult-members, who prepare the food. A successful seller will clear as much as 30$000 a day. From her gross returns, she has to pay her helpers, who in general receive from 40$000 to 60$000 per month each, her rent, and for the fish, chicken, beans, palm-oil, peppers, and other ingredients used in preparing her wares. The older and more established vendors increase their profits by buying in bulk.

The closeness of the relation between food-vending and the sanctions of the candomble becomes apparent when the answer of a priestess is given to the question, "Why is it, when women are initiated, the gods so often advise them to sell foods?" In pointing out that there were various occupations which the "Africans" brought with them, she said, as concerns food-selling, "It is because the Africans brought this over, too, that the gods protect those who engage in this occupation. And the reason the food-sellers dress with their cult beads is that, in the days of the Africans, it was felt that being out on the streets, where there was so much competition and jealousy, one needed the protection of the gods." Hence, by inference, wearing these costumes, which are essentially the dress of the cult-initiates and are to be seen in their most elaborate forms in the cult-centers on ceremonial occasions, gave notice that their wearers had the help of such protectors. Of significance also in this connection, is the fact that for both initiate and affiliate, divination reveals that the "gods" counsel, and encourage entrepreneurial initiative.

One aspect of street-selling that may be noted is the monopoly of what is termed *cabeça de boi* held by the women of the cult-groups. *Cabeça de boi*, literally "ox-head," is a complex that includes not only the skull, brains, and the meat on the head itself, but also the liver, kidneys, lungs, heart, neck and tail. Nothing of this is wasted—even the bones are sold as food for dogs. An established seller of *cabeça de boi* may purchase, on contract, an entire complex each day, but those whose trade is smaller will buy only parts of the whole from an intermediary. One of these intermediaries, a woman who contracted for from between fifteen to twenty heads daily, may be cited. They were purchased at 30$000 each, and were resold to retailers at from 70$000– 80$000 each. It is understandable that such operators are persons of considerable means in terms of their sub-culture; the point to be made here is that many of them are of importance in the candomble world. These traders will also have assistants, often cult-initiates, to whom they have advanced the costs of initiation, and who are repaying their obligations by working them off. Some of the meat is assigned to such younger women to be hawked from house to house. The older established vendors station themselves outside butcher shops, with whom they are not in competition, since these establishments do not deal in *cabeça de boi.* It is stated that, unlike the food sellers, these women are allowed to have their places on the sidewalk without charge, as a friendly act on the part of the butchers, but this could not be checked.

Aside from selling foodstuffs and meat, candomble women form a considerable, if not the preponderant segment of the market vendors, operating both in the permanent enclosed markets and the weekly open air centers. They deal in commodities of all sorts, and are noted for their business acumen—a West African tradition that has been fully retained in this New World center. In addition, they work at the tasks customarily done by women in all Brazilian cities. They are household servants, nursemaids, laundresses and cooks—indeed, they have made Bahian cooking a byword in all Brazil. They are seamstresses and milliners, shop-girls and cashiers. Seen going about their daily tasks, they are indistinguishable from other Bahian women, and only a string of beads at the neck, for her deities, when not hidden inside her blouse, will indicate to the knowing that a woman is a cult member.[3]

As has been stated, the economic activities of male cult-affiliates run the gamut of the occupational scale, with the majority toward its lower ranges. They work as common laborers for building contractors, or on the street railways, or for the municipality; they are porters and cleaners; on a somewhat higher level, they are stevedores, masons, carpenters, drivers of trucks and taxicabs. They are inspectors in the sanitary services, policemen, controllers on the trolley-cars, foremen on the docks, or skilled craftsmen working in factories or in small establishments, sometimes their own, with their apprentices. They are completely integrated into the economic life of the city. This is true even of some of the cult-priests, whose renown enables them to earn their entire incomes, which may be substantial, from their professional work. Some of them, whose cult-centers are on the outskirts of the city, will have *consultórios* in its central portion for the convenience of their clients. Yet even some of these priests participate in the more general economic life, as is evidenced by one who owned and operated a *quitanda,* or small shop, in the heart of the city.

Here, indeed, lies one of the most striking aspects of the acculturative syncretisms that give to Afrobahian life its unity and inner coherence. One of the best-known members of the candomble, who acted as guide and informant for two generations of investigators, was an assistant in the anatomical laboratory of the medical school. Another figure, respected for his cult orthodoxy, was a clerk in one of the municipal bureaus. No incongruity was felt by Afrobahians when a young priest, well-known for his spiritual powers, and head of an influential and prosperous cult-center, who several years before had left medical school to take up his cult obligations, announced that at the bidding of his deity he was about to resume his studies to become a doctor of medicine.

It is obvious that the ability of these men, and of the women as well, to contribute to the cults, and to fulfil their ritual duties, will vary with their economic position. A man with a family who, at the period of this research was earning even twice the minimum wage of 5$000 a day, would have little left over for expenditures of this sort. If illness or other misfortunes made it essential for him to consult the priest or diviner, he would have to borrow the necessary money for the fee, as the Bahian saying goes, "*Candomble não faz nada de graça* —The candomble does nothing free."

A woman without means, or whose relatives cannot afford candomble costs may pledge herself to repay the amount involved over the years. In doing this, she sacrifices status of spiritual gains, and will be at the service of her cult-house until her obligation is discharged. An exception to this is made in cases where an individual is revealed to have unusual supernatural powers, or one to whom has come an important ancestral deity that rarely manifests itself, and will be prized by the cult-group as an addition to their pantheon. Such persons will be carried through initiation by the house itself, on a kind of scholarship. More commonly, however, those whose resources are limited wait until they and their families can amass the sums needed to defray the costs of initiation.

It should be made clear that such cases as have been cited are by no means the rule, since in the main the members and affiliates of the cult-groups are able to make such contributions and payments as they are expected to make. Nor in considering the reciprocal economic ties between the candomble world and the larger community of which it forms a part can we neglect those whose relations with the cults are withheld from general knowledge. In such cases, participation is private, and the principal will be represented by a cult-initiate who acts as his surrogate in the essential rites. The obligations of such persons are discharged through the contributions, often substantial, that they make to the particular group to which they give their allegiance. The rationale for this, which is basic for an understanding of any aspect of the economy of the candomble, whether in its internal or its external relations, is that while the work of the supernatural beings is in large measure that of bringing prosperity and well-being to those who worship them, the relationship is a reciprocal one which, with hard-headed realism, is envisaged in economic terms. The person whose fortune has been enhanced as a result of cult intervention in his behalf must compensate for what he has received with more lavish provision for offerings to the deities, richer accoutrements for the initiate who acts for him, and more generous fees to priests or priestesses and to other cult personnel, if he is to continue to receive the benefits and the supernatural protection that have been vouchsafed him. In essence, then, the candomble must be thought of not only as a socially integrated unit, organized for the worship of the forces that rule the Universe, but in economic terms as an institution which functions pragmatically to protect the best interests of its members and affiliates, with its activities comprising a significant sector of the total economy of the community.

II

If we move to the internal economy of the candomble, we may first of all consider the costs of worship that members and affiliates support. In order to attain perspective on this, we may project some of the ritualistic requirements of cult membership against the economic position of those who belong to the candombles. It will be remembered that though its affiliations may reach high into the strata of Bahian society, the great majority of its active participants belong to the lower strata.[4] At the period of this research, it will be recalled, the minimum daily wage was 5$000, but a more reasonable figure for actual wages of the majority of low-paid workers was reported to be twice that figure, or about 300$000 monthly. Yet a competent seamstress was earning 3$000 or 3$500 a day; female household servants were paid at about the same rates. Craftsmen were paid 10-15$000 a day, clerical and technical aids 400-500$000 monthly, chauffeurs and truckdrivers 400-750$000. Fishing, an important occupation, is sometimes carried on cooperatively, the owner of the boat receiving two shares of the catch. It is seasonal, and earnings vary with the season and with the going market price. Fishermen, on the average, earned somewhat more than common laborers, less than those who perform manual crafts.[5]

If we now turn to the cost of candomble worship, it is apparent that, in terms of such incomes representing the resources of the major portion of the members, even when the contributions of a gainfully employed wife are taken into account, the amounts required for active participation in the cults are not inconsiderable. In these terms, the figures of 7$000, the average daily wage of an ordinary worker, the fee paid the cult official who sacrifices a fowl, or 30$000, almost a week's return for the laborer who received the minimum wage, for the more important sacrificial complex involving a sheep or goat, are seen in proper economic perspective. Nor must it be forgotten that this is only one item in the total cost, which must also include the fee of the cult-head, the cost of the animal and the cooked foods and rum—*cachaça*—or the soft drinks that are also offered the gods, to name but some of the other items. Yet the sums required are not given grudgingly. One man recounted with pride how he had spent more than three *contos* (U.S. $150) for the worship of the deities to whom his wife was vowed, while another said, "When you feed the gods, you are full of life, and you give generously."

The tradition of saving for these expenditures is firmly established, and cult-members look to their families for cooperation in meeting the cost of worshipping the gods that will bring security to them all. Most devotees will have in their homes a small box or jar into which they drop a coin each day, in anticipation of future cult needs, especially the cyclical rites of feeding their personal gods. Certain cooperative aspects of cult spending have developed because of the felt economic need resultant on these obligations. Thus, with an initiation or anniversary rite in prospect, the cult-member and her family will, over the years, if necessary, accumulate the many special costumes, beads and other objects needed for it, sewing, crocheting, raising chickens and ducks, buying mats and pots. Or, the members of a group initiated at the same time will calculate the cost of observing the important ceremonies that mark the third or seventh anniversary of initiation, and each contribute an equal share—something of economic importance when it is noted that the minimal cost of "feeding the god" on these occasions is 400$000. The burden of meeting these costs, moreover, is one reason why the precise calendrical cycle of anniversaries is not strictly followed in observing such rituals. For in cult theology, the gods have a human character that makes it possible to reason and, if necessary, to bargain with them, so that their demands can be reduced to manageable compass, and the more expensive offerings postponed beyond the scheduled time without punishment being exacted.

As documentation of the costs of various rituals, we first reproduce here a memorandum that was tendered a novitiate, before her initiation, by the priestess of her house to show what she must provide. The initiate retained this list to have a record of what was furnished so that she could not at some later date be rebuked with the assertion that special favors were shown her. The list, it should be pointed out, does not include the many new costumes the initiate must provide; nor is the original broken down into the categories given below:

a. *Sacrifices and Accompanying Foodstuffs*

1 goat	beans (black, brown, light brown)
1 turtle	white corn
1 pair guinea-fowl	yellow corn
2 pair pigeons	shrimps
5 cocks	palm-oil
6 hens	onions
9 chicks (4 male, 5 female)	wine
2 snails	rum
African limes	honey
5 kola-nuts	dried beef
5 *orobo* (black African nuts)	dried salt fish
2 *atare* (Guinea pepper)	lard
	flour

b. *Utensils*

1 large water jar	1 stool
2 small water jars	2 pottery cooking-pots
1 medium-sized water jar	2 glazed pots
3 small glazed china dishes	2 frying pans
1 large china dish	4 fire fans
1 covered china dish	2 brooms
6 large plates	1 coffee-pot
1 pair of scissors	1 cooking tripod
1 razor	4 wooden spoons
1 knife	1 grater
1 large washing basin	1 grinding stone
2 small mixing bowls	3 balls of white chalk
1 chamber pot	2 balls of yellow chalk
African soap	3 balls of vari-colored chalk
1 lamp	2 balls of indigo

1 trunk for garments of the deity

For the celebration of the first anniversary of initiation, a rite of relatively minor importance, the following items were provided by the initiate concerned:

1 chicken

1 cock

1 chick (male)

3 bottles of palm oil

1½ kilos light brown beans

1 kilo white corn

3 litres shrimps

2 kola-nuts

½ bottle honey

1 kilo yellow corn

250 grams salt

2$000 worth of cornmeal cakes
   (*acasa*)

2$000 worth of okra

1 yam

½ kilo of onions

3 red china plates

1 white china plate

1 coffee-pot

1 mat

1 ball of white clay

1 large pottery jar

1 package candles

1 medium pottery jar

The "feeding of the gods" that marks the third anniversary of initiation is much more elaborate, as the *nota* given below indicates. Here prices were appended, but the figures given are those of 1937, when the value of the *milreis* in terms of costs of commodities was somewhat higher than in 1942:[6]

1 goat	50$000	1 bottle honey	3$000
6 chickens	10$000	6 litres shrimps	12$000
3 cocks, 6 chicks	21$000	10 bottles palm oil	10$000
1 pair pigeons	5$000	2 kola-nuts	14$000
1 pair guinea fowls	7$000	2 *orobo* (African nuts)	14$000
5 kilos light brown beans	5$000	1 African pepper	4$000
2 kilos white corn	2$000	okra	2$000
3 kilos yellow corn	1$200	herbs (*lingua de vaca*)	2$000
1 kilo black beans	1$000	1 knife	3$000
2 bottles wine	2$000	2 cooking pots	2$500
2 bottles rum	2$000	2 frying pans	5$000
		2 balls colored chalk	——

At the bottom of this list was written a tabulation totalling expenditures, broken down into food, "other goods," and an item entitled chauo, the fee of the cult-head, called the *dinheiro de chão*. This tabulation comes to 207$000, a figure of some variance with the amount of 179$000, the total of the sums in the list itself. In addition, an un-explained item of 85$600 was appended.

The rite of the seventh year anniversary of initiation demands even larger expenditures. This is the occasion on which the initiate reaches senior status, becoming a *vodunsi*, and thereby attaining the knowl-edge that allows worship independent of a given cult-group, if this is desired. It confirms and renews the spiritual power conferred at initia-tion, and is to be considered in some respects as a symbolic reenact-ment of the original initiatory rites. Offerings provided for one such seven-year rite included:

  2 "four-footed animals"—sheep or goats.
  7 cocks
  7 hens
12 chicks
  1 pair each of pigeons, guinea-fowl, and ducks
  1 turtle
  3 kola-nuts
  2 *orobo* (African nuts)
African soap and limes

The foods needed for the rites of initiation, and in similar quantity—beans, corn, palm-oil, honey, wine and the like—and the same utensils, had also to be bought.

In addition to the above, the list gives us some information as to the clothing and linens that must be provided, items which are absent from the *notas* because the novitiate or celebrant of an anniversary brings these to the cult-house for the occasion. The following would be typical, especially since the great majority of cult-initiates are wo-men:

2 new costumes for the deity
2 African cloths
3 lace-trimmed petticoats
3 blouses
1 pair of white slippers

6 new scarves (*ojas*), of cotton and silk
1 "nice" mattress
1 new pillow
towels (usually elaborately embroidered)
new bed linens

Understandably, should the *vodunsi* set up an independent cult-house, the expenditures for the seventh-year anniversary will be much greater, since the deities must individually be given the sacrifices needed to "establish" them in the new center. Space does not permit these to be detailed in all their complexity, but certain summaries can be given which will be useful when compared with the above lists. In one particular case, the sacrificial animals provided were:

For the gods:
- 6 goats
- 7 cocks
- 11 hens
- 3 pair guinea fowl
- 1 pair pigeons
- 1 pair ducks
- 1 snail
- 2 tortoises

For the dead:
- 7 chickens
- 1 goat (if the cult-head of the *vodunsi* had died)

For the drums:
- 1 chicken

The foods furnished for this occasion cost 268$000; the cooking implements, knives, and similar items, 129$000; ritual pottery and other paraphernalia for the shrines of the gods, 95$000; while the cost of the metal objects used in worship, but not in dancing for the deities, was 150$000. This amounts to 642$000, or, at 1942 values, U.S. $32. A minimal estimate for the garments, cloths, and bed-linens listed above would be more than two *contos,* with another *conto* for the sacrificial animals, a total that approximates U.S. $200.00.

The man who is confirmed as an *ogan*[7] supports heavy costs of initiation, a prelude to the recurrent stream of contributions he will be called on to make as time passes. One estimate of the costs of confirmation placed this at 500$000 or more; another held that the cost would be greater than a *conto;* one *ogan*, telling of his own experience, stated he had spent 980$000. Offerings are substantial, as can be seen from the following list:

- 1 goat, or sheep
- 5 hens
- 5 cocks
- 10 chicks
- 1 kola-nut
- 10 bottles of palm-oil

- 2 kilos onions
- 10 litres shrimps
- 1 bottle rum
- 3 bottles of white wine
- 1 bottle of honey
- 5–10$000 worth of okra

1 package of African peppers

In addition, the one confirmed must provide the chair that is a mark of his rank in the cult,[8] which costs a minimum of 100$000, but because of the prestige factor involved would perhaps more often cost about 250$000, while the fee of the cult-head in such a case could scarcely be less than 100$000. If we add the substantial gifts he must give to the woman who acts for him in the initiatory rites he cannot attend because of the demands of his job, the estimates given are entirely reasonable.

III

Nothing is more difficult to learn than the details of candomble income and costs of operation. Heads of cults are by tradition, and because of the nature of their calling, reluctant to discuss such matters, and it is unlikely that even the more important subordinate officers know more than a part of the facts as regards total input and outgo. Whether even priests and priestesses can give overall figures of receipts and expenditures cannot be stated, though it is doubtful if Euroamerican patterns of bookkeeping, except on the most elementary level, have been taken over by the candombles. Certain accounts are kept, however. As we have seen, a prospective initiate is given a list of what is required for initiation, and when this is completed, a bill covering actual expenditures for provisions and costs of services is rendered by the cult-head, and the sum indicated must be repaid before the initiate is a free agent.

In the tightly-knit structure of most candomble groupings, ultimate controls, on any level, and ultimate responsibility rest in the hands of priests and priestesses. Because of this, it is difficult to generalize concerning the economic transactions of the various groupings. Thus, we may take as an example the money given for the drummers at public rites. In some houses, what is collected, which may amount to more than 100$000, is given to the chief drummer, who presents his four or five fellow-drummers with 3$000 or 4$000 each, keeping what remains for himself. But here a complicating factor enters, for the collections are made by cult-initiates under possession or, in the idiom of cult-worship, by one of the gods. In the case of certain deities, all the money, or part of it, will be given the priest or priestess. In one case actually witnessed, the deity instructed the officiating priestess that the sum collected was to be retained by her, and the drummers received nothing. More often, however, the cult-head will, on the day after the rite, give each drummer a small sum as an expression of appreciation, and to ensure that he will be present on the next occasion. But from the point of view of considering such an item in terms of the cult budget, it is apparent that the number of variables that enter are too numerous to draw conclusions of significance for candomble internal economies in general.

Another instance of this can be drawn from the fees paid when sacrifices are to be offered. These can only be performed by the *pegigan*, or *achogun*, who is the first of those who have "the right of the knife," or by one of his assistants. The amounts paid for his services vary; we have noted the figures of one center, 7$000 to kill a chicken, 30$000 for a "four-footed beast"—sheep or goat—and much more on the great occasions when an ox is slaughtered. The fee of the priest or priestess when a rite is performed for a person, the *dinheiro de chão*, "money of the earth," when placed on the ground or "money of the calabash" when put in a gourd, also varies from center to center, with the nature of the ritual, and with the ability of the petitioner to pay. Moreover, out of this money the cult-head will give gifts to various officials of the center, so that the net return is diminished to the degree of generosity shown.

Among the important sources of candomble income are the contributions of the affiliates and members, the cost of whose initiation has already been discussed, known as the *ogans*. These are usually men of substance, who are given honorary rank because of their influence in the city, or are "confirmed" as full participants in the affairs of the group. The primary function of the *ogan* is to serve as sponsor and protector against outside forces, such as officialdom and the police, but they are also expected to make contributions to the center with which they are affiliated when necessary. Thus, for example, in the case of one house where the priest was about to begin the initiation of a new class of novices, each *ogan* was assessed 100$000. Contributions of various kinds are levied on them as need arises, such as money to repair a roof in the cult-center, or to re-build a shrine. Often these contributions are made in a setting conducive to generosity, since giving is often a public function, and the name of each donor, with the amount he has given, is announced to those assembled, so that the prestige that accrues to men whose gifts are large will be assured. Individual gifts of 100$000 have been witnessed, and the total collected at one minor ceremony was more than 300$000—a considerable sum, by then current candomble standards.

Many sources of income are deeply imbedded in the cult-rituals. There is continuous giving of food, and money, and supplementary items of clothing during the long cycles of rites. At the public rituals, such as those where initiates announce their cult-names, for example, contributions are repeatedly requested. Or, there are such instances of institutionalized giving as the "sale" of initiates, which takes place toward the end of the training for cult-membership. In one of these, a play reverting to slavery times is enacted. A woman, who takes the part of an old African, is admitted and states she has been told there are "captives" for sale, and that she has brought her white mistress, who wishes to buy a slave. The initiates are paraded before the "white" woman, whose comments on each are calculated to amuse the audience. When the one she has come to "buy" is produced, the bargaining begins, with mock "haggling" continuing until a price is struck. This is not the place to analyze the complex socio-religious reasons for this "selling" of initiates, since the rite concerns us here only as a source of cult income. In this case, between 100$000 and 200$000 was placed in the calabash of the priestess to redeem the initiate; in another, 80$000 was paid; in still another it was reported than an *ogan* in a famous center paid the very large sum, in terms of cult evaluations, of 800$000. At one actual ceremony, described elsewhere, the prices given for initiates for the several deities were 400$000 for one vowed to Yansan, 350$000 each for those of Ogun, Oshala and Oshossi, and 300$000 each for the devotees of Oshun and Omulu, a total of two *contos* and fifty *milreis*.[9]

There are numerous other ways in which cult income is augmented, some of these involving ingenuous interpretations of earlier requirements in the light of the realities of changing times. Thus, one of the most important precepts requires that the heads of those undergoing initiation, or who are celebrating a seventh-year anniversary of initiation be shaved. But, in the case of a woman initiate who must keep up her customary appearance because of her employment, or who, let us say, has returned to Bahia from her place of residence in Rio de Janeiro for an anniversary ritual, to have the head shaved would result in serious inconvenience. It is therefore possible for her, should divination indicate willingness on the part of the deity, to "buy" her hair, thus at once relieving her of possible conflict between the demands of cult ritual and of her daily life, and providing additional income for the ensuing ceremonies.

Divination and "work"—that is, healing, and the provision of clients with magic that protects them from evil and assures success in their undertakings—provide the principal sources of personal income of the cult head. Fees from divination are not negligible; cult-centers are reported where thirty to forty clients are served daily, at a cost fairly well standardized in the city, of 5$000 per consultation. The candomble group is in the main self-supporting, and its running expenses are met by contributions from members and affiliates, the *ogans* bulking large here. Before an important festa, a public rite, the membership will assess themselves the needed amount, and in many houses it is a matter of pride to be able to give more than one's share. The cost of providing the sacrificial animals and the accompanying provisions and beverages needed for the rituals wherein the deity of the priest or priestess is "fed" and thus the spiritual power of the center itself continued, is also met by the membership, since the fate of each member is so closely tied in with the position and power of the group as a whole. And, as has been indicated, the costs of the rites of initiation and for the continuation of the individual initiate's spiritual rapport with his or her deity must be met by the person concerned.

It is difficult to generalize as to the degree to which the income of the cult-group can be separated from that of its head, since this varies with the traditions of the group, the length of time it has been established, and the personality of its priest or priestess. There is no question that in spiritual matters, ultimate controls rest in the hands of the cult head. On the other hand, the candomble group, often described by its membership as a "society," may be regarded as a cooperative unit; some initiates live at the centers, and there are instances where members receive loans from the "gods," some especially designated by the donors for specific deities, which are repaid without interest, though the recipient, in gratitude to the deity, will add such gifts as he can afford. The well-being of the group is also conceived as being that of the total well-being of its individual members, and there are cases where considerable pressure is laid by the priest on those who belong to the group he heads to work hard, increase earnings and thus enhance the resources and prestige of the candomble as a whole.

In the case of a strong cult-head, all economic as well as all spiritual matters would channel through the hands of this personage, whose judgment would be questioned only by the oldest or most respected members of the group. And certainly there are such priests, whose personal wealth is considerable. Some of their costumes, for example, worn only when, under possession, they dance for their deities at the most important public ceremonies, are in any terms costly. Thus, the value of a single costume of one such priest, with its accompanying jewelled charms, actually seen in ritual use, was estimated at twelve *contos* or, in 1942 values, U.S. $600.00. Yet, even in these cases, it cannot be said what part of income is from the cult-group, and what part from consultations. For even a cult-head whose resources are considerable will show little ostentation, except as regards the rituals of his house, since display of wealth brings on envy, and envy is spiritually dangerous. And here another factor enters; for were the amassing of wealth acknowledged, the logic of cult belief would suggest that it derives from the practice of magic. And since good magic entails the knowledge of bad, and sometimes the use of it, and this is anti-social, a reaction may set in that results in a decline in the prestige and income of the practitioner.

A cult-member who founds a house will own its land, and will dominate it. As time goes on, however, the corporate and cooperative nature of the well-established group will assert itself. There are candombles in Bahia where the cult-head has relatively little to say in the ordering of its economic affairs, this being in the hands of the *ogans*. In some of the older centers, the land itself is vested in the group; in one famous candomble, it passes from mother to daughter or a female collateral as a part of the priestly succession. In the former case, the personal possessions of the cult-head are separate from those of the group; in the latter, they are less sharply differentiated. However, the tightness of the structure of the candomble, as reflected in the loyalties, the spirit of cooperation and sense of identification of the members finds its expression in the economic sphere, and provides the psychological base for the functioning of the group as an economic as well as a socio-religious unit in the Bahian community.

IV

In carrying on field research among the Afrobrazilians, it soon becomes apparent that the internal economy of the candomble has a significance that transcends its surface, workaday meaning, and represents a further instance of adjustment to the system of culturally molded values that characterizes the broader community among which the candomble groups live. In candomble thinking, spiritual power derives essentially from sound knowledge of the ways of the supernatural beings, it is true, but the reinforcement of this knowledge by its implementation in economic terms is also of the first order of importance. This complex of attitudes has a firm traditional base in the system of beliefs and values of the West African past, but the pecuniary evaluations of Africa have been reinforced and given added emphasis by the conventions of Euroamerican orientations toward the role of economic resources in ordering social position.

When one discusses the various candomble groups with Afrobahians, the factor of wealth bulks large in forming judgments as to relative importance of these cult-centers. The length of time a center has been established does enter, though the relationship between this and the opportunity to amass resources is not overlooked by the candomble people themselves in accounting for these differentials. Yet duration of time a center has been functioning is not enough. A notable instance of this is seen in the case of a long established center that, though respected for the knowledge of those who direct it and for its discipline, has been steadily losing ground as its economic position has become more and more precarious. Obviously, the size of the membership of a given group enters, and, in a sense, from the point of view of the causal factors involved, this is circular, in that a spiral in either direction, once set in motion, can bring to a given center gain or loss in resources and the prestige that follows on the command of resources. And here we return to the spiritual base, for it is clear that a series of misfortunes suffered by a center of those affiliated with it is regarded as a sign of disfavor of the gods, and of consequent lessened supernatural control, and potential affiliates tend to turn elsewhere; while success in bringing about desired ends will bring new members, more resources, and enhancement of prestige to the center.

The economic theory of the candomble thus has implicit in it the concept of a kind of equilibrated interplay between the command of resources and the action of the supernatural. As concerns the individual cult-member, this means that the degree of friendly intervention, indifference or hostility on the part of the forces that control his fate and his own personal fortune is mediated by the extent to which he fulfils the ritualistic requirements of worship. In candomble thinking, the degree to which he is prepared to make economic sacrifice is an important factor in bringing him material reward and enhanced status. In terms reminiscent of classical economic theory, he is willing to forego immediate gain for his future benefit. And it is his confidence that the sacrifices he makes will in fact be rewarded—a confidence reinforced by the instances where achievement of goals has in actuality followed on sacrifice and where neglect has brought continued illness and poverty—that is one important source of the strength and persistence of candomble belief.

1. Field work was carried on in Brazil under a grant from the Rockefeller Foundation in 1941–1942, with collaboration of Frances S. Herskovits, whose help has been most valuable in the presentation of this paper. Figures on cost-of-living indexes have been kindly furnished by Professor Yale Brozen.

2. All figures in this paper, unless otherwise indicated, will be given in the *milreis* of 1941–1942, which was at that time quoted as about twenty to the U.S. dollar, and should in this way retain their relative weighting. The inflation following World War II and the lowering in value of the *cruzeiro* that has replaced the *milreis* has resulted in prices and wages being at much higher figures in 1956.

3. PIERSON, D., *Negroes in Brazil*, Chicago, 1942, pp. 298–9, who worked in Bahia in 1935–1937, gives the occupations of the members of one cult-group present at a ceremony he describes. Of the women, 13 were food vendors, 7 seamstresses, 5 laundresses, 5 domestic servants, 1 midwife, while

two looked after the cult-center. Sixteen male affiliates, not enumerated as to occupation, were given as "hucksters, stevedores, day laborers," a porter, a tinsmith, a painter, a baker, a tailor, and a typesetter.

4. Cf. PIERSON, *op. cit.*, pp. 237–238, 309–310. However, the statement made by him in this connection, that "African cultural forms at Bahia are disintegrating at a comparatively rapid rate," has proved to be wide of the mark, as was evident in the flourishing condition of the candomble found during a visit to the city in 1954.

5. These figures are in line with those given for craftsmen and laborers outside the urban centers for a period two years after the data of this research were gathered, as shown in *Brazil, 1943–1944, Recursos, Posibilidades*, Ministério das Relações Exteriores, Rio de Janeiro, 1945, pp. 160–1.

6. Taking the index of wholesale prices for 1948 as 100, the figure for 1937 was 29, and for 1938, 27. For 1953 the index was approximately 190.

7. See below, p. 261.

8. For a description of these chairs, see BASTIDE, R., "A cadeira do Ogan e o poste central," *Bol. lix, Sociologia No. I, Univ. de São Paulo*, 1946, pp. 44–45.

9. A *conto* is a thousand *milreis* (1,000$000), or, under the more recent nomenclature, *cruzeiros*. In 1942, the *conto* was valued at U.S. $50.00.

: VII :

THE WORLD VIEW
OF AN URBAN COMMUNITY

PARAMARIBO, DUTCH GUIANA

The life described is centred largely in the southern portion of the city of Paramaribo, where the Negro population is concentrated . . . but there is no segregation of population groups. . . . In the general idiom of the colony, the term Negro—Nengere—relates to those either actually of full African descent, or who appear to be of full African descent, and to those who, showing some racial mixture, choose to be identified with this Negro group by adhering to the practices which distinguish the Negro population from the rest of the inhabitants of the city. All reference to the beliefs of the town Negroes must, therefore, be held as excluding those mulattoes and others, who representing varying degrees of crossing, participate in the culture of the colony in dress, manner of living and worship. Nor must it be assumed that there are no Negroes, in the Suriname sense of the word, who do not also live according to these patterns of European life; nor that there are no persons who, while following the European form of life in externals, do not also continue certain religious practices peculiar to the Negro group.

Again, it is to be emphasized that in singling out for description here those practices which individualize the Negro group from the rest of the population, it is not suggested that these urban Negroes have not incorporated numberless European and Indian traits. For, in fact, all the more generalized aspects of life will tend, certainly in externals, to emphasize its European character.

(—Abstracted from *Notes on the Culture
of the Paramaribo Negroes*, p. 2.)

All selections in this section are from *Suriname Folklore* [with transcriptions of Suriname songs and musicological analysis by Dr. Kolinski] with Frances S. Herskovits, Columbia University Contributions to Anthropology, XXVII (New York: Columbia University Press, 1936).

The Concept of the Soul*

Of all the supernatural forces which govern the destiny of the individual, none surpasses the role of the *akra*,—the soul—in determining that destiny.[1] The *akra* is a man's ruling spirit, and when it is well disposed toward him guards him against the sinister forces that are set in motion by human enemies, or unfriendly gods. It comes to a man at birth, and dies with him when he dies; and except for its wanderings during a man's sleep, it is with him always, and is faithfully on guard for him, if its dictates are obeyed.

Associated with the *akra* is the *djodjo*,[2] but so little uniformity of opinion exists about the nature of these two forces that we shall give both of the two views most frequently met with. One view holds that the two terms are the names for the two separate souls with which every man is endowed at birth, and while the *akra* remains with the individual, the *djodjo*, which is also the man's shadow, is the wanderer, the soul which goes abroad to see strange things. When a man is about to die, it returns from whatever distant place it had strayed, and dies with him, to become, however, the man's *yorka*,—his ghost. But having been a restless soul during the life of the man, it remains restless after death, and when a man is given improper burial, or when he has led an evil life, this *djodjo*, because of anger toward the world of the living, or because of its inherent evil nature, haunts human dwellings and thoroughfares, and carries with it misfortune and death for the living. It is also said that a man's *djodjo*, in the course of its

* The orthography of African and *taki-taki* words has been simplified. Nasalization, a generalized characteristic of West African speech, but more especially of inland Dahomey, is not indicated.

Vowels: a, e, i, o, and u have the so-called "Italian" values, e.g.

a	as in	father	o	as in	caught
e	" "	let	u	" "	full
i	" "	kindred			

All vowels are sounded.

Consonants: g is always hard, as in get, give, go.

Diphthongs:

ai	as in	eye	ei	as in	say
au	" "	cow	oi	" "	boy

In the text, the apostrophe is not a phonetic symbol, but indicates the elision of a letter or a syllable.

wanderings, may be trapped or imprisoned or shot by a sorcerer; thus
is brought on the slow death of the man to whom it belongs, and the
djodjo becomes the tool of the sorcerer for his death-dealing errands.
In the course of these wanderings, however, the *djodjo* has opportunities to learn secrets, and it is this knowledge that is revealed to man in
dreams, though the revelations are made in symbolic form, and require to be interpreted by those who know the lore of dreams and the
meaning of the symbols.

Yet another name heard for *akra* and *djodjo* is *ye* or *yeye*, and this
is said by those who hold the second view of the matter to be both the
soul and the shadow of the man. This, too, is claimed for the *akra* by
those who hold that *akra* and *djodjo* and *yeye* are synonyms. The *akra*,
they argue, has all the powers ascribed to the *djodjo* and all its attributes, for it goes forth in sleep to visit strange places, and what it
sees, man experiences as dreams; it can be trapped, imprisoned or
shot by a sorcerer, and after death can come to haunt the living as a
yorka; when offended it may decide to leave the individual and set out
on a journey, coming back before the death of the individual to die
with him.

Whether there are two souls or one for each individual, the term
which has greatest currency is *akra* or *'kra*.[3] What does a man know
about his soul? To begin with, there are, apparently, as many categories of souls as there are days of the week.[4] Every individual has
one name which he does not disclose, unless he is consulting a diviner,
and this name is his "day name," of which mention has already been
made. It derives from the day of the week on which a man is born,
and is called his *'kra* name. In discussing causes for divorce, reference
was made to the fact that the soul of a man and a woman may not
agree, and that is because some souls are not compatible. Today, only
those versed in the ancient mythology can trace back how the gods
had fared in their matings in order to understand the cause of these
maladjustments, but of these, few survive. An informant, whose name
is that given to a male child born on Thursday,—*Yao*—indicated that
a Saturday girl would be a congenial mate for him, but not one born
on a Friday. In writing of marriage, we also mentioned that it is held
that a man and a woman born on the same day are rarely successful
in marriage, or any other undertaking involving a partnership. This is
because the two derive their knowledge from the same supernatural
forces, and are equally aware of situations, so that if one uses bad
judgment on occasion, or attempts some deception, the other recog-
nises this instantly, and this makes for friction.

Not alone, however, are souls to be classified according to the days
of the week and the resulting powers which inhere in these days, but

also according to whether they are weak souls, or strong.[5] Several persons told us that because their souls are not strong, if bad magic is planted during the night for some neighbor in the yard, they awake the next morning feeling "like licks all over the body,"—as though they had been flogged. Indeed, a soul lacking in strength is the prey of any force that wishes to control it, and since strength of soul is inherited, the only recourse an individual has to seek to strengthen his 'kra is to resort to a diviner for magic to keep the evil forces away. A strong soul, however desirable it may be, brings difficulties to its possessor. In defining the term akra and its role in the life of the individual, we qualified the fulfilment of that role as conditional upon its being well disposed toward the individual, and upon its having its dictates followed. A promise made to a strong soul, if not carried out, angers the soul, and causes it to seek vengeance, which in extreme form leads its possessor to behave in such anti-social ways as to steal, to destroy property and even to kill. A strong 'kra, if it chooses, may dispute the right of a winti to become a familiar of the individual, so that the winti harasses him and brings him illness.

In order to understand what these promises to the soul are, we must turn to a consideration of the forms which worship of the akra takes. One of the duties which every individual owes his akra is to give it a timely feast.[6] This should be done annually, if a person has the means with which to do it, for the akra refuses to be taken for granted. It must not be thought, however, that debts to the soul are acquitted in as regular a manner as this statement would imply. As a matter of fact, a person delays doing homage to his soul until such a time as he has unmistakable evidence, through some overt manifestation on the part of his soul, that it is displeased and must be placated. So much has this become a truism that when one invites friends to a meal of any kind, gossip at once takes for granted that this is not a casual invitation, but is in effect a "feast" for the person's soul, and at once someone recalls some mishap, actual or imagined, that has occurred to the person giving the "feast," as confirmation of the fact that the 'kra has made its demands on its possessor.

When misadventures come to a person, though his first thought is that his soul is asking for its due, he goes to a diviner to call his soul to discover its specific wishes. A person's 'kra may ask for a feast. It may ask for a gold chain, if the possessor is a woman. It may ask for any item of apparel that has taken its fancy. It may want a bicycle, and we know of a case where a man's 'kra desired an automobile! The usual request, however, is either for a gold chain, in the instances of young women, or a 'kra tafra, a feast for the 'kra, for others. Though the soul refuses to be ignored, it can be reasoned with, and a promise can be made that payment will be given it at some future date. Another device is to give a *to*, a sort of partial payment towards a deferred fulfilment of its demands. All such negotiations are carried on through the diviner, for though all mature individuals know how to serve their souls, it is only the diviner who can call the soul to come into the head of an individual so that it can be questioned. If any but a specialist undertook this, he might not know how to *saka na 'kra*, "dismiss the soul," (especially if in the process of questioning, a cup were placed on the head instead of in the hand, when insanity would ensue). This necessity for a specialist's aid is a general pattern of belief, which is even more in evidence when the manner in which a person works with his *winti* is considered.

To call the *akra*, the person who comes to consult the diviner wears something of which he is extremely fond. He is seated on a *'kra bangi*, —a stool for the soul.[7] The diviner is also seated on a stool. An egg is put into a bowl of rainwater, and someone who is assisting at the ceremony takes a new calabash and throws water all about the person whose *akra* is being called. If a black pot, one of the kind made by Bush-Negro women, is available, this replaces the new calabash, and such a pot may be used many times. The diviner addresses the soul: "*Akra Kwasi*," he says, if the subject, for example, is a man born on Sunday,—"Sunday soul, I speak to you, I beg (pray) you, to hear what your desire is. Thank you, thank you, (please, please), I pray you, prostrating myself, this poor child wishes to know what the good soul has need of." As each word is spoken, water is sprayed from the calabash by the diviner. This is said over and over, until the *akra* comes into the head of its possessor. This is easily recognised by those who are watching, because when this happens, the body begins to tremble, the eyelids grow heavy, and the bowl which is held by the person in his right hand, or on his head, begins to shake from side to side. The diviner, if one is in charge,[8] then begins to question the soul, and the water in the bowl, as it moves from side to side, spills if the answer is "yes" to the question put to it, and does not move if the answer is "no."

Let us suppose that the *akra* has demanded a feast. The diviner then asks it what kind of a feast it desires. It may request that the individual dine alone with it. If that is the case, the table is set for two, one place for the *'kra* and one for its owner. The usual feast consists of a meal of rice, eggs, and chicken. When there is chicken or pigeon, the bones must not be eaten, and when the chicken is divided, care must be taken that the pieces are severed at the joints, so that no bone is broken. If this happens, the whole *'kra tafra* is spoiled. These bones are saved and are put away, serving as "a kind of stop for bad." The food served at such a meal must be eaten with the hands, for no fork or spoon may touch it.[9] Before the person concerned sits down to this meal, the diviner causes him to remove his clothes, and washes him with the contents of a pot containing healing herbs. For the *akra*, these are fragrant leaves, and perfume constitutes an important ingredient that is always added. The diviner uses a hen for the washing which he takes up by the legs and bends back the head until he can hold the animal by its head and legs,[10] in this way making a sponge of the body. This is called washing away the *hebi*, that is to say, the "heaviness" that oppresses a person. Should a hen that has been so used live, it is considered lucky for purposes of breeding, but if it dies, it is never eaten. After this washing, a bottle of beer is poured over the head of the person who had been bathed. This is followed by emptying the contents of a small bottle of sweet liquor and some perfume over him. If the *'kra* asks for a large feast, friends are invited to come at an appointed time, but they are not told why they had been invited, or that the *akra* is in any way concerned. Sometimes, in addition to the meal for the *akra*, a trinket, such as a chain or a ring or a bracelet, may be prescribed. After such a trinket is bought, it must be immersed in a bowl containing weeds and perfume, for purification. This is called *kaser*, or *kasiri*, and is done secretly by the person who has called the *akra*.

Those who are provident, and do not wait until the soul is angered to give it recognition, may perform the ceremony called *pai akra*, a phrase that signifies "to pay the soul," but has the idiomatic meaning of making an offering for the soul. For this a black pot of the type mentioned before is employed for the ceremonial bath, and a new calabash is used to hold the offering. This consists of seven grains of *nengere kondre pepre*, seven half-cent pieces (the smallest Dutch coins); one ell of blue cotton, and sometimes red cotton as well; one bottle of sweet liquor, a few *abongra* (sesame) seeds, and *akansa*. The calabash or pot containing these ingredients is left at a cross-roads, the customary place of sacrifice for all but river and snake gods. If the *akra* is satisfied with what has been given it, "you don't find it when the *akra* take it." Therefore, if the offerings at the cross-roads are undisturbed the next day, it is a sign that what has been given is insufficient and has not met with the *akra's* approval. When this occurs, the person who made the sacrifice at once goes to a diviner. . . .

The *'kra* is also called in cases of illness. The person whose *'kra* is to be summoned is seated. A porcelain cup of which this man or woman is fond, and the kerchief he or she likes best are brought out. The kerchief is rolled into a carrying-pad. The cup is filled with water, and an egg and a Dutch silver 10-cent piece are placed inside it. When the 'kra enters the head, and the diviner questions the soul, the answer is "yes" when the water is spilled toward the questioner, and "no" when it is spilled away from him. The cup and the coin must be retained and the former will be known as *mi 'kra komki*, "my soul's cup."

We have spoken of the particular importance of inviting the souls of children to accompany their possessors to the new home when moving from one place to another. In order to do this it is necessary to go to the place where the child was born, and summon the *akra* from there, for the soul has a strong attachment for the place where its bearer came into the world. The invocation pronounced, is, "*Akra Amba* (for a girl born on Saturday),—Saturday soul, I call you that you do not remain behind." While this is said, rainwater from a new calabash is sprinkled in front of the child's mother, who speaks the invocation, and behind her. A woman performs this ceremony for herself and for her children, but not for her husband, who must do it himself. Belief holds that this is necessary, not alone to show deference to what might be a temperamental soul, but to safeguard the *akra* from being detained by any "bad" *winti* that might live in the yard from which the soul's possessor is moving. When the term "bad *winti*" was spoken in this connection, reference was made to an evil spirit that possessed some tenant in the yard out of which the owners of the souls in question were moving. . . .

We have observed several times that the soul makes demands on its possessor. It must be recognised, in this connection, that a person uses or wears the belongings of his soul, or consumes what food the soul is given. The distinction between what belongs to the person as an individual, and what he keeps as custodian for his *akra*, is nevertheless sharply made. In the first category are those things which a person may dispose of whenever he wishes, and in any way he chooses. With those things in the second category, the property of his soul, he may take no liberties; and if he does dispose of his *'kra's* possessions, punishment is inflicted upon him by the real owner, his *akra*. We witnessed one such instance in the case of a woman who had taken the liberty of pawning a gold chain that belonged to her *akra*. It was in a compound where we were collecting songs, and the season was that of the *winti*-dances, several of which were taking place that same week. As our phonograph was recording songs sacred to the water-gods, we suddenly heard the sound of violent retching outside the cabin where we were at work, and soon a woman entered who was possessed by a *winti*. She was obviously in great pain, and was in ugly temper, swaggering about between her spasms of retching, frowning, glaring at everyone in a hostile fashion, and threatening all who were present. As is customary, we offered her spirit a drink of beer, and she said, "I don't want any gifts from you. I am a strong *Ingi winti* and I can have all the champagne I want from the White man's boats by capsizing your steamers." We were told that this retching was soon expected to bring up blood, because this woman's soul was tormenting her, and turning her friendly *winti*-spirit into an ugly one, in punishment of the pawning of the gold chain belonging to it. She came out of her possession for a few moments, explained that she had lived in British Guiana, and added in perfect English, "I am not insulting you, sir. It is my 'kra troubling me."

When situations of this kind arise, it is believed that the offended soul may force its possessor to steal in order to procure the means for redeeming the pawned article. It is, therefore, the duty of the family to help the individual, and if the family is unwilling or unable to do this, the soul causes the person to break and destroy things. When this happens, and the demands of the soul are such that the family either considers them exorbitant, or beyond any possible means at their disposal, they call a diviner to try to appease the soul, in the manner we have described. Should the soul, however, refuse to be appeased by a partial gift, an attempt is then made to discipline it by having the diviner "tie" it,—that is, they will have him try to subjugate it. In order to do this, a powerful *winti* belonging to the diviner, who in this case, is a priest of that *winti*, is called upon to take the recalcitrant soul in hand. The "tying" is generally done in the following way: The *akra* which is thought greedy is lured to manifest itself by setting before it all kinds of food,—rice, *abongra*, liquor, chicken. White thread is put about this offering of food, and when the soul is called and it goes to take the food which is there before it, the diviner quickly takes up the ends of the thread and ties them into a knot, as he pronounces the words, "Monday soul, I have now tied you." But if the soul is strong and very wrought up, it will beat the *wintiman*, powerful as is his god, and will not allow itself to be "tied." As mentioned when discussing the means men and women have recourse to in order to insure fidelity, this process of "tying" of the soul is employed for other than disciplinary action against an unruly soul, and it can also be utilised to subjugate an orderly soul to the will and machinations of another.

1. The word *akra* or '*kra* derives from the Twi word which has the same meaning.

2. *Djodjo*, perhaps, comes from the Fon, since the root *djo* (a guardian) is contained in the Dahomean word *djoto* (guardian-father), the name

given to one of a person's souls. Cf. Encyc., pp. 35–36. Penard, (I), pp. 159–161.

3. Penard, (I), p. 59, also speaks of two souls, a Mother 'kra and a Father 'kra. We ourselves have heard no reference to these.

4. These day names are so well known that it is not necessary to repeat them here. They are those given in Encyc., p. 501, for Suriname and for the Twi-speaking peoples of the Gold Coast; by Westermann, (I), p. 49 (columns 3 and 4), for the Ewe-speaking peoples of Togo; and by Delafosse (II), p. 133, for the Agni of the Ivory Coast. They have persisted in Jamaica, (Beckwith, I, p. 59) and in other parts of the New World, as witness the Negro names of Cuffy and Cudjo, in use in the south of the United States. They are also found, in translation, as names of Negroes who live in the Sea Islands off the coast of South Carolina, where there are men named "Thursday" or "Saturday."

5. In discussing the concept of the soul with Ashanti informants in the Gold Coast, West Africa, we were told of a belief that prevails there in two kinds of *sunsun*, or supplementary souls, a "light" or weak, impressionable type, and a "heavy" or strong type.

6. In Dahomey a person gives a feast for his soul when the diviner consulted states that his questioning of Destiny has indicated the inquirer's soul desires such a feast to be given.

7. The importance of the stool as something associated with its owner's 'kra has been discussed in detail by Rattray, (II) *passim*. In Dahomey, we found that stools, especially the stools of the king or of chiefs, are of great ceremonial importance.

8. It is not unusual to have an old woman of the family act in place of the diviner, if the cup is held in the hand. This may be a mother, a grandmother, or a maternal aunt.

9. This exemplifies the lag so often found in ceremonial practice when ritual is compared with everyday usage.

10. At the consecration of the drums employed in the great annual ceremonies to the Dahomean sky-deities,—*Mawu, Lisa* and the associated gods of their pantheon—the drummer held the chickens which he passed over the drums in exactly this manner.

Divination

*In order to understand why the Negro [in Paramaribo] val-
ues the Indian diviner, we must glance at his attitude toward
the ranking of Indian, Negro, and White supernatural powers. The logic with which he approaches this problem is that
for himself his own magic—Negro magic—is the strongest,
but that, in certain situations, the magic of the Indian takes
precedence over his own because the Indians, as the autochthonous inhabitants of the land, have the greatest control over
the spirits of earth and water. Of White man's magic, the
reading of the future by means of cards has some vogue.*

*   *   *

The references we have made to divining must already have suggested
that divination plays an important part in the life of the Suriname
town Negroes. Indeed, so impressed are the Paramaribo Negroes
themselves with this, that those who have knowledge of the life of
the Saramacca tribe of Bush-Negroes make the point that there is
greater recourse to divination in the city than in the bush. It was
claimed that among the Saramacca people there are only a few important diviners to be found,—one at the village of *Lombe,* a short
distance south of the rail-head, and several others in the distant village of *Dahome,* on the far upper river—whereas in Paramaribo alone,
there are several times as many, and they are the more skilled. While
to our own knowledge of life in the Suriname bush this statement is
not borne out by actual fact, the significance of such an assertion as
demonstrating the place the Suriname town Negroes give their own
diviners,—despite the superiority ordinarily acceded the Bush-Negroes
in dealing with the supernatural,—is of the first order.

Diviners are called *lukuman,* "those who look." Loosely, however,
all those who deal with the supernatural, whether as diviners or as
workers of evil magic, or as providers of magic which protects, as well
as those who exorcise evil spirits such as ghosts, and those who pacify
personal spirits which have been aroused, are called *Djuka.* Another
name, with the same general implication, is *bonu,*[1] a third *obiaman.*
Conversationally, a practitioner of any one of the above categories is

also referred to as a *wintiman*, or a *wisiman*. When, however, an individual informant is questioned closely, he carefully differentiates these categories. A *lukuman*, he explains, is a diviner who also cures souls. A *wintiman* is one who deals with the spirits called *winti*, the gods, and cures all illnesses sent by these spirits. A *wisiman* is a practitioner of black magic, and as such can if he chooses also cure black magic. The maker of protective charms, if yet finer differentiation is sought, is the *obiaman*, one who deals in *obia*,[2] and the *obiaman* will also at times be designated as the one who cures *wisi*, evil magic. It must be indicated, nevertheless, that in reality this separation of function is most frequently only theoretical, for it is seldom that a man in any one of the categories named is not competent as well in at least one other, and some are skilled in all.

While discussing divination and those who divine, it is also necessary to name the Indian *piaiman*, and the *kartaman*,—literally "cardman,"—the latter of whom may be White or Javanese or Hindu as well as Negro. In order to understand why the Negro values the Indian diviner, we must glance at his attitude toward the ranking of Indian, Negro, and White supernatural powers. The logic with which he approaches this problem is that for himself his own magic,—Negro magic—is the strongest, but that, in certain situations, the magic of the Indian takes precedence over his own, because the Indians, as the autochthonous inhabitants of the land, have the greatest control over the spirits of earth and water. Of White man's magic, the reading of the future by means of cards has some vogue, and anyone, whether White, Hindu, or Javanese, who can tell fortunes with cards, is said to use the White man's method of divining.

When questioning the soul, the answers are given by the tilting of a cup containing water and an egg which rests on the head of the person whose soul is being called, or by the tilting of a cup or bowl, also containing water and an egg, held in the right hand. In both these instances, the diviner uses a folded mat, but sometimes the mat alone is employed. A *lukuman* may also look into a mirror when he reads the future, or he may watch the surface of a basin of water which stands before him, and when the water becomes troubled the spirit is said to have entered it, and the questioning proceeds as it does when the cup placed on the head or held in the hand begins to shake. In all those instances where a mat or its equivalent, a fan, or water in a basin, is used, the answers can only be "yes," or "no." Divining, however, may be done by means of calling upon a *winti* to enter into the body of either the diviner or of the person who came to consult him, and causing this *winti* to speak. Albinos, and those exhibiting strains of albinism, who are called *bonkoru*,[3] are particularly gifted diviners for they are all said to have strong *winti,* and consequently important remedies.[4] If the *winti* is one of African or Indian origin, it is said to "speak tongues," and only the *wintiman,*—the priest or priestess—is able to interpret what is said by the spirit. Certain generalised methods of divination may be mentioned here in passing, which, though they do not need a specialist to perform, may also be employed by a specialist. Thus, a fowl which is being sacrificed either to an individual's *akra* or to a *winti,* is opened and its intestines or testicles are examined to see whether they are white or discolored. If they are white, the omen is one of good luck, while if they are not, the prediction is bad luck. This same test is also used as an ordeal to establish the innocence of a woman who disclaims guilt in adultery. Again, those who are possessed of *Ingi winti* (Indian spirits), especially the water-Indian spirits, are thought to have the gift of divination, even when they are not specialists in the sense that the *lukuman* is a specialist. Certain individuals, as well, at whose birth abnormal phenomena were manifest, such as a caul, or a navel cord entwined about the neck, are thought to have special aptitudes for divination and magical practice. Such persons are encouraged to go through specialized training with an established diviner to fit themselves for this profession.

Divination as practised by the specialist, then, is a matter of training. The knowledge of the technique passes, in the main, from a man to his brother until, the generation exhausted, it is given to one of their sisters' sons. The one chosen is either selected because he is specially intelligent, or because by divination, or in a dream, he is discovered to have special aptitude for the profession. If a father cares, however, he may teach his own son his craft. In the case of women, the knowledge is passed on to sisters, or one of a woman's own daughters or sons; or if a woman has no children, then to the children of a sister. The rule is that the technique of a man is taught to a man, and that of a woman to a woman. It must be made clear that we found no sex division in the types of divination employed by diviners of the two sexes. General practice is to choose a male *lukuman* for illnesses of the soul, but for ills caused by the *winti,* a man or woman practitioner may be selected. There is a way of becoming a *lukuman* other than by inheriting the knowledge and this occurs when an African *komfo*[5] decides to take possession of a man or a woman who has been chosen by him as his fitting medium. It is not necessary that this *komfo*-spirit should have manifested itself actively to the family before. In our ensuing discussion of *winti,* we shall see how certain important spirits are sent to reside in trees and stones by those who die without successors, or whose successors are unwilling to continue the worship of the African gods. It may be that one such spirit

who, while remaining quiescent, had yet continued to identify himself
with the family, might cause a man or woman to go into a state of
possession, and reveal the answers to questions sought of the supernatural. Such a *komfo* needs, to be sure, to prove himself, but once his
reputation for curing and prophesying[6] is established, he is then said to
"*wroko furu moni,*—earn much money" for his possessor.

An illness may be caused by violating a *trefu* [food taboo]. Perhaps
it is an unconscious violation, arising out of the fact that a man's
mother had never told him the name of his true father, and consequently he had been observing food taboos which were not his own
and had been neglecting to observe those which were his, since these
personal food taboos are inherited from the father. The *lukuman* is
consulted, and he both diagnoses the cause of the illness, and names
the foods to be avoided. A person's illnesses or difficulties which bring
him to the diviner may arise out of a violation of the injunctions of
some deity. He may have urinated in that portion of the yard that is
identified as the habitat of the *Gron Mama,*—Earth Mother—of that
particular yard. Or a person may come to the *lukuman* because he has
found a bundle containing porcupine-quills under his door-step, or
one of red and blue cotton, or a broken calabash with evil-smelling
weeds, soiled cloth and thorny bits of wood in it, and these, he knows,
bode him no good. A man consults the *lukuman* to discover why his
rice-crop does not prosper, or he comes to find out who is responsible
for a recent accidental death in his family that is suspected to have
been brought about by other than natural causes. In the last instance,
he waits until after the eighth-day wake has been celebrated, and then
goes to the *lukuman* to have him divine the person who had invoked
black magic to cause the death of his relative. Or it may be such an
incident as was related to us, where a *Yorka,*—a ghost—has manifested
itself, and, through this manifestation, presages trouble.

This incident concerns a man who was sitting one night (about a
week before he told us of the occurrence), drinking beer with some
friends.

He left the table for a few moments, and when he returned, his
friends said they had seen a white hand reach out for his glass. When
he looked, the glass was not there. He had laughed about it, but had
told his mother.[7]

---

1. *Bonu* has, as its derivation, the Fon term *gbo,* a Dahomean word applied to magical charms.

2. According to the suggestion of Professor D. Westermann, the word
obia may be derived from the *Bia* river, a mythologically important river of
the Gold Coast, conceived by the Twi-speaking peoples as a brother of

Tano, the god of all rivers (cf. Cardinall, I, pp. 48–50). The prefix "o" denotes the singular in Twi. Another possible derivation may be from the Efik word '*Mbian* (cf. Talbot, I, pp. 46 ff.), while Sir H. H. Johnstone states "*Obia* seems to be a variant or a corruption of an Efik or Ibo word from the northeast or east of the Niger delta, which simply means 'Doctor.'" Recently Williams (II) has advanced the theory that the word is to be derived from the Twi *obayifo*.

3. Among the Saramacca people albinos are called *Tone* people, that is, they belong to the river gods. In Dahomey such people are said to be sacred to *Lisa*, god of the sun. According to Proyart, p. 197, albinos were sacred in Loango.

4. An informant told of one such remedy that had restored his own health, which consisted of herbs gathered by his mother in the bush, while her moves to pluck now one, now another, were directed by the *winti* of the diviner who, in his own home in the city, sat in a state of possession, shaking a rattle and chanting.

5. *Komfo* is the Ashanti-Fanti word for priest.

6. An especially valued instrument is called "the *komfo* telephone," whose "strong name" is *Kausi*. It is a stick, magically treated, which if concealed in a room, records all that is spoken, and if it is but sprayed with rum and made to hear the proper formula, need only to have one end of it placed against the ear to repeat what it had recorded.

7. The informant's comment at this point carries some significance in terms of acculturation: "All my mother does is go to church. She don't want me to go to *winti*-dances, even to look. But if anything happens, she runs to a *lukuman*."

Gods and Familiar Spirits

A. THE NATURE OF THE *Winti*

A person acquires a winti *in three ways. Most frequently his* winti *comes to him by inheritance—before dying a man or a woman designates the individual to whom his or her* winti *is to go, just as he would designate the disposal of any other possessions. Another possible way to acquire a* winti *is for a spirit itself to choose an individual to possess; this occurs when the* winti *goes to someone not in the line of family inheritance. The third way is through* kunu. *A* winti *acquired in the first two ways is friendly, but one acquired in the third way is an evil* winti.

*   *   *

Divination, then, is an essential factor in the system of beliefs of the Paramaribo town Negroes, for it is through the work of the diviner that all the elements of this system are drawn together, explained, and controlled. These elements are four in number,—the *akra*, or the soul; the *winti*, or the gods; *obia* and *wisi*, or good and evil magic; and the *Yorka*, or the spirits of the dead. Having considered the concept of the soul and its place in the lives of these people, let us now turn to an examination of the nature, manifestations and significance of the *winti*.

"*Winti*," say the Negroes, "mean wind. Wind is every place. Is air (breath). The spirit, too, is everywhere. So we says *winti*." The term, as we shall see, defines the gods and spirits which rule the destiny of the universe.[1] Among the Bush-Negroes, though the word *winti*,—also spoken there as *wenti*, or *wintu*—has the same significance as among the Negroes of Paramaribo, the gods are usually designated by the term *gado*. This latter name is heard in Paramaribo as well, though except in ritual song, it occurs usually in the exclamation "*Mi gado!*" in daily speech. Another term heard is that of *vodun*,[2] (pronounced also *fodun*), though in the city this word has in addition to the specialised meaning of the Saramacca Negroes which makes it a generic name for snake deities, the generalised meaning that makes it synonymous with *winti*. *Vodun* is a word used especially when it is wished to disguise the fact that sacred spirits are being invoked, and in such a case, the play on words, which makes *fodun* mean, in Negro-English, "things that fall down," that is, litter or trash, is utilised. Thus, they sing,

> Wi wani si dem fodun na djari,
> Wi wani si dem, ba.

> We want to see the *fodun* in the yard,
> We want to see them, brother.

A fourth term which has currency is that of *komfo*. When referring to a *komfo*, a person says, "*Mi 'abi wan bigi Nengere-konde komfo*,— I have a great African spirit." *Komfo* is not, however, a synonym for the word *winti*, and is identified only with specialised spirits, among them being those called Indian *winti*. In addition to all these designations, the *winti* songs in the Kromanti language, also give the name *bosum* or *abosmo*[3] for *winti* or god.

Let us examine the types of *winti* that fill the universe of the Suriname town Negro. Though among the Bush-Negroes the term *Massa Gran Gado* (Supreme God) occurs repeatedly in conversation and prayer, it is but seldom that a Sky-god is invoked in Paramaribo.

The only reference there to the Sky is in the *winti* dances to the *Tap-Kromanti*, that is to say, to the Kromanti gods of the Sky, who comprise the seven Thunder gods. These thunder gods are *Tata Yao*,[4] *Tata Aladi* (or *Alada*), *Tata Wese* (or *Muwese*), *Tata Abonuako* (or *Akaobonua*), *Tata Anangka Yao*, *Sofia Bada*,[5] and *Ta S'ranami*.

The Earth gods are headed by the *Mama fo Gron*, the Earth-Mother, who even in ritual is referred to by this euphemism and named only in songs sung by those who are actually under possession. The names given this deity are many, and this is accounted for only partially by the fact that in Paramaribo, as in the bush, deities have their "strong" or *numan* names which may be known only to a few who are initiated, and employed only in ritual.[6] The Earth-Mother possesses a large number of these "strong" names, and this it appears is due to the fact that in Paramaribo are to be found the descendants of persons who derive from various regions of West Africa. Those most frequently heard in ritual are *Asase*,[7] *Agida*, *Aida*, *Waisa*, *Aisa* or *Awanaisa*,[8] and we have listened to persons who perhaps come from families carrying the traditions of two different regions dispute heatedly as to the "true" name of the *Mama fo Gron*. One of these persons, who definitely claims descent from a Dahomean family, insisted that the Dahomean names just given are the correct ones. The point must be made, however, that so feared is the Earth-Mother, and so great are her powers, that there is the utmost reluctance to speak her name, and young people are never encouraged to question about these designations. The names that occur most often for the Earth gods as a group are *Agida*, *Aisa* or *Awanaisa*, *Loko*,[9] and the *Gron Ingi*.

Worship of the *Gron Mama*, or the *Ma fo Doti* (Earth-Mother, or Mother of the Soil) differs from that of most of the other gods, in that while the majority of gods receive offerings from, and are danced for, only by their own devotees, the Earth Mother is a god-head for all *winti* worshippers, whatever their particular gods. To understand this, we must recognise that every plantation, every yard, every locale, is said to have its *Gron Mama*, who may either be a "good spirit," or a "bad spirit," but who in either case must be served. The *Gron Mama* is served by observing the sacred character of the place identified with her habitat, usually a *kankantri*, (silk-cotton tree). That is to say, people refrain from polluting it in any way and also make it offerings of food and drink once a year or more often, if demands upon her are made for special favors. If angered, the *Gron Mama* manifests herself as a snake,—a *Dagowe* or *Aboma*;[10] as an alligator,—*Kaiman*; or as an owl,—*oru-kuku*. If when she appears as a snake, let us say, a person scoffs or says "If I had seen it in time, I'd have killed it," she reappears in the person's house, with an air of challenge, "Here I am.

Kill me, if you like!" She might also appear in his bed at night. She can be appeased with a generous offering of eggs, and a prayer for forgiveness. "*Mama, mi de begi yu nanga saka fasi, mi no du fo ogri.* —Mother, I humble myself and pray you, I had not intended to do harm." If he should have had the misfortune to offend a bad *Gron Mama* who refuses to pardon him, she appears and reappears to challenge him, finally entering his body, and thereupon speaks with the man's voice telling him that she wishes him to become her *hasi*,[11] her devotee. Should he resist her, saying he does not care to have a *winti*, he begins to do unaccountable things,—to steal, to destroy property, to kill. A friendly and well-propitiated *Gron Mama*, however, protects the inhabitants of her domain. Thus, no oath is as binding as one pronounced in her name, which is followed by the swallowing of a few drops of the blood of both parties to the oath, to which some earth had been added; nor is any threat as dangerous as that of invoking the vengeance of the *Gron Mama*. Thus we heard a Negro woman say in anger to a man of Indian-White descent, "*Luku bon, mi nanga yu habi na sref'-srefi Gron Mama.*—Take care, I and you have the selfsame Earth Mother."

The most prevalent types of *winti* among women in particular are those associated with the snake, and since these enter into all the categories of *winti*, we list them after the gods of the Sky and Earth. Of these we have *Dagowe*,[12] *Papa, Vodun, Hei-gron, Aboma, Aninino*,[13] *Alado, Sinero, Korowena, Kwenda, Tobochina,* and *Cheno*. The term *Dagowe* often serves, in the town, as a generic term for all the snake spirits, though the *Dagowe* snake, properly speaking, is one of the constrictor group found in the colony, and is believed by the natives to inhabit both land and water. This is, of course, good observation on their part, for this characteristic of all snakes of the boa type is well-known. Not all snakes are sacred, yet no one will kill a snake. In support of this it is said that the snake itself, whether *Dagowe*, *Aboma* (boa constrictor), or any other, is not a god, but only a potential carrier of a god, and therefore if someone kills a *Dagowe*, the snake itself, once dead, takes no steps to punish its murderer, but those who worship it see that the *Dagowe* is avenged.[14] "They send *wisi*,"—that is, bad magic or poison. There are those, however, who hold that the *Dagowe* snake in particular is the *winti* itself, for if a person kills a *Dagowe* snake, the *winti* enters the abdomen, causing it to swell, and brings eventual death to the killer. In point of fact there is no sharp distinction between the Earth deities and the Snake spirits; indeed, not alone the Earth spirits, but any spirit, may manifest itself in the form of a snake.

Though the *Dagowe* may take possession of either a man or a woman, the *Papa* snake possesses only women. The explanation given was,—"Do you know why the *Papa* God doesn't possess men? Because men don't make (i.e., give birth to) children." Vodun is said to be greater in power than the *Papa* spirit, while *Hei-gron* surpasses all in strength. For this snake, which occupies mountainous regions, is thought to be the incarnation of ghostly spirits,—"When a *Yorka* goes into an *Aboma* and catches a human being, that is *Hei-gron*." [15] Thus we see an illustration of the belief that ancestors, as well as gods, may use snakes as vehicles for exercising their power over human destiny. It is in this that is constituted the essential importance of the snake-cult to the Suriname town Negroes.

A fourth group of *winti* are those which are associated with the river. This group, as all others, overlap the Snake gods, since the constrictor lives in the water as well as on land. However, there are other gods, among them the *kaiman*, which are peculiar to the rivers alone. The river-gods are headed by the *Liba-Mama*, or *Watra-Mama*, respectively Mother of the River, or Mother of the Water, who, again, is not referred to by name. Among the Saramacca tribe of Bush-Negroes, the river-gods go under the generic name of *Tone*, and this name, like the name from the interior for the gods in general, is also sometimes employed in Paramaribo.[16] In one instance at least, when a woman under possession was singing to what she called *Ingi*,—Indian—*winti*, she sang,

> The *Tone* spirits are in the river-e
> The *Tone* spirits are in the river-o
> The river *Vodun* crush me,
> The *Tone* spirits are in the river-o
> The river *Kwenda* crush me,
> The *Tone* spirits are in the river-o
> The River-Mother crushes me,
> The *Tone* spirits are in the river-o.

The *Tone*, it is said, are the river *Dagowe*, and all these are included in the term "water-*Ingi*." One of these river spirits sung to is called *Abo*, and the rest are the *Ingi* spirits, *Yanki*, *Kobisi*, *Frepsi*, among others. We have already commented upon the powers ascribed to the Indian spirits. This is definitely in the African tradition, and follows what seems to be a deep-seated African pattern of belief which is manifest practically throughout all of West Africa, if not in other portions of the continent as well.[17] Among the Saramacca Bush-Negroes, little reference is made to Indian spirits, for here the tradition exists that the ancient ancestors had themselves cleared the land, deepened the channels of the river, and caused the great forests to spring up.

Next, in the list of Paramaribo deities, come the *Kromanti*[18] gods. These comprise *Opete*,[19] the vulture; *Tigri*,[20] the jaguar, sometimes called *Dyebi* or *Dyadya; Obia-Kromanti; Nengere-kondre Kromanti* (African *Kromanti*); *Busi-Kromanti* (Bush *Kromanti*); and *Ondro-watra Kromanti* (the *Kromanti* spirits who live under the water).[21] The thunder deities, of which we have spoken, are also classed in this *Kromanti* group. The designation *Kromanti*, as used in Paramaribo, though often employed as a synonym for "African" gods, is, nevertheless, the name for a distinct category, and seems to relate to warrior and disciplinary elements in nature. Thus comment is made that *Kromanti* dancing is *hebi*,—"difficult"—that is, "strong," or dangerous. *Kromanti* devotees are immune to bullet wounds; when they are under possession a knife cannot cut them, thorns cannot lacerate their flesh, or fire burn them, or glass cut them. The *Kromanti winti* are conceived as powerful spirits, who when they possess human beings, cause them to speak African words not intelligible to the uninitiated.

In still another category are to be found the gods of the bush. The most dreaded of these are the *Akantamasu*, who live in anthills. There are thought to be three types of these,—those who live in the ground, those who live in trees, and those who live in holes. Another group of bush-spirits are the *Apuku*, the little people of the bush. In town, though this name is heard both in reference and in song, the designation for these is also *Bakru*. There is no uniform opinion, however, that the two are identical. Those who hold that they are make the distinction that there are *Bakru* whom "God" makes, and those are the *Apuku;* and there are *Bakru* whom sorcerers make, and those are the messengers of black magic. Whether we consider these as two groups or one, reference is made to the "little people" in both instances. Belief also exists that there is a group of *Apuku* who live in the water. This, however, seems to have little currency in general knowledge or in ritual practice, and would appear to be a belief that, at most, is restricted to one group of Negroes.[22] Another of these bush spirits is that of the *kankantri*, the silk-cotton tree.[23] There are differing opinions as to why this tree is sacred. One view is that it is worshipped as the home of the Earth-Mother, another because the tree itself has a *winti* known as *Kankantri winti*, which at times sends out a "fireman" who is seen as a wave of flame that disappears if someone stands watching it fixedly. Another holds that the silk-cotton tree is important because people who die without having heirs to whom to leave their *winti* send these *winti* to live in silk-cotton trees. A fourth is that the tree is sacred only because the *Dagowe* snake lives in it, and that when food is placed as an offering at the foot of one of these trees, it is not for any spirit in the tree itself, but for the spirit of the *Dagowe*.

These, then, are the principal categories of deities which the Paramaribo Negroes worship. Through matings between these *winti*, however, there result offspring who give rise if not to categories which are distinctly new, then to new alignments in behavior and function of these resulting gods, since they inherit their powers and attributes from both parents. For the *winti* are thought of as living in families. The only direct reference to this in the city is to the seven Thunder gods we have named, who are spoken of as *"na sebi opruru brada,—* the seven thunder brothers." In discussing dancing for the snake *winti*, we shall see the point made that male snakes mate with the Earth gods, and the female snakes with the deities of the Sky.

Some of the *winti* that are not classifiable under the categories we have mentioned can be comprised under the heading *Nengere-kondre winti*,—African spirits. Foremost among these is *Leba*, about whom two different concepts exist.[24] One of these is that *Leba* is the god of the cross-roads.[25] The second opinion holds that *Leba* "is like a lock against bad spirits," and that it is a *winti* left in a tree by some person who either had no children or relatives to whom he might leave the *winti*, or who did not feel that these children or relatives would worship the *winti* properly. When such *winti* consent to leave the family in peace and reside in a tree, they become *Leba*, and they manifest themselves in the form of tattered old women or, when invisible, are heard in the night as a wind. If a *Leba* chooses, it can allow evil to enter the yard it guards, just as it can, when it wishes, prevent evil from entering. It is offended by having soiled water thrown at it. At night, inhabitants of a yard go in a roundabout way in order to avoid the particular tree where the spirit is said to reside. The two beliefs merge in the concept of it as a spirit constantly on guard, the one idea being that *Leba* guards the cross-roads, and the other that he inhabits the yard and keeps evil from it. Another of these African *winti* is *Akabrewa*, and still another is called *Adyanti-wai*, sometimes also known as Fire-*winti*, because of the fact that, under possession, the devotees of this deity dance in the fire.

A person acquires a *winti* in one of three ways. Most frequently his *winti* comes to him by inheritance; that is to say, before dying, a man or a woman designates the individual to whom his or her *winti* are to go just as he would designate the disposal of any other possessions. Usually, succession in the instance of *winti* is from men to men and from women to women, so that a man first wills his *winti* to his next eldest brother, and a woman to the sister who follows her. There are, however, exceptions to this manner of passing on the custody and worship of the familial *winti*. If an individual, whose death is approaching, has many *winti*,—we have heard the fact referred to with pride that an ancestor of one informant had as many as ninety-seven *winti* —and the sister or brother in line to succeed is old or ill, such a relative is passed over for someone younger who is physically more capable to perform the rites necessary to worship the family spirits. This need for physical strength in the worship of the *winti* is referred to constantly, since dancing is the governing element in this worship. Should that strength be lacking in any one individual, several members of the family are called upon, each to take over several of the *winti* to be inherited. In those cases where the person who is about to die is the last of his generation, the *winti* are passed to daughters, if it is a woman who is disposing of her inheritance, or to a sister's sons, if it is a man. If a woman has no daughters of her own, her *winti* are inherited by her sisters' daughters, though, if she chooses, she may give any of her *winti* to her sons. In the same way, a man, if he chooses, may pass down his *winti* to his own sons, or even to his daughters. This occurs, in the main, only when there are no proper heirs, and is to be regarded as the exceptional procedure.

Another way in which a *winti* is acquired is for a spirit itself to choose the individual whom it wishes to possess. "Living with someone doesn't give a person *winti*, unless the *winti* likes him. Some people do get their *winti* that way. Some get theirs at a *winti* play. This happens when a *winti* likes a person and decides to come to him." When this occurs, it is said that the *winti* has met and loved the one whom it has chosen, and has decided to stay with him. Thus, when, in family inheritance, the *winti* goes to someone not in the customary line of succession, such a choice on the part of the god is said to have taken place. However, such a choice by the *winti*, as is indicated in our informant's statement, need not be within a given family. The spirit may decide to leave the family and go to a stranger, and we ourselves were earnestly warned against memorizing the words of *winti*-songs and singing them, lest the spirits, flattered by this attention, decide to possess us, and make us their devotees. The choice of worshippers by the *winti* themselves is said to be occurring with special frequency in more recent times, because the *winti* are so often dissatisfied with the descendants of their traditional devotees as potential worshippers. This is the case, for example, when the persons in line for succession to a given *winti* or group of *winti* have become active members of one of the Christian churches.

The third way in which a person obtains a *winti* is by *wisi* or *kunu*. A *winti* which comes to an individual in the first two ways described is friendly to its devotee, and when worshipped properly helps him keep his health, earn a living, gain the good-will of his neighbors, and relish life. But one acquired in this third manner is an evil *winti*, that seeks to bring its devotee illness, poverty, misfortune, and death. These evil spirits can only be appeased by doing their will, or by getting medicine which will send them away. Those brought to a person through *wisi* are sent at the behest of some enemy. *Kunu*, in town as in the bush, is the vengeance meted out by gods and ancestors for violation of traditional codes of moral behavior. In the city the concept of *kunu* is not as powerful a disciplinary force as it is in the bush, since the belief in its validity is not as strong in Paramaribo as in the interior. Yet even in the city the crime of incest, or that of killing a sacred snake without giving it ritual burial, and of killing by black magic, are held to be punishable by *kunu*. The form this takes is to punish not so much the perpetrator of the crime, as members of his family in the female line, from generation to generation, thus bringing his line to an end, or, at best, seeing his family reduced to poverty. This punishment by *kunu*, for the town Negroes, takes the form of the coming of a *winti* as an enemy. If a snake is killed, a snake spirit comes; if incest is committed or evil magic employed, any type of *winti* may come.

In this connection a further point relating to the concept of *winti* must be made, and that is that a *winti* may at the same time be both a good and an evil spirit. The fact is that the logic of the Negroes of Paramaribo holds that no spirit is either good or evil in the absolute sense. This concept of the absence of a spirit which is wholly good or completely evil enters here in a more subtle way. For while it generally follows that a spirit is friendly if it is worshipped, unfriendly if it is neglected, and evil if it has been sent to do evil, a spirit may be temperamentally as inconstant as human beings are inconstant. A whim may make one of them disposed to overlook an offense, and a whim may cause the same spirit to bring accident to a person who has not been guilty of serious neglect. There are *winti* such as the *Akanta-masu* who may be said to be friendly spirits only in the negative sense; that is, when they are not angered they abide in the deep bush, and allow the person possessed of them to live in peace. But all *Akanta-masu* spirits that are inherited are thought to have originally come into the family as the result of the operation of a *kunu*.

1. This identification of the gods and spirits with wind or air was found by us in Dahomey, where the Fon word *djo*, which means wind, is often employed as the term for "god."

2. *Vodun* in Dahomey is the term for "deity."

3. This is, of course, the Gold Coast *obosom*, the Twi word for god.

4. *Tata* means "father."

5. *Bade* is youngest and most powerful member of the *So* (Thunder) pantheon of Dahomey. In Dorsainvil's list (p. 39), *Zofi-Bade* appears as one of the voodoo gods in the Haitian pantheon.

6. In all West Africa, every deity, to say nothing of human beings, especially kings and chiefs, have these "strong" names which are employed only on ceremonial occasions.

7. *Asase* is the Gold Coast name for the Earth deity.

8. In Fon, *Ai* is the term for "earth," and occurs in sacred names.

9. In Dahomey and among the Yoruba, *Loko* (*Iroko*) is the name of a sacred tree. The *Loko* tree in Dahomey, however, is a deity in the *Mawu-Lisa* pantheon, and has totemic associations for many sibs, as well.

10. Kongo *mboma*, python.

11. Lit. horse; in Haiti *choual* (*cheval*) is used with the same significance.

12. *Dagowe* is the Suriname equivalent of *Dagbe*, an Ewe-Fon word also used to designate a sacred snake. *Dangbe* is similarly employed in Haiti (Parsons, I, and Dorsainvil). Dan is the Fon term for a kind of serpent-like mobility, and is applied not only to snakes, but to a spirit which manifests itself in anything that is undulating.

13. This is the sacred python, *Onini*, of the Ashanti.

14. This follows Dahomean practice, where, if someone by a willful act does what is hateful to a *vodun*, the members of all the *vodun* cults go into a state of frantic possession, shouting the name of the guilty one at all the crossroads and at the shrines of all the gods, until a purification dance is held. This last takes place when the *vodun* is avenged, that is, when the offender is dead or insane.

15. This statement reveals the identity of the *Hei-gron* snake spirit with the Dahomean deity called *Dambala Hwedo*, which also takes the form of a serpent that lives in mountains and is a manifestation of the spirit of an ancient ancestor.

16. Through a transposition of vowels, it is possible that the *Twi* name for the most sacred of all rivers, *Tano*, the parent of numerous deities, has here become *Tone*. Cf. Rattray, (II), passim, and Cardinal, (I), pp. 49 ff. It is also to be remarked that the Fon word *to* means "water."

17. See on this point, Delafosse, (I), ch. V., especially the section entitled "Le Régime Foncier." The same attitude as is described here is found on the part of the Dahomeans toward the spirits of those persons who represent the aboriginal inhabitants of their country.

18. This term is derived from the Gold Coast. It is a well-known fact that one group of slaves were called Coromantines, and there was a kingdom of Coromantyn in the present colony of the Gold Coast. The word is well known in Jamaica and throughout the West Indies. Thus, Edwards, vol. ii, p. 75, speaks of "the Koromantyn, or Gold Coast, Negroes . . ." For an ingenious theory as to the origin of the New World significance of the term see Williams (I), p. 9.

19. *Opete* is a Twi word for vulture, and is in use among the Ashanti-Fanti peoples of the Gold Coast. The sacred character of the vulture is widespread in West Africa and among the New World Negroes. In Dahomey, Togoland, and the Gold Coast the vulture is the messenger who

takes sacrifies to the gods; the vulture is sacred in Jamaica; and even in the Sea Islands of the United States to "jump Jim Crow" is to dance a vulture-dance.

20. The leopard is sacred in all of West Africa, where it is often identified with royalty. In Dahomey it is the totem animal of the royal sib and is thus accorded the rank of a powerful deity.

21. These are not to be confused with the river spirits proper.

22. Possibly the Dahomean *toxosu* cult is here found merely as a vague tradition.

23. The silk-cotton tree is sacred throughout West Africa, and in Dahomey is revered because the souls of ancestors are held to have taken their residence in them.

24. This bespeaks the fact that in this deity as he is envisaged in Suriname there appears to have been a merging of the attributes given him in the beliefs of two distinct regions in Africa.

25. *Legba* is the deification of accident in Dahomey, and is universally worshipped as the divine trickster. *Legba* is worshipped in Haiti, (cf. Parsons, I, pp. 65–67). *Legba*, under the Yoruba name of *Elegbara*, is worshipped in Cuba, (Ortiz, I, p. 66–67), and in Brazil.

B. THE WORSHIP OF THE WINTI

Those who can afford [it] . . . go up the river and either dance on one of the plantations, where the prohibitions of the city do not exist, or better still, arrange . . . [worship of the winti in the bush]. This last, of course, is most costly of all, for it involves not only paying the drummers and buying all the sacrifices to the person's own winti, but also furnishing the things needed to propitiate the Earth-Mother and other Earth gods as well as the god of the crossroads . . . in order that the winti be allowed to come and dance, and evil spirits be kept at bay. Finally, those who hold a dance must sacrifice to the ancestors. . . .

* * *

We have discussed the nature of the *winti*, the types of *winti* that are found, and the manner in which these spirits are acquired. In our consideration of the pattern of their worship, let us first view the phenomenon of the *winti* as it is thought to manifest itself in the growing child who is a potential devotee of his family's gods. For example, we watched a two-year-old girl playing in the yard where her mother lives, and saw how any vessel filled with water attracted her attention, and how if it was large enough, she climbed into it and splashed about. It was soon said in the yard that when she grew up she would have a strong water Indian (*watra Ingi*) god, and what at first seemed to be mere pleasantry at the child's attraction for water, soon became apparent as a serious expression of belief. The mother of the child had Indian *winti*, and though she was not yet obliged to worship it regularly, since her own mother, the child's grandmother, was still alive, the *winti* had already manifested itself to her, and the opinion was held that if the grandmother lived long enough for the child to be of an age to dance when the grandmother died, the *winti* would go to the child rather than to the mother of the child. Thereafter when choosing gifts for her little daughter, the mother bought red beads, or figured red prints, or a small red kerchief, since red is sacred to the water gods.

Again, bad tempered children are spoken of as having dormant Tiger spirits, and at times, especially if reference is being made to a boy, this is said with pride. Or if a child behaves badly and breaks things, the mother may say, in disgust, "Ah! She's going to have *Bakru winti!*" It must be made clear, however, that praise or blame is not associated only with the *winti*. For the *akra* is called upon to take foremost responsibility for personality traits, and a good-tempered child is generally said merely to have a good '*kra*, or a bad-tempered child to have a bad one. However, no matter what aptitudes for the worship of a given type of *winti* a child shows either in general behavior, or in special ability to remember and sing the songs of that *winti*, or to drum its rhythms, or to dance its dance-steps, we know of only one instance where any belief was held in the active presence of a *winti* in a child under the age of puberty. This case was that of a boy about seven years old, who already was under the influence of a *Leba* spirit. Once a year his mother gives an offering at the cross-roads to the child's spirit, putting into a calabash a pipe filled with tobacco, some corn, *akansa*, *asogri*, and a torn blouse. If she neglects to do this, then with the coming of the new year the child rolls on the ground and screams, as he had done the first time, two years back, when the presence of his *Leba* spirit was discovered.

Let us give another instance of the manner in which it is discovered that a child, when of age, will be possessed by a god. An informant, whose grandmother was said to have come from *Demakuku*,[1] dreamed, when a young child, that someone came to tell her she would be taken to Africa. They then went together on foot through the bush for a long time, until they came to a "big" house, where hung a "big" bell. A very black, stout woman was sitting there. She wore a black *pangi*,—tunic—and a colored cloth over her breasts. When our informant awoke and told her mother of her dream, her aunt, who was present, informed them that the informant's grandmother had *Nengere-kondre Kromanti winti*,—African[2] Kromanti *winti*—which she would "catch" when she grew up. While still a child, she had had yet another proof that this *winti* would come to her, for once when she was ill she again dreamed that she was taken to Africa. When she arrived there, she saw several very black men stamping leaves on a mat. These leaves when sufficiently crushed were put in water, and with this water she was washed. When she awoke, she felt better, and soon grew well. This *winti*, however, did not come to her immediately after these dreams, for, except in rare instances, it is not until after the age of puberty that the person destined to be possessed by a *winti* actually begins his worship by dancing for it under possession. This woman has today six *winti* in all; two snake gods, one male and one female, that came to her from a maternal aunt; this African *winti* from her grandmother; *Aisa, Loango,* and *Papa Ingi* from her mother.

How does a person learn the manner of worship of his *winti*? Those who have *winti*, when questioned, say no formal instruction is given. When the *winti* enters the individual, it is the spirit itself who sings the songs, speaks the tongues, and dances the dances. That this is an accepted belief is illustrated by the comments heard at *winti* dances, where if a devotee dances unusually well, it is said "Her *winti* dances splendidly." Again, when one of the *winti* priestesses was induced to sing some sacred songs for our phonograph, the words never corresponded exactly to those we ourselves had taken down during the actual ceremonies which this woman had led. The explanation of this was that at the dance it was the *winti* that sang, while before the phonograph, the priestess could at best only reproduce such fragments of the songs sung by the gods as remained in her memory. Often, when asking a man or a woman who was an acknowledged devotee of a *winti* to sing the songs of that *winti*, the answer was, "I know these songs only when the *winti* comes, because it is the *winti* who sings them." It must be recognised that in the refusal often lay the fear that if the songs were sung, possession would come on, as we have seen it come on when an informant, himself choosing the songs he wished to sing for the phonograph, sang those of his own *winti*.[3] It is not strange the belief exists that in the performance of ritual songs, dances, and drumming, it is the *winti* who perform. Given a situation where the children, from their earliest years, are held to be potentially capable of possession by a given spirit, and where they have, from time to time, witnessed the dances, heard the songs, and listened to the drum-rhythms for the *winti*,[4] it follows that when the traditionally accept-able time comes for them to be possessed by these spirits, they dance and sing as a result of unconscious habituation; not as novices, but as though they were being directed by a force within them.

This belief in the performance by the *winti* itself cannot be said to be universal, for we have the statement of one man, at least, that he went through formal training for his *winti*. This man, who is now in his late twenties, told how when he was fourteen years old his mother informed him that he had *Arawaki Ingi winti* (an Arawak In-dian spirit), saying she had learned of it in a dream. She began to teach him the dance-steps for this *winti*, and not until after a year of intermittent instruction was he ready to dance. During this period she also taught him the make-up for the spirit that was to possess him, and the songs to be sung in worshipping it. One other instance which contravenes the general explanation given comes from our own ob-servation. At a *winti* dance, as the devotees of the *Tap'-Kromanti* spirit were dancing under possession, there was one young woman who danced with awkward hesitation. Observing this, the priestess in charge, herself possessed, came over to the young woman and, since speech is forbidden under possession, stepped lightly on the young woman's foot to call her attention to her presence; then, dancing at her side, showed her the steps and gestures.[5]

Let us return to the case of the man who had Arawak Indian *winti*, and see what, other than the steps of the dances and the words and melodies of the songs, it was incumbent upon him to know in order to worship his *winti*. One factor which entered his life with the coming of the *winti* was the observance of its *trefu*. In his particular case, this necessitated the abstinence from eating beef, or pork, or a certain kind of fish. "*Na winti dati a teki da kau fo hem 'asi.*—That *winti* has taken the cow for its medium." No food cooked by a menstruating woman could be eaten by him, for this is the deadliest taboo of all for the *winti*. —"No, no! No *winti* can eat food prepared by a menstruating woman. If the *winti* eats food prepared by a menstruating woman, it will spoil. It cannot work any more." Since red is the sacred color for the Arawak Indian *winti*, the new devotee wore about his person something of that color to please his *winti*. There was no other ritual of systematised worship, except that when he embarked on a journey, he made a sac-rifice of some kind to the *winti*, to ask of it support and protection.

Some of the foods that are forbidden by other *winti* are as follows: persons who worship the *Papa-winti* do not eat plantains or bananas.

The *Kromanti* gods forbid smoking in their presence. "*Kromanti no lobi smoku. Efu suma smoki pe den dansi Kromanti, dan yu habi tumusi trobi.—Kromanti* does not like smoke. If someone smokes where they dance *Kromanti,* then you have much trouble." Those who worship *Aisa* do not eat the flesh of the peccary, nor of a species of deer described to us as having a spreading hoof. The *Tigri* devotees refrain from eating meat not freshly killed.

The *winti* also prescribe the offerings that are pleasing to them. For example, all *winti* demand that the rice given them as sacrifice be *kriori* (creole, or native-grown) rice, and not the imported kind. They demand that the food be cooked with *obia-fatu,*—oil that comes from indigenous palm trees, and not imported oil. The *Kromanti* gods and the ancestors require rum, but to the Earth gods rum is hateful, and only sweet drinks such as molasses, or syrups, or a mixture of sugar and the bitter and sweet almond, called *orshadi* are given, though beer is also acceptable to them. Each *winti,* too, is said to come to a special part of the body of its devotee, and if angered by neglect, it is that portion of the body that the *winti* attacks when it sets out to bring illness to a follower. Thus, the snake deities, the *Akantamasu winti,* and the *Apuku winti* "*nyam bere,*"—eat the belly; the *Opete* "eats" the eyes; while the *Kromanti winti* attack the head and bring fever to the heart. Each *winti,* in addition, has a color that is sacred to it. White is the color of the Thunder gods, blue is the *Kromanti* color. Red is for the *Ingi* gods, brown is for the *Akantamasu,* while *Leba,* dancing in tatters, wears black or dark brown.

Those who are possessed by the *winti* are called, as we have seen, the '*asi* of the *winti.*[6] An '*asi* waits for his *winti* to manifest its desire to be worshipped before entering on its ritual. In the city this makes for difficulties, for since early slave days, the *winti* dances have been forbidden. Consequently, in the city of Paramaribo there is not the freedom to dance for the *winti* that exists in the bush, and that the working out of the system of *winti*-worship demands. Among the Bush-Negroes, where this freedom is had, when a devotee feels his *gado* asking for dancing,—this is manifested by restlessness and nervous tension,—he begins to wash for the spirit, daubs himself with white clay, and waits until the day of the week sacred to the god to dance. In Paramaribo this is impossible, and the restrictions have made, among other things, for the desuetude into which the custom of observing the day sacred to each individual *winti* has fallen, at least insofar as general dancing is concerned. In setting the day for *winti* cures, however, the *wintiman* does wait for the day sacred to the *winti.*

Under recent official rulings, dances have been decreed to be legal in the city four times a year. One of these legalized dances is held the first of July to celebrate the emancipation of the Negroes from slavery; another the first part of August, in celebration of the birthday of the Queen-Mother of Holland;[7] the third, during which the most important *winti* plays of the year take place, is held in celebration of the Queen's birthday, and on this occasion the festivities cover a period of about a week; the fourth celebrates the end of the year, and occurs the last week in December. There are those who dance for their *winti* at each of these dances,—who, in fact, appear every night and dance as long as the dances go on. Since giving a dance for the *winti* involves expense, many persons dance only at one of these dances, or at a series of dances given during one of these legally sanctioned intervals. There are other people, however, whose *winti* are not appeased even though they dance for them at all of these four annual dance-cycles. Such *winti* demand further dancing during the year. Those who can afford to indulge their *winti* in their desire to be thus worshipped frequently go up the river and either dance on one of the plantations, where the prohibitions of the city do not exist, or better still, arrange for a dance in worship of their own *winti* somewhere in the bush away from the city. This last, of course, is most costly of all, for it involves not only paying the drummers and buying all the sacrifices to the person's own *winti*, but also furnishing the things needed to propitiate the Earth-Mother and other Earth gods as well as the god of the cross-roads, all of whom must have their sacrifices in order that the *winti* be allowed by them to come and dance, and evil spirits be kept at bay. Finally, those who hold a dance must sacrifice to the ancestors so these may share the offerings and the dances for the ancestral *winti*.

If the *'asi* who is troubled by an insistent *winti* cannot afford to provide his god with one of these costly special dances, and his *winti* is amenable to persuasion, he gives an offering of food, and asks for its forbearance until such time as he can find the means to worship it properly. If it is not willing to wait, he arranges for a surreptitious *winti* dance in his own yard or in that of the *wintiman*, and provides an ordinary bass drum, or more probably a calabash upturned in a basin of water. A reasonable *winti* accepts the exigencies of the situation which demand the use of a substitute for the sacred drum, and is appeased when its *'asi* dances to it. It is also possible for a devotee who is troubled by his *winti* to come and dance at a special dance that another provides for the curing of an illness brought on by *winti*, for, except at those dances that are held away from the city, the *winti*-cures but rarely take place at these four stated dancing-periods.

As one informant put it, "After the Queen's birthday, I will have to see to the pacifying of my *winti*. On the Queen's day each one looks after his own, the *wintiman*, too."

. . . .

The point has been made that the essential mode of worship of the *winti* is dancing for it, and that the need to dance for the *winti* manifests itself in possession. It will make for clarity in understanding the phenomenon of possession as it exists in Paramaribo, and the attitudes toward it, if we cite specific instances we ourselves witnessed.

One of the possessions we saw was that of a woman in her early twenties, who was on her way to market.[8] She was alone, and as she walked, her body shook and trembled, and the muscles of her face twitched. She talked as she went on, greeting in the name of her *winti* those who passed her, announcing her *winti's* "strong" names, and her own "strong" name. She was possessed by the *Papa* god. Before she reached the market, her trembling became more violent, and suddenly she fell to the ground and began crawling and rolling face downward. She emitted falsetto sounds, which turned into shrieks when some women tried to bring her to her feet. A crowd soon gathered, and an old woman who herself had a *Papa* god came from the market with something for her to drink. After several minutes, in which all those who surrounded the woman showed anxiety lest the police come, she was lifted into a passing automobile and taken home. Those, however, who did not know the woman sufficiently well to be concerned whether the police came or not, joked about the incident, for though according to religious belief the *winti* alone was accountable for this performance, the actual situation presented an amusing scene in the marketplace which was well relished.

This latter attitude toward the phenomenon of possession we have seen expressed during the tensest moments of a dance, and illustrates a fundamental point of view toward worship. The sense of immediacy which frequent possession by the *winti* engenders, though it gives an experience of the most valid kind to those who go through it, brings with it neither sanctimoniousness nor solemnity. This is evidenced also in the directness of the prayers that are sung or spoken, in the reasoning with the *winti* whose wants are too exacting, in the tradition of calling upon the *winti's* sense of fair play in difficult times to induce it to forego demands it has made for dancing or sacrifices. The *winti*, indeed, partake of much of the character of human beings, and while they are respected and feared, little of awe enters into their worship, except in times of stress, when the spirits show themselves implacable.[9]

Another case of possession occurred on the street near our hotel. The possessed woman was brought into the courtyard, threw herself on the ground, and lay moaning and foaming at the mouth. In this instance, possession was by the *Akantamasu*, god of the ant hill. However, the woman had a strong alcoholic breath, and this puzzled the bystanders for a moment, for they could not decide whether intoxication or possession was the cause of the attack. But the white foam at the mouth was for them an unmistakable sign that it was the latter, and the alcoholic breath was at once attributed to the fact that under the malign influence of this particular god the possessed woman had been drinking. This time there was very little levity on the part of the bystanders, for the *Akantamasu winti* is dreaded by those who have it, and when it manifests itself, calls forth a feeling of pity. A woman who herself had many *winti* brought water for the possessed one, and soothed her with gentle speech, bathing her hair and face. Recovery from this possession was slow; the woman whose god had seized her lay in the courtyard for more than an hour before she regained consciousness. Finally, however, she was brought to her feet, and with the aid of several of the women who had remained with her, was taken home. She looked physically exhausted, but it was explained that *"A sa kisi hem srefi te a kaba dansi fo 'a winti.*—She will recover after dancing for her *winti."*

The third instance of possession not brought on during ritual dancing occurred in our room, while we were working on tales and songs with an informant. Two of the songs which he had given as *kot' singi*[10] were *Kromanti* songs, and as he sang them for the phonograph he became extremely nervous. He asked for a cigar, and chewed it as he went on to tell two ghost stories. Then he got up and began pacing the floor, until he suddenly turned and asked for a Bush-Negro drum, which he knew we had collected in the interior, saying he wanted to sing into the phonograph with a drum accompaniment. As soon as he had finished these songs, which he sang loudly, the drum was taken from him with the explanation that it was too late to record any more songs, for he was then fully possessed, and the situation demanded that he be calmed.[11] The drum obviously fascinated him, for he stood looking at it fixedly, and then he walked toward it. He himself, however, did not wish to allow his possession to get out of bounds, and he stood beside it struggling for self-control against the new African *komfo* that troubled him. This *komfo*, when once calmed and made at home by his *akra*,—it was at the time being opposed by his soul in taking possession of the informant, because this *komfo* would become his *basi-winti*, his governing *winti*,—would make of him an important priest. The time had not yet come to see to its calming, however. The following day, when we discussed this possession with him, he explained that it is possible to check the coming on of possession by taking measures to allay the restlessness of the troubling *winti* with a promise of a future dance. Within a day we had an opportunity of verifying this, for both he and his aunt, who had told us in advance that they would not dance at a certain ceremony to which they escorted us, actually did not dance.[12] The woman remained seated beside us, though when her own *winti* were called, she did not participate in the singing. The man, hearing his *winti* called, rose and paced back and forth on the road which flanked the yard where the dance was held, and the people who watched him go shook their heads and laughed. They knew the symptoms of possession, and were scornful of his attempt to frustrate his *winti*.

When possession occurs without the necessary preparation for dancing, it is because the *winti* is forcing its wishes to become known. In other words, it is a sign that the *winti* has been angered because of improper worship, and since what the *winti* exacts is, above all, dancing for it,—the offerings which are a part of the necessary preparation for the *winti*-dance accompany such dancing as a matter of course—sudden possession comes when its 'asi has either denied the *winti* expression through dancing, or has not given it full release.

1. We were unable to localise this term in Dahomey, where, according to the Suriname people who spoke of *Demakaku*, this village is supposed to be located. According to Encyc., p. 1, a reference to "Doemakoekoe Negers" is made by F. W. Hostmann, in volume II, p. 250 of his work entitled "Over de beschaving van negers in Amerika door kolonisatie met Europeanen," published in Amsterdam, 1850, while on p. 638 they are referred to as cannibals.

2. Rattray (V, p. 145), gives the following: "*Abibirim*, Africa, lit., among the blacks, the black man's country." This would explain the Suriname usage of *Nengere-kondre*—"Negro country"—for "Africa."

3. The fact must not be overlooked that there is also a disinclination to discuss these matters with a White person because of the fear that the spirit itself would resent such a discussion with a member of the race that had forbidden *winti* dances.

4. *Winti* songs are never introduced as work-songs, or sung for diversion. If they are sung while at work, or about the house, it is either that a ritual is being performed, or that the *winti* is clamoring for worship.

5. The same technique of instruction is employed in Dahomey, where for each two or three novitiates an older initiated member of the cult dances beside them.

6. *'Asi* is literally translated as "horse" by Paramaribo Negroes who are asked its meaning, and they say that it denotes the one who "carries" the *winti*. Some persons add to this the meaning "servant," i.e., of the *winti*. However, the word is identical with the Fon-Ewe word for "wife,"—*asi*—which, in Togo and Dahomey, is employed in religious terminology to denote "wives of the gods," i.e., worshippers. Thus, a follower of Mawu is called *Mawusi*, one of Legba, *Legbasi*. On the Gold Coast, the Ashanti employ the term *oponko*, "horse" for worshipper, hence the telescoping of the Fon-Ewe word, and the Ashanti usage into the word *'asi*, which is Negro-English for "horse," accounts for the translation so often given.

7. In Nigeria, as in Suriname, the word "play" is usually employed for "dance" or "ceremony." Cf. Talbot, (II), vol. ii and iii, *passim*.

8. Whether it is chance that the instances we cite occurred a short time before the sanctioned period of dancing in Paramaribo, we cannot say, for our stay in the colony coincided with this time.

9. We have found the same attitude toward the gods among Negroes in the Suriname bush, in the West Indies, and in West Africa itself.

10. These songs are used to "cut" Anansi stories.

11. As a matter of fact, by this time a crowd had collected in the street in front of the hotel, and the talk ran that White people were dancing for their *winti*. Our gratitude goes once more to Miss Gans for her forbearance in this, as in other situations incidental to ethnological inquiry.

12. This is practised in Haiti as well, where a worshipper will *marré* his *mâit' tête*, i.e. bind his controling deity, before going to a dance at which he does not wish to be possessed.

C. WINTI MALADIES AND WINTI CURES

The view persists . . . that there are fevers that the White doctor can treat, and those that he is powerless to cure. For this last type of fevers, therefore, the lukuman, the wintiman or the obiaman must be called in, since these ailments are of supernatural origin, and it is only a supernatural remedy that can cure those who have succumbed to them.

*   *   *

There are other ways, often more drastic than through possession, that a *winti* makes known its displeasure. It may make its *'asi* so ill-tempered that he will tear his own clothes to shreds and break whatever is in his house. It may even cause its *'asi* to steal, in order to obtain money necessary to provide the proper offerings and the necessities utilised when preparing for a dance. It will, above all, bring illness to the individual himself and to members of his family. The sequence of any of these punishments is not fixed, for any of them may occur in a more or less aggravated form as a first sign of displeasure, this depending largely upon the powers attributed to the *winti* itself. When such misfortunes occur, it is usual for the more immediate members of the family to call together the more distant relations to discuss what should be done. At such times, contributions are made to enable the family to satisfy the familial *winti*. An attempt may be made to have a *wintiman* call the *winti* to reason with the spirit on behalf of the family, and to offer it some small sacrifices to appease it temporarily. If the *winti* refuses to be pacified on those terms, a *winti*-play is given in order to cure the person who is being troubled. This ritual is called *seti winti*,—pacifying the *winti*.

Before discussing *winti* curing, let us return to the informant who was being claimed by an African *komfo* as its *'asi* for an example of how the need for such a cure arises. This *winti* came from Demakuku, in Africa and is traced by our informant through five generations of his ancestry. "It is not a little one," he said of it proudly, though at the time he knew but little about it,—only, in fact, that it did not drink rum, but wished sweet liquors, and that it troubled him when he worked for other people, especially when those others were men darker than himself. One of the things he does under possession, and which he did when he was possessed in our hotel room, is to write the language of his *winti*. We reproduce a sample written while in a state of possession.[1] Since leaving Suriname, we have had several letters from him which contained this writing, included, he explained, as a greeting from his *winti* to us. Objectively considered, the symbols he employs are consistent, and we have seen him write them with ease. He has not yet solved for himself the meaning of this writing, for he still questions us about the peoples in Africa who know how to write, though he assures us that once the *winti* is pacified, it will make known to him the meaning of the symbols, and their origin.

This man's difficulties in having his *winti* pacified are many. Most important of all is that of getting the money necessary to engage a *wintiman* to do this pacifying, and to provide for the essentials of such a ceremony. This should cost about fifty guilders, a sum still beyond his reach. In addition, in his present condition he has a grave distrust of the *lukuman*, feeling that once they discover how powerful a *winti* it is, they may give him medicine to "spoil" it, and thus eliminate a powerful rival. Moreover, since this *winti*, powerful as it is, would become the *basi winti,* the master of all the *winti* whose devotee he is, his *akra* sees in it a challenge to its own power over the man, for a powerful *winti* such as this would seek to subordinate the will of the *akra* to its own will, and therefore, the *akra* is reluctant to yield it the right to take possession of the man.

What constitutes a *winti* cure? All curing, whether of possession such as we have described, or of illness, includes in its regime the need of bathing the body. This bathing is said to "cool" the body, and the phrase "to cool" means "to set at peace." Each individual *winti* has herbs which are especially sacred to it. These are put in water, and to this is added white chalk, washing blue (to represent indigo), African pepper and other ingredients according to the *winti* that is to be "washed for." Among these sacred herbs are the *sangrafu, manu-sneki wiwiri, uma-sneki wiwiri, blaka-uma wiwiri,*[2] *korsu wiwiri, aneisi wiwiri, abongra* seeds, and *sibi wiwiri.* The person to be washed is stripped, and the washing is done either with a black or a white cock, used as a sponge, or some bread is employed for the same purpose. "Bread is more better, because bread come from the skin of God." If a cock is used, it is killed after the ceremony, and, as is the case when divining is done at a *winti*-dance, if its testicles are white the omen is held favorable and the person under treatment will be cured, but if black, the person will not recover. After this washing, and before a cure can be effected, the *winti* must be worshipped with dancing. While it is best that dancing be done by the person possessed by the *winti,* it is not unusual, especially where the patient is too old, or too ill, or has become so Europeanised that he is not familiar with the proper dance-steps, to find someone else to dance for him. Most frequently this other is the *wintiman,* who, as priest of the *winti,* may be either a man or a woman.

Not all the *winti* can be dealt with so simply. We were told the story of a woman who is unable to dance for her *winti* because her husband is a pastor of one of the Christian churches. The wife's *winti* so dislikes the husband that it harasses him and even threatens to kill him. This woman is described as handsome, and as a good wife when her *winti* does not trouble her, but she becomes violent when her *winti* comes, and she was once known to have struck her husband so hard a blow on the head while under the influence of the *winti* that he was in the hospital for some weeks. Sometimes her *winti,* in anger, puts the children out on the road in the rain, and the husband seldom dares enter his house when he finds his wife possessed by her *winti.* When the *winti* leaves her, she has no memory of having done any of these things. And the belief of most Negroes in Paramaribo is that if those, who like this woman give their *winti* no outlet in danc-ing, persist in their course, they will go insane. This, in fact, is the Paramaribo Negro's explanation of insanity, as given us by more than one informant. And though most often this is deplored, we have heard the fact mentioned with astonishment mingled with admiration that there are some who take up the religion of the Europeans so fervently that, in spite of their knowledge that insanity is in store for them, they still refuse to dance for the *winti*. This power of the *winti* to punish those who refuse to worship it is never questioned, and the conviction gives rise to a number of folkloristic beliefs.

A favorite theme of this folkloristic type has to do with the case of a policeman who was sent by the authorities to stop a *winti*-dance. It is told that upon hearing the drums play, his own *winti* possessed him. Stripping off his clothes, he joined the circle of dancers, and danced not only all that night, but remained at the *winti*-play until its end five days later. Another tale concerns a woman in the colony, who, to all appearances, is white. She came to a dance to satisfy her *winti*, and when the *winti* possessed her, she turned black, and remained black until her *winti* was appeased. Then, slowly, the deep pigmentation faded out and she was once more white. Still another story concerns a White woman whom a White man brought to see a *winti*-dance. When the drums played for the Snake gods, the *winti* seized her. She began to tremble and to twitch like the others who were possessed, and pulling out the hatpins from her hat, flung them and the hat into the bush, and joined the dancers, rolling on the ground as did the devotees of the snake. "It was the *winti* dancing. That's why she knew how." So strong is this belief, that White people who are interested in the cult of the *winti* are themselves said to be possessed of a spirit of which they may know nothing. In their own homes, belief holds, White people give *winti*-dances, but so disguised that only the expert eyes of the servants, who know what *winti* is, recognise them as such. For instance, instead of *winti* drums, snare-drums are used, and the violin and such other instruments as com-plete the White man's orchestra are substituted for rattle and gong. But after the dancing, which is but ordinary party-dancing of the White people, is in full swing, it becomes *winti*-dancing, and the special evidence in one such case cited was that some of the women present wore red petticoats! [3]

In all situations which arise out of the unfriendliness of a *winti* toward his *'asi* and the family of the *'asi*, it is important to deal with the *winti* amicably. Those who, let us say, choose insanity for themselves rather than "serve the Devil" are thought to be selfish, for, in accepting insanity for themselves, they are by no means ridding the family of the *winti* which, deserted, becomes an enemy, and will seek to enter the body of one member after another.

Those about to die, therefore, who wish to prevent the harassing of their descendants by unfriendly *winti*, call upon their *winti* to name the price at which they will withdraw from the family and leave it in peace. Mothers, especially, do this to save such of their children for whom belief in *winti* has lost its old validity. These negotiations with the *winti* are called *meki wan sweri*,—"swearing an oath"—or as an informant whose English was excellent, said, "Making a contract with the *winti*." Through the *wintiman*, the *winti* is asked to name its own conditions upon which it will consent to release the family. A woman, then, let us say, who wishes a *winti* to leave the family at her death, and the *wintiman* who is to question the *winti* are seated on benches. The *wintiman*, with rattle and to the accompaniment of drums, brings the *winti* into that part of the body of the woman where the *winti* is localised. The *wintiman* addresses the *winti*: "Your *'asi* is getting old. She has no one to whom to leave you. She wishes to pay you to leave her children in peace. I am here to find out what payment you ask." The answer may be that the *winti* demands a dinner, or a big feast, or liquor,—some *winti* are less exacting than others. The *winti* is also asked where it wishes to be sent. Usually, the place it elects to enter is a tree, and the tree preferred is the *kankantri*. A person who is thoughtful of his neighbors does not leave his *winti* in a tree in the city, but sends it to a *kankantri* on the outskirts of the city.

When the *winti* called *Adyanti-wai* was called to name the conditions upon which it would release a woman, it expressed the wish to leave the colony and to go back to Africa. "They made a little corial, and they put in a bottle of beer, some *switi sopi* (liqueurs), some *orshadi*, rice, *Nengere kondre pepre*, some white, blue, and red cotton, about an ell of each, and thirty-two cents (Dutch). At night, the little corial was taken in a boat to the harbor. We waited for the falling tide, and the *wintiman* said, 'We made an oath that you would leave the body of your *'asi* Afi now. She is getting old. Her children do not care to serve you. We are giving you the payment you asked for. It is here in the corial. You are in the corial. We beg you to go back to your own country. We beg you to leave the family of this *'asi* in peace.' Then they put the corial in the water, and it floated out to sea in the direction of Africa."

No *winti* that comes to a family as a *kunu* can, however, be disposed of in this manner.

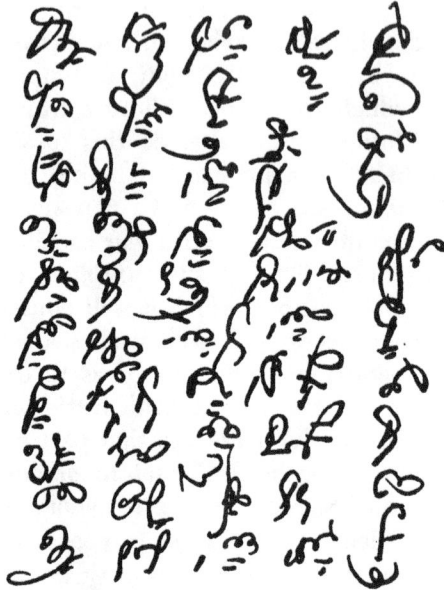

Writing produced under a state of possession by Winti.

Normal handwriting of the same individual.

1. Shown on page 304.
2. *Cordia Graveolens* H. B. K. Fam. *Borraginaceae.* (Encyc., p. 229).
3. This tendency on the part of *winti*-worshippers to infer their own kind of belief from behavior that has nothing to do with the *winti* is illustrated by the question asked us by one informant who wanted to know what kind of *winti* the Negroes of the United States worship. On being told that they are Christians, he exclaimed, "But I saw a *winti* dancing in your country!" Further questioning brought out the fact that, at the cinema, he had seen the Charleston danced.

Magic, Good, and Evil

There are two explanations why it was easier . . . under slavery to retain beliefs in divination and magic . . . and to pass them on to descendants, than to continue aboriginal worship. In the first place, these are matters that involve no public rituals and can therefore be carried out in the privacy of a cabin, or an isolated spot in the open country-side. More than this . . . the forms of African magic and European magic—and the general concept that it is possible to fortell coming events—differ only in detail. That this unconscious recognition of affinity was present among Europeans as well as Africans is illustrated by the well-documented fear that slave-owners had of the magic powers of their slaves.

* * *

A. OBIA—THE TAPU AND THE OPO

Of the four phenomena which define the world of the supernatural for the Paramaribo Negroes, we have thus far described two, the manifestation and role of the *akra*, (the soul) and of the *winti* (the gods). The third phenomenon concerns magic, good and evil. The generic term for good magic, as among the Saramacca Bush-Negroes, is *obia*, and for evil magic, *wisi*. But whereas the word *wisi* has general currency when reference is made to evil magic, the more usual name for good magic in Paramaribo is "luck" rather than *obia*. That is, people are spoken of as "buying luck" or "wearing luck," and comments are heard about the importance of carrying one's "luck" when walking alone at night, when going on a journey, when wooing a woman, or seeking work, or combating the effect of black magic.

More specifically, however, this "luck" is divided into two distinct types, the *tapu* and the *opo*. It is when we consider these two designations, indeed, that we come to the twofold aspect of good magic. A *tapu* is good magic which acts as a defensive instrument against evil. Thus, there are *tapu* against *Yorka* (ghosts), against *bakru,* (sorcerers'

Trinidad Village (with Frances S. Herskovits) New York: A. A. Knopf, Inc., 1946. p. 311

emissaries), against poison, against slander, against sterility and impotence, and against illness of the soul. In fact, a *tapu* can be provided for any ill within the range of human experience. The *opo*, on the other hand, is called into play to procure for an individual certain definite ends. It is an aggressive force, and it is the offensive factor in the concept of good magic.

The *opo*, in its use as a supernatural instrument to procure positive ends for its owner, is often asked to accomplish such ends to the definite disadvantage of other people. From the point of view of the group, these disadvantages may assume, if not a criminal character, certainly one that is anti-social in nature. That this does not escape the attention of the people themselves is evidenced by the fact that they recognise the *opo* as a marginal instrument between good and evil magic. We heard this point raised several times, one view holding that since the *opo* requires a ghost to act as its agent, it is *wisi*, another maintaining that the *opo* serves to better oneself, and takes that for its primary function as against the function of *wisi*, whose essential purpose is to bring harm to another.

An *opo*, then, is conceived as a supernatural agent which works on the will of others to make that will favorable to the owner of the *opo*. Examples of such *opo* are those which use as a base a piece of paper on which appears the handwriting of a White man. This paper, when combined with other elements, forms a charm for working on the will of White persons, and such charms are called *Bakra opo* and form in themselves an entire category of magical devices. Since a charm possessing blanket power to achieve any end, in all situations, is not deemed to have much efficacy, a special *opo* must be procured for each occasion of sufficient importance to warrant the expenditure of the amount necessary to secure it. One of these *Bakra opo* might be bought to secure a desired job from a White man; another for a case that is pending in court before a White judge, to bring a judgment favorable to its possessor. A *Bakra opo* might also be acquired to conceal irregularities in keeping the larder, or the mercantile stock of a White employer.

There are other categories of *opo*. People buy love *opo*, that is, either *uman* (female), or *man* (male) *opo*, which make it impossible for the men or women held desirable by the owners of the *opo* to resist their attentions. There are hunting *opo*, *opo* for trade, *opo* to help a person win at cards when played for money, and *opo* to make it impossible for a police officer to arrest its owner.—"When a person has a true-true *opo*," in this instance it was an *opo* against the interruption of a *winti* dance, "the policeman cannot beat him. He cannot do it at all. The *opo* does not give him the right. I saw it twice already. The policeman himself began to dance, and he forgot what he came to do. The opo said, 'Pengere, pengere, don't come here today' . . . 'Pengere' is the *obia*-language for a policeman with his weapon." A very famous *opo* that has earned a great deal of money for its owners is called *bambakula*, and is said to have been brought from Africa.

An *opo* may be some medicine in a bottle which, as in the *karta-opo*, or in the *man* or *uma opo*, for example, the individual puts on his person,—on his hair or his hands or some other part of his body—before embarking on the adventure he wishes to engage in; or it may be a charm to be worn on the person, or carried in a pocket, or kept in the house, and used in conjunction with a medicine. Each *tapu* and each *opo* has its own *trefu*, and sometimes an *opo* or a *tapu* may have several of them, for it is these food taboos which individualise the *opo* or the *tapu* for each owner, and assure him that his charm will remain potent. Thus, if someone, suspecting that a *tapu* was impeding his black magic, were to seek to nullify its effectiveness, he would be unable to spoil it if he did not know the proper *trefu*. On the other hand, violation of a *trefu* spoils an *opo*.

We have seen how the *sweri*,—the compact—sealed between an individual and his *winti*, resulted in the release of that individual's family from its obligation to serve the *winti*. This concept of making a *sweri* with a supernatural force is operative in magic also. An *opo* which once freed a sentenced man from jail involved such a compact made between the prisoner and a bird. The *opo* was worked with the head of a cock, and was called *kakaforu opo*. The compact specified that at the next cock crow the man was to be set free, and it is told that this occurred. This *opo* could have been made with any bird instructed to enter the cell, and when the bird found its freedom, the man would also have found his freedom. Such power is given to a bird by the maker of the *opo*, and is based on a formula, such as where the man makes seven cuts on a calabash, gives seven cuts to the man for whom the charm is being made, and says, "Well, you see, I did not cut you any more than I cut the man, so I throw you away under the water. Well, you see, the person who gets you under the water to do something to you, that one can do something to the man, too." This same principle of sealing a compact applies both to the *tapu* as well as to the *opo* and is also operative in *wisi*. What special supernatural agencies stand behind this compact is not clear, but it is generally attributed to the power of the *basi-winti* of the practitioner.[1]

Though we have spoken of the *tapu* as a passive agent, there are times when, in its defensive role, it issues positive warnings to its possessor. We have already spoken of the belief that if a drink which had black magic in it were taken up by a person who had a *tapu* against *wisi*, the glass would break. There are also *tapu* in the form of metal arm-bands, which contract when danger threatens to warn the wearers. Variants of this general type are *segribui* (silver link bracelets) which have been ceremonially cleansed in herbs, iron anklets or toe rings, and belts on which cauries or small white buttons are sewed. All of these, when felt to tighten, tell their owners that not only is black magic set against them, but that the *wisi* is actually entering into these *tapu*. Another form of *tapu* is that of "getting a *koti*." This consists of several small incisions which are made anywhere on the body, and into which medicine is rubbed. An example of this was had in the story of the calabash and the man who was cut seven times. These *koti* are specialised in power. There are *Yorka-koti* which insure to the possessor of them the harmlessness of ghosts; there are *Bakru-koti*, which protect against these "little people"; cuts are also made against illnesses, and to prevent anyone from calling away a person's soul.[2]

A *tapu* of this type that has attracted the widest attention in the literature is the *sneki-koti*.[3] Belief in this immunizing agent against snake bite, and in its curative powers if given after the serpent has struck (it may either be taken internally or in a cut), is not only held by the Negroes but by many of the Europeans resident in the colony. This remedy of the Bush-Negroes is said to be made out of the roasted powdered head of a venomous snake, and is sold to the people of the town. We have heard many persons testify to its efficacy, but whether their belief is validated in fact, or whether it is only of folkloristic value, is not our concern here. That this belief is firmly held is significant for our study, and we may quote an incident related to us illustrative of the manner in which faith in the remedy is kept alive. The person who recounted this anecdote was at one time a plantation-overseer whose station was not far from Paramaribo. One day, during his absence in the city, a poisonous snake bit a Javanese woman who was working on the plantation. The natives who were present did everything possible for this woman, but her condition grew steadily worse, and, toward evening, it seemed certain that she would die. It was at this time that the plantation manager returned. Going to his medicine stores, he took out some of this *koti*, mixed it with liquor, and forced it down the unconscious woman's throat. She soon began to revive, and early the next morning was at work again. This *koti*, it must be noted, is believed to be a preventive in other than the prophylactic sense, for belief has it that if a person with *sneki-koti* encounters a poisonous snake, the snake, recoiling from the influence of the *koti*, glides out of his way.

There is yet another aspect of *obia* to which reference has been made in several connections, and this is its curative power. The internal and external application of various ingredients added to a base of herbs, white clay, washing-blue (for indigo), and other similar substances which have for their purpose curing disease, are all actuated by the principle of supernatural aid that is implicit in the belief in *obia*. We shall see, in the case of black magic, how the Paramaribo Negro does not differentiate between the chemical operation of an actual poison and the supernatural actuation of a charm that has as its end the bringing of evil to another. The same evaluation of cause and effect holds also in the case of *obia*, where the work of chemicals and formulae are for purposes of good magic, and not evil. No efficacy is thought inherent in any medicine except insofar as such medicine is actuated by the power of *obia*, and so strong is this belief that, while the natives of Paramaribo do avail themselves of the expert medical services which are at their disposal, they do not fail to complement the White man's cures with their own *obia* remedies. The view persists, however, that there are fevers that the White doctor can treat, and those that he is powerless to cure. For this last type of fevers, therefore, the *lukuman*, the *wintiman*, or the *obiaman* must be called in, since these ailments are of supernatural origin, and it is only a supernatural remedy that can cure those who have succumbed to them.

1. It will be remembered, in the case of our informant whose *basi-winti* made him write in a script that he could not explain, how it would be this *winti* that would make an *obiaman* or a *wintiman* of him. In Haiti such compacts are called *engagements*.

2. These cuts are given in Haiti for similar purposes. (And in Brazil where they are said to "fechar corpo," e.g., seal the body.—Ed.)

3. The most recent contribution to the discussion of *sneki-koti*, in which the literature is critically summarised, is that of Benjamins.

B. WISI AND BAKRU

For protection against wisi, *a person may go to any luku-man, but actually selects a* lukuman *who is known to be versed in the ways of* wisi. *For in the logic of Paramaribo Ne-groes, it is those familiar with the practices of black magic who know its cure. . . . As a direct concept* wisi *is abhor-rent . . . but as a measure of recourse in the hands of the weak against the strong, it has the sympathy of all.*

*   *   *

If *obia,* then, is good magic, *wisi* is the magic that brings evil. "Wisi *wroko nanga Yorka—Wisi* works through ghosts," and in manifesta-tions of black magic it is not so much the ingredients which go into the making of black magic as the deadly carrying agent which kills. The control of ghosts for these errands is obtained by *wisi*-men in the following manner. It is thought that the souls of men, like the *winti,* may belong to the earth, to the water, to the air. In order to procure a carrier for black magic, a *wisiman* will call out the soul of a living person and shoot it; if it is a soul of the air, he will imprison it in a tree; if it is a soul belonging to the earth, he will bury it in the ground; or he may destroy it in the water, if it is a soul which in its wanderings would make for the water. A person whose soul had been so treated sickens and soon dies. It is then that the *wisiman* claims this soul, mak-ing it his agent through which he accomplishes his ends. Other souls are obtained by digging up a recently buried body and taking from it some hair or a finger, and calling the ghost of the one who has died to enter into this. Some souls are brought under the control of a *wisi-man* by stealing some of the water in which a corpse had been washed and summoning the *Yorka* to enter the water. A ghost obtained in any of these ways becomes the slave of the *wisiman,* and does his bidding.[1] It is made to animate the *bakru,* to enter fowls, to go into inanimate objects such as wood or clothing, to enter into herbs, or earth, or water in order to carry sickness or death where it is directed to go, and it is the *Yorka,* too, that actuates the poison put into an enemy's drink or food.

Before discussing *wisi* itself, it is necessary to consider two examples of what may be termed "marginal" *wisi.* These are a form of *opo* designed to enrich their owners, but since this is accomplished at the cost of the lives of the growing children of the family, native opinion classifies them as *wisi*. One such *opo*, less condemned by public opinion than the second, is that of the purchase of a snake,—the *Dagowe*, or *Aboma*—from a *wisiman*, to keep in the house for "luck." Whether acquired by the man or the woman of the household, such a snake serves all those who live in the same cabin with it. It is kept under the bed, or in some hidden corner, and is fed on eggs. Such snakes are said to exact as many as fifty eggs a day, and the *Aboma* requires yet more in order to be satisfied. The owner, however, is well repaid for such lavishness in terms of wealth,—money, and the prized things which money buys, such as bracelets, *koto-yaki*, kerchiefs, and earrings. Not only must this snake be well fed in order that it may not leave the household, and the "luck" leave with it, but it must have assurance of the owner's affection for it, and in proof of this, the owner must speak to it at night in terms of endearment. When children are born to such a household, the snake soon grows jealous of the attention paid them, and kills them. Actually, then, it is held that the owner of such an *opo* sacrifices his children to his personal ambitions.[2]

"Do one snake in the house bring luck? I knows a lady sitting in the market now. She got one *Dagowe* snake in she house. She sell fish, but sometimes one-two month she don't sit in the market at all, but she got plenty gold bracelet on all two hand, and chain, and plenty, plenty money. Everybody say the snake bring she money."

The second "marginal" case of *wisi* concerns the acquisition of *bakru* for "luck." This special use of the *bakru* is so classified, under the definition that it is designed to enhance one's own position, rather than as a direct instrument of evil magic against a specific individual. "If you want luck, you go to a *wisiman* and tell him what you want. Husband, some woman's husband, automobile, plenty money, bracelets. You pay a hundred or two hundred guilders and go home." After a short interval, the *wisiman* comes at night and brings two children, a boy and a girl, who have the appearance of very black two-year-olds, except that their heads are large. These are, however, not children, but *bakru*, creatures fashioned by the *wisiman* himself, and each is but half flesh,—the other half of the body is of wood. They have human voices, and human speech, and are given to teasing, which they do to trick and disarm people. Those who own them keep them under the bed, or locked in an empty room, and there they feed and care for them. They do not need to be clothed, however, for the garment they wear when they are brought to their owner, a checked blue and white dress, they never outgrow, or wear out. If they are struck, they turn to receive the blow on the wooden side. Sometimes, when one looks under the bed, the *bakru* are not there. That occurs because they have gone to amuse themselves on the road. They are not always visible on the road, but even when they are invisible, one senses their presence as a hot wind. A person who meets a *bakru* on the road strikes it only if he has a long stick, and above all "if he got luck with him for bad spirit." A man who has no "luck" and strikes a *bakru* dies. The *bakru*, however, never die; even if one were to see them stretched out lifeless on the ground, they would not be dead. If a person returns later, nothing is to be found, for the *bakru* only simulate death, and once left alone, they return to the cemetery where their home is. . . .

Aside from the marginally sinister duties which the *bakru* and the snakes perform, these "little people" have the more important rôle of carrying magic that is only evil in character. The *bakru*, who play a major part in the performance of *wisi*, are created by *wisi*-men out of the portions of bodies of the dead which, as we have said, come from a disinterred corpse, or a finger, or some hair taken from a corpse. These figures are made animate by injecting into them a dead soul, for it is said of *bakru*, as of *wisi* in general, "*Bakru wroko nanga Yorka,* —The *bakru* work through a ghost," or "*Bakru wroko nanga Djombi. Na Djombi nanga na Yorka na srefsref sani.*—The *bakru* works with the *Djombi*. The *Djombi* and the *Yorka* are the self-same thing." Thus, one informant, who said he was a *doro-sei pikin*, an illegitimate child, explained why he was an only child. The legally married wife of his father had sent a *bakru* to his mother. "*Dati ben de wa wisi fo tap' hem bere. Dat' meki mi mama no kisi pikin noit' moro.*—That was a *wisi* to stop pregnancy. That is why my mother never had any more children." Sterility, indeed, is usually said to be the work of *bakru*. Another incident, given by a woman, told how when she was a girl a neighbor in the yard where she lived found a snow-white chicken underneath her table. This neighbor called together the women of the yard to find out to whom this chicken belonged, but no one claimed it. The woman then took a broom and struck it. There was one cry from the chicken, and it disappeared. Later that day, this woman and a rival of hers met on a plantation where they were both trying to sell fish. The other fell upon her and beat her, without her having the power to lift a finger in her own defense, though she had had a reputation of holding her own against men. "That was the *bakru* the other had sent her. The *bakru* make the woman come weak." Late that same night, when they were all sitting on their doorsteps, a *bakru* appeared at the gate of the yard. It could not enter, however, because there was a *winti* guarding the yard. "That *winti* was one lock to keep away bad things." This *winti* was lodged in a tree close to the entrance of the yard, and was a *Leba*.

Another example of *wisi* which occurred during our stay was that sent against a friend of one of our informants, who, working about town, stepped on a nail late one afternoon, and by nine o'clock that night was dead. A death such as this could be explained only as caused by *wisi*. When the body was placed in the coffin a candle and some other objects, unknown to the church officials who were present, were put with the corpse. This was done to make the spirit of the dead come back to tell who had killed him. The dead person was expected to appear in a dream to name his enemy. Sometimes, instead of placing the candle and other objects in the coffin, or in addition to putting them there, the corpse is placed face downwards, and is so instructed that not before the spirit of the dead comes and reveals the one responsible for his death will his body be able to turn over and rest. In addition to this, in the case just cited, the parents of the dead man were waiting for the important wake of the eighth night after death to be held, after which they would be free to consult a *lukuman* as to the cause of their son's death.

Wisi is worked by the use of menstrual cloths, perspiration, hair, finger-nail clippings, and wearing apparel that has touched the body of the person against whom evil magic is designed. These act as substitutes for the individual himself, and whatever form of destruction is intended is told to a ghost or the *bakru* animated by a ghost, who puts it into execution. *Wisi*, like *obia*, involves the pronouncing of a formula which, magically endowed, makes clear that the object belonging to the person against whom the magic is directed is being used to represent the person himself, and that whatever is done to this representational object shall befall the person meant to be harmed. A simpler form of *wisi*, which involves slow illness rather than death, is to place a broken basin containing faded, evil-smelling weeds, thorny bits of wood, pins, porcupine quills, or other pointed objects, or toads either living or dead, in the center of the yard where the person against whom the evil is designed lives, or at the door of his cabin. In the morning, when this is discovered, an immediate alarm is raised, and no effort is spared to find the perpetrator of the deed. If he is found, he is taken before a magistrate and imprisoned as a *wisiman*. If this is not possible, recourse is had to the *lukuman* to find out what must be done to ward off the effects of this *wisi*, and, according to the prescription given, the person will set up a *tapu*, or will wash, or will appeal to his *winti* or his *akra* to save him, or if the *wisi* had already entered his body, he will see that it is exorcized. Indeed, even if the *wisiman* is discovered and imprisoned, this procedure would be gone through to insure the purification of the yard and its inhabitants from the bad effects of the *wisi*.

For protection against *wisi*, a person may go to any *lukuman*, but actually selects a *lukuman* who is known to be versed in the ways of *wisi*. For in the logic of Paramaribo Negroes, it is those familiar with the practices of black magic who know its cure. Perhaps in this logic lies the key to the fact that though there is an abstract differentiation made between *lukuman, wintiman, obiaman,* and *wisiman,* actually the practitioner of black magic can cure, and the *obiaman,* whose duty it is to heal and to furnish protective magic, also supplies people with *opo* to enrich them at the expense of others. This, in a more attenuated fashion, holds for the *wintiman* and the *lukuman.* It is also because of these factors that, in order to practice his craft, a man invariably familiarises himself with all these branches of knowledge of the traffic with the supernatural. As a direct concept *wisi* is abhorrent to everyone, but as a measure of recourse in the hands of the weak against the strong, it has the sympathy of all.

Curing *wisi* involves exorcising the bad spirit that has been instructed to enter the individual whose death is sought. The idiom for this is to *puru wisi,* to "remove" the evil magic. The ritual for this varies, though the principal elements of the exorcism include the knowledge of calling the spirit and forcing it to speak, and of driving it from the body of the person it has attacked. The ceremony of the final driving out of the spirit takes place at the cross-roads, for the cross-roads is a "place where bad and good must cross." Before the cure is begun, an offering is made at the cross-roads for *Ma Leba. . . .*

1. This is similar to the Haitian concept of *zombi* (Cf. Parsons, I, pp. 178–179), though the *zombi* is more specialised in the work it can do for the sorcerer. The term *zombi* is not used in Suriname, but when we described the Haitian concept to one Paramaribo Negro, he said that tradition had it that in Africa a *wisiman* could dig up the body of a person who, apparently deceased, was really only bewitched, and could sell the body, now without a soul, to some far-off land. We were able to confirm the validity of this tradition in Dahomey.

2. This concept is paralleled by the Haitian belief in the *baka,* though the Haitian *baka* also resemble in some respects the Suriname *bakru.*

The Spirits of the Dead

A. THE YORKA AS AN ANCESTOR

The Yorka, as a friendly ancestor, is worshipped at harvest-time, at the close of the year, at wakes, at the opening of winti dances, and on special occasions—for a particular enterprise, or, for special intervention with the gods, as during childbirth, or in times of drought. . . . in the daily life . . . such awareness of the existence and importance of the Yorka . . . is not of the good Yorka but of those who do evil.

❋　　❋　　❋

The fourth element in the supernatural world as it is conceived by the Paramaribo Negro is the *Yorka*,[1] or ghost. The *Yorka*, it is said, never dies, and a person's *Yorka* is good or evil according to the character of the man when he was alive. The life the *Yorka* lead is not visualised as quiescent. The good *Yorka*, when appealed to, helps the members of his family, warding off evilly disposed ghosts, working with the gods of the Earth for a good harvest, interceding in behalf of the living members of his group with deities who may be angry, counseling the family in dreams, and bringing them well-being and good fortune. If evil, a *Yorka* harasses the living, bringing illness, bad luck and death. A *Yorka* may enter the body of a member of his own family, or of a family not his own, even when not acting under the instructions of a *wisiman*. And a *Yorka* may turn into an animal and haunt a cabin, or a yard, or a road.

Even though the *Yorka* can appear in many guises, no trouble is spared when a corpse is prepared for burial to dress it in such a way so that later, when the *Yorka* walks abroad, it can be identified. This consists in stopping up the nose with cotton so that when it speaks, "*A n'e taki kring,*—It does not talk clean," that is, its speech is nasal. Cotton is put into the ears and a folded white kerchief is tied about the head to hold the jaw in place. Since ghosts are known to dislike gunpowder, firecrackers are an important element in all the *tapu* against *Yorka*, and when there is a death, though ceremonial shooting is not permitted in the city, firecrackers are placed before the bier and lighted, in this case performing not only the ritual of honoring the dead, but above all, serving to drive away the bad *Yorka* that might cluster about the corpse. Care is also taken that the *Yorka* does not come back to claim the living for whom the person who has just died has felt affection. Thus string is used to measure each of his children, and the pieces of string are put into the coffin as substitute companions, or several knots are made in one piece of string, each marking the size of a child, or the young children are passed across the coffin three times as a gesture of separation. The man's most intimate friend also addresses the deceased as he lies in his coffin, telling the dead man that they had been friends, but now their friendship is at an end, for the dead must associate with the dead and the living with the living.[2]

For the good *Yorka* the wake serves to entertain the recent dead, as well as the spirits of those other dead that may care to come. There is propitiation of these good *Yorka*, with offerings of food and dancing at the opening of *winti* dances; there are offerings of food, and the lighting of a lamp for them when the year draws to a close, or at the anniversary of the death of those who have died not long before; and, finally, the *Yorka* eat of the first crops, especially of staples such as rice. "When you plant rice, the first rice you must not eat. Then you boil some. Then you throw (it) away on the ground. If you can afford it, you give a dance. I saw when this was not done. There was no second crop from that field." When rice offered the *Yorka* is cooked, neither salt nor pepper is put in, for the dead must not eat salt.

This offering is given for the Earth Mother as well as for the ancestors, for both of these must eat of first fruits if the fields are to prosper. Nor is this the only instance where Earth and Ancestors are associated in ritual. For example, one dance for the Earth[3] is called *banya*, and that for the Ancestors is termed *baka-futu-banya* = back-foot *banya*. For the *baka-futu-banya*, food is given the ancestors before the dance takes place. "*Yu teki en yu bori aleisi nanga foru di no hab' sotu, no hab' pepre. Da' yu trowe lontu 'a dyari.[4] Dan yu teki 'afu, pot na ini wa' baki. Efi yu wani, yu poti wa pikinso sopi. Da' yu saka a wa presi, pe suma n'e si. Da' yu gi dansi. Ef suma habi Yorka winti, a wer' weiti nanga kakumbe angisa.* You take and you cook rice and chicken, which has neither salt nor pepper. Then you throw some away about the yard. Then you put half in a basin. If you like, you add a little rum. Then you put it down somewhere, where no one sees it. Then you give a dance. If someone has *Yorka winti*, he is dressed in white, and he wears the kerchief of the dead."[5]

The *Yorka* are also given food when they are called upon to help a person, that is, when the *lukuman* or the *wisiman* goes to the cemetery and calls the *Yorka* to find out what food and other offerings it wishes for help on a special venture on which a member of the family is embarking. The usual offerings in such a case are rum and white rice grown in the colony, and cooked without salt. "*Mi no sabi san ede, ma noit' i ben poti sotu te i boru nanyam gi Yorka.*—I do not know why, but you never put salt in the food you cook to give a *Yorka*." [6]

B. THE YORKA AS AN ENEMY GHOST

The *Yorka*, then, as a friendly ancestor, is worshipped at harvest-time, at the close of the year, at wakes, at the opening of *winti*-dances, and on special occasions when its services are sought in behalf of a particular enterprise, or for special intervention with the gods, as during childbirth, or in times of drought. At the same time, it should be made clear that in the daily life of the individual, such awareness of the existence and importance of the *Yorka* which a person may have is not of the good *Yorka* but of those who do evil. The association of the ghost with *wisi*, and the danger from those ghosts who, because not satisfied with the rites offered them, have become evilly intentioned, is sufficient to explain this attitude. Thus it is that so many of the *Yorka* stories,—and in these as a cycle, the bad *Yorka* is chiefly referred to—bring out the point of the danger of being abroad alone at night. When going home late from *winti*-dances, we were led away from certain thoroughfares, and went a roundabout way to avoid a corner, or a tree, or a house, because these were known to be "bad" places,—that is to say, they were haunted. At least two persons accompanied us home, so that, in returning to their own homes, they would not have to walk the streets alone. The hours that are dangerous are midday, from 5:30 to 6:30 in the evening, and from 12:30 to 1:30 at night.

Many tales of such encounters are current. A few months before our first stay in the colony, a taxi-driver, a friend of the teller of this tale, was in his cab at eleven o'clock at night near a motion-picture house, when two young women "dressed in pink, like for church" asked him to drive them home. They made a price with him of one guilder fifty cents, and indicated a road leading past the cemetery as the one that led to their house. When he had passed the cemetery, he turned to them to get the exact directions, but there was no one in the car. The man was sick with fever for months after. "He went to the hospital, but they couldn't do anything for him. A *wisiman* cured him. He had no 'luck' with him, because, if he had a *tapu*, the *Yorka* couldn't come in his car." In another case, a hunter on his way to the bush before dawn met, on several mornings, a tall White man dressed in white with silver buttons on his coat. One morning this man stood on the road with arms outstretched blocking the hunter's way. The hunter turned back and loaded his gun with a special bullet, and though his wife pleaded with him not to go out that day, he went back. The man was still there, standing as before, arms outstretched. The hunter shot at the man, but took fright, and ran home. Later, when it grew light, he went once more to see what was there, and he found a large white cat lying in the road. "It was the bad spirit of a White man. Everybody went to look at the cat. It was big, like a dog. A policeman made a black man throw it in the river. The man didn't get sick because he had a good *tapu*, but he was afraid."

The *Yorka* who enters the body of a living person does not kill outright. "*Na Yorka, a no kan kiri yu wan-tron. A kiri yu pikin a pikin, ma fos' a shwax yu.*—The *Yorka* cannot kill you all at once. It kills little by little, but first it weakens you." One man told of an instance of a *Yorka* that had entered a man's body. When the *Yorka* was in him, he spoke like a woman, for the ghost was that of a woman. This same man told of having heard the voice of a *Yorka* in a girl. It was a male ghost, who kept saying, "I'm going to kill her. There's nothing you can do." This girl, however, did not die because a *wintiman* exorcised the *Yorka*. This was done by beating the girl as she was given a cleansing bath at the cross-roads. One such attempt at a cure, however, ended disastrously, according to this man, for it was interrupted by a police officer who arrested the entire party, and the girl died.

When a *Yorka* has entered a person and must be exorcised, the person who is possessed is seated on a bench and a white sheet is put over him. A drum begins to play,—often in town it must be an improvisation of a real drum. The *bonu*, or *wintiman*, who does the exorcising, sings

> The cemetery is clothed in white,
> You shall not sit down there,
> The *Yorka* sits there,
> The *Yorka* sits there.

This is repeated until the possessed person, hidden by the white sheet, begins to tremble. The man who does the exorcising addresses the spirit, and orders it to leave. The *Yorka* answers nasally, "*No, mi n'e gowel Mi basi pai mi. Ef yu wani mi gowe, da' yu pai mi baka.*—No, I will not go away! My master has paid me. If you want me to go away, you must pay me again." The one who is in charge of the ceremony asks "*San yu bas' pai yu?*—What did your master pay you?" "*Fo kopro sensi, nanga sebi-ai nengere-kondre pepre, nanga dri pis' kreti. Dan yu mu tyari go poti na sabana. Efi yu no poti 'a sabana, mi n'e gowe. Mi broko yu neki.*—Four copper cents, and seven grains of African pepper, with three pieces of *kreti*(?). Then you must take

them and put them in the cemetery. If you don't put them in the cemetery, I won't go away. I will break your neck." The one exorcising sings

> A sabana den teki yu,
> A sabana yu sa go baka,
> Tide a kaba fo yu.

> From the graveyard they took you,
> To the graveyard you will return,
> Today you are through.

He then comes forward with a cord of twisted white cotton, seizes
by the hair the person who is being treated, and ties the cord around
it. This symbolizes tying the *Yorka*. After several songs, he loosens the
hair, and puts the cord quickly into a bottle. "*Na Yorka a-i ko na ini na
tetei.*—The *Yorka* comes into the cord." He then corks up the bottle.
"*Na batra kom hebi leiki fa a ben de libi suma na ini.*—The bottle becomes heavy, as though there were a human being inside it." This
bottle is carried to the river, and thrown in. If someone were to take
up the bottle and open it, the *Yorka* would at once enter into that
person, and possess him.

Not all possession by the *Yorka* is dangerous, for there are friendly
ancestral *Yorka* who on occasion seek out a descendant and enter his
body to demand offerings and dancing. This occurs at the *baka-futu-
banya* dances at the end of the year, when those so possessed dress in
white, tie a kerchief about their faces, and stop up their ears and
nostrils with cotton, and dance. This dress is necessary because while
the *Yorka* possess them, they cease to be themselves, and become the
Yorka. Each family generally has some member to whom an important
ancestor so manifests himself.

1. *Yorka* is a Carib Indian word (Encyc., p. 393).
2. Among the Saramacca tribe of Bush-Negroes, at one funeral we witnessed, the dead man was separated from his family, from the Kromanti
group, and from his village.
3. This is actually a social dance which Earth deities and ancestors are
felt to enjoy. The Martinique cycle of dances in Haiti resembles the Suriname *banya*.
4. At this point the informant interpolated the explanation that if no
people are about, the food is thrown down anywhere at all, but if it is a
yard where other people live, then the food is thrown where no one sees it.
5. This means that the kerchief is tied so that it goes over the head and
under the chin, in the manner in which a white kerchief is put about the
head of the corpse to make it easy to identify a ghost as such.
6. This idea that the dead must not be "fed" salt in offerings to them is
prevalent in many Negro cultures of West Africa and the New World. To
our knowledge, Haiti is one of the New World exceptions.

: VIII :

REINTERPRETATIONS

‖‖‖

African Gods and Catholic Saints
in New World Negro Belief [1]

*. . . the data show quite clearly to what an extent the inner
logic of the aboriginal African cultures of the Negroes, when
brought in contact with foreign traditions, worked out to
achieve an end that, despite the handicaps of slavery, has
been relatively the same wherever the forces making for
change have been comparable.*

❊   ❊   ❊

The tendency of native peoples who have had long contact with
Catholicism to achieve a syncretism between their aboriginal religious
beliefs and the doctrines and rituals of the Church has received notice
in the case of various folk. Best known in this connection are the
Indians of Central America, Mexico, and the southwestern part of the
United States, where the phenomenon has been emphasized in the
literature. The somewhat more thoroughgoing assimilation of Christian
and pagan beliefs which has taken place among New World Negroes
has, however, gone in large measure unrecognized. In Mexico and
among some Indian tribes of the Southwest, assimilation has generally
taken the form of the survival of aboriginal custom in a system of
belief and ritual practices the outer forms of which are predominantly
Catholic. In the case of the New World Negroes who live under
Catholic influence in Brazil, Cuba and Haiti, however, the exchange
has been less one-sided, and the elements ancestral to the present-day
organization of worship have been retained in immediately recognizable
form.

American Anthropologist, New Series, XXXIX, no. 4 (1937), 635–43.

This phenomenon has been studied with care in Cuba and Brazil,[2] and somewhat less systematically in Haiti.[3] In all three countries it is marked by the following characteristics: the Negroes profess nominal Catholicism while at the same time they belong to "fetish cults" which are under the direction of priests whose functions are essentially African and whose training follows more or less well recognized channels of instruction and initiation; the ceremonialism and ideology of these "fetish cults" exhibit Catholic elements more or less prominently; and everywhere specific identifications are made between African gods and Catholic Saints.

It is the last of these characteristics that will be treated in this paper, since here can be most immediately recognized the manner in which these Negroes, in responding to the acculturative process, have succeeded in achieving, at least in their religious life, a synthesis between aboriginal African patterns and the European traditions to which they have been exposed.[4] The emphasis, as far as actual data are concerned, will be placed on information gathered in the course of field work in Haiti; but because of the resemblance between Haitian syncretization of African gods and Catholic saints and that found in Cuba and Brazil, the material from these countries will also be summarized to permit comparisons.

The historical background of the phenomenon is obvious, since efforts were made everywhere in the New World to convert the slaves to Christianity, and in Haiti, at least, baptism into the Catholic church was required for all those who were unloaded from the holds of the slave ships. In Cuba and Brazil, as in Haiti, the course of history has enabled Catholicism to continue to play a major role in the life of the people as their official religion. And it is this fact, together with the present day vestiges of the fear, constantly present in the minds of the Europeans during the time of slavery, that the African cults offered a focus for revolt, that explains the inferior social position held by these "fetish cults" wherever they are found. It is here also that explanation may be sought for the conditions under which African rituals are carried on, since at best they obtain but passive acquiescence on the part of the authorities and, more often, must be conducted under the greatest secrecy.

In the case of these African religious systems, handicapped by social scorn and official disapprobation, the followers are almost inevitably split into local groups, each of which is dominated by the personality of the priest whose individual powers furnish the principal drive toward any outer organization the cult-group under his charge may achieve. This in turn makes it difficult to maintain anything more than a local hierarchy of priests, and is reflected in a resulting confusion of theological concept. Hence in all these countries a general frame of reference concerning the supernatural has been handed down from Africa, and within this a variety of beliefs and modes of worship exist.

In the Haitian *vodun* cult, this takes the form of differences of opinion not alone from region to region, but within a given region even between members of the same group concerning such details of cult belief and practice as the names of deities, modes of ritual procedure, or the genealogies of the gods, to say nothing of concepts regarding the powers and attributes of the African spirits in their relation to one another and to the total pantheon. As a case in point, there may be cited the three separate lists of names of deities which were collected in Haiti from a single valley in the interior, the valley of Mirebalais. When these three lists were compared with each other[5] and with the published roster of names of *vodun* deities given by Dorsainvil,[6] it was seen that while certain designations were found in all lists, there were extreme divergencies as well. Some names were present in all of them, it is true, and these represented the more important deities worshipped over the whole of Haiti, being gods derived from Dahomey and, to a lesser extent, from Nigeria and those other cultures of West Africa which have predominated in determining the form and functions of Haitian *vodun* worship. But the differences between these lists were much greater than the resemblances; and since this had to do only with names of gods, it is not strange that in identifying deities with Catholic saints, an even greater divergence of opinion was found.

Two methods were employed in the field to obtain this material. In some cases African deities were equated with Catholic saints in the course of discussions of general theological problems, or, as has been done in Brazil,[7] invocations of songs were recorded which coupled the name of a given saint with that of its corresponding pagan god. The other means used to obtain this information was more direct. As elsewhere in the New World the imagination of the Negroes seems to have been taken by the ordinary chromolithographs found widely distributed in Catholic countries, which depict the saints and are hung in the houses of the faithful. It was possible to present a collection of these *images*, as they are termed in Haiti, to the natives and to obtain information concerning the manner in which the saints are envisaged by the people, and those *loa* or African deities they are believed to represent, by asking the necessary questions.

We may now turn to the correspondences themselves. Legba, the god who in Dahomey guards crossroads and entrances to temples, compounds, and villages, is widely worshipped in Haiti where, as in Dahomey, he must "open the path" for all other supernatural powers and hence is given the first offering in any Haitian *vodun* ceremony. Legba is believed by most persons to be the same as St. Anthony, for the reason that St. Anthony is represented on the *images* as an old man, poorly dressed, carrying a wand which supports him as he walks. Some hold that Legba is St. Peter, on the basis of the eminently logical reason that St. Peter, like Legba, is the keeper of keys and opens the door. By most persons, however, St. Peter is usually believed to be a *loa*, or *vodun* deity, without any African designation, being called the *loa* St. Pierre, though this again is disputed, the *loa* St. Pierre being held by still others to constitute the spirit that validates the neolithic celts which in Haiti as in other parts of the New World and in Africa, are held sacred as "thunderstones."

Damballa, the Dahomean rainbow-serpent deity, is one of the most widely worshipped and important Haitian *vodun* god. The question of the active existence of the serpent cult in Haiti is one which cannot be considered in this place, but to the extent that it does exist either in actuality or in the sacredness with which serpents are regarded, their worship is undoubtedly associated with this god Damballa, who also retains his aboriginal character of being the rainbow. The saint identified with Damballa is St. Patrick, on whose *image* serpents are depicted. Following this logic further, Moses is held to be the "father of Damballa" because of the miracle he performed before Pharaoh when he threw down his staff on the ground and turned it into a serpent.

The Ogun *loa* include several gods who are generally regarded as brothers. Ogun Ferraille is held to be St. James, while Ogun Balandjo, a deity who gives "remedies" to cure the sick, is identified with St. Joseph because the picture of this saint shows him holding a child, his hand raised in the blessing which heals. Gran' Erzilie is by most persons believed to be Mater Dolorosa, though one informant expressed the belief that this saint is another *loa* named Erzilie Freda Dahomey. The wide-spread identification of Gran' Erzilie with Mater Dolorosa, however, is based on the attributes accorded the African goddess, since she is believed to be the richest of all the deities, so that the chromolithographic representation of Mater Dolorosa showing her as richly clothed, surrounded by many evidences of great wealth, and wearing many rings and necklaces, is quite in keeping with the wealthiness of Gran' Erzilie. The Dahomean sea god, who has retained his aboriginal function in Haiti, is equated with St. Expeditius. The *marassa*, spirits of twins, are believed to be the twin saints Cosmas and Damien, and St. Nicholas, because of the figures of children on his representations, is regarded as the "protector of the *marassa*." Simbi, who unlike the deities of predominantly Dahomean origin already mentioned is a Congo god, is believed by some to be St. Andrew, though others state that this saint is Azaka Mede, a *loa* which clearly derives its name from that of the river across which Dahomean belief holds that all dead must pass to reach the next world. One special member of the Simbi group, Simbi en Deux Eaux, is believed to be the equivalent of St. Anthony the Hermit, although this again is disputed by those who hold this saint is rather the *loa* named 'Ti Jean Petro.

The Haitian, however, does not stop merely at identifying saints with African gods, for saints are occasionally themselves conceived as *loa*, or as natural phenomena such as the sun, moon, and stars, which are regarded as saints and occasionally worshipped. Thus St. Louis, the patron of the town of Mirebalais where this field work was carried on, is a *loa* in his own right. Similarly two of the kings who figure in the *image* that depicts the Adoration of the Christ Child, Balthazar and Gaspar, are also held to be *vodun* deities. La Sirène, a character derived from European mythology, is believed to be a water goddess and is identified with Nôtre Dame de Grâce, while the *loa* Kpanyol, or Spanish *loa*, is equated with Nôtre Dame d'Alta Gracia.

St. John the Baptist is a powerful nature spirit worshipped as the *loa* St. Jean Baptiste, and is believed to control the thunder and lightning. The chromolithograph depicts this saint as a sweet-faced child holding a lamb, in striking contrast to the great power he is supposed to wield, and the irresponsibility that characterises his actions. Yet this identification becomes understandable when it is realized that in Dahomean mythology, which has influenced so much of Haitian belief, as in Yoruba concept, the ram is the emblem of the god of thunder; while the basis of the conception of the *loa* St. Jean Baptiste as the thunderer becomes even clearer when it is pointed out that the ram is the sacrificial animal of this *loa* in Haiti. The following myth is told of this deity:

On a given day of the year, God permits each saint to have control over the universe. St. John the Baptist, however, is so irresponsible, and his rage so violent, that God fears for the consequences were he allowed to exert his power on his day. Plying him with drink the day before, he is therefore made so drunk that when he falls asleep he does not awaken until the day after. When he is told his day has already passed, his rage is terrible, and he causes great storms to flay the earth; and it is a commonplace in Mirebalais that this day is marked by tempests of almost hurricane proportions, with great displays of thunder and lightning. Though he can do some damage, his power is now limited, however, to his own sphere.

Concerning the tendency to regard the phenomena of nature as supernatural beings we find St. Soleil (St. Sun), Ste. la Lune (St. Moon), Sts. Etoiles (Sts. Stars) and Ste. la Terre (St. Earth) among those worshipped under this category. Even the conception of a force such as the power that can bring reverses to a man may be anthropomorphized and worshipped, as the belief in the existence of a supernatural being known as St. Bouleversé indicates. An *oraison* to this "Saint," well known throughout Haiti, reads as follows:

Saint Bouleversé, vous qui avez le pouvoir de bouleverser la terre, vous êtes un saint et moi, je suis un pêcheur, je vous invoque et vous prends pour mon patron dès aujourd'hui. Je vous envoie chercher un tel; bouleversez sa tête, bouleversez sa mémoire, bouleversez sa pensée, bouleversez sa maison, bouleversez pour moi mes ennemis visibles et invisibles; faites éclater sur eux la foudre et la tempête.

En l'honneur du Saint Bouleversé dites trois Pater et trois Ave Maria.

Satan, je te renonce, si tu viens de la part du démon, que le démon t'emporte et te jette dans l'abîme et dans l'infernal séjour.

Bête méchante, langue de vipère, langue penicieuse, si tu viens de la part de Dieu pour me tromper, il faut que tu marches de terre en terre, de coin en coin, de village en village, de maison en maison, d'emplois en emplois comme le juif errant, l'insulteur de Jésus Christ.

Seigneur, mon Dieu, viens chercher à perdre un tel, afin qu'il soit disparu devant moi comme la foudre et la tempête.

The data which have been sketched from Haiti will be strikingly familiar to those conversant with the literature on Cuba and Brazil, though the names of the Haitian deities will be unfamiliar to them, and the correspondences, Catholic saint for saint, and African god for god, somewhat different. Thus Legba, the Dahomean trickster held to be St. Anthony or St. Peter in Haiti, appears under his Yoruba name Elegbara, being held in Brazil to be the equivalent of the Devil, and of the Blessed Souls in Purgatory or the Anima Sola in Cuba. Shango, identified with Santa Barbara both in Brazil and Cuba, is not represented in Haiti by his Dahomean counterpart, Xevioso; it is to be remarked, however, that in Dahomey itself, among those natives of the city of Abomey who are members of the Catholic Church, this same identification is made between Xevioso and Santa Barbara. Mawu, the Great God of the Dahomeans, has not been retained in Haiti in the way in which Obatala, her Yoruba counterpart, has lived on in Brazil and Cuba, and though the Nigerian-Dahomean Ogun (designated Gu in Dahomey) has persisted in all three countries, differences are found in the saints with which he is identified in each. The table that accompanies this discussion shows in concise form the reconciliations that have been effected between gods and saints. It has been abstracted from the available literature on Brazil, Cuba, and Haiti, and in addition is supplemented by data recorded during fieldwork in the latter country.

CORRESPONDENCE BETWEEN AFRICAN GODS AND CATHOLIC
SAINTS IN BRAZIL, CUBA, AND HAITI*

African deities as found in:	Brazil	Cuba	Haiti
Obatala		(O) Virgen de las Mercedes; the Most Sacred Sacrament; Christ on the Cross	
Obatala; Orisalá; Orixala (Oxalá)	(I) (N) (R) "Nosso Senhor de Bomfim" at Bahia; (N) Saint Anne; (R) "Senhor do Bomfim" at Rio ("because of the influence of Bahia")		
Grande Mambo Batala			(M) Saint Anne
Shango	(I) (N) (R) Santa Barbara at Bahia; (R) St. Michael the Archangel at Rio; (R) St. Jerome (the husband of Santa Barbara) at Bahia (see Yansan below)	(O) Santa Barbara	
Elegbara, Elegua, Alegua		(O) "Animas benditas del Purgatorio"; "Anima Sola"	
Legba			(M) (H) St. Anthony; (W) (H?) St. Peter
Esú	(I) (N) (R) the Devil		
Ogun	(I) (R) St. George, at Rio; (N) St. Jerome; (I) (N) (R) St. Anthony, at Bahia	(O) St. Peter	
Ogun Balandjo			(M) St. James the Elder; (H) St. Joseph
Ogun Ferraille			(H) St. James
Osun	(N) Virgin Mary; N.D. de Cándeias	(O) Virgin de la Caridad del Cobre	
Yemanjá	(N) Virgin Mary; (R) N.S. de Rosario (at Bahia); N. D. de Conceição (at Rio)	(O) Virgin de Regla	
Maitresse Erzulie; Erzilie; Erzilie Freda Dahomey			(M) (S) the Holy Virgin; especially the Holy Virgin of the Nativity; (P) Santa Barbara (?); (H) Mater Dolorosa
Saponam	(I) the Sacred Sacrament		
Osa-Osê (Oxóssi)	(I) (N) (R) St. George, at Bahia; (R) St. Sebastian, at Rio	(O) St. Alberto; (occasionally) St. Hubert	
Ololu; Omolú	(R) St. Bento	(O) St. John the Baptist	
Agomme Tonnere			(M) St. John the Baptist
Ibeji (Brazil and Cuba); Marassa (Haiti)	(R) Sts. Cosmas and Damien		(H) Sts. Cosmas and Damien
Father of the Marassa			(H) St. Nicholas
Orumbíla (Odumbila?)		(O) St. Francisco	
Loco	(R) St. Francisco		
Babayú Ayí		(O) St. Lazarus	
Ifa	(R) the Most Sacred Sacrament		
Yansan (wife of Shango)	(R) Santa Barbara (wife of St. Jerome)		

African deities as found in:	Brazil	Cuba	Haiti
Damballa		(W) (H) St. Patrick	
Father of Damballa		(H) Moses	
Pierre d'Ambala		(M) St. Peter	
loa St. Pierre		(H) St. Peter	
Agwe		(H) St. Expeditius	
Roi d'Agoueseau		(M) St. Louis (King of France)	
Daguy Bologuay		(M) St. Joseph	
la Sirène		(M) the Assumption; (H) N.D. de Grace	
loa Christalline		(H) Ste. Philomena	
Adamisil Wedo		(H) Ste. Anne	
loa Kpanyol		(H) N.D. de Alta Gracia	
Aizan		(H) Christ (?)	
Simbi		(H) St. Andrew	
Simbi en Deax Eaux		(H) St. Anthony the Hermit	
Azaka Mede		(H) St. Andrew (?)	
'Ti Jean Petro		(H) St. Anthony the Hermit (?)	

* In this table, the initials before the names of the saints indicate the sources from which the correspondences have been derived:

(H) Herskovits, field data (see also *Life in a Haitian Valley*, Ch. 14).

(I) Ignace, *op. cit.*

(M) Price-Mars, *op. cit.*

(S) Seabrook, W. B., *The Magic Island* (New York, 1929).

(W) Wirkus, F., and D. Taney, *The White King of la Gonave* (New York, 1931).

(N) Nina-Rodrigues, *op. cit.*

(O) Ortiz, *op. cit.*

(P) Parsons, *op. cit.*

(R) Ramos, *op. cit.*

In a sense, the disparities that exist between the identifications made by the Negroes who live in different countries emphasize the theoretical importance of the materials presented in this paper. Were a given African god everywhere found to be identified with the same Catholic saint, there would be great probability that this had resulted from contacts between slaves subsequent to their arrival in the New World, and thus represented a diffusion from one country to another. As it is, there can be little question that these syncretizations have developed independently in each region where they are found. In the two lands where gods of the same African (Yoruba) tribe predominantly survive —Brazil and Cuba—distance and the absence of historic contacts of any significance make any other explanation untenable. And though Haiti is relatively close to Cuba, the fewness of the contacts between the Negroes of the two countries except in very recent times, added to the fact that in the syntheses that have been achieved in each country the gods of different African tribes figure, make the same point. Considered as a whole, therefore, the data show quite clearly to what an extent the inner logic of the aboriginal African cultures of the Negroes, when brought in contact with foreign traditions, worked out to achieve an end that, despite the handicaps of slavery, has been relatively the same wherever the forces making for change have been comparable.

1. Presented to the Second Afro-Brazilian Congress, Bahia, Brazil, November 15–20, 1936,

2. For Cuba: Fernando Ortiz, *Los Negros Brujos;* for Brazil: Nina-Rod-rigues, *L'Animisme Fétichiste des Nègres de Bahia* (Bahia, 1900), Etienne Ignace, *Le fétichisme des nègres du Bresil* (Anthropos, Vol. 3, pp. 881–904, 1908), Arthur Ramos, *O Negro Brasileiro* (Rio de Janeiro, 1934), especially Chap. 5.

3. Price-Mars, *Ainsi Parla l'Oncle . . . Essais d'Ethnographie* (Port-au-Prince, 1928), and E. C. Parsons, *Spirit Cult in Hayti* (Journal, Société des Américanistes, Vol. 20, pp. 157–70, 1928).

4. In Haiti this synthesis marks practically all phases of the life of the Negro peasant; there is no reason to assume that a similar assimilation has not taken place in Cuba and Brazil. Except for folk-lore, however, all studies of Negro life in these latter countries have been almost exclusively con-cerned with religious practices.

5. M. J. Herskovits, *Life in a Haitian Valley* (New York, 1937), pp. 309–19. The setting of the special traits of Haitian culture described here is to be found in this volume, Parts II and III.

6. J. B. Dorsainvil, *Vodun et Névrose* (Port-au-Prince, 1931), pp. 174–75.

7. E.g., Ramos, *op. cit.,* pp. 121, 125, etc.

The Trinidad Shouters

PROTESTANT-AFRICAN SYNTHESIS

Contrasting with the simplicity, and often poverty of the physical setting of this worship, is the richness in concept of identification of the worshipper with the "Spirit," with "Glory," with the "Holy Ghos'." . . . Mournin' groun' is the term used to designate a kind of retreat either literally or figuratively "in de bush," at which Shouters are initiated into the mysteries of their faith, obtain and later renew the power of their "gifts" or receive higher powers. . . . When the Shouters are com-pared to other groups in Toco, they are equated not so much with churches as with "orders," and they are often referred to as a lodge . . . some of the more obvious reasons being the internal organization, the intense feeling of unity . . . the canons of mutual aid, the discipline, the ritual handshake, and the ways in which at funerals of adherents, the group takes charge.

o o o

Shouters groups are small, and from the exterior their places of worship are hard to distinguish from nearby dwellings. One such "temple," as their churches are termed, situated atop a hill, was the center of a kind of compound where some of those who supported it also lived. It was a small rectangular building with mud walls, a dirt floor, and a thatched roof.

Inside, toward the rear was a series of benches, with an aisle down the center. Across the front of the small room a low rail ran along the outer edge of a shallow platform on which were chairs for the preacher or other church officials, and the altar. One cross hung against the wall, and another was attached to the railing on the left of the opening at its center. At the extreme right was a pulpit on which at night services a candle burned. Inserted at the base of the thatch was a flag of pale violet, while directly beneath the large cross was the altar, a table covered with a cloth, on which were a candle and four vases filled with white flowers.

Directly in line with the opening leading to the platform was the ritually-significant central post of the house. It was whitewashed, and at its base were a lighted candle, a large brass bell with a wooden handle, a Bible, and flowers in a jam jar, similar to those on the altar. Extending outward from the post to mark the cardinal points, four crosses were chalked on the dirt floor, with the long arm of each cross toward the post. Chalked designs appeared also in front of the entrances to the church. The plan of this church is as follows:

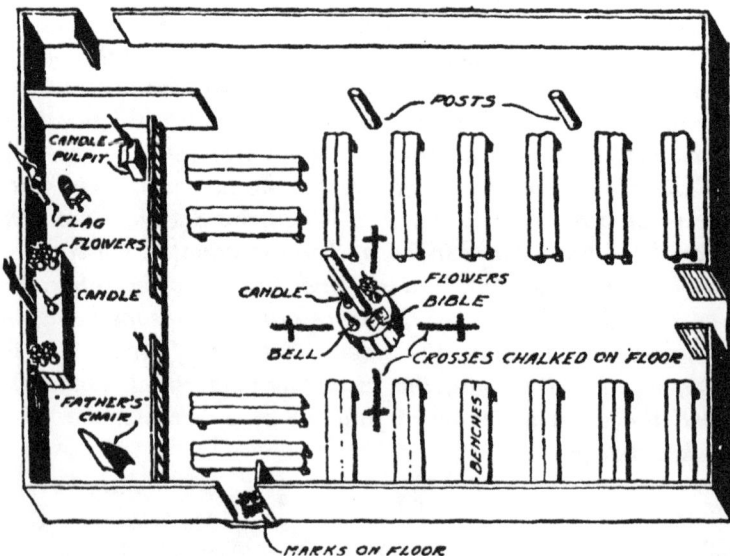

This particular "temple" was soon to be vacated, despite the fact that the rent paid by the group, one dollar a month, was twice the sum that would ordinarily be charged for it. The plot was owned jointly by a brother and sister, and though the woman had no objection to this congregation remaining there, her brother, a devout Catholic, would have no Shouters on his land. The group was therefore building a new "temple," on land owned by another man, where they were to be allowed to remain until they had accumulated the money to buy it.

Another "temple," in a locality some distance from Toco was situated on the periphery of the town. Here was to be observed a sizeable compound with a number of thatched houses in the clearing, on both sides of a path leading to the church. From these houses protruded poles, with flags of various colors on them, and there were at least two outdoor shrines, with candles burning in them. The "temple," or "tent," as the church itself was called, was much like its Toco counterpart, though more solidly built, with straw thatch of the finest workmanship and mud walls painted a blue-grey.

Since this second "temple," which serves a larger and more established congregation, probably was as elaborate as any Shouters' center to be found, it will be described in some detail. At each corner of the room was a semicircular altar, consisting of four steps, each top step holding a lighted candle and a vase of flowers. The principal altar, facing the entrance, had a great cross in low relief against the wall, and a smaller wooden cross on either side of it. Separating this altar from the rest of the church was a wooden railing similar to that in the Toco church. The central post was here set in a high circular altar consisting of seven steps on which rested a large bell, a candle, and flowers in a vase. The benches to accommodate worshippers and spectators were ranged behind the central post, facing the main altar, and along the side walls. Flags of many colors hung over the principal and subsidiary altars, and were attached to the central post.

II

Contrasting with the simplicity, and often poverty of the physical setting of this worship, is the richness in concept of identification of the worshipper with "the Spirit," with "Glory," with the "Holy Ghos'." The "Spirit" actually touches the worshipper with an unseen hand, and a shiver electrifies his body, causing him first to stiffen, then to begin to shake. The "Spirit" fills him with joy, causing him to dance, to speak in tongues, to prophesy, to "see." The worshipper sings a hymn of joy that had never before been sung, and thereafter there is a "spiritual hymn" that all will sing, as

> Give me wings,
> Let me fly to Glory;
> Only the pure of heart,
> Dear Jesus.

This will be sung to a melody so full of verve that it will lift the congregation to its feet dancing.

But entering into this identification are psychological factors which lie outside the mystic, other-worldly emotions. A worshipper who lives a good life has tangible symbols that can be looked to to achieve tangible benefits for his everyday well-being. More than this, from his mournin' experiences, which will be detailed in succeeding pages, he emerges with "gifts" which define for each humble worshipper in supernatural terms a specific task, or series of tasks in the fabric of church organization.

Baptism, proving, mournin', the phenomenon of possession by the "Spirit," the physical manifestations of such possession in the shaking, the dancing, the speaking in tongues, the bringing back of spiritual gifts are all at the core of the Shouters worship everywhere. The resemblances from group to group are significant, because each congregation is autonomous, and no supervisory body sees to it that in organization—or dogma—the separate churches maintain any degree of unity.

But while variations in pattern do occur everywhere, it is possible to draw generalizations about cult structure and practices in broad terms. Leadership and discipline are outstanding features of the worship, and leadership always vests in one who exerts his controls because of the supernatural powers that are his by endowment and continuous seeking. This individual may be a man or woman, may be termed "teacher" or "preacher," or "father" or "mother" of the flock. Regardless of the strength of the personality of the leader, he is responsible in varying degrees to his associates; on the other hand, his congregation, depending largely on his relationship with leaders of Shouting groups elsewhere, may be self-sufficient or may have relatively close affiliations with other churches, even where no inconsiderable distances separate them.

The most important functionaries, however, are always the "father" or "mother," the "teacher," the "preacher," and the "prover." The franchise of these offices derives from the quality of their visionary experiences, especially as these manifest themselves in the mournin' ground, and the continuing power they demonstrate as they fulfill their tasks. The most inclusive list of "gifts" recorded was given by a woman, herself "teacher" and head of her group, who is reputed to be endowed with great spiritual power. This list demonstrates how the proliferation of "gifts" serves to integrate each church member into the organization of worship as a purposeful unit in the play of forces that rule the lives of men. In presenting this list, the "work" expected of each member endowed with a specific "gift" will follow the version of this "teacher." Unless otherwise stated, persons of either sex may be conceived as functioning in these duties:

preacher—one who preaches and, at times, "interprets" the Bible.

teacher—one who teaches the meanings of dreams and visions, and "sees things." "Some teachers don' know how to point proper, or don' want to point them correct. I look at them, say, 'But I can see you in the spirit. You have a high call. As soon as I lay hands upon you, you are wise already.'"

prover—"He is there to prove the good from the bad in the church. You say you are a teacher, well, you've got to write an' the prover proves it. To be a prover, you must say something about this writing, spiritual writing."

leader—"He leads the children to the water," where the one who is going to baptize new members awaits them. He may also preach in the church.

divine healer—"Heals everything, with the aid of divine power." In this list, he is differentiated from the

healer—who was set down as a person who merely "heals diseases," and whose title is synonymous with that of *doctor*.

captain—"He sails the camp," like the captain of a ship. "He begins everything, has everything fixed."

pastor—the father of the church.

shepherd—"Who takes care of the children."

shepherdess—"When you come to church, find you a seat, an' if there is anything you need they must let you have it. Shepherdess can also lead a prayer meeting." Just as there is an assistant teacher and a teacher, so there is a leader and a shepherd. "The shepherd must be very bright, yes? Can be brighter than the leader, can do mysterious things. The shepherdess, too."

pumper—"Help you when you go down to seek the spirit, to really bring something back. When the pumper pumps, sometimes he hear Mother Earth speak to him and tell him what to do." The explanation went further: "That is about spiritual work of the church. Not about curing."

diver—"Anything that down, he would get up. It's when the spirit leaves them and goes away (i.e., among members of the church)." Or, "The spirit takes them away and he brings it up." It was made clear that this did not involve curing in the sense of recovering the soul of a person that has been "taken away" by the black magic set by an enemy.

prophet—one who prophesies things "of the past and the future."

apostle—"Jesus' messengers, who saw his miracles." They prophesy, teach, "an' heal, too. They're higher than the prophet."

queen—"She can be queen of teachers, queen over the spirits. I mean they have got to take orders from her so. She can prove, too."

fortune-teller—"Tell you things of the spirit, an' many different things, also. It's like an astronomer." A fortune-teller, however, it was explained, cannot prophesy the "things of heaven," or read the stars and the moon. A prophet is higher than a fortune-teller. "Fortune-teller read you, the man. Prophet read the writing in the sky."

surveyra—surveys the camp where mournin' is held, and designates the water for baptism. "What does it mean to survey the camp? It's the four corners you want, for you have to know the center. When the leader wants to do his work, he must know the center. If a strange Baptis' visit you, you make your sign inside, he makes it outside. Then you see if he is a good man and know the Baptis' secret. Then you shake hands, you glad." The "surveyra" also keeps out the evil being called *sukuyan*, or vampire.

judge—"Higher than prover, but something like him. If you are wrong in doing spiritual things, then the judge is higher than everything —than teacher, or leader or preacher. If the judge calls another, an' he don' come, he'll suspend him, an' then put a penalty. He mus' fast, an' then gets a pardon." His powers go farther. "He can flog even a teacher. But he does this at a particular (secret) meeting. The children (the congregation) won' be there, won' hear about it."

nurse—"That's a woman alone. She cleans the church, puts flowers around." During the services it is she who, in accordance with the instructions given by the "mother" of the church, goes to each corner, "watering the field."

Such are some of the "gifts," or "vocations," or "spiritual tasks" as these are variously called, that are found in different Shouters groups. This list does not exhaust the tale of the gifts named by persons affiliated with other groups, a few of which may be mentioned. These would include the gift of the *philosopher,* "who tells of something expected to come," or the *artist*, "who draws the signs" made in white on the floor of a church, or the *revealer*, "who reveals things in the Bible," or the *searching warrant*, "who can tell you when the spirit of God is coming; lays hands on a mischievous person. Anything secret he will put his hands on it; and when there's a bashfulness toward the spirit of God, he comes to you and the bashfulness leaves you."

Outsiders who discuss the Shouters mention their discipline as often as their spiritual power. Not only religious behavior, but everyday conduct of those within the community is scruntinized and regularized. "Baptists don' like cards. Don' like too much rum. Don' like running around with women. Livin' is all right, but steady. If he married and wrangle, don' like it. Better livin' steady and nice with another, because marry not sustain always. That's why a young man work to become a member, we ask, 'You married? Livin' with woman? Intend to begin livin'?' If he say 'No,' we won't have him. Say, 'You is gentleman in the day. What you doin' at night?' Same with woman. Say, 'You not old. You a human being, what you doing then?'"

Several persons spoke of an officer of the Shouters groups called a watchman, whose task is to know what is "going on" among the members, and particularly to learn and verify gossip about wrong-doing. "They chastise you in open church for it," it was stated. "You have to kneel down and then they chastise." At times, too, the spirit will come to a member who will testify, "Sister Mary or Brother John is living in sin." To accept chastisement when guilty is regarded as a test of willingness to live in accordance with the principles of the sect, for one who is "a frivolous person" will, under these circumstances, leave the church before permitting himself to be flogged or otherwise humbled.

The office of *"prover"* is another cited by outsiders discussing the strictness with which Shouters hold their members in line, and see that the tenets of the good life are not violated. One person even maintained that there is a head prover to test the provers—something not borne out by the statements of Shouters themselves, but indicative of opinions held by others concerning Shouter discipline. The *prover* has a wand which, "have something in it. Say it's the spirit." It is put to the head of each member three times. "You begin to shake. If you fall down, a sister call out, 'Prover, flog her, she fall from grace.'" They "prove" the entire membership, and perhaps find one or two of these who, after their punishment, are termed penitents. For a time, penitents sit alone in the church, and wear special clothes. "If they're women, they wears a blue dress with a white collar, like a nurse." Then, later, at a meeting in the "teacher's" house, they are questioned. "Then they have to tell, an' promise not to do it again."

As a consequence of this discipline, and the impression made on the community by the retelling of incidents that come to popular attention, the Shouters enjoy a reputation of great probity. "Wednesday night meeting flog you self, till you bawl (if you have done wrong). Outsiders see it, yes? But if they're seeing it too much, then they shut the windows. Member get three chances; then if they do wrong again, cut him off." Inner controls, as described by a "teacher," reinforce this reputation of discipline and rectitude by intervening officially in internal feuds that might bring members before the law. For "the church judge things between members. Don' like court at all; try to settle things between ourselves. I'm strict, yes! If I say, they do so." The view of the younger men and women was that the flesh is too weak at their age to live in such grace as this worship demands, but that it is a way of life they hoped one day to attain.

III

Most Shouters come to seek membership in the church as the result of a dream-experience. Two of these experiences may be given here. One man, the "father" of a Toco Shouting church, had come to Trinidad from St. Vincent some four decades before. There he was a Wesleyan (Methodist), but because this denomination was not represented in Toco, he attended the Anglican services. "Say we all was sinners. It was like they beat me. I couldn't go there." So he "stayed at home, studied, studied. All the different churches, all say they tell the true word. I study, say, 'Lord, I want to serve you. Which you true children?'"

"One day," his tale continued, "I dream. A white man come hol' up two fingers. A fine lookin' man. I look at his face an' down to his feet, then I begin to look from the feet up. When I come to about here (showing his side), I know it the Savior. I say, 'Lord, which one has the true word?' He show the two fingers, say, 'They there.' Say, 'Which one, Lord?' He say 'Choose.' I choose, and then I know it's the Baptis', the spiritual." And since then, his search for the truth having been successful, he like St. John "bring the light." He added that his religion made him happy, that it filled him with joy. "When the body is fill with joy, it move, it shake. If I got up one mornin' an' didn't feel like shoutin', then I know the Lord is not with me. I would know something was wrong."

To another man, who had lived earlier in Tobago, the call likewise came in a dream. He had had many conversations with the leader of a Shouters' group, and one day, while ill, he dreamed he was thrown out of a boat in which he was sailing. "The sea was dry and level. You could see everywhere, to Port-of-Spain, even to London." He was on shore near the Galera light-house, east of Toco, where many people stood in line, moving out over the sea until they reached Christ, "the place of Glory." Some went to the right, some to the left, "But glory be, when I got there I go to the right-hand, not to the lef'. Go to glory with Jesus." Those who went to the left are "gone to the devil-imps, an' burn night an' day." So he knew he was among the saved.

Let us follow the subsequent behavior of this man. Next morning he packed his clothes and followed his mentor to a house in the country, some distance from Toco, "though he didn't wan' to take me." However, after some urging "He take me. We trottin', goin' an' when we meet the house, he wife get some 'dust grass' put it in the water," and then tied it about his aching feet, which had "come big, boy! It swell wit' the distance." After he had rested, he began to work for his teacher— "clean the yard, draw water, work in the estate"—until, since his visions continued, he was taken to be baptized. After this, he went to mournin' groun', thus becoming a full member of the group, and returned to Toco, where he has been active in Shouter circles ever since, though it was bruited about he was falling from grace for being unfaithful to his keeper.

The decision to be baptized may thus come to a person as the result of a dream or vision. Baptism is the first step in the chain of rituals that are to be thought of as a process of initiation into the Shouters sect, an image that becomes the more apt when it is pointed out that for the community as a whole the Shouters are regarded as "an order like the Rose of Sharon" or other secret societies.

Dreams and visions are said by some to be of equal weight in this process, while others hold them to be of different quality, though of equal importance. "There can be dreams and visions, though children only have dreams. Dreams mean something, but God sends visions so you know what to do." God sent the vision that led to the baptism of the man who volunteered these opinions. "When you get a vision like this, you got to baptize. You got to obey." Otherwise God punishes with sickness. "Is the Angel self speak to you, the Angel of Christ! He show you the spot where you are to baptize even, whether fresh river or the sea." Rivers were likened to the Jordan—"Any river is the Jordan. You have to be born again. Born again mean remerge. Remerge mean baptize." Sometimes, according to a statement by another cult-member, the teacher may have the vision, and inform the candidate, or the candidate may have a dream and the teacher interprets it in the manner in which dreams sometimes have to be interpreted. In any event, the importance of prior interest in the cult is recognized. "If Baptist appeal to you, it's a voice inside you speaking to you. It's the voice of God. We calls it getting converted."

When a man or woman comes to the teacher with his vision or dream, and offers himself as a candidate for baptism, he undergoes a period of instruction that some say lasts for three months, others three weeks, a month, or longer, depending on the candidate. During this time he goes to the teacher every other night, and must lead a life worthy of his new calling. "If he's single, can't live in fornication, but if he's married, goes on livin'." The teacher gives him a chapter, or part of a chapter of the Bible, or a psalm to read "all by himself." The Spirit of God may come while he is reading, and he begins to pray.

This is an important—probably the most important—aspect of the pre-baptismal training, for "everyone who receives baptism has a *hymn,* a *psalm* and a *chapter* that is his . . ." which cause him to "receive the spirit, and when he testify with a candle, he start with that hymn." For to the question, "Why do some shake and others don't, when a hymn is sung?" the answer came, "If my hymn is sung, I'm happy. If another hymn is sung, if it's connected with mine, it would move me. But if it wasn't either of these, I wouldn't feel it." The speaker added, "Sometimes a hymn move everybody. We say 'Spirit of God come like a wind.'" It is recognized also that individual differences may not be disregarded at any stage in affiliation. "When members are deeper down, it's easier for them to get the Spirit. But some are self-starters, while some need corkin' up," and some, "Oh, the spirit love them too much, come too quick, rush to them!"

The baptismal meeting begins at the church or the home of a member. It is usually held on a Saturday, and lasts the entire night. The eyes of the candidates are bound early in the proceedings, about nine or ten o'clock, "to prevent them from looking around." There are prayers and hymns, and the teacher addresses them, exhorting them to give their hearts to God, and to pray sincerely; which they do while the congregation sings softly in accompaniment. Coffee and refreshments are served to all about midnight, and there is a recess of an hour or two. "Let them cool off now. Some teachers let them sleep, but others only let them rest. Prayin' is quieted down now, too."

At about this stage the baptismal rite which occasioned the series of arrests and subsequent trial of Shouters shortly before the period of this research, was interrupted by the police. The testimony of one of the officers, as given before the court, may be quoted here from the transcript as a first-hand account of the nature of the proceeding in the ceremonies immediately before the arrests were made: "I heard singing and shouting. . . . I noticed a woman serving coffee, some drinking coffee and some singing. I saw five persons sitting on a bench. Their eyes and heads were bandaged with white cloth and they had lighted candles in their hands. They were moving their bodies from side to side and grunting. I noticed . . . [the leader] . . . reading from a paper in her hand and holding a woman in one hand who was jumping. I noticed . . . [one of her assistants] . . . with a small stick making signs and touching the heads of the persons sitting on the bench. . . ."

At about four o'clock the group start their march to the river, or the spot on the sea-shore where the baptizing—which must always take place in "living" water—is to be carried out. They take the bands off the eyes of the candidates, and all "march singin'," the leader first, staff in hand. Attendants greatly outnumber candidates. The "surveyra" tries the depth of the water, and plants a cross there, while the teacher enters to consecrate the water, as all sing and pray. Then, shortly before dawn, baptizing begins. Each candidate, holding a lighted candle, is immersed three times. "There are miracles, yes? Some go in with it lighted, come up with it lighted." But to all, the Spirit comes. The elder who performs the rite, it was pointed out, gives nothing when he baptizes. "It's Christ who gives, for the Bible say, 'A sign shall follow you,' an' that sign is the power of the Holy Ghos'. If you heart clean, you get the power clean, if not, you get it partly. But after you receive the Holy Ghos', you cannot keep still at all. You feel a j'y (joy) within you, an' at the mention of God, the power shake you."

Afterwards, the candidates are taken to the "tent"—a thatched shelter—to rest and partake of fruit and other refreshments before returning to the church, and to "give thanks." Later that morning, at the church, they sleep, and some of them may have further visions that often tell them they must undertake the next step, the rites of the mournin' groun', specifying also the period they must spend there to obtain the "gift" they are destined to receive.

Should those having undergone the rite of baptism feel hunger, they are fed during the day, but many of them go without food, resting while they await their consecration at the seven o'clock services. At that time their heads, hands, and feet are washed, the face, head, palms of the hands and soles of the feet are anointed with oil, and they are given sacred water to drink. "They read the orders to them: Remember the Baptism morning; remember the Baptism, remember the three drops of water (symbolizing Father, Son and Holy Ghost) given you." Then, the day's services over, they are free to return to their homes.

IV

Mournin' groun' is the term used to designate a kind of retreat either literally or figuratively "in de bush," at which Shouters are initiated into the mysteries of their faith, obtain and later renew the power of their "gifts," or receive higher powers. "We call it mournin' because they fast there. Don' wash," said one teacher; and another, "We mourn for sins. Go there, and ol' person die, new person born in Christ." It was also said, "Long time ago people they call 'converted' had mourning, but didn't baptize. That was dangerous. On their way [to Glory] they saw too many things, met too many things. It hurt them sometimes too much after they got back."

The period of time required varies with the individual. "They do what they're told by the Spirit, but sometimes the Spirit says they must stay longer than they plan, fourteen days and not seven, or even twenty-one." Where there are no special instructions from a spirit to follow, mourning begins at night. At midnight, "you set them," putting bands about the eyes of those in mourning, and causing them to lie on pallets of straw, or banana or bread-fruit or bamboo leaves. "Wash today an' band them. Then they don' get washing till the bands are off. They are bathe' right through with consecrated water. Some don' sleep at all," during the days of retreat.

When they tire of lying, they are placed on their knees, or are brought to a sitting position, and their arms are rubbed to help the circulation. "The mother of the church must be there to help," and women with the gift of nurse, who look after those mourning as they would after children. "There's a bell to ring if you want to ease yourself, but you must do this inside, an' not go out." The leader is in the same house. "He know your thoughts, an' if your spirit isn't going beating the pass (path) to the other world he may flog you." Another person commented, "If you do something wrong, the Spirit lick you. Spirit bound to lick you before you get it. . . . Spirit send some to Africa, learn to talk language, African language. Some to India, learn to talk like Indian. Some to China, learn to talk Chinese." But in answer to a question as to whether the Spirit is Jesus, or St. John, or the Virgin, the only answer was "No, it's another spirit."

Each morning those in retreat are "called up for prayer." They are given milk and a little sweet rice to eat. "When an African spirit get to them they ask for *kuku* (an African dish made of cassava). Sometimes spirit don' allow them to use a plate. Have a calabash. They eat and drink out of it. Have a spoon—they bring spoon, fork, plate, glass, towel—but don' use it. At times the spirit ask for a knife put under their head. Then, when they travellin', there's three people then, not one. The knife, fork, an' spoon are not to eat with. The knife cuts away the path, the fork clears it, the spoon digs." There are continuous prayers and instruction. Each Saint who appears to a mourner tells "what things he don' like to eat. Some don' like smoke, some other things."

"Spiritual tasks" are shown them. "Reading, not the Bible, but religious books" that pertain to the Bible, such as "The Manual of Devotion," "The Guide to God," "Pilgrim's Progress," "The Prince of the House of David," and the "chapter of the Bible with wisdom, called Book of Maccabees." Those mourning are conceived as "travelling a path" to Glory, as many of the images already quoted indicate. From their travels, they "bring the psalms they want read, new hymns, chapters (of the Bible). The members of the congregation come there to build them up, help them in prayin'." Sometimes a message for the teacher, or the church, or for things to be done for them is brought back from this journey to "Glory," and "They call what they see," as they kneel, or sit or lie.

At the end of the period, most of them know such "gifts" as it is their lot to possess—if it is their first time in the mournin' groun'—or, if they had been through mourning before, the higher gift which gives them greater status in the church. One teacher compared the gifts that are acquired to the education of a child. "There are seven standards in the spiritual world. After each mournin', you get higher gift." One man, the Father of his church, held a different conception of the purpose of repeating the mourning experience. "If you been to mournin' before the 'power' gets cold; [after a time] you got to go again to hear what the spirit will tell." Still another view made the point that it is possible to return from a second or third visit to the mourning ground reduced in spiritual powers rather than augmented. This would result only, however, "if your life is not correct."

Not all are successful. "Some mourn and bring nothin'. Mistress Small mourn *six* times. Bring nothin'. They flogs her enough." Others who have had the same experience are not so persevering. "Mistress Brooks went once, come back with nothin'. Don' mourn again, just stop being member." The gifts they bring back have to be "sealed in writing." Members who go in more than once "come out of each mournin' with a new name for each new gift. They have saints' names—John, Joseph—even for a woman."

When the mourners emerge from their retreat, they are received back into the church in an important ceremony. First of all they are bathed by the teachers and "nurse," and are fed. Each then is told the head-bands to be worn—bands assigned by the teacher in accordance with the dreams and visions she, or the mourner, or both have had. These bands differ in color in accordance with the quality of a person's spirit. Over all of them, however, is worn the "baptism band," of white, that covered the eyes during the rituals when the member was baptized, so that outsiders do not know of the three or seven colored bands each mourner may wear. Three bands are worn at the ceremony of emergence.

Symbolic significance of the bands associates white with purity; yellow with glory; red with power—"It's the blood of Jesus"—green with peace; blue and pink with truth; mauve with mystery; and black and brown with "power, air power, African."

The color symbolism was further developed by one teacher as representing specific relationships to specific saints of the church. It was not possible to obtain from other sources corroboration of so close an association of the saints with the "spiritual Baptist" worship, lacking which it is offered as an extreme deviant from orthodox Baptist or other Protestant practice. The list which appears below is therefore given as it was detailed by this teacher.

COLOR	FEMALE	MALE
brown	St. Mount Carmel	St. Joseph, St. Michael, St. Anthony
green	Lady St. Anne	St. Patrick
red	St. Catherine	St. John
yellow	Mysteries of God, Glory	Ascension
blue	Immaculate Conception, St. Mary, Mother of Christ, St. Theresa	Ezekiel
white	purity—the dove purity—the Holy Spirit	
black	"I forget the name of the Saint in black."	Resurrection, Death

With each mourner wearing three bands, then, the white on top, "like batteries of a torch (flashlight)—three batteries, but only one light," and carrying two bouquets, each with five candles for the Virgin, they march in procession three times about the church. The standard bearer, the shepherd, and the leader are first, then comes the priest. Those who have been in the mourning ground are next, followed by the teacher, the congregation, and finally the pastor. The church is decorated this Sunday night, for it is a festive occasion. "Have same as bride." This was elaborated: "If man come for king and has money, get fine things for him, and a crown."

When prayers are over, the mourners who are seated at the altar are called upon in turn "to give their tracts." Each, addressed by his new name which he has brought back from mournin', stands before the congregation and says in salutation, "Good night, brothers and sisters. Good night, teacher." The band on the forehead protects the eyes, now, from the unaccustomed light. The mourner sings or speaks, as he is impelled to do by his spirit. "If he must give a hymn first, he gives it." But before he speaks or sings, he is anointed by the "priest." "They get oil that smells nice. And when they are consecrated, they smoke incense for them." Sometimes when a tract is given—that is, a sermon is preached or a testimonial offered—"the spirit is manifest in the camp." Then all rejoice at the power this mourner has brought back, and though happenings of this kind prolong the ceremony— "sometimes it last till two o'clock"—none of those who have emerged from the mournin' groun' may forego this rite.

Before the newly emerged mourners are ready to resume the secular tasks of their daily lives, they must be protected from the ill effects of a too hurried transition from the trance-like state of mournin', and consequently they remain secluded for several days more—three, if there are people at home to care for them, otherwise nine days. "They mustn't handle a knife or cutlass, or spend money. It would hurt their sight."

v

Because the Shouters sect is proscribed by law, it is understandably not easy for an outsider to attain a position of confidence which permits him to be present at services where possession occurs. Except for minor deviations from conventional patterns, notably the chalked symbols found on the church floor, and the pouring of water in the four corners, nothing in the regular Sunday or Wednesday services differentiates them from services held at any legally approved Baptist church. The decorous behavior of the congregation, the nature of the sermon, the type of prayers offered at such services are, as a matter of fact, far closer to European conventions of religious behavior than that of the American Negro "shouting" churches, North or South.

The music heard at such a service illustrates this point. Shouters, like those of other evangelical denominations, sing and enjoy singing what they term "Sankeys,"—the hymns from the well-known Sankey and Moody hymn-book. These songs are sung as written, but the manner of singing emphasizes a certain lugubrious quality by means of drawn notes and slurs from one tone to another, rendered at full voice, and with a kind of paradoxical enthusiasm by the singers.

The memory of the song-leaders—the more important officials of the congregation—is prodigious, for in each rendition, every verse of the hymn being sung is exacted, and the volume of sound increases from verse to verse as the congregation solidifies its attack on the melody. A passage from the diary kept during this field research may be cited to illustrate the perplexing question which this singing posed when the setting of the dimly lit bare church with its earthen floor

Jesus, Lover of My Soul

brought to mind services in equally humble settings in the United States: "What is baffling is the miracle that produced the American spirituals, and the historical reasons for the acceptance by the folk in these islands of the hymns just as the Whites sing them."

But just as the essential rites of the cult are carried on beneath an overlay of conventionalized decorum, so these "Sankeys" also mask more vigorous musical forms. This was disclosed when a recording was being made of the hymn "Jesus, Lover of My Soul," as part of a collection of songs which had as its object to cover the total range of Toco music, in which the Sankeys, whatever their derivation and affiliation, are of such importance. After two verses, the singers, continuing the melody, began to change their rhythm, introducing hand-clapping as the tempo became faster, until the hymn was transmuted into a swing idiom which in the proper setting would result in the spirit possession that was simulated in the sounds made by the singers on the record. All this is apparent in the transcription of the song, as given here:

Also to be encountered on closer acquaintance are the "spiritual"

hymns that, as mentioned, are improvisations dictated by "the spirit."
It is told, "The spiritual hymns are the shoutin' hymns. It's the spirit
sing it, give the words, the lure." A few examples of the verses will
show the nature of these improvisations:

> "Where are you been
> When de firs' trumpet soun'?
> Where are you been
> An' it soun' so loud,
> An' it soun' so hard,
> As to wake up de dead?
> Where are you been
> When de firs' trumpet soun'?"

> "We shall wear a starry crown,
> In the mornin', praise the Lord!
> We shall wear a crown,
> A hallelujah crown,
> Oh, yes!"

> "Me mother (brother, sister) dis mornin'
> She gone along home.
> She gone away to Glory,
> She gone along home."

In the rituals of the sect, as well, the restraints that impress on
initial acquaintance are found to give way to vigorous, energetic forms
of worship that, as has been pointed out, have an emotional appeal
even for those not themselves Shouters, because its expression is in
an idiom that flows out of the beliefs of the membership, and is
equally understandable to those who come as spectators.

Descriptions may now be given of some of the services that were
witnessed—a Sunday-night prayer-meeting, a Sunday morning
"preachin'," the dedication of the site for a new "temple," and a Sunday night service where the full range of Shouters rituals was present.

The evening prayer and testimonial meeting that consituted the first
contact with any Shouters group, was inordinately subdued, with
barely audible interpolations from the congregation to punctuate the
pauses in sermon and testimonials, and the singing of the Sankeys giving forth a heavy, doleful, dragging effect. On this occasion, there
were some fifteen to eighteen people present. The vigor of the singing
and the excellence of the voices were the only distinguishing things
about the rendition of the six hymns that were sung. Singing was always done standing up; when there was a prayer, everyone knelt
facing the altar. All were barefooted, and most of the women wore
white kerchiefs.

Prayers and testimonials gave the same quotations from the Bible heard in American Negro churches. The rambling discourse laid emphasis on being saved and, as a distinctive turn, emphasized how Jesus was as poor as they were, but that their poverty would not stand in their way of attaining grace. The preacher testified first; then there was a hymn; then the "Father" of the church spoke, an able speaker, and a moving one, describing their poverty and their persecution, with obvious reference to the court action taken recently against the Shouters. Next the stout teacher who sat with her back to the altar, facing the congregation "testified"; then a hymn; then a prayer by a lad who knelt and held a candle as he half-chanted his rhythmic and almost metered plea; then a hymn; and finally another half-chanted benediction by the "Mother" of the church. There was no collection, and no request for offerings.

At the Sunday morning "preachin'" and the dedication later that day there was at least an approach to "shaking." Somewhat greater confidence in the presence of outsiders, and the participation of a visiting preacher of some renown in Shouting circles, perhaps accounted for this. At eleven o'clock, when the service was to begin, the people were just assembling. The women, who came in white dresses and hats, went behind the little church-building to change their hats for white head-kerchiefs, while most of them put white aprons over their dresses. The men wore clean clothing, in most cases white coats. Two of the women wore lavender dresses, one was in a brown dress, and two wore blue nursemaid uniforms. "Naked red they don' wear," was said of the dress of these churchgoers, "but white with red flowers they love too much."

As the services began, shoes were removed, but not stockings or socks, and in kneeling to pray, a handkerchief was spread on the ground to protect the clean clothing. The church was spotlessly clean, with freshly laundered cloths on tables and altar. What had appeared a white flag over the altar turned out to be pale violet in daylight; the crosses about the center pole and the designs at the doors were not newly chalked for the occasion. At the base of the center pole was a jam jar filled with flowers, the bell, and an unlighted candle, but not the Bible that had been lying behind it the other evening. A lighted candle stood on the altar, that had its four vases of flowers.

The visiting preacher, who with the Father of the church appeared at about 11:15, was from a town near San Fernando. He changed into a clean white gown, with a white cord which was knotted several times with the ends hanging down the side. As the services opened there were fourteen people present, but the little place filled somewhat as the ritual went on, and at the end there were at least twenty-five adults and about ten children, who comported themselves much as they pleased, though noiselessly, while several of them slept.

An invocation was followed by a hymn—the preacher reading the entire text, then lining out the first half of every stanza. Several prayers by women, each followed by a hymn, preceded the prayer by the Father of the church. His "Thank you's" for blessings received, were in a quiet, conversational manner, as if the beings he addressed were close at hand and asked for neither rhetoric nor oratory. After the next hymn, the congregation remained standing while the Gloria, in English, was repeated by all.

Seats were resumed for the first scripture reading, which concerned the law (Exodus 21:5, 6) that a Hebrew servant must go free after six years of service; but that if his master had given him a wife who had borne him children, and he wished to remain with his family, he must be taken before the judges, and say "I will serve my master, I will not go free," whereupon a hole is to be bored in his ear with an awl "and he shall serve him forever." Again a hymn marked the interval between the first and the second scripture reading, this time from Paul's Epistles, then followed the Credo, in English, recited by all standing, and yet another hymn.

Sermon, hymn, benediction, and collection succeeded each other in orderly sequence, both preacher and congregation restrained, with but one emotional passage where allusion was made to the persecution of the group. The only observable evidences of nervousness were that one woman who entered the church while a hymn was in progress, knelt down in the aisle and began to "jerk," but quickly controlled herself; while another began to pat the ground; doubling the time of a hymn, and then quieting down. Services were over at 12:55, an early dismissal for this group, called for by reason of the scheduled rite of consecration of the site for their new church, at half-past three.

The visiting preacher also officiated at the dedication of the new "temple" being built by this group. The site was up a bypath, removed from the main road, on a sharply sloping hill, so that one side of it was a deep trench, behind a central mound of earth yet to be excavated. At the northwest corner a post hole had been dug, and at about the center of the north side was a small table, covered with a clean white cloth on which were a jar with water and flowers, and the bell; behind this stood the preacher as he began the services. The Father stood near the post hole; the members of the congregation, more numerous than at the morning service, stood grouped nearby. A number of playing children were about including a little boy not yet four years old, who was responding with the "Amens" and "Hallelujahs" during the prayers, and repeating the Lord's Prayer after the preacher, with all the assurance of a full-fledged member of the group.

The service began at 3:40 with the customary alternation of hymns, prayers, hymns, then the reading of the psalms, followed by another hymn, and a discourse by the preacher, based on the concept that consecrating ground must be secondary to consecrating people. With lighted white candle in one hand, and the bell in the other, the stout teacher next accompanied the Mother of the church to the four corners of the excavation, where she rang the bell three times as the Mother three times poured water from the jam jar holding the flowers. The preacher accompanied by four additional persons proceeded to dedicate the same four corners, reading a psalm, and offering up a prayer at each corner.

Emotion was shown when the Mother, praying at the southeastern corner, came to ask God's favor for the Father of the church. Her voice broke and she cried out "Oh, Father! Oh! Father . . . !" but the embankment intervened so that it was not possible to see whether she "shook" or not. Similarly, after making the tour of the four corners, the preacher stood just west of the unexcavated mound of earth, saying, "I shall take this for the center," and the Father himself prayed. Deeply moved, his shaking threw him from a kneeling to a sitting position, but he recovered quickly and continued with his prayer.

A number of details were recorded. Only those who offered up prayers knelt, and no shoes were removed. Care was taken to observe what offerings would be put into the hole with the "cornerstone," which was a block of wood, but the only one observed was a three-penny piece, tossed into the hole by one of the men present who stepped up just before the four-by-four post was lowered. The benediction was at 4:45, and as it ended and the handshaking with the preacher began, the shouting hymn, "Of the Church and the Chapel" was started. This was the accompaniment to the ritual handshake exchanged with everyone present, three downward shakes of the right hand, then the hands elevated above the head, the touching of the left breast of first one and then the other party to the handshake, and a final downward shake.

VI

To have pressed the Toco Shouters for permission to visit those ceremonies where they worship their God in a manner proscribed by law would have been unfair. It is enough to say here that for these rites they go elsewhere, carrying out the services where "shouting," properly speaking, can be indulged in, as is not possible in their own "temple," situated in so small a community and so close to a main road.

The description of the Shouting service which follows, therefore, recounts the worship of a group in another town not far from Toco. This congregation, like others in the area, has liaison with Shouters of the whole northeastern portion of the Island; acquaintance with a number of its members and officers, made and renewed in Toco itself, made possible attendance at this ritual. It is worthy of note that, despite the remoteness of the "temple" from a main road, an efficient watch-dog gave notice during the services, when anyone approached, while along the path leading to the compound where the "temple" was situated, watchers were stationed.

At 6:30, the beginning of the service, the teacher chalked a design on the floor inside the entrance door. At the same time she started a hymn. Candles were lighted and passed around to those who needed them to read their hymn-books, and as the singing went on and more people began to drift in, all possible places were "consecrated"—the four corner altars, the principal altar and the one at the base of the central post, the doors and windows—by pouring water from the flower-glass three times at each place, and ringing the big bell three times. Water was also thrown on the floor about the central altar at each cardinal point of the compass, and in front of the subsidiary altars. Song succeeded song—all slow Sankeys—with the group becoming steadily larger and the teacher supervising quietly and efficiently.

A singer went down on his knees and gave the first prayer, interspersed with songs and following the pattern, by now familiar, of using verses from hymns to fill in or, in the instance of one or two younger men, to give them an interval to overcome reserve. When the singer rose, candle and flowers in hand, he went over to a young woman in a grey dress who proved to be the teacher's most gifted disciple, herself leader of a church. With her, and later with the teacher and one or two others, this man shook hands, in the ceremonial "proving" manner, already described, and from this woman in grey he received a curtsy as he finished. It should be added that during the period of preparation the teacher did "writing" along a candle, which was used by all those later possessed by the "spirit."

The singing was not so "warm" as the leader wished it to be, and she called out "Sing, children!" telling the song leader not to "do any cold turkey." This had the immediate effect of producing singing of such fervor that the leader for a moment began to shake. By this time the room had filled. Among those present were a Hindu woman and her daughter, who did not participate in the service except by joining in the hymn-singing from time to time, and who left early. At about eight o'clock, the teacher herself began to pray. The singer had been succeeded by one of the other men, who carried on effectively in a soft voice that rarely went up in volume. Taking the candle and flowers from him after the approved handshaking, putting out the light and relighting the candle from the "eternal light" at the central altar, the teacher went to the door where her shepherd's crook—full size, and beautifully made of dark wood—was hanging, and took a place in front of the railing at the extreme right, where she had a seat and from which she thenceforth directed proceedings. Kneeling in this corner, facing the central altar, she offered up one of the rambling prayers characteristic of these meetings, punctuated with song in which the members joined, and dropping into "tongues" several times for some minutes at a time.

Her manner of praying was quiet, and with no apparent effort she roused her congregation to a high pitch of excitement. When her prayer, which took about fifteen minutes—not much longer than that of the others—was ended, and the song that followed it was in progress, she walked to the central altar and rang the bell there three times. Next the flowers and candle went to her disciple, who prayed in a loud voice for some time, and also stimulated some spirited singing. Then she, too, rang the bell at the central altar three times, and returned the candle to the teacher who handed it to a young lad who was quite aroused—his hand went backward and forward constantly in a sidewise motion. The congregation of perhaps fifty sang the hymns that punctuated his prayer with an enthusiasm thus far not equalled.

At this time, too, the "jazzing" of a Sankey hymn at an actual service was first heard—the people here carrying the melodic line sung slightly faster, while the song-leader and a few others ornamented it with harmonized "ram-bam-bam, bam, bam, ram-a-bam," simulating drums and making the song irresistible to patting feet, and hand-clapping. It was sung toward the end of this youth's "testimony," when, overcome by the spirit, he danced on his knees, moving backing and forward in a kind of body-swing while he also "danced" the candle and glass with flowers which he held.

He staggered to his feet, drenched with perspiration. After his handshakes, the teacher gave the candle and glass to an elderly man, also a teacher, who moved to one side to pray facing the main altar, first inspecting the maroon flag. Since he had forgotten to remove his shoes, this was done for him as he knelt. His disjointed effort did not stimulate the group as had the prayer that preceded it, but the hymns that he introduced were well sung.

The teacher now gave candle and flowers to a tall young man at the other end of the church, who began in a halting, hesitant manner, with words issuing forth with difficulty. He went over the words of several songs before he could speak, until "he catch de spirit," it was whispered; as he went on, his rising eloquence caused the choruses of response to swell. The hymn on which he ended was sung over and over until it gradually fell into a swinging dance rhythm, and brought about the second possession of the evening. The youth who had prayed and afterwards knelt and danced, now danced again, as did some of the men who had been sitting on the bench along the side wall.

One man in particular, who from time to time had shown signs of possession, and had shaken violently but had been restrained by the teacher, was now allowed to dance part way down the west side of the church toward the other possessed young man, while the song leader shook a bit and did a kind of foot-patting dance that gave a further basic rhythm to the massed song. The teacher also began to shake, and danced toward the other end of the church, but all evening her "possessions" in which she shook and threw herself from one foot to another, hopping to regain her balance, seemed to rob her of none of her awareness of the things about her—an awareness that was not present in any of the others except, on one occasion, perhaps, that of the song leader. It was almost 8:45, and the teacher passed the flowers in their glass and the candle to her disciple, who now held a Bible, and who was to "read the lesson," which was the chapter that set forth the miracle of the loaves and fishes.

Before she began, the leader handed her the bell, which she held with one hand on top of the Bible; the candle and flowers were in the other. She read well, though the reading dropped into Negro-English often enough, and then she preached for about twenty minutes. Her discourse was made up of the customary weaving together of quotations from the Bible and the words of hymns, and contained many requests for remission of sin. Once or twice she "talked tongues."

As she finished, she knelt in front of the central altar and began to pray. The singing became hotter and hotter, and the young man who had been dancing earlier resumed his dance. This time the response from the congregation was electric. Then men on the side bench were dancing; one of them, like the teacher herself, went shaking clear around the central altar, hopping on one foot, until he settled into his dance step. The singer shook and danced alternately; two women in white danced and shook in place; while a church assistant in training, her head bound with a kerchief, who watched the door, also shook in place—hands clenched, arms half-raised, her angular frame shaken by a continuous quivering of the arms that extended itself to the entire body. What happened to the hymn that "bring a strong spirit to rejoice everybody" was as interesting musically as the dancing was dramatically, for it almost disappeared in the "ram-bam-i-bam-bam" of the full-throated song leader.

After a time, most of the dancers began to quiet down, but one of them continued to grow more and more excited, and "got the spirit" strongly, continuing to cry in the rhythm of the song that was no longer being sung, as it had been succeeded by another prayer, intended as a final one. The visiting male teacher got him to kneel while he was still shaking and crying out, and then forced a Bible into his hands. Gradually the possessed man calmed down sufficiently to be able to testify when the candle and flowers were handed him by the teacher. His intense possession at an hour so late in the service presented a special problem, for since the spirit had entered him, he had to testify no matter what the time, and the ten o'clock deadline of the law had already passed.

This last prayer, though an anticlimax to the dance of a few moments before, proved to be the most moving incident of the entire evening. The man could barely speak, and the candle shook in his hand causing the hot wax to drop on his upper arm and on the floor. He seemed obsessed by a sense of guilt, and his broken pleas for forgiveness were more coherent, more marked, and far less a matter of phrases than those of any of the others. As he prayed the teacher began a hymn, softly, so that the sound of his words was progressively blurred by the voices of the congregation repeating the hymn again and again in a sustained crescendo that finally drowned the voice of the supplicant, until he arose and gave his hand in the "proving" handshake that must end any possession. Again, he was barely able to control his shaking, though the teacher's caressing gestures did much to help him regain control of himself. After "proving" the disciple and several other members, his state of possession passed completely, and the services were brought to a close, at about 10:30, with the recital of the Credo and some other liturgical passages.

What Is "Voodoo"?

The best evidence of the socially normal nature of pos-
session is the existence of rules governing its incidence which
are well understood by all. . . . The gods are known to their
worshippers, and the duties owed them. . . . The reward for
the performance of these duties is good health, good harvests,
and the goodwill of fellow-men; the punishment for neglect
is corresponding ill fortune.

❋ ❋ ❋

More than any other single term, the word "voodoo" is called to
mind whenever mention is made of Haiti. Conceived as a grim system of African practices, it has come to be identified with fantastic
rites and to serve as a symbol of daring excursions into the esoteric.
Its dark mysteries have been so stressed that it has become customary
to think of the Haitians as living in a universe of psychological terror.

What, then, is "voodoo"? "Voodoo," or Vodun, as it will be termed
here, following native pronunciation, is a complex of African belief
and ritual governing in large measure the religious life of the Haitian
peasantry.

In Dahomey, the ancient West African kingdom whence the term
has come, Vodun means "god" and is a general name for all deities.
This source of the word has long been known. For instance, M. L.
E. Moreau de St.-Mery, in his work *Description topographique, phy-*
sique, civile, et historique de la partie française de l'Isle Saint-Dom-
ingue (Philadelphia, 1797 and 1798), wrote:

"According to the Arada Negroes, the real followers of Vaudaux in
the colony . . . *Vaudaux* signifies an all powerful and super-natural
being on which depend all the events that come to pass on this globe."

Two historical facts must be kept constantly in mind. The first is
that Vodun derives from a background of African theology and ceremonialism. The second is that Haiti's Negroes have continuously been
subjected to the influence of Catholicism during the centuries that
have passed since their introduction into the island.

Tomorrow, III, no. 1 (1954), 11–20. Abridged from chapter 8 of Herskovits'
Life in a Haitian Valley (New York: Knopf, 1937).

Yet another point may prove suggestive in providing a useful point of view for an analysis of the Vodun cult. This bears upon a difficulty, impossible and happily unnecessary to resolve, in the field study of religion. This difficulty arises out of the degree of variation in answers to questions dealing with the same point. These answers differ not only according to the status of the individual in the cult, since layman and priest have understandably different concepts of the functions of deities, but also according to the extent to which an individual has, or is indifferent to, religious interests.

A fundamental fallacy results from the fact that except where there is an officially sanctioned theology—which makes for dogma, and often for perfunctory worship, in contrast with the living dynamic nature of Haitian peasant belief and ritual—there are no "real" answers to questions in the field of religion. The student pursuing the "correct" statement will find that, no matter how painstaking his method and how extensive his precautions, the versions of different persons can never be entirely reconciled, unless a false appearance of truth is given to his findings.

If the underlying philosophy of the universe held by the Haitian is summarized, as it can be abstracted from his expressions of belief and from his observed behavior, this philosophy might be phrased somewhat as follows: The ruler of the universe is God, its Creator, who shares this task with His son Jesus, the saints of the Church, and the Holy Ghost. Man has been endowed with a soul, and the soul, which has come from God, returns to God for judgment and, if necessary, for punishment at the end of its sojourn on earth.

From Africa—*Guinée*—the Negroes brought other deities, termed variously *loa, mystères,* or *saints,* and these deities have been inherited through succeeding generations by the descendants of those who brought them to Haiti. The specific function of the African spirits in the Haitian system was given in the following terms by one of their devotees:

"The loa are occupied with men, their task is to cure. They can make a person work better than he otherwise would. When the loa possess people, they give helpful advice. But they cannot do the things that God does. They can protect a garden, but they cannot make a garden grow, for streams, rain and thunder come from God."

Another statement clearly shows the same concept: "God made the loa, but did not make them so they might do evil. When a man purchases a loa for money, that spirit will do evil as well as good, but God becomes angry and will not accept these bad spirits into the sky, and He drives them away."

The most striking element in the Vodun cult is the manner in which the gods are said to "possess" their devotees. Despite the fact that this is the aspect of Haitian religion that seems to the casual observer its least restrained and least disciplined, possession occurs according to well-defined rules and under specifically defined circumstances.

When a person is possessed for the first time, the spirit which is said to animate him is known as a *loa bossal,* an "untamed" god. The word *bossal,* which in the early days was applied to newly arrived Africans, has always been a term of contumely, and today the same feeling-tone is continued through the belief that since all things in the universe are subject to observable regulation, and animals and plants and human beings must all live according to these rules, the loa, as members of society, may not manifest the unrestrained and often dangerous traits of unpredictable behavior which characterize them before they have been "baptized" and thus brought under proper control.

Baptism of a deity most often occurs when a boy or girl is possessed by a family loa, especially if it is one which gives that knowledge of healing and divination meant by the word *connaissance.* Sometimes, though not always, this possession is violent, and the prospective devotee rages about the house, destroying whatever comes to hand. On occasion, since custom frowns on possession at a ceremony not given by the family of the one possessed, possessions of this kind mean either that the loa needs baptism; or that, being baptized, its devotee has been negligent in serving the god.

No actual rite of baptism of a loa—or, as it is also termed, of *lavé tête,* "washing the head"—was witnessed by this writer, but the account of the ceremony given here, obtained independently from several persons, represents an adequate exposition of the rite as performed in the town of Mirebalais. A room is prepared where the person whose loa is to be baptized must remain for three days. The mat or bed on which the neophyte rests is covered with fresh sheets and pillow-cases, and three changes of clothing are made ready, one of which must be entirely new for the last day of the ceremony. These are in the color of the god being "baptized"; that is, if the loa were revealed to be such a one as Damballa, Aida Wedo, or Gran' Erzilie, everything would be white, but if it were Gran' Siligbo, the colors would be blue and white: if Ogun, everything would be red; if Ossange, blue: where the god is one of the Pétro suite, such as 'Ti Kita or Bosu, everything would be black.

During the three days' "retreat" the one whose loa is being consecrated lies alone. All day long the men and women of the family sit in the next room or outside the house, singing and praying, though at night they sleep, since "this is not a wake." They not only sing the songs sacred to the loa being baptized, but also the canticles of the Virgin, while prayers of the Church are recited under the leadership of the *prêt' savanne*, the "bush-priest" whose ability to read the prayers makes him an essential figure in all Vodun rites. They may from time to time have "a little procession" about the room where the novitiate lies, when small banners in the color of the god are carried. Soft drinks and a *mangé sec*—a "dry" offering—are given the god, and white tapers and an oil lamp are lighted. Chicken and rice may also be cooked for any god except Gede, while chocolate and rice with milk are favored, since it is said "the loa loves desserts"—a commentary on the very immediate and human character of these spirits.

The actual baptism, or "washing of the head," is performed on the third day of the ceremony by a Vodun priest or priestess who is a member of the family, though any member who has important loa and the necessary *connaissance* may officiate if the membership of the family includes no priest. As at any baptism, there must be a godfather and godmother, and preference is given those who are the parents of twins or are themselves twins. The officiant must be possessed at the time, since, it is said, "one loa baptizes another."

Leaves of the basilique tree are steeped in perfumed cold water, and the hands of the one who baptizes are first immersed in the liquid; then, while songs of the loa and canticles of the Virgin are sung, he washes the head of the person to be baptized. Possession occurs immediately, and the new devotee lies back, half conscious, while all others kneel, seeking word from the loa to learn if it is satisfied. If an affirmative answer is given, all retire, the person possessed remaining in the room to sleep through the night. A "ball," but not a Vodun dance, may celebrate the event either the next day or later, but this is not obligatory, and most often those present, after eating, quietly disperse.

The following day, the one who has been baptized goes to the family place of worship and greets those who have helped him. Only one further rite is necessary, and this solely when the loa bossal is revealed to be a hostile god. Then the loa, after having been baptized, is "restrained" by being placed in a jar and buried, so it cannot later emerge and trouble the family of the one to whom it has come.

To have a baptized loa merely means that the worship of the loa is thereafter carried on in regular form. The worshipper learns how to *marré*, or "tie" his spirit, so as to enjoy the social aspects of a Vodun dance without fear that his loa will come unbidden. He gives it small offerings from time to time, and if it becomes insistent, or if his family is being troubled by its gods, he takes full part in the rituals that are staged.

In native idiom, a person when possessed is "mounted" by his god, and thereafter becomes his *ch'wal*, or "horse." A devotee may come under the influence of a number of spirits during a single ceremony or dance, one loa succeeding another. The first deity that ever came to a person, however, for him constitutes the chief of his gods—his *mait' tête*—and the leader of any deities which may subsequently possess him. It is this loa alone that is "baptized," and this one alone "taken from his head" at his death; and, as far as he is concerned, all his other gods are under the control of this *mait tête*, so that any agreement which he may enter into with this principal spirit must be respected by all the others.

Fundamentally, in Haitian peasant thought, to be possessed by a loa means that an individual's spirit is literally dispossessed by that of the god. Personalities undergo radical change in accordance with the nature of the deity, while even the sex of the one possessed is disregarded if it differs from that of the god, so that, for example, a woman "mounted" by Ogun is always addressed as Papa Ogun. One wears the colors of the god and the ornaments he likes, eating and drinking those things he prefers, and otherwise manifesting his peculiar characteristics—rolling on the earth, if possessed by Damballa or chattering incessantly if by Gede.

Not everyone, by any means, is subject to states of possession. If the existence of individual differences in the capacity for religious expression is recognized, it becomes apparent that while some react to the supernatural with immediate and overwhelming emotion, and others, though incapable of as deep a response, do sense the mysteries of possession, there are still others who go through life without ever feeling this religious "thrill." In native explanation, it is the former to whom the gods manifest themselves, who become the *ch'wal* of their loa; while to the latter the deities never make themselves known.

Scientifically, the phenomenon of possession in Negro cultures, at least, is as yet unsatisfactorily explained, largely because of the almost complete absence of adequate reports on the background and incidence of specific cases. Perhaps the most satisfactory approach to its understanding is through a consideration of it in terms of differences in nervous instability, which may be thought of as predisposing different persons to experience the religious thrill in different degrees; or, in other terms, by reference to their differing susceptibility to suggestion.

One must reject an hypothesis which attempts to explain the Vodun of Haiti in terms of the neuroses, even when, as in the admirable exposition of Dr. J. C. Dorsainvil in *Vodou et Névrose* (Port-au-Prince, 1931), the approach neglects neither accepted genetic theory in stressing the inheritance of neurotic tendencies in voduist family lines, nor the important historical forces which have been operative. For in terms of the patterns of Haitian religion, possession is not abnormal, but normal; it is set in its cultural mold as are all other phases of conventional living. That it gives release from psychic tension does not altar the case; neither does the fact that it offers a way to the satisfaction of unfulfilled desires, as when the god, speaking through a woman under possession, demands a necklace or bracelet which, though forever the property of the god, will be worn by his devotee.

These facts merely emphasize the compensatory character of the phenomenon. The social situation of the individual also enters; some undoubtedly simulate possession for the attention it brings them, while a person who experiences no serious difficulties in the course of his life is perhaps never called upon to ask whether or not he is properly serving his gods; is never placed in a situation for which possession would be a release. Hence to consider all possession as something which falls within the range of psychopathology is to approach it handicapped by a fundamental misconception.

The best evidence of the socially normal nature of possession is the existence of rules governing its incidence which are well understood by all. Not everyone who is a *ch'wal* may become possessed at any dance or *service*, for the gods, if properly under control, are permitted to come only to members of the family giving the rite. If a loa persists in dancing at a Vodun dance given by another family, it is either one of these loa bossal already described, or a loa *vagabond*, and may be scolded by the *hungan*: "You must not come here! You are not wanted! Go home where you belong!"

The passion with which a person resists his god, when he feels possession coming on at a rite not given by his own family, is particularly instructive. Men have been seen holding so tightly to the rafters of the shelter under which the dance was being held that the muscles of their forearms formed great cords, while beads of perspiration rolled down their foreheads. A person who must live away from his family for a long time usually takes steps to "feed" his loa in order to satisfy it, for it is more important to give offerings to the spirits than to dance for them. He therefore either quietly prepares a sacrifice of cereals and liquor in his own room or sends money home so that his loa may be "fed" at the family habitation, and his absence explained to it.

When Vodun deities were discussed in Mirebalais during the writer's visit, most often two "companies" of them were mentioned, the Rada and the Pétro "squads."

From comparatively early times the impression has been given that certain of these classes of gods perform only good, and others evil. Nothing could be further from the truth than this attempt to read European concept into Haitian ideology, for though some gods are feared far more than others, and some generally regarded with affection, even these latter bring great harm to a neglectful devotee, while the gods whose power validates the most malignant magic may, in certain situations, work for the good of their worshippers.

For while a general principle in the cult of the dead is that in the normal course of events those who die deliver up their souls to God, making the care for these souls primarily a concern of the Church, it is recognized that there are others who become loa. This occurs when an individual, usually a priest or priestess of the Vodun cult, who during his lifetime was known to possess great supernatural power, dies without having had his loa "withdrawn from his head." Burdened by these spirits, and therefore unable to get to God, his soul goes to the bottom of a stream, there to remain until, becoming impatient, it demands to be taken out. A ceremony then brings back the tortured soul and makes of it a *"loa nan canarie—a loa in a jar"*— which thereafter acts as a guard for its family.

There is little agreement as to the place of residence of the loa. In general, it is believed that they come from Guinée each time they are called, returning when they have, in the native idiom, "descended from the heads of their horses"—that is, when the possession of their devotees has ceased. Those "under the water," however, being Haitians, remain in Haiti for seven years until the ceremony just mentioned, of putting them *nan canarie,* has been performed, when they, like the other loa, return to Guinée. At the same time, all recognize the African character of the loa, whether they be gods brought from Africa or Créole loa from Haiti itself.

Worship of the loa is directed by priests of the cult. The terms *papaloi* and *mamaloi* as designations for male and female priests, almost universally employed by non-Haitian writers, are practically unknown in Mirebalais, where, as in most regions of Haiti, a priest is called a *hungan,* a priestess a *mambu.*

An important function of the *hungan* or *mambu* is to foretell the future, and it is as a diviner that the Vodun priest or priestess is most often employed. No major rite would be considered by a family unless divination were resorted to, but consultation is made for a far wider range of affairs than those of a purely religious nature. No proposed undertaking of any importance in the secular field is begun without visiting a diviner to discover whether or not the fates are propitious. When divining, the priest is usually under possession by his gods, but other methods, such as gazing into a crystal or basin of water, may also be employed.

Under the hungan and mambu are assistants called *hunsi*, or sometimes, in the case of men, termed *adjanikon*. In some parts of Haiti, particularly in the plain of the Cul-de-Sac and the Southern peninsula, there are degrees of initiation for the hunsi, which include the ordeal by fire that makes them *hunsi kanzo*. In Mirebalais, however, the *kanzo* rite, though known by name, is neither required nor performed. The hunsi and adjanikon know the rituals in a general way, hold and wave the banners used to salute the gods, sing the songs for the loa, aid in bringing the possessed dancers out of their possessions, and perform such other ritual tasks as helping the officiating hungan. Some members of the cult group have special ability to sing large numbers of the ritual songs for any loa which may be called, while others perform the animal sacrifices. It is among these male assistants that the most expert drummers are found.

This, then, constitutes an outline of that system of belief included under the term Vodun. Once more, in summary, it may be emphasized that Vodun is neither the practice of black magic, nor the unorganized pathological hysteria it is so often represented to be. The gods are known to their worshippers, and the duties owed them are equally well understood. The reward for the performance of these duties is good health, good harvests, and the goodwill of fellow-men; the punishment for neglect is corresponding ill fortune. On this basis of belief is erected the ceremonial of worship.

Index

community life, and Brazilian cult group, 229-47
comparison, role in ethnographic research, 71-81
compensation mechanisms in Negro cultures, 137-44
Congo, Brazilians from, 200; slaving in, 116
Congo-Angola cult groups, 219
conservatism, cultural, 56-57
continuum of New World Africanisms, 5-6, 50-56
cooking, African influence on American, 172-73; of Bahian cult members, 252
Cornwall and Jamaica General Advertiser, 116
"Coromantynes," 10
costs of cult life, 248-65 *passim*
Courlander recordings, 32
Creoles, Haitian, 26, 108-10; of Sierra Leone, 27
Cruickshank, J. G., quoted, 97-98
Cuba, African patterns in, 31, 53; studies on Negro culture of, 29-30; syncretism of African gods with Catholic saints in, 321-22, 326-28
"Cuffee" day-name, 8
cults, ancestor-worshiping, 84-88; in Brazil, 199-265; caboclo, 185, 195, 201, 219; candomble, 226-65; cult-houses of, 202-204, 229; deities syncretized with Catholic saints, 78-79, 203-14 *passim*, 321-28; drummers' importance in, 183-96; economic aspects of, 248-65; "fetish," 322; hysterical, 173-74; initiation rites, 205-206; interrelations among, 243; *panan* ritual of Brazilian, 217-26; priest and priestesses of, 17-18, 119-20, 202-206, 230-38, 260-65, 360-61; registration figures on, 201; social organization of, 226-47; in southernmost Brazil, 199-215; Trinidad Shouters, 329-53; vitality of, 201; vodun of Haiti, 354-61; *see also* gods and goddesses; religion; rituals
culture, Africanisms in American, 5-6, 50-56, 77, 168-74, 199-215; African's contribution to New World, 124-25, 168-74; Afroamerican as contributing to African, 12-23; Afroamerican research as contributing to theory of, 78-80, 145-55; anthropological vs. social study of, 129-33; borrowing in, 48, 56-59; conservatism and, 56-57; contact, 49-50; data available on Negro's, 4-5; dynamics of, 72-81, 145-55; ethnographic study of, 72-81; ethnohistorical study of, 49-50; focus in, 13-15, 51-52, 59, 79; as learned, 56-57, 147-51; need for rounded approach to study of, 246-47; "plantation America" sphere of, 126-27; problems in study of, 1-4; psychology of, 145-55; and reinter-

pretation, 13, 15-16, 35-38, 57-58, 79; retention of, 13, 15-16, 35-38, 56-58; slavery's effect on, 55-56; syncretisms and, 57-58; tenacity of, 13-14, 80
cures, magical, 299-304, 309
currency of West African tribes, 118
Cussy, M. de, 104
customs, Africanisms of majority survive while minority traditions vanish, 98; folk, 176-78; of Southern U.S. as influenced by African, 172-74; *see also* culture

Dagowe, 283-84, 311
Dahomey, attitude toward twins, 19; game in, 20; infant care compared with Ashanti's, 151-52; influence on New World cultures, 26, 200-201; kings' rationalization as compensation mechanism, 143-44; religious syncretism in, 326; ritual for ancestors, 86-88; slaving in, 50, 83-88, 117-19; studies of family structure, 64-65
Damballa, 324
dances, *avogan* in market place, 138; as compensation mechanism for psychological repressions, 135, 138; "Danse Congo," 135; drummers', 194; legalized, in Paramaribo, 295; possession cured by, 290-301 *passim*; and subconscious aesthetic patterns, 148
"day name," 269
dead, Brazilian cult of, 212-13; Haitian cult of, 360; Yorka as spirit of, 315-19
definitions, needed in Negro folklore, 176
deities, *see* gods and goddesses
Denis, Lorimer, 30
divination, by cult heads, 205; by Haitian vodun cult, 360-61; by Indians, 277, by *lukuman*, 276-79; in Paramaribo, 276-79; souls called by, 270-71; training for, 278-79
djodjo, 268, 269
documents on slavery, preservation of, 33-34
Donnan, Elizabeth, 28, 95-97, 115, 116
Dorsainvil, J. C., 30, 323, 358
double entendre, significance in folklore, 181
dreams, importance to Shouters, 336-37
drummers, religious functions of, 20-21; role in Afrobrazilian cults, 183-96; role in social organization, 45
drums, of Afrobrazilian cults, 183-96; cost of, 249-50; of Porto Alegre cults, 210
DuBois, W. E. B., 28
Dutch Guiana, Africanisms in, 5-6, 50-51, 53; Bush-Negro art of, 157-67; Paramaribo Negroes' view of supernatural world, 267-319; psychic re-

www.ingramcontent.com/pod-product-compliance
Lightning Source LLC
Chambersburg PA
CBHW021544260326
41914CB00001B/160